About Island Press

Island Press is the only nonprofit organization in the United States whose principal purpose is the publication of books on environmental issues and natural resource management. We provide solutions-oriented information to professionals, public officials, business and community leaders, and concerned citizens who are shaping responses to environmental problems.

In 1994, Island Press celebrated its tenth anniversary as the leading provider of timely and practical books that take a multidisciplinary approach to critical environmental concerns. Our growing list of titles reflects our commitment to bringing the best of an expanding body of literature to the environmental community throughout North America and the world.

Support for Island Press is provided by The Geraldine R. Dodge Foundation, The Energy Foundation, The Ford Foundation, The George Gund Foundation, William and Flora Hewlett Foundation, The John D. and Catherine T. McArthur Foundation, The Andrew W. Mellon Foundation, The Joyce Mertz-Gilmore Foundation, The New-Land Foundation, The Pew Charitable Trusts, The Rockefeller Brothers Fund, The Tides Foundation, Turner Foundation, Inc., The Rockefeller Philanthropic Collaborative, Inc., and individual donors.

About the Rural Economic Policy Program

Established in 1985, the Rural Economic Policy Program (REPP) fosters collaborative learning and innovation to advance rural community and economic development in the United States. REPP aims to help rural decisionmakers better understand how local choices and opportunities fit into the larger economy, and to speed the adoption of a comprehensive set of public and private initiatives that will sustain rural progress and improve the lives of rural people. Headquartered at The Aspen Institute in Washington, D.C., REPP is funded by The Ford and W.K. Kellogg Foundations. The Aspen Institute is an international organization whose programs enhance the ability of leaders in business, government, the nonprofit sector, academia, and the media to understand and act upon the issues that challenge the national and international community.

For more information about REPP publications, please write to: Rural Economic Policy Program, The Aspen Institute, 1333 New Hampshire Avenue, NW, Suite 1070, Washington, DC 20036. Or Call REPP Program Assistant Diane Morton at 202/736-5804.

Rural Development in the United States

Rural Development in the United States

CONNECTING THEORY, PRACTICE, AND POSSIBILITIES

William A. Galston
Karen J. Baehler
Rural Economic Policy Program

ISLAND PRESS

WASHINGTON, D.C. / COVELO, CALIFORNIA

Writing and research for this publication was made possible by support from The Ford Foundation and the Rural Economic Policy Program of the Aspen Institute.

Library of Congress Cataloging-in-Publication Data
Galston, William A., 1947–
  Rural development in the United States : connecting theory, practice and possibilities / by William A. Galston and Karen J. Baehler.
      p. cm.
  Includes bibliographical references and index.
  ISBN 1-55963-326-3 (pbk.)
  1. Rural development—United States.   2. United States—Rural conditions.   I. Baehler, Karen J.   II. Title.
  HN90.C6G35 1995
  307.1′412′0973—dc20   94-41685
                                                                     CIP

Printed on recycled, acid-free paper ∞ ♲
Manufactured in the United States of America
10 9 8 7 6 5 4 3 2 1

Contents

Part II. U.S. Rural Development: A Sectoral Analysis   77

Preface

The purpose of this book is to initiate the construction of a new model that can guide and integrate rural economic development policy in the United States during the 1990s and beyond. The models of the past—New Deal-style, large-scale federal public investment; industrial attraction campaigns; resource exploitation strategies—have all produced disappointing results. No new consensus has emerged to replace them. Thus, *Rural Development in the United States* is intended to serve as a catalyst for new thinking. It will address the basic questions: Where do we go from here? On what foundations can we build new approaches?

Toward that end, the book synthesizes and analyzes much of the theoretical and practical literature on rural economic development and related issues from the past two decades. The book will be a first step toward overcoming the fragmentation and isolation that have characterized U.S. rural development research. We have assembled the best of what is being thought and done in U.S. rural development, and we have placed it in the broadest possible theoretical, historical, and geographical context. We offer suggestions as to what we now know and what we still need to learn. Throughout, we will view the rural economy against the backdrop of national and global economic trends.

The book is divided into two parts. Part I lays out a theoretical, conceptual, and historical framework. Part II surveys research and practice in key sectors of rural America. The conclusion summarizes our principal findings within an understanding of rural American economics, politics, and society as inextricably embedded in, and shaped by, a rapidly changing global order.

This book is intended for theoreticians and economic development practitioners, policy makers, and experts. In particular, it is for:

individuals and organizations involved with federal, state, and local economic and industrial policy making;

participants in different sectors of the rural economy and society, including both the public and private sectors and community-based organizations;

academic experts in economic development, rural affairs, and public policy; and

experts in emerging issues of concern to the rural economy and society such as telecommunications and deregulation.

Perhaps the most conspicuous, and to us unexpected, feature of our analysis is the path that it travels from broad theory and prediction to detailed strategy and tactics. Taking as our point of departure the perspective of economic and social change spurred by global competition and information highways, we conclude that initiatives fueled by local deliberation and entrepreneurship, public as well as private, offer the best chance for rural development in the contemporary fiscal and political context.

This book was for the most part completed in 1992, shortly before one of the authors (William A. Galston) went on temporary leave from the University of Maryland at College Park to serve in the Clinton administration as Deputy Assistant to the President for Domestic Policy. In these circumstances, it is necessary to state that the views expressed in this book are those of the authors alone and should not be taken as representing the policies, current or prospective, of the President, of the United States Department of Agriculture, or of any other agency of the executive branch of the U.S. government.

We have reviewed our manuscript carefully in light of some key events of the past two years. While these events are broadly consistent with our overall thesis, it seems useful to take note of them in this preface.

To begin with, the movement toward a competitive global economy, which served as the basis of our analysis of rural America, has sharply accelerated. The completion and final passage of NAFTA and GATT, progress toward opening Asian-Pacific markets, the commitment to move toward hemispheric free trade announced at the Summit of the Americas—all these and more are signs that our economic future will be even more tightly linked to the free flow of goods, services, and innovation across national boundaries.

Second, it is even clearer than it was two years ago that along with global competition, the information revolution is a key driving force of economic and social change. In particular, the emerging telecommunication network—the "information superhighway"—is swiftly reconfiguring the structure and location of economic activities. A mounting body of evidence suggests that modern telecommunications can effectively and affordably lower the barriers of distance and remote isolation that crippled so many rural communities during the 1980s. It must therefore be a key goal of rural policy for the remainder of this century and beyond to ensure maximum feasible rural participation in basic telecommunications infrastructure such as fiberoptic cables.

Third, pressures to reduce the federal budget deficit have intensified. The five-year budget plan proposed by President Clinton early in 1993 and passed by the congress with some modifications in August of that year has set the deficit on a multiyear declining course for the first time since the Truman administration. The November 1994 elections set the stage for further reductions in federal spending. In these circumstances, overall federal investments in rural development are unlikely to increase significantly (if at all); the need for programmatic innovation is even greater than it was two years ago.

Fourth, support for a total rethinking of relations between the national government and other levels of the federal system has risen sharply. Governors, local officials, and many members of Congress (on both sides of the aisle) are calling for a sweeping reconfiguration of institutional structures and overall responsibilities. Ideas such as program consolidation, devolution of authority, relaxation of statutory and regulatory micromanagement, and accountability for results rather than inputs—ideas pioneered by the National Performance Review under the leadership of Vice President Gore—have now moved center-stage. If proposals for revised rural development strategies are to receive a respectful hearing, they must take these new themes fully into account.

Acknowledgments

A survey of this scope and complexity could not have been completed without the assistance of numerous individuals' expertise in various aspects of rural development. We are indebted to Susan Sechler for her patient but firm nurturance of this project, and to DeWitt John and the other staff members of the Aspen Institute's Rural Economic Policy Program for their encouragement and insights. We are also, and especially, grateful to the Ford Foundation for its generous support of this multiyear undertaking, and for its gentle tolerance of the many delays we encountered in bringing it to the finish line.

Over the years, numerous members of the Economic Research Service of USDA assisted us with literature and advice. Ruy Teixeira generously shared with us draft essays on rural labor market and education issues, and survey articles by Kenneth Deavers provided indispensable guidance for our overall inquiry. Without the staff at the National Agricultural Library, John Kane in particular, we could never have found our way through the perplexing maze of materials pertaining to rural development.

Finally, we wish to pay tribute to the extraordinary assemblage of rural scholars and experts who gathered at the Aspen Institute on February 28–March 1, 1991 to review the first draft of this book. In addition to Susan Sechler, DeWitt John, and Kenneth Deavers, they included Bonnie Thornton Dill, William Duncan, Cornelia Butler Flora, Amy Glasmeier, Alain de Janvry, Maureen Kennedy, Katharine McKee, Priscilla Salant, Alton Thompson, and Ann R. Tickamyer. Their friendly but pointed suggestions provided precisely the road-map we needed for the comprehensive revisions undertaken in order to produce a document that fulfills the goals we present in our preface.

William A. Galston
Karen J. Baehler
Washington, D.C.

PART I

Background and Framework

s the United States heads toward the new century, there is a palpable sense of exhaustion with the policies of the past. The New Deal liberalism that defined and dominated our politics from the 1930s through the 1960s is ancient history. In the wake of the November 1994 elections, the new conservatism that took shape in the 1970s and assumed power in the 1980s may be tested once again. Though the American people are often cautious about deviating from the status quo, they believe that our national problems are serious and growing. But they have lost confidence in public policies and institutions as tools for resolving these problems. The need for new thinking is evident, as is the demand for it. What is lacking is the supply.

Rural development is no exception to this broad picture. Existing public policies have failed to halt, let alone reverse, stagnation and decline. The only alternative to abandonment is innovation, theoretical and practical. We must ask: On what foundations can we build new approaches? Where do we go from here?

This book addresses these questions. We say "address" rather than "answer" because we are painfully aware of the limitations inherent in any such effort: disputed theories, incomplete research, contestable data, the fog that shrouds every attempt to peer into the future. Still, we are confident that progress can be made.

The Research Context

As we pore over mounds of literature on U.S. rural development, we are struck by two main features above all: its fragmentation and its isolation. Fragmentation takes many forms. Individual pieces of research in the relevant academic disciplines (economics, sociology, anthropology, political science, area studies, social theory) have not been brought into fruitful conjunction with one another. Research and practice remain largely separated, at mutual cost. United States rural development literature is also isolated. Three dimensions stand out: Particular research is inadequately linked to broader theoretical frameworks; U.S. rural development is not often studied in relation to either advanced industrial nations or developing countries; and the "embeddedness" (as opposed to the isolation) of rural America in national and international trends is insufficiently emphasized.

We offer this book as a first step toward overcoming these difficulties. We have assembled the best of what is being thought and done in U.S. rural development and placed it in the broadest possible theoretical, historical, and geographical context. We offer some suggestions as to what we now know and what we still need to learn. Our hope is that in those instances where we have not been able to forge plausible connections and interpretations, we have provided the material and stimulus for the reader to go further.

Rural Places

Early on in discussions such as this, it is customary to invoke the "diversity" of rural America. And in an important sense, rightly so. The differences are enormous whether one looks at history, at geography, at climate, at ways in which families make a living: The contrasts between dairying New England and the humid poverty of the Delta; between besieged Midwestern farming communities and the forbidding semi-aridity of the mining Southwest; between the moist timber-dependent Northwest and the ranching West. Alongside this diversity, however, there is an idealistic sense in which rural America constitutes a unity. The obvious point of departure is the contrast between rural and urban, but we must try to understand with some precision what that contrast is intended to mean. Rural life has stood for something particular and special, a symbolic representation of the desire to be at one with the land.

Rural place is ideally defined by its three fundamental characteristics. The first is a *relation to nature*, in which the human use of natural objects and processes is guided by notions of balance, affection, and care. Earth, water, and resources are all reshaped by human contrivance, but with a steady awareness of their limits and of the need to ensure their continued existence over time.[1] The antithesis of this relation is behavior that ravages, exploits, and depletes—for example, through strip-mining, or patterns of farming and timbering that accelerate soil erosion, or settlements that drain underground water tables.

The second characteristic is a *relation to other human beings*, in which individuals and families come to know one another intimately, assist one another in time of need, and trust one another enough to cooperate in pursuit of goals that cannot be attained through solitary endeavor.[2] The antithesis of this relation is the image of urban life as anonymous, fiercely competitive, and devoid of the felt impulse of mutual aid. (This image was fixed for all time when New York City's Kitty Genovese was assaulted within view and earshot of dozens of her neighbors, not one of whom came to her defense or even telephoned the police.)

The third characteristic is a *relation to history*. In this conception, rural places enjoy a special stability over time. Not only do neighbors come to know one another well, but children can expect to take their parents' place in the community and to live and die where they were born. Individuals are linked to their place, and to each other, by narratives of family and community.[3] The antithesis of this relation is an image of urban life as transitory, migratory, and utterly lacking in shared memories.

These special relations may be considered as rural "ideology" because of their complex correspondence to the facts. The foregoing contrasts do not map neatly onto the distinction between rural and urban life; neighborhoods around midcentury steel mills have often been depicted in ways that closely resemble images of rural communities. Moreover, aspects of rural life in which there exists heedless exploitation of resources, feuds between neighbors, and the boredom of young people cannot be denied.

Still, this "rural ideology" does clarify certain real and powerful tensions in American life. One of these is the conflict between market- and place-oriented development. Markets prize innovation, require mobility, and, as social theorists have noted since the onset of the Industrial Revolution, act as a solvent on established social relations. But while market activities have profound effects on human communities, those effects are typically not intended or even in view. For example, competition promotes continuing technological changes that increase productivity; consequently, the number of people needed to produce specific commodities or goods is reduced. This, in turn, reduces the number of people who can make a living in a given community, inducing an outflow of young people from that community. The human costs, individual and collective, of market-induced changes do not register in the classic market calculus.

For that reason, one of the prime functions of modern politics is to deliberate on the consequences the market treats as "externalities." In the course of such deliberations, members of the community may well face a tradeoff between levels of individual self-interest and the extent to which their community preserves its characteristic pattern of social relations. Should communities welcome Wal-Marts, which offer a wider range of goods at lower prices, if their advent means the death-knell of Main Street small businesses? There is no single correct answer to such questions, but they cannot be effectively considered within a market framework devoid of opportunities for conscious political reflection and choice. Often the legal reach of local communities is too narrow to encompass the full range of relevant market processes, a structural feature of American federalism that exacerbates the tension under discussion.

That is not to say that politics and markets are necessarily antithetical. Indeed, political processes can be used to address market imbalances through regulations or taxes that serve to compel market agents to "internalize the externalities" and take into account the wider or long-term consequences of the acts. The point is that unfettered market processes are likely to erode the stability and integrity of many local communities.

The difficulty, and this leads to the second central tension, is that American culture does not give priority to place, that is, to intimate and enduring human communities. Alongside the desire for connection is the yearning for unencumbered freedom; along with the desire for stability is the lure of the road. These tensions may be affected by history, but they are also a matter of temperament. In the course of chronicling his "migrant childhood," Wallace Stegner describes his feelings when he left the Canadian town where he had "stayed long enough to put down roots and develop associations and memories and friends and a degree of self-confidence":

> I departed from Saskatchewan mourning what we had left behind and scared of what we were heading toward, and one look at my mother told me she was feeling the same way. My father and brother were leaning out of the car, exhilarated by how the fenceposts flew by on the smooth dirt road along the South Bench. They leaned and watched the roadside as if they were afraid Great Falls might flash by at any second, and they might miss it. But I was at heart a nester, like my mother. I loved the place I was losing, the place that years of our lives had worn smooth.[4]

As Stegner puts it in a wonderfully moving letter to his long-dead mother, "You believed in all the beauties and strengths and human associations of place; my father believed only in movement."[5]

The point is not a root-and-branch rejection of American individualism, the perennial desire for freedom and motion. On the contrary, like de Tocqueville before him, Stegner traces much of what is distinct and positive in America to its habitual impatience and restlessness, and he is under no illusion that these traits will disappear any time soon. The point is rather that, taken to an extreme, a mobility that undermines place ends by defeating its own aspirations:

> The rootlessness that expresses energy and a thirst for the new and an aspiration toward freedom and personal fulfillment has just as often been a curse. Migrants deprive themselves of the physical and spiritual bonds that develop within a place and a society. Our migratoriness has hindered us from becoming a people of communities and traditions.... It has robbed us of the gods who make places holy. It has cut off individuals and families and communities from memory and the continuum of time. It has left at least some of us with a kind of spiritual pellagra, a deficiency disease, a hungering for the ties of a rich and stable social order.... American individualism, much celebrated and cherished, has developed without its essential

corrective, which is belonging. Freedom, when found, can turn out
to be airless and unsustaining.[6]

Communitarianism is not the silver-bullet solution for America's spiritual
ills. But for many Americans, including a large number of rural Americans,
the self-willed cosmopolitan bricolage celebrated by contemporary postmod-
ernists simply will not do. For these Americans, who feel Stegner's hunger
particularly keenly, the question is how communities rooted in place may be
sustained when the market forces render them impotent.

This is an essential context within which discussions of U.S. rural development ought to be conducted. Rural development involves economic
growth, to be sure; but that growth is understood as a means, not just to increased prosperity, but also to the maintenance of community-in-place.
When national and global market forces erode local economic bases, communities must find or grow new ones. They undertake economic development, not for its own sake, but in order to survive. Of course, the process of
development cannot be wholly harnessed to the purposes of local community. In contemporary circumstances, the logic of development enmeshes localities in complex, imperfectly controllable national and global forces. The
question in each case is how much unwanted change must be accepted at the
cost of survival.

In the course of a lifetime's study of rural America, Calvin Beale has visited
thousands of rural communities. Outside the small town of Galesville,
Wisconsin, he found a billboard that proclaims, "WELCOME TO
GALESVILLE, The Garden of Eden. Industry Invited." He comments:

> Here, in a nutshell, the basic modern dilemma of rural America is
> expressed. On one hand there is the ardent assertion of the idyllic,
> fulfilling quality that life in a small community can have, but then
> tempered by the necessity to invite the serpent of industry into the
> garden if people are to have the means to live there.[7]

In the course of this book, we shall discuss the growth sectors and strategies available to contemporary rural communities. But we will treat them, as
Calvin Beale suggests, not as ends in themselves, but as alternative means for
living, or continuing to live, in places that are not only chosen but cherished.

1

Rural America in the 1990s: Trends and Choices

As is now clearly established, the rural renaissance of the 1970s turned into the rural bust of the 1980s. Both extractive industries and routine manufacturing, on which many rural areas are heavily dependent, experienced severe recessions in the early and middle part of the decade, and the subsequent partial revival of production in these sectors was not accompanied by a commensurate revival of employment. Meanwhile, the growth sectors of the national economy—high-tech manufacturing, knowledge-intensive industries, business services—became increasingly concentrated in urban areas.

The difficulties rural America experienced in the 1980s were in large measure the product of vast shifts in the national and international economy. Nonetheless, federal government policies during this period also contributed to the reemergence of rural disadvantage. For much of the decade, the macroeconomic regime produced currency distortions that impeded rural exports, as well as persistent high real interest rates to which the rural economy proved vulnerable. Deregulation in transportation and telecommunications wiped out long-standing implicit cross-subsidies to rural areas. Federal spending patterns, particularly in defense, tilted toward metropolitan areas, and the bias of federal rural dollars toward agriculture and current consumption was not conducive to long-term economic growth.[1]

The overall consequence of shifting economic trends and public policies for rural America in the 1980s has been summarized by Kenneth Deavers: "The recovery that began in 1982 [was] long and fairly strong in terms of compound annual rates of growth in GNP and employment... Nevertheless, in contrast with earlier periods, strong national growth ... contributed little to improving the relative performance of the rural economy."[2] The elements making up this dramatic divergence can be measured along a number of key dimensions.

• **Employment** Between 1979 and 1987, metropolitan area employment grew by 18 percent, while rural employment grew by only 8 percent.

• **Unemployment** Between 1979 and 1987, annual rural unemployment rates ranged between 1 percent and 2.5 percent higher than metro rates.

• **Income** The ratio of rural to metro per capita incomes declined from 77 percent at the end of the 1970s to only 73 percent in 1987, the lowest level since 1970.

• **Wages** After adjusting for inflation, average annual earnings per job fell 8 percent ($1700) in rural areas between 1979 and 1987, versus only 2 percent ($450) for metro areas. As a result, the metro/rural gap grew from $5000 to nearly $6200.[3]

• **Earnings Penalty** In 1974, the ratio of metro to rural earnings was quite similar across educational categories, rising only gradually from 1.08 for individuals with eighth-grade education to 1.14 for college graduates. By 1986, while the ratio for the eighth-grade educated was 1.18, the ratio for college graduates approached 1.40. In short, returns to education increased much faster in metro than in rural areas.

• **Poverty** The rural poverty rate soared to 18 percent between 1979 and 1982, and remained stuck at nearly that level throughout the ensuing economic recovery. By the late 1980s, the rural poverty rate was nearly 50 percent higher than for metro areas. Today, 51 percent of rural residents fall in the two poorest quintiles; the comparable urban number is 37 percent.

Not surprisingly, rates for the working poor (the characteristic form of rural poverty) also increased dramatically. In 1979, 32 percent of rural workers earned below the poverty line for a family of four, compared with 23 percent of urban workers. By 1987, the percentage of rural lower earners had risen by 10 points, to 42 percent, versus a six-point rise to 29 percent for urban lower earnings.[4] The poverty rate for rural families in which the head of household worked rose from 7.6 to 10 percent during this period, twice as high as the rate for corresponding metro families.[5]

• **Population** While the rural growth rate had exceeded the metro rate by almost 40 percent in the 1970s, it fell to less than half the metro rate through the 1980s. By the mid-1980s, annual out-migration from rural areas reached nearly 500,000, a rate substantially above the annual average for the 1950s and 1960s. More than one-half of all rural counties actually lost population during this period. And in large measure because of the shifts in educational earnings penalties summarized above, "rural

out-migration is not only age specific but education specific. As a consequence, many of the rural citizens most important to future rural development are leaving rural America."[6] Although the most recent analysis of
rural population trends in the late 1980s suggests that the worst of the
out-migration to urban areas is now behind us, rural population growth
continues to lag well behind that of metro areas, and the inequality between rural winners and losers continues to widen.[7]

While it is too early to reach definitive conclusions, the available fragmen-
tary evidence suggests that recent rural population trends are inversely correlated to community size: On average, the smallest towns have been hardest
hit, and mid-sized communities have come closer to holding their own. In
Iowa, for example, the 680 small towns with population under 1000 lost
about 35 percent of their retail trade during the 1980s, and their population
losses were disproportionately concentrated in the younger age groups.[8]
Overall, 72 percent of towns with fewer than 2500 inhabitants decreased in
population during the 1980s.

We should also note the continuing impact of location on rural population trends. Given previous research demonstrating the importance of metro
adjacency for rural county growth in the 1950s, 1960s, and 1970s, it is hardly
surprising that it turned out to be so significant in the 1980s, a decade so
markedly favorable for metropolitan areas. During 1979–88, employment in
rural counties adjacent to metropolitan areas grew at more than twice the rate
of nonadjacent counties.[9]

These aggregates conceal significant disparities: When metropolitan areas
fared quite poorly during this period, the rural areas near them tended to
follow suit. Still, the past decade may be viewed as a vindication of at least a
moderate version of central place theory. One of the great challenges of the
1990s and beyond is therefore to devise new forms of urban–rural linkage
that can substitute for geographical adjacency. The extension of modern
telecommunications to remote rural areas can play a key role in overcoming
long-standing problems of distance and location. Failing this, the prospects
for many small, remote communities will remain far from bright.

The markedly adverse trends of the 1980s do not imply that rural
America should be given up for lost. To begin with, there are signs that these
trends have largely run their course. The overvalued dollar that impeded exports has been replaced by a much cheaper dollar. The recently ratified
General Agreement on Tariffs and Trade (GATT) should mean new markets
and fairer treatment for a wide range of rural American products. The defense budget increases of the 1980s, which shifted rural tax dollars to metro-
politan-based contractors, have been reversed. The increased competitive-

ness of the U.S. manufacturing sector appears to have halted the rapid decline in manufacturing employment, on which much of rural America still depends. Overall, the recession of 1990–92 hit urban areas harder than it did rural areas, and metropolitan unemployment rates now exceed those in rural areas. And as we noted previously, the rate of rural population loss appears to have slowed significantly in many areas and in other areas to have reversed outright.

Nor should we overlook the vital role that rural America continues to play in the U.S. economy and society. Today, rural America is home to 21 percent of the U.S. population, supplies 18 percent of its jobs, and generates 14 percent of its earnings.

The structure of the rural economy increasingly resembles that of the nation as a whole. Services provide more than half of all nonmetropolitan employment, manufacturing slightly less than one-fifth, and agriculture less than one-tenth. Indeed, during the past 20 years the percentage of the rural workforce engaged in farming has been cut virtually in half, and only about five million people (less than 10 percent of the rural population) live on farms.

Notwithstanding some favorable trends in, and the important contributions of, rural America, many significant problems persist. Key indicators such as per capita income, real earnings per job, and rates of college completion remain far lower in rural counties than in metropolitan areas. (Real earnings per rural job in the early 1990s were significantly lower than in the late 1970s.) Almost one-quarter of all rural counties are persistently poor, with poverty rates in excess of 20 percent since at least the 1960s. Rural job generation continues at only half the pace of metropolitan areas. Increases in agricultural productivity continue to outpace growth in demand, producing continued downward pressure on agricultural employment. Rural manufacturing—much of which is routine, low-skill, and low-wage—remains exposed to international competition. And the nearly one-fifth of rural jobs that depend on government activities may prove vulnerable to pressure for reducing the size and scope of the federal government.

The National/Global Context

The shifting rural trends we have just sketched cannot be understood, and should not be studied, in a vacuum: U.S. rural society and economy are now exposed, as never before, to powerful national and international forces. Three major developments must be considered.

To begin with, the primary products economy is now significantly detached from the industrial economy. In classic business cycle theory, a decline in agriculture and raw materials is soon followed by a serious crisis in industry. Yet throughout much of the 1980s, a prolonged primary-product depression had little effect on the broader economy. Because materials constitute a small, and declining, portion of the GNP of advanced countries, even sharp declines in output and income have at most marginal overall effects.

This progressive marginalization of primary products in industrialized nations is unlikely to be reversed, in part because other countries proved unexpectedly able to increase their agricultural and materials output in the 1970s and 1980s, but more fundamentally because materials are decreasingly important as inputs for production. Peter Drucker offers the following examples: Materials and energy constituted 60 percent of the costs of the representative industrial product of the 1920s—the automobile—versus 2 percent for the representative industrial product of the 1980s—the semiconductor microchip. Copper wires with a materials/energy content of close to 80 percent are being replaced in telephone cables by glass fiber with a materials/energy content of 10 percent.[10]

These are long-term trends. With the exception of wartime, the amount of raw material needed per unit of economic output has been dropping throughout the twentieth century. A study by the International Monetary Fund calculates the annual decline as 1.25 percent (compounded).[11] While there may be temporal local or sectoral exceptions to these broad trends, rural strategies premised on sustainably rising demand and prices for primary products overall have no serious chance of succeeding.

The decreasing importance of raw materials has consequences for the entire U.S. economy, not just rural America. In a path-breaking article, Gavin Wright has shown that the rise of the United States to industrial supremacy rested heavily on relative price and supply advantages in nonreproducible natural resources. Since then, the integration of world markets for resources has significantly eroded those advantages. As Wright observes, these resources are now commodities rather than factor endowments. An important issue facing the U.S. economy, then, is whether it can find new sources of competitiveness to replace this vanishing advantage, an issue complicated by the increasing mobility of technology and information.[12]

The second key development is the wedge that has been driven between production and employment throughout traditional economic sectors. This is a familiar phenomenon in U.S. agriculture, where tremendous advances in output have been accomplished with ever-shrinking numbers of producers. There is no reason to expect the increase in agricultural productivity to slow. If anything, biotechnological advances may increase the rate of increase during the 1990s.

Somewhat less familiar, but just as important, is the spread of this inexorable logic of productivity to the manufacturing sector over the past 15 years. U.S. manufacturing production has risen by roughly half, but manufacturing employment during this period has declined. The much-discussed U.S. productivity crisis has been largely confined to the service sector; our manufacturing productivity has risen by more than 2 percent annually since 1982, a rate that has accelerated in recent years.

This trend is also long-term. The ratio of blue-collar workers in the total labor force was one in three in the 1920s, one in four in the 1950s, less than one in six today, and likely to be at most one in 10 by the year 2010. This decrease, which implies a continuing decline in the absolute number of U.S. manufacturing workers, will coincide with continuing large increases in manufacturing output and exports. Indeed, rapidly rising productivity is a condition for such increases, because without it no industry can hope to remain competitive internationally.[13]

Once again, the moral for rural America is clear. Both agriculture/raw materials and manufacturing will continue to shrink their employment. Absent heroic assumptions about the future location of manufacturing plants, there is no possibility that routine production jobs can absorb excess rural workers in the 1990s as they did to some extent in the 1970s. If trends toward rising rural unemployment, as well as population exodus, are to be reversed, answers must be sought elsewhere.

The third development affecting economic growth concerns investment, particularly in innovation and people. During much of the 1980s, U.S. investment fell behind that of our major competitors, leading to a decline in the key capital/worker ratio.[14] In 1989, Japanese investments in plant and equipment per worker were three times as large as those in the United States.[15]

Several factors account for this shortfall: U.S. personal savings fell to historic lows, while the federal budget deficit soared. Total national savings (individuals, corporations, governments) fell from 17.4 percent of GNP in the late 1970s to only 11.3 percent in the late 1980s.[16] High real interest rates raised the cost of capital above that of our major economic competitors, discouraging investments other than those yielding substantial short-term returns. What would otherwise have been an outright clash between investment and consumption was muted considerably by an influx of capital from abroad, notably Europe and Japan.

In this respect, the remaining years of the twentieth century are likely to be quite different. Under pressure of political change, the days of heavy U.S. reliance on external investment capital are rapidly drawing to a close. Germany is turning its attention to the capital requirements of assistance to the former Soviet republic, Eastern European reconstruction, and its own increasingly painful and costly reunification. The rest of Europe is following suit, a tendency likely to be accelerated by European integration and by the difficulties encountered in the Uruguay round of GATT negotiations. For its part, Japan now confronts demands for increased domestic spending (public and private) in a context reconfigured by a shattering stock market crash, troubled financial institutions, higher interest rates, an aging population, and the declining savings propensity of its households.[17] As a result, the productivity-enhancing investments the United States needs will have to be financed to a much greater degree out of domestic savings. This implies some combination of increased private and public savings.

It also implies a much slower rate of debt accumulation. During the 1980s, debt of all kinds (government, corporate, and consumer) rose to unsustainably high levels. The 1990–92 recession already forced bankruptcies and restructurings, a diminished willingness on the part of households to take on new debt, and a much more cautious attitude toward debt creation on the part of financial institutions hard-pressed by failing loans and tightened government regulation.

To make matters even harder, increased private savings will have to come directly out of household earnings at a time when median wages are stagnating and when family incomes are less likely to be supplemented by capital gains. The range of expert disagreement is fairly wide, but no model predicts real estate price rises during the 1990s at anything approaching the levels of the 1980s. In 1991 alone, the sagging residential housing market wiped out the net equity of many middle-class families. Nor can the stock market be expected to triple as it did during the decade of the 1980s.

Some of the increased investment the United States needs will have to come from the public sector. But this will be hard to accomplish. Pressure for spending cuts at the federal level continues to intensify. While the federal domestic program retrenchment of the 1980s was substantially counterbalanced by expanded state and local activity, this is most unlikely to recur in the 1990s. Instead, we appear to be entering a period of simultaneous pressure on public budgets at every level. Finally, as noted above, public faith in governmental honesty and efficacy stands at historic lows.

The implications of all this for U.S. rural development are clear and sobering. Incremental public funds will be very hard to come by; pressures on (and struggles over) existing resources are bound to intensify. As is the case in other areas, demands will escalate for stricter accountability as well as demonstrable results, and there is likely to be an expanding market for more efficient, less bureaucratic forms of public sector activity, a process policy analyst David Osborne has labeled "reinventing government"[18] and that has been pursued by the National Performance Review under the leadership of Vice President Gore.

The need to compete more effectively in the international economy will give an edge to public programs that can be justified as investments in long-term productivity and growth over efforts to promote equity. Rural strategies will have to be defended primarily as contributions to overall national well-being rather than in place-specific terms. But national and local advantage may not converge. For example, human capital investment makes eminent sense as a national strategy, but it cannot succeed in staunching the outflow of trained young people from rural communities unless rates of return to human capital are simultaneously increased in these communities—a goal that may prove far harder to justify in national terms, let alone achieve.[19]

The implication to be drawn from these broad trends is clear: Rural America has entered a new era in which innovation may not guarantee success, but status quo policies will ensure failure. The challenge in the years ahead is to shape new strategies responsive to both rural realities and changing national and global circumstances.

Rural Comparative Advantage

To have any chance of succeeding, these new strategies must be built on a realistic assessment of the rural comparative advantage. Early in U.S. history, the development of rural America rested primarily on place-specific resource advantages: land, timber, and minerals. The central rural disadvantage, the obstacle of distance, was overcome in part by natural location factors (such as long, navigable rivers) and in part by publicly guided development of communication and transportation systems. These advantages have not disappeared, but their significance has been steadily eroded by changes in technology, related factors of production, and the composition of final demand.

In the 1960s and 1970s, the primary basis of rural comparative advantage shifted from resources to factors such as cheap land, low-cost labor, relatively relaxed regulations, and weak or nonexistent unions. Combined with a new burst of public investment in transportation (the interstate highway system), these advantages spurred a significant expansion of routine manufacturing in rural America. From 1960 to 1980, the rural share of manufacturing employment rose from 21 to 27 percent.

But these advantages, too, have been eroded by economic change. The importance of land costs in plant siting decisions has diminished, and in a global marketplace with fully mobile capital, cheaper labor can be found and employed outside our borders.[20] In the longer term, there is good reason to believe that labor will continue to shrink as a component of manufacturing costs and, therefore, as a determinant of production siting.

During the 1980s, rural America appears to have entered its third major phase. The kinds of natural characteristics regarded as "amenity values" by retirees, vacationers, and certain businesses have emerged as the chief new source of rural comparative advantage. We may speculate that this relative advantage may have been widened by declining amenities in many urban areas. Rural places with substantial locational assets have commanded the lion's share of rural population and employment gains.

There is however a downside. The same characteristics—lower population size and density—that give some rural areas amenity value frequently limit opportunities for development in other areas. Three factors are key. First, lower size and density make it difficult, and in some cases impossible, to achieve significant local diversification, which leaves communities, and even entire regions, highly vulnerable to downturns in their prime economic base. Second, these factors are correlated with larger average distances between individuals as well as between economic activities, which raises costs of communication and transportation. Information is typically harder to get than in urban areas, and transaction costs are higher.[21] The deregulatory wave of the 1980s increased the rural disadvantage in transportation costs. Not surprisingly, rural counties that are adjacent to metropolitan areas did far better than did remote counties during the past decade. Third, successful amenity-based development may eventually erode the original advantage, as population size and density increase and amenity values decline.

As Emery Castle has observed, the financial costs associated with overcoming distance are not a linear function of distance. Technological change and infrastructure development can do a great deal to reduce the costs of geographical distance. Still, he notes, "The economic welfare of the more sparsely populated areas is linked with, and dependent upon, economic activity in the more densely populated areas . . . It is not a coincidence that the most prosperous rural areas have close economic links with other parts of the world and the large urban centers."[22] This thesis, ardently expounded by Jane Jacobs, suggests that a central challenge for U.S. rural development will be to conceptualize, and put in place, new kinds of linkages between metropolitan areas and remote communities. Absent such innovations, the prospects for remote communities without significant natural amenities can only be regarded as bleak.

Collective Action Failures

The foregoing should not be misinterpreted as an argument that the decline witnessed throughout so much of rural America in the past decade is the inevitable consequence of irrefutable national and international trends. We urge a more complex thesis: While these broad trends do set the agenda and restrict options, the outcomes for rural areas reflect the choices made among available options, as well as the forms of collective action used to implement these choices.

In modern societies, broadly speaking, there are three principal ways in which individuals can organize themselves collectively to get things done. The oldest of these, politics, is the sphere of authority in which the legitimacy, office, persuasiveness, or power of some persons induces others to accept their judgment and command as the basis of action.[23] Since the eighteenth century, a second sphere has emerged, the market, governed by the principle of exchange: transactions that leave all parties better off (as they themselves define their own well-being) than they were. The third sphere is that of civil society, which encompasses all voluntary associations based on shared principles, loyalties, or sentiments: families, churches, neighborhood groups, nonprofit or charitable organizations, and so on.[24]

Like the market, civil society can only exist if the sphere of politics is not overbearing. Markets and civil societies are thus linked to what may be called the liberal principle that government should, for reasons of efficacy as well as morality, be limited in crucial respects.

Armed with this simple but serviceable trichotomy, we can now tell a story about the main currents of modern American history. The New Deal represented the victory of politics over both the market, alleged to have produced fatal economic imbalances, and civil society, which had proved unequal to the task of coping with the human consequences of market failure. Programs such as the NRA, AAA, WPA, and CCC reflected the belief that the market could not be trusted to generate enough jobs for workers or appropriate prices for goods. At the same time, Social Security, unemployment benefits, and AFDC emerged to assist, and in considerable measure to replace, voluntary associations swamped by the Great Depression.

New Deal liberalism was the dominant paradigm for two generations. But by the end of the 1960s, there was a growing sense among both policy elites and the general public that the incremental gains stemming from further expansion of politics were being purchased at excessive cost. The conservative movement, which culminated in the election of Ronald Reagan, in part represented the desire to roll back politics in favor of market transactions and the activities of voluntary groups. The decade of the 1980s represented a sustained effort to do just that. We are now in a position to evaluate what we have gained, lost, and learned (or perhaps relearned.)

The market, we see, is a remarkable mechanism for transmitting information and for inducing change. It promotes efficiency, generates wealth, fosters individual mobility and opportunity, and increases personal freedom. These considerable advantages help explain why the market attained almost iconic status among the nations throwing off the legacy of Stalinism in the late 1980s.

But there are entries in the debit column as well. The market is insensitive to the distribution of income and wealth among economic classes and geographical locations; indeed, there are indications that under contemporary conditions it tends to exacerbate preexisting disparities. Left to its own devices, the market does little to alleviate the burdens of the changes it induces; witness the struggles of communities and regions dependent on declining industries such as steel, autos, and mining. To individuals as well as firms, the market presents various entry barriers that are bound to have unequal impacts on different social groups—especially when educational attainment commands an increasing premium. The market is structured by rules that it neither creates nor enforces; if the political sphere does not exercise its authority, inefficiencies and scandals result. The market, it turns out, does not achieve a self-regulating balance between private consumption and private investment or, for that matter, between the short term and the long term. Added to all these difficulties rediscovered during the past decade are the classic kinds of market failures known, if perhaps underestimated, all along: imperfect information, externalities not factored into prices, and the inadequate provision of public goods that undergird sustainable economic growth.[25]

We have argued that the conservative movement of the past two decades represented a revolt against politics in the name of both the market and civil society. But a tension has emerged between these two antipolitical commitments. The sustained, rapid, and inexorable changes produced by the market do not support and, indeed, may weaken the intermediary social groupings that require cohesion, stability, and trust. The unintended victims of the market's "creative destruction" include families, neighborhoods, and communities as well as inefficient and unresponsive firms.

This is not a new lesson, of course. It has been a staple of European social commentary since the Industrial Revolution. But the traditional American view, expressed classically in de Tocqueville's *Democracy in America,* has been more hopeful: that the variegated web of voluntary associations comprising civil society would be strong enough to counterbalance the excesses of market-based individualism as well as of political centralization.[26] We are now learning that the market may have to be restrained by other means as well if civil society is to flourish.

And flourish it should. During the past decade, voluntary associations have performed remarkably in areas such as education, housing, and neighborhood safety—frequently in the face of problems seemingly impervious to standard political and market mechanisms. Alongside these successes, however, have been troubling difficulties of scale and strength. In many instances, associations have been unable to mount efforts equal to the size of the problems; churches and advocacy groups, for example, have not been able to shelter all the homeless. Nor have associations been able to counteract the effects of broad economic and social trends that have overwhelmed many families and communities. Vigorous civil society is a necessary but not sufficient condition of social health.[27]

While the experience of the 1980s has muted some enthusiasm for markets, it did little to restore confidence in politics as a mode of collective action. By and large, the American people continue to equate the political sphere with the mode of government activity characteristic of the New Deal: a labor-intensive, self-regarding, unresponsive bureaucracy, captured by special interests at the expense of the general interest. In addition, this bureaucracy is wedded to old programs at the expense of new needs, with a seemingly unlimited appetite for consuming public funds but a limited capacity (at best) for resolving public problems. In the judgment of many, "government failure" is just as probable, indeed just as pervasive, as "market failure."

These sobering conclusions are hardly confined to the United States. In a wide-ranging review of postwar international efforts, Anne O. Krueger comments: "One of the lessons of experience with development is that governments are not omniscient, selfless, social guardians. . . . One must ask why economists were ever comfortable with the simultaneous beliefs that individuals in the private sector act in their self-interest and that individuals in the public sector are motivated by a Benthamite vision of social justice."[28] As Krueger notes, this disillusionment about the benevolence and efficacy of government has led to some important insights: "First, when economic policies create something that is to be allocated at less than its value by any sort of government process, resources will be used in an effort to capture the rights to the items of value. Second, whenever a government policy has clearly identifiable beneficiaries and/or victims, those groups will tend to organize in support or opposition to the policies and then lobby for increasing the value of the gains or reducing the value of the losses."[29]

The analytical framework developed in this section illuminates the current plight of rural America. On the one hand, market forces on balance did not promote rural development during the 1980s, and the unchecked market's indifference to issues of geographic distribution was nowhere more clearly demonstrated. Nor, in spite of heroic efforts, was rural civil society able to address effectively the problems with which it was confronted. Churches, communities, and support groups ministered to distress and occasionally warded off worst-case outcomes, but without reversing underlying negative trends. The public sector, finally, did no better: In spite of unprecedented spending on programs regarded as "rural," the federal government did little to improve the long-term prospects of rural families and communities.

This last point is perhaps the least obvious and requires further elaboration. James Bonnen has argued that U.S. rural policy is a classic example of government failure. The reason, he contends, is that during the past century the political economy of rural America was institutionalized around key industries rather than communities. For much of the period, this political configuration was not too damaging. But in the crisis of the Great Depression, Congress created legislation that for the most part provided selective goods to specific groups, usually agricultural. This evoked a mobilization of agricultural interest groups to defend and expand public benefits (as Krueger's model predicts) at precisely the time that the agricultural sector was rapidly shrinking in terms of rural population and economic output. The result has been the domination of national rural policy by an increasingly narrow and unrepresentative segment of rural America.[30]

The inadequacy of rural political institutions has been exacerbated by population mobility. One consequence is obvious and well known: As rural residents leave their communities in search of opportunity elsewhere, the rural population declines as a percentage of the total, decreasing its representation in state and national legislative bodies. This trend was accelerated by the one-person one-vote Supreme Court decisions of the 1960s, which left the U.S. Senate as the last bastion of rural over-representation.

Another consequence of population mobility is less obvious, but just as important: the weakening of internal forces pushing for change. As Albert Hirschman has argued, "exit" and "voice" constitute the two major forms of response to organizational decline. Individuals dissatisfied with the performance of firms or communities can choose either to leave or to stay and speak out for reform. The problem is that the availability of the exit option tends to inhibit the development of effective voice.[31] Exit serves as a safety valve that removes the most energetic and upwardly mobile members of the community, leaving behind a stratified mix of those who are relatively satisfied with the status quo and those too old, weak, or downtrodden to muster an effective protest against it. (A number of studies suggest that the portions of Europe with the highest rates of migration during the nineteenth century were less prone than others to social protest and violence.)

One difficulty, particularly acute in the U.S. context, is that voice is labor-intensive over an extended period and typically requires coordinated action with others, while exit is a once-and-for-all act that can be performed by isolated persons or families. Effective voice—collective action through politics—faces special impediments in a country whose public culture celebrates mobility and individualism. Still, an initial display of political effectiveness can serve as a magnet, inducing some who would otherwise leave to believe in the possibility of local improvement. This suggests that "public entrepreneurship" must play a key role in the revitalization of rural America.

Conclusion: Rural America in the 1990s

We must not overlook the powerful national and international winds now buffeting so many rural communities, but neither should we slight the ways in which, even in the face of these inhospitable conditions, skilled hands at the public helm can artfully tack and move forward.

In this complex interplay between structure and agency, it is important to maintain the distinction between macrolevel trends and microlevel choices. What is true in the aggregate may not be valid for individual communities. For example, within an overall pattern of stagnation, opportunities for local growth may nonetheless persist. The point is that a sounder understanding of broad developments will create a context in which policy analysts and local decision-makers can more realistically evaluate the odds of success for each of the options before them. Rural communities need not always "go with the flow," but they should at least understand the nature of that flow.

Let us summarize the consequences for research and public policy that flow from this thesis. Each of these propositions will receive more detailed treatment later in the book.

1. As we have seen, the pressures of international competition will force steady productivity increases in agriculture, natural resources, and manufacturing, driving even deeper the wedge between output and employment. If there is to be any hope of maintaining, let alone expanding, the rural job base, local communities and national policy must turn increasingly toward the substantially nontraded sectors of the economy such as the retiring elderly, tourism, and the siting of government activities. This new emphasis is consistent with the shift of rural comparative advantage to a third phase, one that emphasizes amenities rather than natural resources or the costs of production.

2. The fiscal crisis of the public sphere, which has now spread to every level of the federal system, means that large new rural programs are impossible and that continuing pressure on existing programs is inevitable. This is a situation that cries out for innovation in the basic structure of public action. Government programs must increasingly employ cost-effective, nonbureaucratic mechanisms, and they must use public resources to catalyze action in the private sector and in rural communities. As one analyst has put it, contemporary government can steer the boat, but it can't row.

3. The continuing, perhaps even enhanced importance of rural linkage to thriving metropolitan areas means that efforts must be intensified to find effective functional substitutes for the geographical fact of adjacency.

Rural policy must focus on implements such as advanced telecommunications that could give rural communities more complete, timely access to information, and it must lower existing barriers to fuller rural participation in the most vigorously growing parts of the economy.[32]

4. The emerging importance of size for community survival suggests that institutional change is essential. Small rural communities must seek to break down political boundaries and form new cooperative political units for education, service delivery, and public entrepreneurship—units that more closely correspond to the real scope of contemporary rural economic and social life. Recent trends suggest that only through such consolidation can many of the smallest communities hope to avoid continuing decline and eventual extinction.

5. The progressive globalization of advanced economies has led many analysts to conclude that the skills and cumulative learning of the work force are the new keys to competitiveness, the real sources of the "wealth of nations" in the next century. While there is debate as to the rate at which new and enhanced work-force skills will have to come on-stream, the basic conjecture is widely accepted. It does not follow, however, that what enhances national wealth will necessarily benefit particular regions. There are many reasons for local communities and the federal government to embark on a new partnership to upgrade education and training. But rural communities should be under no illusion that such initiatives by themselves will suffice to create local job opportunities and staunch the outflow of young people.[33]

2

Development: A Conceptual Framework

This chapter attempts to bring some order to the vague and conflicting ideas that are typical of discussions of development. Throughout, our focus is on development as a normative concept—as a set of goals and processes that are (or are thought to be) positively related to individual and social well-being. However, a significant point is that to advocate development is to favor change. Development alters the status quo; it will therefore be opposed by those who are satisfied with, or benefit directly from, the current state of affairs, or who believe that any alteration is likely to be a detriment.

Development as a Social Goal

There are three kinds of social goals. The first may be called "single-valued." Goals of this sort contain only one relevant dimension, and goal attainment is measured as progress along that dimension. For example, when a litigator struggles to win a big case or when a scientist works day and night to crack an experimental puzzle, the single value—victory in the one case, knowledge in the other—may be the only thing that matters.

The second kind of goal is "dominant-valued." In these instances, the goal may be defined along multiple dimensions, but one of them must be preferred in case of conflict among them. For example, some people say they want a society that is both free of drugs and respectful of civil liberties but that no drug control strategy is permissible if it violates civil liberties. It is not that they are indifferent to drug control, but rather that civil liberties enjoy a priority.

The third kind of social goal is "multi-valued." Goals of this sort contain two or more dimensions of evaluation, no one of which enjoys absolute priority. In case of conflict, the task is to determine appropriate tradeoffs among them. During this process, concepts such as "balance" and "diminishing returns" will typically come into play. The philosopher James Fishkin has termed such multivalued goals "ideals without an ideal" and has located them at the midpoint of a spectrum extending from moral absolutism at one extreme to moral subjectivism at the other.

Over the past four decades, we suggest, the concept of development in the international sphere has evolved from the first, through the second, to the third of these social goals. In the immediate postwar period, development was typically understood as the single value of economic growth. But by the early 1970s many agreed with Robert S. McNamara, then president of the World Bank, that the "critical issue within developing countries is not simply the pace of growth but the nature of growth." Even when these nations exceeded GNP targets, the "social impact of that growth was so severely skewed, and the number of individuals all but passed by so immense, that the simple statistical achievement was misleading."

During much of the 1970s, not surprisingly, official priorities shifted toward issues of distributive equity and basic needs, though such equity and need did not replace the goal of economic growth. The noted economist and social philosopher Amartya Sen helped crystallize this movement through the distinction between (on the one hand) economic growth and (on the other) substantive indicators of human well-being, such as infant mortality, longevity, physical growth, health, education, and opportunities:

> [The] real limitations of traditional development economics arose not from the choice of means to the end of economic growth, but in the insufficient recognition that economic growth was no more than a means to other objectives. The point is not the same as saying that growth does not matter. It may matter a great deal, but, if it does, this is because of some associated benefits that are realized in the process of economic growth.

At roughly the same time that economic growth was being reconceptualized as the means to, rather than the goal of, development and was supplemented by concepts of equity and basic needs, the development discussion was dramatically broadening along other dimensions as well. In 1969, for example, a meeting chaired by Gunnar Myrdal was convened to clarify "the role of social factors in development" and produced a report that proposed a "more unified treatment" of "the development process as a complex whole." One of the key participants, Benjamin Higgins, explained that this new approach began by rejecting GNP growth as the sole objective of development and instead "stressed the need to plan directly and simultaneously for all objectives of development with full cognizance of interactions and feedbacks among them." As he later observed:

When "development" comes to mean all elements of human life that contribute to human welfare, including nutrition, health, shelter, employment, the physical environment, the sociocultural environment or quality of life, and such matters as participation in the decision-making process, a sense of human dignity, of belonging, etc., standard neo-classical and neo-Keynesian economics has only a limited contribution to make to development policy and planning.[1]

The economic historian H.W. Arndt has argued that these and related proposals received at best a mixed reception both within the expert community and among economic and political elites in Third World countries. Arndt goes so far as to characterize the story of the 1970s as "the rise and fall of social objectives as the dominant theme in the development debate."[2] Nonetheless, the discussion of that period tapped some deep insights and left an important residue—the understanding of development as a multidimensional phenomenon.

This new understanding is not without problems. As the concept of development has become more complex, it has become less precise. A typical contemporary commentator suggests: "The starting point for talking about development is our vision of what society should be like; how men and women should live and how they should get along; how groups can coexist; how the values of our society can be maintained and enhanced."[3] Aside from the inherent difficulties of such visionary thinking, understandings of "what society should be like" are likely to vary from society to society. As Arndt observes: "So diverse have the interpretations of 'development' become that one sometimes wonders whether it now stands for anything more substantial than everyone's own utopia."[4] Still, we suggest that certain core elements tend to recur in most contemporary accounts.

Development: Specific Features
Economic Growth

While development cannot be equated with steadily increasing incomes, it is hardly imaginable without income growth. In many societies, even a highly egalitarian distribution of current income and wealth would leave large populations well below levels of resources generally thought acceptable. In such circumstances, only increases in aggregate income and wealth would hold hope of improving the lot of the least advantaged. This suggests that the moral logic of growth may be different in wealthier societies.[5]

If economic growth is part of the solution, then "poverty" must be considered part of the problem. This seems obvious, but it is by no means uncontested. For example, Gandhi opposed modernization of the Indian economy on traditional religious grounds: "A man is not necessarily happy because he is rich, or unhappy because he is poor. . . . Millions will always remain poor." As Tolstoy forcibly reminded his contemporaries, the New Testament is replete with similar sentiments—a point Alexander Solzhenitsyn has urged on both the West and his fellow countrymen in our own times.

Wolfgang Sachs has argued that global poverty "was discovered after the Second World War; before 1940 it was not an issue." The Western economic concept of poverty "was used to define whole peoples, not according to what they are and want to be, but according to what they lack and what they are expected to become. Economic disdain has thus taken the place of colonial contempt."

In place of the gross concept of poverty, Sachs invites us to distinguish among frugality, destitution, and scarcity. Frugality is a "mark of cultures free from the frenzy of accumulation. The necessities of life are mostly won from subsistence production with only the smaller part being purchased on the market. . . . Despite being in the 'low-income bracket,' no one goes hungry. . . . 'Poverty' here is a way of life maintained by a culture which recognizes and cultivates a state of sufficiency." Destitution emerges without that state of sufficiency, when frugality, so understood, is deprived of its social and material foundation: "Along with community ties, land, forest, and water are the most important prerequisites for subsistence without money. As soon as they are taken away or destroyed, destitution lurks." And scarcity emerges when those who are no longer to live in a regime of frugality are plunged into a money economy: "Their capacity to achieve through their own efforts gradually fades, while at the same time their desires, fueled by glimpses of high society, spiral toward infinity; this scissors-like effect of want is what characterizes modern poverty."[6]

Sachs' distinctions possess considerable historical and sociological force, for they mirror the experiences of communities in the contemporary Third World and those in the eighteenth–nineteenth century Industrial Revolution. These distinctions were also experienced in the U.S. South and Appalachia after World War I. These societies were compelled by circumstances beyond their control—in particular, by destitution—to make the transition from subsistence to scarcity. Still, the immediate critical force of his categories is limited by what appears to be historical irreversibility: Once the subsistence option has been foreclosed, rightly or wrongly, the only alternative to what Sachs calls "modern poverty" as a permanent condition is some version of development that holds out the promise of relieving poverty.

Equity

Having to choose between poverty and development brings the discussion full circle. The moral imperative of ameliorating poverty lay at the heart of the initial postwar development impulse. It was the perceived failure of economic growth strategies to meet that imperative that engendered the focus on distributional equity characteristic of the 1970s. While the specific equity strategies of that period encountered resistance and rejection, a residue survived and has become a defining element of acceptable development. The thesis in its most general form runs as follows: Growth strategies that unfairly impact on the least advantaged members of the community cannot be justified and should not be implemented. As we attempt to make the concept of "unfair impact" more specific, different versions of the thesis emerge.

The "No-Harm" Principle

The weakest, but by no means trivial, version of the "unfair impact" concept requires that during the process of overall economic growth, the well-being of the worst-off members of the community cannot be allowed to decrease. This would require, in turn, either that policies with that effect be ruled out or that effective strategies for compensating the losers be built into the initial policy design.

Although it seems limited and abstract, the no-harm principle could call into question strategies that systematically tilt in favor of cities and against rural communities—for example, by holding prices paid to rural producers at artificially low levels—unless it could be shown that poverty is disproportionately concentrated in urban areas. It could also restrict policies of "primitive accumulation," in which the least well off are made to suffer further privations today in anticipation of a more prosperous tomorrow.

The Maximin Principle

A somewhat more ambitious definition of equity is the maximin principle. Associated in recent decades with the work of John Rawls, this principle states that policies must be evaluated in light of their impact on the least advantaged members of the community. Specifically, if we are faced with a choice between policies A and B, this principle directs us to select the policy that maximizes the well-being of the worst-off individuals or groups. Inequalities are acceptable only to the extent that they in fact serve to improve the lot of these worst-off member. An important consequence of the maximin principle is that it reduces the goal of maximizing overall growth to secondary status: A higher-growth trajectory is preferred to lower growth only if faster growth is best for those at the bottom.

The Equalization Principle

A third, and in some respects the most stringent, equity principle is that of equalization, which judges economic policies with reference to their impact on the relative spread between the most and least advantaged groups in society. According to this principle, no policy may be adopted that increases the gap between the top and the bottom: Small "trickle down" effects are unacceptable if they result from the enrichment of elites.

It should be noted that maximin focuses on the absolute wealth and income position of the least advantaged, while equalization emphasizes relative position. Under maximin, individuals and groups are assumed to compare their current position with their previous and expected future positions; under equalization, they are assumed to compare themselves with others in their society. The maximin principle, therefore, is broadly consistent with "basic needs" approaches, while the equalization principle is more nearly compatible with approaches that stress relations among economic well-being, social status, and political power.

This distinction draws our attention to the risks attendant on any one-dimensional conceptualization of "poverty." A useful corrective is to be found in the work of Robert Chambers. Drawing on extensive experience in Third World nations, Chambers offers a description of "integrated rural poverty" that reflects "clusters of disadvantage." These clusters are typically characterized by five related and mutually reinforcing features. Disadvantaged rural households and communities are "poor" in that they lack assets of all kinds; "physically weak" in that there is a high ratio of dependents to able-bodied adults; "isolated" in that transportation, communication, and cultural links with other regions are inadequate; "vulnerable" in that the unit has few buffers against contingencies; and "powerless" in that their knowledge of, and ability to use, legal and political structures to their advantage is at best limited.[7] While alternative accounts to Chambers' can readily be imagined, it seems to us that he has at least sketched the space that a more fully realized theory of rural development must occupy.[8]

For Whom?

The criteria of growth and equity raise the question: Growth and equity for whom? It is conceivable that a particular community might experience both growth and increasing equity, but accompanied by—or even at the cost of—a dramatically shrinking population. We would hesitate to classify such a community as an example of successful development, and our reluctance would increase if the population decline were compelled by the absence of adequate economic opportunities.

At a minimum, adequate development requires the provision of suitable opportunities for the children of current adult members of the community. Towns in which the majority of graduating high school students are faced with a choice between emigration and unemployment can hardly be regarded as models of successful development.[9] This criterion suggests a relationship between development and indigenous birth rates.

More generally, for the wide range of societies in which income, wealth, and social respectability are critically influenced by access to employment, jobs stand out as a key indicator of opportunity. When jobs available to current community residents are seriously inadequate, quantitatively or qualitatively, basic development criteria cannot be met.

An important aspect of qualitative job opportunity is that of occupational diversity. If individuals vary widely in talents and inclinations, then societies with limited ranges of occupational choices are likely to be experienced by many residents as stifling. Intrinsic to the norm of successful "social" development, we might say, is adequate scope for "personal" development through satisfying and meaningful work. As Jane Jacobs puts it, "It is natural for human beings to build new kinds of work and skills on earlier kinds because the capacity to do this is naturally built right into us." Thus, she concludes, "An economy that contains few different sorts of niches for people's differing skills, interests, and imaginations is not efficient."[10]

There is also an empirical argument for diversity: Under contemporary circumstances in which localities are increasingly embedded in systems of national and even international competition, a significant portion of a community's economy and social structure is exposed to the possibility of significant, rapid, and unpredictable change.

We propose the following thesis: A high level of diversity makes it more likely that communities will be able to respond successfully to decline. This is so for a very simple reason: Diversity reduces the impact of decline in any single sector and provides a fusion of resources in other sectors that can be mobilized either to restore or replace the endangered part. Beyond a certain point an increase in diversity may decrease the organization's ability to oversee its affairs and to reach consensus on collective action. However, development based on a single sector poses risks for a community that may well be judged unacceptable.[11]

Successful development implies an expansion of opportunity such that new entrants into the community can be accommodated. In modern history, communities typically classified as developing have tended to generate job opportunities in excess of indigenous population growth, and thus to become magnets for immigration.

The phenomenon of population mobility does, however, raise another aspect of the "for whom?" issue. It is possible, and at many times in the United

States and elsewhere it has been the case, that particular local communities will experience opportunity deficits while the national community of which they are a part will have an opportunity surplus. If the aggregate level of opportunity is more than adequate and there are no legal or institutional barriers to individual movement from deficit to surplus region, how might the development process be judged inadequate?

At the transnational level, let us suppose one country is running an opportunity surplus while its neighbor is in deficit, and there are no barriers to mobility. Is there a problem? Yes, there is. First, in many cases the immigrants will not be treated as full members of the host nation, a distinction that can produce serious consequences in the event of economic or social disruption. Second, movement across national barriers typically entails profound linguistic and cultural dislocations as well as disruptions in patterns of social relations. Such changes are not always bad in the long run, but they do engender significant pressure on the immigrants' sense of their personal identity.

Both of these transnational phenomena are considerably attenuated in cases of intranational mobility. The latter typically does not threaten one's status as a member of the wider community; indeed, as in the case of the post-World War I black exodus from the South, it may actually enhance that status.[12] Nor need it produce the same degree of pressure on identity, for linguistic and cultural differences are usually less significant within than across national boundaries—setting aside for the moment cases in which nations contain a multiplicity of deeply separate ethnic and linguistic subcommunities.

Social Continuity

In offering the foregoing argument, we do not mean to suggest that the strains engendered by national mobility are trivial. When purchased at the price of geographical disruption, enhanced economic opportunity is frequently experienced as a mixed blessing. For many individuals, the opportunity to remain in a relatively stable community is an intrinsic element of their well-being. Indeed, social theorists have long argued that community membership is a key to forming and maintaining personal identity and, quite possibly, identification with others.

Our conclusion is that if social and cultural continuity are both intrinsic and instrumental advantages, and if such continuity is strongly correlated with geographical continuity, then an important normative argument for place-sensitive development policies emerges. This is not to say that community membership is always a good thing, since not all communities are created equal. If a particular community is so constituted as to breed extremes of violence, injustice, or oppression, its alteration is desirable.

Let us assume, however, that large numbers of communities with widely varying characteristics meet basic ethical standards. For them as participants as well as for us as observers, the choice between disruption through mobility and disruption through local cultural change is an unpalatable one. Far better would be an outcome in which a substantial measure of growth in economic opportunity is achieved in a manner consistent with substantial stability of culture and society.

But is this possible? Not according to the so-called institutionalist theorists of development—chiefly C.E. Ayres, Simon Kuznets, and John R. Commons—who found their inspiration in the work of the economist and social theorist Thorstein Veblen. Following Veblen (and Marx before him), institutionalists distinguish between "modes of production" and "social relations." Improved production, the source of increased income and wealth, is driven by gains in knowledge and technology within social systems that have the capacity to accept and utilize these gains.

Therein, say the institutionalists, lies the crux of the problem: Not all societies can achieve this; some communities are structurally open to, while others structurally resist, modern forms of knowledge and technique. In the former cases, economic growth is broadly consistent with existing social relations; in the latter, growth means disruptive social change. Reflecting on the disappointing results of post-World War II international development efforts, Kuznet put it this way:

> The transformation of an undeveloped into a developed country is not merely the mechanical addition of a stock of physical capital; it is a thoroughgoing revolution in the patterns of life . . . and must overcome the resistance of a whole complex of established interests and values.[13]

One can accept the institutionalists' general point about development—culture matters—without accepting their restrictive views that only certain kinds of cultures are compatible with development. Not too many decades ago it was fashionable to argue that "traditional" Asian societies whose cultural beliefs had been shaped by Hindu, Buddhist, or Confucian religions were largely debarred from participating in processes of development. Now we find that the "Asian Drama" described so disconsolately by Myrdal has taken an unexpectedly positive course. The "Protestant ethic" Max Weber placed at the center of modernizing change has been both relocated to Eastern cultures and questioned more radically in principle: Perhaps Eastern-style cultural solidarity is more conducive to key features of long-term development such as growth and equity than is Western/Protestant-style individualism. So far has this shift gone that James Fallows recently felt compelled to write a book arguing that the United States could in fact surmount its economic and social challenges without adopting the norms of Japanese society![14]

It is not our purpose here to resolve the complex relation between culture and development, but only to indicate that development is compatible with a much wider range of cultures than was once supposed. To bring this abstraction down to earth: If we hypothesize that cultural differences between U.S. cities and rural areas are modest by international standards, it is unlikely that rural development in the United States requires deep cultural changes. Within broad limits, the desire for continuity can be squared with strategies of development; the more important obstacles lie elsewhere.

Long-Range Self-Sufficiency

Whatever its other features may be, a key criterion of successful development is what we will call long-range self-sufficiency. By this we do not mean autarky; it would be absurd to identify development with sealed off, inward-looking communities. The idea is rather that developed communities can sustain themselves through either indigenous activities or exchange relationships with other communities. The antithesis of long-range self-sufficiency, then, is permanent dependence on external supports.

A metaphor may help clarify this idea. Prematurely born infants frequently suffer from inadequate lung development and must be surrounded with special equipment designed to assist their breathing. The purpose of the equipment is to help them reach the point at which they can breathe on their own—the point, that is, at which their lungs are adequately developed. The temporary assistance achieves its goal when it renders its presence unnecessary.

Much the same may be said of development strategies. Developing communities may need significant transfusions of external capital, technical assistance, institution-building advice, and other assistance, but they can hardly be regarded as developed unless, over time, they become progressively more able to do without such external support, or to give the outside supplier full value in return. There is thus a difference in principle between grants and loans. A regime of endless grants or subsidies is incompatible with development, while loans reflect the expectation that the borrower will eventually attain self-sufficiency in the sense of being able to return full value to the lender.

We wish to emphasize that this is not an argument against long-duration or even permanent subsidies to groups, regions, or even nations. It is rather a conceptual point: To the extent that subsidies of this nature are required, the program in question falls under the heading of social policy (or peacekeeping and world order in some international cases) rather than development per se.

Nor do we wish to understate the complexities involved in determining when groups or activities are in fact being "subsidized." Macrodecisions—for example, to socialize specific overhead costs or to create particular regulatory frameworks—may well create regimes in which particular activities flourish without visible public support while others languish. The phenomenon of "cost-shifting" that pervades so many spheres of U.S. life is but one of the consequences. In our judgment, the refinement and practical employment of full social cost accounting in the evaluation of public policy is long overdue. Once some definition of "subsidy" is accepted as part of a broader theoretical structure, the goals of development are incompatible with the existence of permanent subsidies.

Sustainability

As more than one commentator has observed, "sustainability" has become a buzzword for environmentally sensitive development in the 1980s and 1990s. The concept describes rather than resolves conflicts between environmental concerns and other development-related values.[15] Still, it seems to demonstrate an important set of considerations for development.

The notion of sustainability as we shall employ it is rooted in the fact that development is, or at least is intended to be, a process both lengthy and cumulative. The question therefore arises whether any given development strategy is self-reinforcing or self-undermining—that is, whether it can serve as the basis for an extended cumulative process or rather contains the seeds of its own demise.

This distinction is particularly clear in the area of the environment. A strategy of agricultural development may be self-undermining if it, for example, depletes the water table or rapidly erodes fertile topsoil. A strategy of resource development may be self-undermining if renewable resources such as trees are not systematically replaced or finite, unrenewable resources are treated as infinite and inexhaustible.[16] A strategy of industrial development may be unsustainable if it leads to a level of pollution that undermines the health and productivity of workers.

While the notion of sustainability finds its most natural home in the environment, wider application is possible. For example, a development strategy may be judged unsustainable if it imposes a level of stress that exceeds the capacity of the political institution that must devise and implement it. The strategy may require these institutions to receive and process more information than they can handle, or to manage more processes than they can control, to employ more coercion than is available, or to mobilize a broader base of support than can readily be mustered. Relatedly, a development strategy may be judged culturally unsustainable if its implementation brings about a confrontation with deeply held social and moral beliefs.

Underlying these various applications of sustainability is the notion that, as an extended, cumulative process, development requires the simultaneous mutual support of numerous systems—ecological, political, cultural, and others. As a dimension of development, sustainability functions as a cautionary note more than as a strict criterion. When taken seriously, it sensitizes those who carry out development strategies to the system stresses these strategies may engender and suggests the wisdom of building in feedback mechanisms that can monitor levels of stress and trigger midcourse corrections before systems self-destruct.

The need for feedback mechanisms is part of a broader consideration. Because it is subject to a complex process over an extended time, the developing entity will experience, sequentially, a wide variety of shifting circumstances. The ability to respond and adapt is therefore crucial. Conversely the incapacity to react to change—whether by an inability to recognize the fact of change or by rigid adherence to a single course of action—is almost certain to prove self-undermining.

Political Responsiveness

Political responsiveness is a vital dimension of development. Development plans that do not over time gain and maintain widespread support can only be implemented through coercion. The extreme example is the forced collectivization and industrialization of the Soviet Union in the 1930s, but there are many others extending back to the dawn of the Industrial Revolution. To the extent that we are committed to forms of collective life that minimize coercion, responsiveness to individual interests and beliefs must be built into our concept of development. A politically responsive community is desirable not only because economic and social processes of change are sustained over time, but also because it is advantageous in and of itself. Whatever its other strengths and accomplishments, we would resist calling a massively coercive society "developed."

We must be careful, however, not to construe responsiveness too narrowly. Formally democratic institutions represent one path to responsiveness. But we cannot rule out the possibility that other kinds of political institutions may also serve to take the people's wishes and interests into account. Because a community is governed through tribal mechanisms, a council of notables, or a traditional monarchy, we cannot conclude that responsiveness has yielded to coercion. It may well be that democratic institutions are much more likely to reach adequate levels of responsiveness. It does not follow that political democracy is a necessary part of the concept of development.

What is part of the concept, it seems to us, is the notion of respect, both self- and mutual. It may be that certain forms of economic growth reinforce class distinctions and make it more difficult for members of subordinated groups to consider themselves full, equal, independent members of the community. So, for example, some critics have charged that tourism-based strategies create jobs by turning locals into menial servants or, alternatively, into objects of cultural display. This raises, but does not resolve, the question of how closely an absence of respect is correlated with particular occupational and social structures.

Development and Tradeoffs

We argued at the outset that the goal of development was best understood as multivalued—that is, as consisting of multiple dimensions no one of which enjoys absolute dominance over the others. It follows that whenever plural goals cannot simultaneously be met, some way of trading off one against the others must be found.

We are now in a better position to understand what this might entail. We have already discussed the potential strains between cultural continuity and other aspects of development. And if our conception of development embraces some idea of equity as well as growth, then the familiar possibility of tensions between these goals arises.[17]

Another much discussed conflict within development is between growth and sustainability. This has been taken by some as the occasion for revisiting and revising our conception of growth in the belief that if we come to a better understanding of growth, the need to sacrifice valuable features of the environment may be reduced.

Implications for U.S. Rural Development

The concepts of development sketched in this chapter are of wide application and constitute a general framework for analysis. We now offer a general characterization of what might be termed the center of gravity of U.S. rural political culture. We are under no illusions that our description is valid for every rural community or for every group within particular communities. Nonetheless, we believe that these remarks provide a commonsense baseline for evaluating U.S. rural policies and possibilities.

Keeping in mind local variations, it seems reasonable to assume that U.S. rural communities share many of the basic cultural dispositions that characterize the United States generally. We may safely assume, to begin with, that they place a positive value on economic growth. This assumption is strengthened by the fact that (as Joyce Appleby and others have shown) since the beginning of American history, rural communities were not oriented inward to subsistence and autarky but rather have been integrated into an emerging continental and even international market economy.[18]

These rural communities, moreover, have strong feelings concerning the "growth for whom?" question. Most of them have experienced, close up, the consequences of population decline: shuttered main streets as business volume decreases; frayed generational ties as high school graduates depart; a general atmosphere of exclusion from the more dynamic mainstream. With the steady erosion of population, the problem of limited jobs and opportunity continues.[19] They therefore believe that to be judged successful, development must provide for, at the very least, population stability.

To the best of our knowledge, there is no compelling reason to believe that U.S. rural attitudes toward poverty and equity are significantly different from those of Americans generally. As foreign observers have noted at least since de Tocqueville's time, Americans are on average noticeably less solidaristic and economically redistributionist than are Europeans. Norms of independence apply at least as strongly at the individual as at the community level. In times of deep and pervasive hardship, these norms are to some extent supplanted. During the Great Depression, for example, the initial tendency of the unemployed to blame themselves for their plight was eventually overlaid by explanations at the level of economic and social structure. The classic theme of moral individualism—people get what they deserve for good or ill—was diluted by the rise of what might be called "There but for the grace of God go I" sentiments. At some point, the community ceased to regard the down-and-out as "they" and began to think of them as "we." Without this shift, the construction of the modern U.S. welfare state would not have been politically feasible.

But while the concern for social justice in rural America may not have risen appreciably during the past generation, interest in sustainability almost certainly has. Questions of depletion, pollution, and renewability are now part of the consciousness of ordinary citizens as well as policy makers. This does not mean that sustainability enjoys an absolute priority, or even relative dominance, vis-a-vis other aspects of development. Loggers will protest safeguards for old-growth forests that may cost them their jobs; farmers will object to what they see as overblown and excessively intrusive protection for wetlands. Still, in the course of framing development strategies, there is on balance a greater willingness to take the future into account (as opposed to 30 years ago) and to consider tradeoffs with real costs attached.

We come, finally, to the issue of political responsiveness. The fact that the United States is a representative democracy and that its Constitution guarantees a "republican form of government" sets limits to the tradeoffs between responsiveness and other dimensions of development that can be entertained within the American context. Still, the history of this century reveals some important changes.

For more than 30 years, one man (Robert Moses) was able to exercise near-plenipotentiary power over key aspects of development in New York City and its environs—a pattern repeated in gentler forms in many urban areas governed by an informal coalition of local notables.[20] During the 1960s, the federal government sought with only modest success to increase the element of public participation in urban development efforts, and the federal programs spearheading this initiative were subsequently scaled back or eliminated altogether. Still, the urban ferment of the 1960s has left an important residue: Political elites now find it useful and sometimes necessary to consult more widely and to construct procedures that provide neighborhoods with channels of protest against externally imposed changes. (In this regard, the contrast between urban highway siting today and 30 years ago is instructive.)

Several recent studies indicate that political responsiveness is positively correlated with successful local development strategies. This is especially true when communities are undergoing severe stress and must somehow mobilize internal resources and allocate sacrifice to effect change. This research points to the optimistic conclusion that the relations between political and other dimensions of development can be one of mutual reinforcement rather than painful tradeoffs. Whatever may be true in developing countries,[21] enhanced political responsiveness and economic development appear to go hand in hand in rural America. We shall return to this issue in Chapter 4.

3

Development: An Economic Process

In this chapter we turn from our conceptual framework to focus more directly on development as an economic process. To create a context for considering the issues facing U.S. rural development, we cast our net widely. We start by asking what can be learned from the theory and practice of Third World development, from contemporary analyses of global economic change, and from competing theories of rural economic change.

Third World Economic Development, 1950–1990

At first glance it may seem that the relevance of Third World development efforts for rural America is limited at best. After all, differences of initial income levels, of history and culture, and of social and political structure are vast. The contextual difference is equally fundamental: The development challenges facing rural America take place within an already urbanized, industrialized country, not within a political community struggling to move a largely peasant population into a modern socioeconomy. Nevertheless, there is something of significance to be learned from a brief glance at the theory and practice of Third World development over the past 40 years.

We have divided this history into three phases: (1) post-World War II reliance on the public sector, (2) the neoclassical revival, and (3) governmental activism.

Reliance on Public Sector

The first phase of economic development in the Third World, which began shortly after World War II, was characterized by a high degree of reliance on planned public sector activity. This emphasis is not hard to explain. Key experiences of the 1930s—in particular the Great Depression, the Keynesian revolution, and the apparent success of forced industrialization in the Soviet

Union—had combined to undermine confidence in market mechanisms and to boost the prestige of government. The leading events of the 1940s pushed farther in this direction. World War II, after all, had been won in large measure through a massive mobilization of resources led by the public sector, and the Marshall Plan had successfully jump-started the stalled economies of Western Europe.[1]

These experiences were supported by a conceptual structure with roots in classical theory: the idea of market failures. In other words, whenever the conditions of perfect competition fail to obtain in practice, market transactions may fail to produce optimal results. For example: Information may be imperfect; certain costs or benefits of particular transactions may not be met by the transacting parties, but may be externalized (as in water pollution caused by a manufacturing plant); transaction costs may be steep; monopoly distortions may exist; structural obstacles may impede full responses to price signals; institutional preconditions for long-term risk-taking may be absent; factor shortages may prevent productive investments; public goods needed for economic growth may not be fully supplied.[2] Because one or more of these circumstances almost always exists, the theory of market failure was ardently embraced as a guide to practice.

Beyond government success and market failure, another factor supporting confidence in the public sector was a broad agreement on the nature of development. The goal was to improve the lot of impoverished peoples through aggregate economic growth. The prime obstacle to rapid, sustainable growth was the shortage of capital stemming from the inability of poor countries to raise internal funds. The solution was externally supplied capital, judiciously invested in large projects that would break through the vicious circle of poverty. And because "social overhead capital" (transportation, communications, power, urban infrastructure, and the like) had to be in place before private entrepreneurs or foreign governments could be expected to commit directly productive capital, investment allocation required the intervention of governments and sometimes of multilateral agencies.[3]

Concerning this consensus, doubts soon arose on two fronts. During the 1950s, a number of economists showed that the contribution of capital to GNP growth was far smaller than had been supposed. Rather, "residual factors" such as advancing knowledge, technical skills, social learning, and organizational improvements were key.[4] At roughly the same time, Albert Hirschman questioned the thesis that factor shortage was the obstacle to economic growth. Every organization, he suggested, contains significant amounts of "slack": underutilized human and material resources. The main task of development, then, is to prompt action that creatively uses what is already available.[5]

Other difficulties were less theoretical. Orthodox development strategies seemed in practice to experience four kinds of failure. There was, first, failure at the heart of the enterprise: Many projects, particularly investments in "social overhead," did not induce the kind of self-sustaining growth they were intended to produce. The issue thus arose as to how, if at all, particular economic activities were causally connected to others. Some appeared relatively self-contained, even sterile, while others seemed to trigger chain reactions. Hirschman formalized this insight in the concept of linkages: "Backward" linkages occur when the appearance of product X stimulates the production of Y, needed as an input for X, and "forward" linkages occur when X serves as a more efficient input for final product Z. This conceptual structure led in turn to empirical questions concerning the kinds of activities that were most likely to induce the desired chain reactions.[6]

Beyond failures of growth were failures of equity. The perception that even rapid rates of growth in developing countries had failed to benefit individuals and communities at the bottom of the socioeconomic ladder became widespread. Indeed, it was argued, income gaps were widening, ratios of inequality were increasing, and the poorest of the poor were finding themselves even worse off. These perceptions led to a new emphasis on inequality, poverty, and basic needs as appropriate subjects of direct attention.[7] This raised, in turn, the question of whether development could be understood simply as economic policy or, rather, required a mix of social policy and perhaps even structural institutional reform as well.[8]

Another level of failure was cultural. The impact of economic development on existing cultural patterns had been anticipated to some extent, but the degree of distress and resistance it was to engender had been underestimated. Development strategies led by Western governments or Western-dominated multilateral agencies came to be perceived in many quarters as assaults on the cultural identity of developing countries. Not surprisingly, rising popular ambivalence soon found intellectual expression.[9]

A final level of failure was political. Early thinkers had assumed that economic growth would go hand in hand with political democratization. But events turned out far differently, especially in Africa and Latin America, giving rise to theories of authoritarian government as the likely accompaniment of rapid industrialization.[10]

An important arena of conflict throughout this early period was the relationship between trade and development. Classical economists had endorsed unfettered trade as in the best interests of all parties. While rejecting the classical preference for markets over the public sector, the first wave of development economics had retained what Hirschman calls the "mutual benefit assumption": the belief that relations between developed and developing nations could be shaped to serve the interests of both.[11] The problem was that inequalities between these two groups of nations had the effect of transferring most of the benefits of unfettered trade to the more powerful nation. Scholars such as Raul Prebisch and Gunnar Myrdal argued that while the terms of trade for Third World primary products were increasingly adverse, open trade regimes had the effect of destroying traditional production and strangling infant industries—trends that combined to leave developing countries impoverished and dependent.[12] The solution was restriction on imports, designed to protect domestic markets and to give infant industries a fair chance to mature.[13]

A number of Latin American countries instituted or expanded the strategy of "import substitution." It quickly encountered difficulties. To the extent that domestic industries required foreign inputs, protectionism raised their costs. Meanwhile, inattention to exports restricted the ability of these countries to accumulate foreign exchange needed to finance imports and also deprived them of the dynamic benefits of international trade. During the 1960s, on the other hand, a lengthening list of countries outside Latin America, particularly in Asia, were attaining sustained high growth rates through outward-oriented export policies.[14]

The Neoclassical Revival

The events catalogued above set the stage for the second phase of development economics, which may be termed the neoclassical revival. The negative element of this revival was a theoretical effort to replace market failure with a new understanding of "government failure." As Anne Krueger, one of the leaders of this new movement, argues, early development economists had assumed that the government would behave as a "benevolent social guardian, in the Fabian Socialist tradition. . . . [But] one must ask why economists were ever comfortable with the simultaneous beliefs that individuals in the private sector act in their self-interest and that individuals in the public sector are motivated by a Benthamite vision of social justice." It is more realistic, she suggests, to assume that individuals within the public sector are as concerned with their self-interest (survival, promotion, reelection) as those in the private sector, and that agencies are likely to be captured by, or to represent, special interests rather than the national interest.[15]

Government activity diverted by individual self-interest also has perverse effects on nongovernmental behavior. Two such governmental activities are of particular importance. First, government actions tend to encourage "rent-seeking behavior": Individuals will spend resources to capture property rights or nonmarket advantages created by the government. Mrinal Datta-Chauduri, no enemy of government-led development, spells out the consequences for India's private manufacturing sector, which operates under a system of bureaucratic rationing: "With the legal barriers to entry instituted by the licensing system, they do not have much incentive for either cost reduction or quality improvement. Their perceptions, as businessmen, become more and more fixed toward cornering the rents associated with the distribution of licenses."[16]

Second, the intervention of government will tend to produce or strengthen interest groups that seek to defend publicly conferred advantages. The classic (pluralistic) model is that already existing groups induce the government to create these advantages. But as Krueger observes, "It also frequently happens that, once an intervention starts—regardless of motive—those benefitting from it organize to exert political pressure to maintain and increase their benefits."[17]

Table 1

Problems of State Intervention[18]

Individuals may know more about their own preferences and circumstances than the government.

Government planning may increase risk by pointing everyone in the same direction—governments may make bigger mistakes than markets.

Government planning may be more rigid and inflexible than private decision-making since complex decision-making machinery may be involved in government.

Government may be incapable of administering detailed plans.

Government controls may stifle private sector individual initiative if there are many bureaucratic obstacles.

Organizations and individuals require incentives to work, innovate, control costs, and allocate efficiently; the disciplines and rewards of the market cannot easily be replicated within public enterprises and organizations.

Different levels and parts of government may be poorly coordinated in the absence of equilibrating signals provided by the market, particularly where groups or regions with different interests are involved.

Markets place constraints on what can be achieved by government. For example, resale of commodities on black markets and activities in the informal sector can disrupt rationing or other nonlinear pricing or taxation schemes.

Controls create resource-using ("rent-seeking" or "directly unproductive") activities to influence those controls through lobbying or corruption.

Planning may be manipulated by privileged and powerful groups. Such groups may actually be created or strengthened by the public planning process itself.

Governments may be dominated by narrow-interest groups pursuing their own welfare and sometimes actively hostile to large sections of the population.

This negative thrust of neoclassicism, the critique of government intervention, leads directly to its positive recommendations. To begin with, government must restrict its activities, primarily the provision of large-scale public goods, to areas in which it arguably has an advantage. This is particularly important because government is not costless and absorbs not only resources but administrative talent and energy that are typically in short supply in developing areas. Second, there is a general presumption in favor of liberalization, external and internal. Trade should be liberalized, and direct involvement in manufacturing, credit allocation, and licensing should be minimized. Third, when government activity seems justified in principle, that activity should be organized so as to minimize administrative bureaucratic mechanisms and reduce incentives for rent-seeking behavior. For example, tariffs are preferable to import quotas.[19]

We mentioned earlier that the contrast between the relative failure of Latin American development and the rapid growth attained by many Asian nations had helped clear the way for the neoclassical revival. It is not surprising, then, that unpersuaded scholars turned to a closer examination of Asian success stories. In a detailed study, for example, Larry Westphal was able to show that South Korea's rapid advance was based on a combination of export promotion and protection for infant industries. Each of these taken individually required significant levels of government activism, as did efforts to coordinate them. On balance, Westphal concludes, "selective intervention has greatly contributed to Korea's remarkable success . . . by accelerating the rate of growth with little if any compensating loss in efficiency."[20]

Westphal's proposed explanation is important. He suggests that market imperfections associated with technological change, generally thought to be negligible, are in fact very significant. Because the mere possession of technology guarantees neither understanding of it nor its adaptation to local circumstances, technology is far from perfectly tradable. The returns from particular technological investments may thus be largely unattainable by individual market agents. Thus, if appropriately used, "selective intervention may greatly increase a country's ability to capture dynamic economies associated with the introduction and exploitation of modern technology."[21]

Looking at successes in India as well as South Korea, Datta-Chauduri arrives at a parallel conclusion. India established state-run sales outlets to distribute products produced in local communities, and this network became involved in the dissemination of information, product designs, and production techniques. Similarly, South Korean trading companies horizontally integrate a number of exchange-related activities, including marketing, communications, and technology transfer. The common element justifying these activities and contributing to their effectiveness is the existence of important externalities in information-processing and other exchange-related activities. Institutions designed to capture and share these externalities thus constitute the vital "soft infrastructure" of developing market economies.[22]

The point of these and other case studies is to demonstrate that the area of market failure in modern economies may be wider than is commonly supposed by the revivalists and that government is not as consistently hamhanded as its critics suppose.

Governmental Activism

In recent years, this counterthrust has been broadened into what may be described as the third phase of postwar development economics. "Bringing the state back in" could well serve as the slogan for this emerging movement. Its core premises can be summarized as follows:

1. The neoclassical critique of trade protection/import substitution as a model for development is distinguishable from, and does not logically or empirically entail, the broader critique of governmental activism. In fact, successful export-oriented policies are compatible with—may even be strengthened by—infant industry protection and other government interventions in the domestic economy. Moreover, not all export strategies are created equal. The kinds of benefits achieved through the expansion of manufacturing exports are probably not available for most primary products.[23]

2. Although the neoclassical critique of government failure represents a valuable corrective to earlier naiveté, it does not rule out the existence of the market failures that justified government intervention in the first place. If anything, recent economic theory and experience have tended to expand the sphere in which market failures may be expected.[24]

3. The relative weight to be attached to government failure versus market failure does not permit a general answer. It is an empirical rather than theoretical question, the answer to which depends on specific circumstances. All the following factors (and more) bear decisively on the form of collective action a particular society is best advised to employ: the kinds of growth one seeks to achieve, the nature of the market failures to be overcome, the institutional capacity of governments embedded within distinctive histories and culture.[25]

4. In most cases of successful development, including the industrialization push in all the now-rich countries, public interventions in everything from legal structures to credit were numerous and significant. It

is therefore not evident that the burden of proof should be borne entirely by those advocating public sector policies.[26]

5. The conflict between public and private initiatives should not be overstated. Well-designed public projects can "crowd in" rather than displace private investment. Conversely, infant industry protection policies cannot in the long run provide world-class costs and variety unless domestically produced goods become competitive in world markets.[27]

In short, beyond their classic social functions in the areas of basic needs, distribution, and citizenship, public institutions and policies have important economic roles to play: They must overcome market failures, internalize costs and benefits omitted from private-sector decision making, and address collective action problems by making available the provision of public goods that would not be optimally supplied through the market.

To define appropriate roles in principle, however, is only the beginning of the argument. To move from principles to concrete practice, a solid case must be offered that proposed public programs will not be captured and subverted by private or bureaucratic interests. In this connection, institutional and policy innovations designed to overcome the defects of the traditional top-down bureaucratic state will prove essential. (For fuller discussion, see Chapter 4.)

Implications for Rural Development

The purpose of this excursion was not to investigate the history of Third World development for its own sake, but rather to determine what relevant lessons, if any, might be drawn from it for U.S. rural development. Bearing in mind all the caveats, stated earlier, about key contextual differences, the following inferences from the Third World to the U.S. rural case are plausible.

1. There is no excuse for naiveté about the public sector—about the likely motives of either the providers or the beneficiaries of government programs. The omnipresent threat of government failure means that advocates of public activity must discharge an initial burden of proof. It also means that programs must be designed to minimize, so far as possible, incentives for unproductive behavior.

2. What we typically call "economic development" is in practice divisible into two categories: (1) self-sustaining economic growth and (2) social policy designed to provide the requisites of existence and citizenship to

all. While the former can help provide the wherewithal for the latter, we should be under no illusions that growth by itself will fulfill basic needs.

3. The provision of infrastructure, and more generally of "social overhead capital," occupies an ambiguous status between growth and social policy. While there is some evidence that infrastructure is a condition for private sector growth, and even that it can encourage private sector investment, it is highly unlikely that the totality of infrastructure spending can be justified along these lines. To some extent, access to public infrastructure is part of a social definition of what it means to be a full and equal member of the community.

4. The justification of public sector activity as a contributor to self-sustaining economic growth rests largely on the identification of market failures. Students of U.S. rural development should therefore devote increased energy to the documentation of rural market failure, with special attention to questions of access to information transaction costs, marketing, and technology acquisition.

5. The traditional emphasis on "hard" factors of production such as capital and human resources should be supplemented by an increased focus on "soft" factors—institutions that facilitate social learning and collective action. Rather than stressing external provision of resources, students of rural development should employ Hirschman's conception of slack to investigate—and where possible inventory—underutilized rural resources and to devise strategies that encourage local residents to mobilize those resources. Public entrepreneurship helps provide a context for private entrepreneurship.

6. Rural development professionals should focus on linkages—that is, seek out economic activities that are likely to trigger chains of related activities. In this connection, it should be noted that studies over the past two decades have shown that enterprises originating within a specific locality have a greater tendency to develop linkages than do those attracted from the outside.[28] This is but one reason among many for giving "attraction efforts" a subordinate position within overall development strategies.

7. As a general matter, autarkic or inward-looking development strategies are unlikely to succeed. Rural areas must instead seek out productive connections with vibrant external economies that can help stimulate local activities. They must ask themselves what kinds of new products, services, or amenities can be developed for export. As we shall see in Part II,

however, the traditional notion of exports must be broadened to include more than the physical transfer of goods, or even the electronic transmission of information and services.

During the past decade, many observers have noted that successful economic development strategies have combined vigorous export promotion with systematic protection for infant industries. It is at this point that the lack of similarities between sovereign nations and subnational regions becomes most striking. Relations between rural and nonrural regions differ structurally from relations between nations. In contemporary circumstances, rural regions do not have the ability to restrict imports from other parts of their country, and they lack independent currencies whose fluctuations could signal, and help reverse, weaknesses in exports.[29] Jane Jacobs compares the relationship among national policies to a group of people "who are all properly equipped with diaphragms and lungs but who share only one brain-stem breathing center." Even though they may be engaged in different activities with varying oxygen requirements, they will all receive the same simultaneous breathing signals based on aggregate (or more precisely, average) demand. The result will be to overload some systems and stifle others.[30]

The obvious retort is that regions also get the benefit of membership in larger national markets. For example, in spite of constant interregional conflict over tariffs and national monetary policy, the states that banded together to form the United States benefitted enormously from the creation of a unified continental market without the divisions engendered by tariffs, quotas, and currency distortions. There can be little doubt that the creation of just such a market was one of the major objectives of the supporters of the 1787 Constitution.

However, this retort, though qualitatively valid, does not decide the issue. More than 30 years ago, Gunnar Myrdal and Albert Hirschman independently developed the distinction between two effects, pointing in opposite directions, that spatial economic units have on one another. Consider two such units, A and B, the former wealthier than the latter. In a market in which transfers of labor, capital, and technology are unrestrained, their interaction may help "spread" A's wealth to B. Alternatively, it may further exacerbate the "polarization" between them. No general economic theory can tell us which effect will predominate in specific circumstance.[31]

It is clear, however, that poorer regions will have better prospects if they can somehow enjoy the best of both worlds: unfettered participation in external markets plus some degree of internal protection. This suggests the need for regional "equivalents of sovereignty." Possibilities include national corporation income tax deductions for investments in poorer regions (the equivalent in some respects of a tariff); expanded local credit autonomy; local, state, and regional variations in tax policy; subnational trade relations with foreign countries; preferential exchange rates for poorer regions' international exports.[32]

Lessons from Global Economic Change

These considerations lead directly to the second of our topics in this chapter: the significance of global economic change for our understanding of U.S. rural development. The initial point concerns the definition of economic entities. Since Adam Smith's time, and even before his time, it has been assumed that the "nation" is the basic economic unit—hence titles such as "The Wealth of Nations" and concepts such as the "Gross National Product." But in recent years the primacy of the nation has been attacked, so to speak, from above and from below. Drucker notes the rise of three supranational forces: (1) multinational regions, such as the European Economic Community; (2) the world economy of money, credit, and investment flows, organized from information that knows no national boundaries; and (3) transnational enterprises that view the entire developed world as one location for producing, and one market for selling, an enormous range of goods and services.[33]

Working from the other direction, Jane Jacobs has advanced the city-region as the preferred unit for analyzing and conducting economic life:

> Nations are political and military entities . . . But it doesn't necessarily follow from this that they are also the basic, salient entities of economic life or that they are particularly useful for probing the mysteries of economic structure, the reasons for rise and decline of wealth. . . . Once we remove the blinders of the mercantilist tautology and try looking at the real economic world in its own right rather than as a dependent artifact of politics, we can't avoid seeing that most nations are composed of collections or grab-bags of very different economies.[34]

There is, of course, no reason why Drucker and Jacobs cannot both be on to something, and in fact they are. We suggest, therefore, that rural policy must be framed with an awareness of the extent to which the nation is no longer the sole, or even the prime, site for wealth formation. Here are only the most obvious points: (1) Cooperation among firms in the form of flexible manufacturing networks may point to subnational regions as crucial economic units.[35] (2) To the extent that production is carried out by transnational firms, managements will constantly be comparing U.S. rural sites with potential locations around the globe. (3) The political/administrative structure of rising multinational regions such as the European Community may well have an effect on site selection, above and beyond general economic considerations.

Even if we retain the nation-state as our unit of analysis, we must alter our understanding of the sources of national wealth. The following considerations seem fundamental.

Work Force

Robert Reich has argued that as every advanced economy becomes global, skills and cumulative learning of the work force become the key to national competitiveness. In fact, American competitiveness should be defined as the capacity of American workers to add value to the world economy. The reason, he asserts, is that every other factor of production—capital, state-of-the-art factories, technology—is mobile and interchangeable. A work force that is knowledgeable and skilled at performing complex tasks is thus the key to attracting long-term investment in productive facilities.[36]

While Reich's point is important and broadly valid, it must be qualified. To begin: Skilled labor is mobile across national as well as regional lines, giving rise to significant externalities. This leakage is particularly significant for developing countries that make large investment in education and training, only to see much of it vanish in a much-discussed "brain drain." This phenomenon has led one prominent student of development, the economist Jagdish Bhagwati, to propose that developed countries should impose a supplementary income tax on the earnings of skilled immigrants from developing countries and remit the proceeds to their countries of origin, permitting those countries to achieve a fair return on their human resource investments.[37] Although dealing with such leakages across regional rather than national lines poses some additional practical problems, the general point remains valid.

There is at least one other respect in which Reich's emphasis must be qualified: skilled workers may be the raw material of the modern economy, but skilled management is needed to organize, motivate, and direct them. A decade ago, for example, it was fashionable to blame the poor quality and low productivity of U.S. automobile factories on various deficiencies of U.S. assembly-line workers. Then, during the 1980s, an increasing number of Japanese automobile firms established full production plants in the United States. Within a remarkably short time, there was no quality or productivity gap between these plants and their Japan-based counterparts. The critical variable, evidently, was not the skill of individual workers but rather the ability to manage them.[38]

These caveats notwithstanding, a more modest version of Reich's thesis seems incontrovertible: Although worker skills and training do not constitute a sufficient condition for national or regional competitiveness, they are a necessary condition.[39] Economic development strategies must therefore concentrate on investing in human resources and on establishing mechanisms that enable the public sector investor to gain the returns from such investments.

Innovation and Entrepreneurship

More than half a century ago, Joseph Schumpeter argued that innovation was the prime source of economic growth. While Keynesian macroeconomists have been unable to give a plausible account of innovation within the structure of their theory (in the jargon, it is treated as an exogenous variable), recent empirical studies on the determinants of economic growth have strongly supported Schumpeter's hypothesis.[40]

Innovation has two faces, which may be called "creation" and "diffusion." Creation is simply the conceptual development of new products, production processes, and mechanisms of distribution, while diffusion is the effective implementation of these conceptual breakthroughs by private firms or public sector institutions. A substantial body of evidence now exists that the fastest growing nations in the past two decades have been those that proved most adept at diffusion. The United States, by contrast, has remained the world leader in the creation of innovation but has fallen far behind in diffusion.

Explanations are multiple. They include "free-rider" phenomena—the ability of nations focusing on diffusion to appropriate U.S. conceptual breakthroughs at relatively low cost. Management failures are also important: Notoriously, key products such as VCRs were developed in the United States but successfully commercialized elsewhere. But more important than either of these is the fact that innovation has externalities that those investing in it cannot fully appropriate for themselves. Successful public sector efforts enhance the willingness of private firms to invest in innovation without tilting the playing field or "picking winners and losers."[41]

The central role of innovation has important implications for U.S. rural development. Jane Jacobs argues that both the creation and diffusion of innovation are essentially metropolitan functions and that rural regions are bound therefore to remain dependent and vulnerable.[42] The case for cities as centers of innovation–creation seems hard to deny. A key issue for rural areas is whether they can learn to do a better job of implementing innovation developed elsewhere, in a manner that creates new rural employment possibilities for workers displaced by technological change. As we saw in the previous section, well-focused public programs that share information ("technology extension"), generate rural networks, and create economies of scale can make a difference.

Another possible niche for rural areas is in incremental innovation, as distinguished from the large breakthroughs symbolized by, for example, the VCR. Some critics of U.S. business point to a lack of interest in the continuous improvement of existing products and processes. These small innovations, which affect variables such as quality, durability, and ease of production, can add up to lower costs and greater market share. Although most rural facilities lack the capacity for large discontinuous discoveries, they may have a better chance of contributing to the more mundane, but vitally important, process of incremental improvement.

Comparative Advantage

The classic Ricardian theory views comparative advantage as relatively static, dictated by natural factors such as land, raw materials, climate, and population. More recent theory, however, characterizes comparative advantage as dynamic—that is, as affected by changes in technique and managerial know-how as well as by patterns of public investment. Moreover, trade may spur import-substitution by demonstrating the existence of local markets for particular products and by permitting learning in the form of reverse engineering.[43]

A corollary of this shift is that comparative advantage may be created: A geographic unit may make a conscious choice about the economic areas in which it achieves a competitive edge. This choice will of course be constrained in various ways: Barriers of distance and remoteness may prevent some rural areas from participating in certain parts of the domestic economy; regions with near full employment are unlikely to succeed in new labor-intensive production; nations with small internal markets may find it difficult to break into already crowded sectors of the international economy, even if they protect their infant industries. Still, the range of options is wide.

These facts give rise to public entrepreneurship as a central fact of modern economic growth. Even if we are accustomed to thinking of individual entrepreneurship as a component of success, we are less familiar with the parallels between firms and political jurisdictions. Communities, regions, and even nations can frame strategic economic plans and achieve excellence in specific economic sectors through deliberate public choice.[44] We shall return to this theme in Chapter 4.

Time Horizons

During the past decade, there has been a growing awareness that both individuals and organizations can make suboptimal allocations of resources between the present and the future. Individuals can prefer excessive consumption to personal savings; firms can focus on the next quarter's profit at the expense of long-term market share; governments can bloat income-maintenance programs while starving public investment in infrastructure, research, and development. A central challenge of modern economic development is to create mechanisms that maintain a wise balance between present needs and future progress. For example, tax laws can have a major effect on the choice between consumption and investment as well as among alternative investment possibilities.

The distinction between consumption and investment bears directly on U.S. rural areas. As Kenneth Deavers has pointed out, the composition of federal spending in urban and rural areas is quite different: Rural areas receive a larger share of federal funds in the form of transfer payments and current consumption. For example, per capita federal spending on higher education and research was more than twice as high in urban as in rural areas. Further, the evidence suggests that federal spending in such areas as farm price support and income maintenance tends to squeeze out programs directed toward long-term investment.[45] An important task for U.S. rural development, therefore, is to reorient programs in a manner that promotes economic growth over the long haul.

Theories of Rural Economic Change

To account for observed rural economic change over the past three decades, a number of theories and models have been proposed. In 1967, Brian J.L. Berry examined the applicability of trade, location, and export/staple theories to rural growth.[46] In 1989, Steven Kale updated and expanded Berry's analysis.[47] The following theories and models draw heavily on the work of these two authors.

Income Equalization Model

This model assumes that capital and labor are perfectly mobile and will move to areas where the highest returns are obtained: Workers will migrate from low-wage to high-wage regions, while capital will flow in the opposite direction, leading to an eventual convergence of incomes among regions.

The assumption of equalized income has been shown empirically to be unrealistic and the usefulness of this model has decreased. While considerable wage-induced movement from rural to urban areas has occurred, income differences have persisted and, as we have seen, have even expanded over the past decade. Lack of information and ties to family and community are among the reasons cited. It would also appear, although the evidence is somewhat less clear, that high information and transaction costs have impeded the operation of rural capital markets.

This model also raises deeper questions about labor mobility. A number of studies have indicated that such mobility increases rather than decreases regional disparities because migrants generally comprise a higher percentage of individuals with education and desire for economic improvement; those left behind may be unsuited for a wide range of economic activities or may be out of the work force altogether.[48] In the course of a striking transnational survey, Jane Jacobs concludes that out-migration from regions with limited opportunities has no effect on their stagnant economies other than to shrink them. In practice, she suggests, there is very little evidence of the equilibrating mechanisms posited by factor equalization theories.[49]

Unbalanced Growth Models

As we have seen, Hirschman, Myrdal, and others have developed models of unbalanced growth. Because of initial advantages in location, transportation, labor, or other factors, growth occurs more rapidly in certain areas than in others, resulting in a polarization of capital, income, opportunity, and overall standard of living between more- and less-developed regions. Eventually, however, growth at the core leads to expanded demand for goods and services produced at the periphery. If these spread effects outweigh the polarization effects, peripheral areas begin to grow.

As applied to U.S. rural areas, the unbalanced growth model has been less than successful, for a number of reasons. Demand for rural products typically does not rise as rapidly as income. Indeed, with technological substitution it may even fall. Further, the ability of rural areas to meet demand from urban growth poles at competitive prices will frequently depend on rising inputs of productivity-enhancing technologies, generating more surplus rural labor. And finally, there is no guarantee that growing urban areas will continue to purchase from domestic rural areas. In a global economy with declining transport costs, Mexican tomatoes and Zairean copper will take market share away from U.S. producers.

Beyond these empirical considerations lie more general doubts about the application of unbalanced growth models to rural development. Jane Jacobs, for example, argues that all self-sustaining economic growth occurs in cities and their regions—that is, in those counties typically categorized as "metro-adjacent." She would not be surprised by—indeed, she more or less predicted—the strong correlation between adjacency and growth in the 1980s. These "active" economies generate growth through continual processes of innovation and improvisation, sustained by the size, diversity, and contiguity of cities' populations, which leads to an increased capacity to substitute internal production for previously imported goods. "Passive" economies, by contrast, do not generate internal growth, produce only a narrow and relatively static range of exports, and remain dependent on other economies for all other goods—or do without them altogether.

Jacobs' argument is cast in nontechnical, even polemical language, but in substance it resembles, and tacitly draws upon, well-established lines of scholarship. For example, as Kenneth Deavers observes, "Central place theory, perhaps the most powerful concept of regional science, suggests that rural territory with low population density, limited economies of scale, greater distance to markets, information, and technology, and fewer opportunities for specialization, will probably always lag behind larger urban places in a purely market-driven economy."[50]

Jacobs' understanding of economic growth leads her to a pronounced pessimism about the entire enterprise of rural economic development. She argues that rural areas (supply regions) are almost bound to be stunted and vulnerable to resource depletion, technological substitution, and foreign competition. Further, she claims that the most prominent rural development strategies (reliance on raw materials, industrial attraction, outside investment, and the basic-needs approach pursued by the World Bank under Robert MacNamara) are demonstrably ineffective. These strategies may, up to a point, transfer enough income to rural areas to relieve the worst of human misery. But that is all they can do. In particular, they cannot generate sustainable economic growth.

While Jacobs' argument is hardly supportive of rural development, it is not a complete dead end. Rather, it suggests that rural areas cannot take off economically unless they somehow become part of a city region. There are three ways in which this might occur. First, technological changes in transportation and communication might expand the functional meaning of adjacency.[51] Second, separated rural communities might be able to "federate" in ways that replicate key aspects of urban areas. Third, rural communities might generate their own growth poles, in the form of newly developed import-replacing cities.

Jacobs is skeptical about the chances of accelerating this third strategy through direct public action. She denies that self-sustaining cities can be planned and built on the analogy of a military operation. Rather, they must arise through a largely spontaneous process of creative innovation that leads to new ways of producing for export. Development, she insists, is not an infusion of external wealth, is not a collection of production tools, but rather is a commitment to the process of indigenous change within a context that can sustain that process.

Jacobs' argument suggests the need for a focused research agenda. For example, what does the record of the past three decades reveal concerning efforts to create regional "growth poles"?[52] It also sounds a cautionary note about expansive hopes for rural development: Whatever steps may be feasible to expand adjacency, certain areas are almost certain to remain remote "bypassed places." Public assistance can help the residents of such places lead better lives, but this social policy should not be confused with strategies for achieving self-sustaining economic growth.

Export Base Model

Jacobs' emphasis on import-substitution can easily be confused with the failed inward-looking protectionist policies followed by many Latin American nations a generation ago. In fact, she proposes a cycle in which the capacity to export successfully enables a city to earn an increasing volume of diverse imports, for which it subsequently devises its own replacements.[53]

Beginning with Douglass North, a number of economists have developed theories of the first phase of that cycle.[54] The core proposition is that regional economies develop because of demands for commodities produced for export to consumers outside the region. Demand growth in these "basic" export sectors triggers intrasectoral increases in employment and income as well as linkages to other sectors in the regional economy.

Export base theory undoubtedly illuminates past patterns of rural growth and decline. In practice, it is frequently easy to identify the core of a rural community's economy and to trace the impact of falling demand for basic exports on other economic sectors within the community (coal and copper, for example).

There are however two difficulties with this model as a guide to future rural economic development. First, it does not come to grips with Jacobs' key point: Exports that do not stimulate import substitution and economic diversification leave their communities highly vulnerable to resource depletion, technological substitution, and external competition. Local consumer services that feed off exports represent a multiplication, not amelioration, of this essential vulnerability.

Second, as we will show in Part II, our understanding of the "base" available to rural areas must be expanded. In the 1990s and beyond, local earnings derived from the in-migration (temporary or permanent) of individuals with assured income sources are likely to prove increasingly important relative to earnings from the export of goods and services.

Product Cycle Model

As Kale notes, the product cycle is perhaps the most widely used explanation of rural economic growth during the 1960s and 1970s. A product's life cycle is said to pass through three stages: innovation, growth, and standardization. The first two stages are predominantly urban functions, but the third, "routine production," can and does filter down to more peripheral rural areas where labor and other costs are relatively low.

There is little doubt about the utility of this model in understanding the post-1950s rural manufacturing surge, as well as current patterns of rural employment.[55] It is less promising, however, as a guide to future rural development. To begin with, as the past decade proved, routine manufacturing is increasingly likely to be located in other countries with even lower costs than those available in rural America. There is little hope that recent declines in rural manufacturing employment will be reversed. Further, even if routine manufacturing does remain, international competition will tend to depress the wages it commands relative to those in other economic sectors. To the extent that U.S. rural communities continue to depend on routine manufacturing, wage and income differentials between rural and urban areas are likely to increase during the 1990s. We expand on these themes in Chapter 4.[56]

Location Models

Based on neoclassical revival economic theory, location theories focus on distance and the costs of overcoming it. Typically, these theories regard transportation as the most important factor determining the location of economic activities.

As Kale notes, location models have been particularly useful for analyzing rural development in cases in which their underlying assumptions are empirically valid—in particular, for economic activities characterized by large amounts of weight or bulk lost during the processing of materials. Many such activities are located in rural areas.[57]

There are, however, a number of considerations that reduce the overall utility of location theory in its classic form. To begin with, the determinants of location have shifted in response to economic change. More than 20 years ago, Edgar Hoover was already able to sketch these changes: (1) Costs of physical transport of heavy and bulky goods are diminishing in importance relative to speedy, flexible transportation of high-valued goods and to communications—that is, the transmission of intangible goods and information. (2) Access to markets has increased in importance relative to access to raw materials and energy. (3) Amenities are of increasing importance. (4) There is an increasing degree of dependence on particular industries and services locally supplied by other industries, institutions, and public bodies, and therefore more emphasis on the "external economies" of locations that possess such features.[58]

Next, even broad measures of cost fail to explain locational decisions and patterns below the level of large regions. For example, Peter Doeringer and David Terkla have recently shown that while traditional cost variables, in conjunction with national sectoral growth patterns, explain two-thirds of the variation in economic growth among the states, they explained only about one-quarter of intrastate (regional or community) growth.[59] We shall return to this disjunction in Chapter 10.

Finally, as Robinson emphasizes, classic location theory is essentially microeconomic, directed toward explaining locational decisions of individual firms. The relationship between such micro-decisions and macro-outcomes— community or regional growth—is mediated by linkage effects and by even less tangible path-dependencies: For example, one firm's locational decision may well affect the decisions of others, even if there are no measurable externalities.[60]

Still, provided care is taken to avoid fallacies of composition, specific insights can help explain broader phenomena. Robinson, for example, suggests a tripartite division of economic activity. In the first category, the costs of transport and economies of scale are such that a national or international market can be served from a single center. In the second, these factors are such that a wide region can be served, but over greater distances marginal economies of scale are insufficient to offset increasing costs of transport. In the third, the ratio of transport costs to scale economies is so high that the activities must be conducted on a local basis.[61] More broadly, it has been proposed that locational outcomes are a function of a wide range of factors: sectoral considerations based on available resources and production techniques, constraints produced by the immobility of key factors of production, agglomeration economies, and individual locational preferences.[62]

Conclusion

This brief review of theoretical explanations for rural economic performance suggests useful conclusions. To begin with, theories are no better than their underlying assumptions. All too often, the lust for parsimony dominates the need for accuracy. To be more useful, these theories must travel some distance along the continuum from the abstract to the definitive.

Second, these theories must be updated to reflect broad patterns of economic change—for example, the shifting balance between transportation and communications as determinants of economic location, the enhanced role of technology in economic growth, and evolving definitions of regional comparative advantage.

Third, more attention must be paid to relations between macro- and micro-level phenomena. We would put it this way: Macroanalysis helps determine the likely "flow" of economic activity, while microanalysis helps determine the place of specific firms and communities within that flow. Macroanalysis can help assess the odds that a particular development strategy will succeed, but even long odds can be overcome in certain circumstances. The point is that firms and communities should be able to assess, at least in rough terms, the prospects of specific strategies before embarking on them.

Finally, while our survey of rural growth theories suggests that on the whole Jane Jacobs' approach is the most nearly adequate, it too must be modified to take recent economic and political changes into account. For example, the expansion of the welfare state has produced large classes of individuals whose entitlement incomes are not linked to current economic activities. For specific communities, the import of such individuals can to some extent serve as an alternative to the export of goods and services. Indeed, the income-stream they bring with them can serve as a growth pole for the goods and services they demand.

4

Development: A Political Strategy

Introduction: Action versus Inaction in Rural Development

A prime motive for this study of rural development is the widespread belief that current conditions and trends in much of rural America are unsatisfactory and that current efforts are unlikely to produce significant improvements. This raises the key question: What is to be done?

One possible answer is, nothing. It may be argued that, given the nature of the contemporary global economy, a substantial measure of rural decline is unavoidable—or, to put it more bluntly, avoidable only at increasingly unaffordable cost. This fatalistic position tends to equate rural programs with social initiatives that drain the national community, and with preservationist/protectionist strategies that maintain income or employment for specific groups at the expense of the overall national interest. From this perspective, rural development simply does not contribute to the "wealth of nations."

As we saw in Chapters 2 and 3, there are two lines of response. The first is to concede the economic argument but nonetheless insist that policies can be justified on other grounds. Consider an analogy. During much of the twentieth century, black Americans had the option of leaving areas in which they were denied the right to vote in favor of communities in which they could freely exercise that right. There was a mobility-based solution to the lack of equal political opportunity. Yet this "solution" came to be seen as inadequate. As citizens, individuals are entitled to certain rights, whatever their geographic location within the national community. Therefore, the national community is committed to the interventions and costs required to guarantee these rights. Similarly, it may be argued, the nation should ensure basic economic opportunities to all residents, regardless of their location.

Whatever the abstract merits of this approach, it runs up against some powerful realities. To begin with, the idea of mobility as the source of economic opportunity is deeply rooted in the U.S. political culture—not surprising for a country that originated in the creation of a continental market and grew by becoming a nation of immigrants. Further, in contemporary circumstances of stagnant personal incomes, public support for overt policies of geographical redistribution is unlikely to increase from current low levels.

Given these facts, a second, more promising approach is to look for ways in which programs directed toward U.S. rural areas can be justified as promoting the national interest. Two elements of such a strategy are clear. The first emphasizes the costs of neglect. Precisely because the United States is a mobile society, local underinvestment in people will have consequences for society at large. For example, if large numbers of poorly educated rural residents migrate to cities during a period of shrinking demand for unskilled labor, the social and economic effects will be severe. And to the extent that the preservation of certain rural amenities and options is viewed as a national public good, support can be mobilized for environmental and other policies directed toward rural areas.[1]

However effective these arguments, they are at best limited in scope. The second element emphasizes the benefits of action rather than the costs of inaction. It rests on the proposition that rural decline represents the underutilization of resources that could contribute far more than they do at present to national income and opportunity—that is, U.S. rural communities present a classic case of "organizational slack." A recent study of successful development suggests that the ability to "see advantages where others see only liabilities" can be crucial: idle infrastructure, physical plants, and human resources furnish opportunities for innovation.[2] From this standpoint, community mobilization and visionary public entrepreneurship may emerge as keys to rural development for the 1990s.

Institutions and Strategies

As described above, there are justifications for intervention in rural development. The scope of problems, as we have seen, is large. Yet there is a perception that current rural programs are not doing the job. What follows is an inventory and evaluation of the usual responses to this perception.

1. *Within the current institutional framework, improve existing efforts by reforming programs and/or increasing funding.* No doubt some gains can be realized along these lines. For example, a recent study has documented specific changes that would enable FmHA rural development programs

to achieve more of their stated objectives.[3] Still, no serious observers believe that the benefits of modest reform would be commensurate with the scope of the rural problems outlined in the opening discussion of Part I.

2. *Within the public sector, sort out and shift responsibilities among the different levels of federal government.* Under this approach, each level of government would assume primary responsibility in those areas in which it possesses a clear comparative advantage. One sketch of such a strategy goes as follows: The national government should concentrate its efforts on macroeconomic management and on what might be termed "national public goods," such as improved transportation and communications and a more secure financial system. State governments should focus on state public goods and on creating an encouraging climate for local and private sector activity. Localities should emphasize the kind of "public entrepreneurship" that identifies the needs, resources, and opportunities of specific communities.[4]

The case for moving in this direction is especially powerful in the current context. Today, for the first time since the Great Depression, available resources at all three levels of the federal system are shrinking. The logic of increasing efficiency by acknowledging different levels of public comparative advantage seems hard to rebut.

While the effort to move in this direction is well worth making, significant progress may prove difficult. Whatever their current merits, existing federal categorical programs are sustained by entrenched bureaucracies and interest groups. Moreover, considerable ideological and interest group support remains for the top-down, command-and-control federal organization structures left over from the Depression and World War II. The efficacy of this support may well be put to the test in the years just ahead, as both the executive branch and the congress promote strategies of devolution to states and localities.

3. *Shift responsibilities among the basic forms of collective action.* As indicated in Chapter 1, three forms of collective action have continuing power in the contemporary United States: governments, markets, and voluntary associations. At the national level, the 1980s represented a revolt against governmental expansion and favored increased reliance on the private and voluntary sectors. During the early 1990s, as tax rates soar and revenues wither, anti-government sentiment is spreading to the state and local level. Increased reliance on market delivery of services, or "privatization," is one consequence and enhanced roles for charitable and nonprofit organizations is another.

While these developments have yielded gains in some areas, they are no panacea for rural ills. On balance, the rural decline of the 1980s owed more to the unfettered operation of market forces than to "market failures," and rural voluntary associations were unable to serve as effective counterweights. This is not an argument against correcting whatever rural market failures may exist—for example, those stemming from high information and transaction costs—or against bolstering the efforts of churches, charities, and foundations. It is an argument against any easy confidence that by tilting away from the public sector these shifts will, by themselves, produce acceptable results.

4. *Forge new relationships between forms of collective action.* Along with shifts of responsibility among forms of collective action, alliances between these forms emerged as a significant development during the 1980s. In the space of just a few years, "public–private partnership" moved from innovation to cliché. State-level ventures such as the Michigan Strategic Fund and Pennsylvania's Industrial Resource Centers appear to have forged effective new links between public and private capital.[5]

But the possibilities are even more diverse than these success stories would indicate. New cooperative ventures were formed between nonprofit enterprises and the public sector. Witness the takeover of the Chelsea, Massachusetts public school system by Boston University. Businessman Eugene Lang's pledge of scholarship support to an inner-city sixth-grade class has been emulated by other private-sector philanthropists. Or consider the remarkable triadic collaboration across public, private, and voluntary sector lines that made possible the successful development of suburban-style single family housing in the notorious Charlotte Street neighborhood of the South Bronx.

Such alliances were hardly unknown in the rural America of the 1980s. Foundations supported energetic not-for-profit intermediary organizations such as MDC, Inc., the Center for Rural Affairs, and the Mountain Association for Community Economic Development (MACED). Many localities have created local development organizations: private, not-for-profit entities designed to pursue public purposes. These organizations may be viewed as hybrids containing elements of all three forms of collective action.[6]

These new partnerships scored some important local successes during the 1980s. Still, the decade closed on a note of perplexity and doubt: Solid evaluations were rare; the scale of success was inadequate to counteract trends; and replicability of "best practices" across community lines had yet to be established.[7]

5. Reinvent collective action. In recent years, a radical reexamination of large organizations has been taking shape. Peter Drucker has argued that the expanded role of knowledge and information in modern society is in the process of changing the criteria for successful collective action. The private sector has found that it must abandon command-and-control management styles in favor of more egalitarian collegial relations, shrink the number of managerial layers, and acknowledge the enhanced power of knowledge-bearing employees as specialists. The military metaphor of the business organization must be replaced by the orchestral metaphor. According to classic organization theory,

> ...there should be several "group vice president conductors" and perhaps a half-dozen "division VP conductors." But there is only one conductor—and every one of the musicians, each a high-grade specialist, plays directly to that person, without an intermediary.[8]

The impact of knowledge and information on the public sector, Drucker argues, will be equally dramatic. The hierarchical bureaucracy characteristic of government from Bismarck through the New Deal craves monopoly, innovates grudgingly, and discards outdated programs and structures with great difficulty. The rapid diffusion of knowledge and information, by contrast, undermines monopoly, fosters an accelerated pace of innovation, and demands the ceaseless replacement of what worked yesterday with what is needed for tomorrow.[9]

In recent years, a number of policy analysts and practitioners have applied Drucker's basic framework to state and local development. Doug Ross, for example, has distinguished three "waves" of development activities. The first wave, industrial attraction, scored significant successes in the 1950s and 1960s but was undermined by the globalization of manufacturing competition in the 1970s. The second wave, characteristic of state programs in the 1980s, emphasized internal, homegrown cultivation of new and expanding businesses through such initiatives as applied research centers and grants, new mechanisms to help meet business capital needs, assistance in applying and commercializing new technologies, education reform, and public efforts to improve work force quality and productivity.

It is important, of course, not to take the distinction between the first and second waves too literally. After all, external attraction and internal cultivation can be complementary as well as competing strategies, and at least one important study suggests that successful rural communities tend to employ both.[10]

As Ross tells the story, by the end of the decade of the '80s a number of state and local "second wave" leaders were convinced that their goals were correct but that their chosen means were flawed. They began to wonder whether the public programs they had initiated were adequate to the scope of the problems they were addressing—whether they were making a big enough difference. Doubts also arose about the degree of integration and accountability the new programs were achieving. These misgivings could be generalized into a critique of New Deal/Great Society strategies for meeting broad challenges: In contemporary circumstances, traditional public programs were bound to be hampered by inadequate scale, lack of competition, and limited feedback.

In response to these difficulties, concludes Ross, a "third wave" of development is now underway. To achieve competition, this strategy rejects the old model of the public sector as monopoly supplier and tries instead to enhance choice among multiple suppliers. To achieve integration, the new strategy rejects the model of top-down coordination, relying instead on incentives to suppliers and information for customers. To achieve scale, the public sector seeks to encourage nonpublic activity, replacing direct action with policies of leverage and engagement. To achieve accountability, new programs are designed to measure public demand for, and satisfaction with, public programs and to link that demand to the level of programmatic resources.[11]

David Osborne, a leading student of public sector innovation, has attempted to translate this new strategy into a list of new rules for the public sector, collectively entitled "reinventing government." Among them:

- To address problems of public sector scale (programs too small, bureaucracies too large), government should be used to "steer" rather than "row" the ship of state, using ends (goals) rather than means (rules) to drive public sector organizations.

- To foster public sector dynamism and innovation, authority within government should be decentralized and citizens should be given maximum control over the services they receive.

- To foster public sector efficiency and effectiveness, administrative mechanisms should be replaced with market mechanisms whenever possible. This means more competition among service providers, more choice for service consumers, the substitution of public "investment" for public "spending," and a meaningful linking of outlay levels to results.

As Osborne sums up his case:

Competition, funding tied to results, customer choice, investment—all are characteristics of functioning markets. In a complex and rapidly changing world, in which our ability to access information is almost unlimited, markets are often more efficient and effective than administrative processes. But market mechanisms are only half the equation. Markets are impersonal. Markets are unforgiving. Even the most carefully structured markets tend to create inequitable outcomes. That is why we need the other half of the equation: the empowerment of communities.[12]

Development: Overcoming Political and Cultural Obstacles

Community empowerment is more than an equity issue. Precisely because public sector resources and capacities are typically inadequate to the scale of public problems, solutions require the effective mobilization of both private and voluntary efforts. We have learned that to surmount the challenges of the late twentieth century, we must involve "all the community's resources, not just those of government."[13]

This crucial proposition, drawn from a qualitative analysis of public organization, is increasingly supported by the quantitative analysis of local economies. A 1989 national Governor's Association study of patterns of community employment change found that standard factors explained only 17 percent of the variation.[14] An article published in 1990 shows that while two-thirds of the state-level variation in employment growth can be explained by a combination of traditional cost variables and national growth trends, only one-quarter of the local variation can be thus explained.[15] A survey of international applications of standard factor analysis to local growth concludes that "a large proportion of per capita income increase remains unexplained. This residual can only be attributed to . . . social and institutional factors."[16] Kenneth Deavers notes that "while we can explain most of the variation in levels of development among counties at a point in time (typically the r^2 for such studies are in the 0.7 to 0.8 range), models attempting to explain rates of change in income employment at the county level over time are much less successful. It is usual for them to exhibit r^2 in the range of 0.2 or less." Deavers goes on to invoke a distinction between "objective" growth factors, typically used by economists, and "subjective" factors regarded as important by social scientists. He calls for much greater precision in specifying and measuring the impact of the latter: "Simply adopting a name for the unexplained residual in our regression equations is not a very useful contribution."[17]

Can we be more precise about these factors? A survey published in 1990 focuses on intangibles such as local vision, flexibility, adaptability, civic commitment, and community organization.[18] After examining 48 high-growth counties, the National Governors' Association study identified eight "keys" to local success, among which were a "pro-growth" attitude, a well-organized partnership of local leaders, and sustained long-term development efforts.[19] In a parallel study, Jan and Cornelia Flora examined a number of relatively successful Great Plains rural communities. A number of common attributes emerged, among which were acceptance of public controversy, willingness to invest their own resources in the future, ability to acquire information and direct it to the community, and the presence of a flexible and dispersed community leadership.[20]

While not directly focused on rural communities, a recent article comparing strategies and outcomes in four medium-sized northeastern industrial cities suggests some relevant generalizations. Among the necessary conditions for success are the general public perception of a crisis situation, effective leadership that enjoys broad-based support, and a credible vision of a better future.[21]

The examination of failure can also be instructive. Michael Hibbard has examined the inability of Oakridge, Oregon, a town with a population of about 3500, to adjust effectively to a precipitous decline in the logging and forest products industries. He identified a number of key explanatory factors: a school system that breeds passivity and docility rather than innovation and entrepreneurship; a gulf between leaders and followers; a strong ethic of individualistic self-reliance; and, perhaps most important, the inability to tolerate the kind of public controversy that inevitably attends the early stages of efforts to chart a shared future requiring collective action. As Hibbard observes:

> This may be effective for everyday social intercourse, but it is crippling to public decision making. The enforced public amiability makes it impossible to carry out the public dialogue necessary for realistic community. The people of Oakridge have been socialized not to disagree publicly, so it is impossible to have a meaningful debate on community development alternatives.[22]

Hibbard concludes that effective mobilization for community development begins with creating an appropriate structure that contributes to the sense of having a common fate over which a significant measure of control can be exercised—a thesis that dovetails neatly with James Fallows' emphasis on the "radius of trust" and the sense of "controlled destiny."[23]

In practice, the importance of political structure and public culture for rural development entails a number of difficulties. To begin with, communities (and nations, for that matter) can be very slow to recognize that they are in crisis. The obvious risks of change often blind community members to the real costs of maintaining the status quo.

Second, the mere existence, and even perception, of shared community interests in change may not suffice to precipitate the creation of needed public structures and strategies. As Mancur Olson pointed out in his classic study, rational self-interested individuals will not necessarily act collectively to further what are in fact their shared interests. The welfare of the community is a public good that, like many others, will tend to be suboptimally supplied. To help close this gap, a structure of organization and leadership is needed that can authoritatively allocate selective benefits to individual members of the community. But this functional requirement is not a "demand" that automatically generates its own "supply"; public as well as private entrepreneurship may be in short supply.[24]

Finally, the emphasis on the importance of public culture and belief can breed a kind of fatalism. It is easy to think of these variables as external and resistant to rapid change—in particular, through deliberate transformative efforts. As Coffey and Polese observe:

> When we speak of such objectives as the emergence of entrepreneurship, the stimulation of indigenous talents, or the awakening of regional solidarity, we are basically speaking of social changes the origins of which we do not fully understand.... In strictly political terms, it is far easier for decision makers to deal with problems of infrastructure and capital rather than become involved with policies designed to alter a population's behavior and perceptions, especially since such policies are at the same time less visible, less immediate, and less predictable.[25]

In spite of these difficulties, it is a mistake to think of culture as a fixed, permanent obstacle to development. Fallows offers the sobering example of a pre-World War I expert's opinion that Japanese easy-goingness in economic matters, the lack of concern with time, would prove intractable.[26] In *Asian Drama,* Gunnar Myrdal offered a cultural explanation for India's alleged lack of development success at precisely the moment when India was poised to achieve unprecedented agricultural self-sufficiency and a dramatic expansion of its middle class.

Still, political structure and culture do represent real hindrances in many circumstances. What are the alternatives to fatalism? We see four options.

1. A crisis can become so acute that the community can no longer deny its existence, cost/benefit perceptions may shift massively against the status quo, and cultural constraints on change are decisively weakened. Something of this sort happened in the United States at the depth of the Great Depression and made possible a range of institutional and programmatic innovation. But while this option is important analytically

(for example, acute downturns may be preferable to slow decline), its policy relevance is less evident; it is difficult to imagine politically acceptable ways of engineering crises for the purpose of promoting needed change.

2. Cultural and institutional obstacles to change can be swept away by external intervention. Witness the post-World War II U.S. occupation of Germany and Japan, which laid the foundations for economic resurgence in the context of political democracy. And national intervention in state and local affairs throughout the South during the 1960s contributed to the surge of regional economic development in the following two decades. Here again, the policy relevance for contemporary communities is limited: Whatever the severity of the problems they face, their character is not such as to legitimize forcible external intervention.

3. The internal forces needed to overcome cultural and institutional obstacles can be decisively strengthened through appropriately structured external incentives. For example, at a time when postwar Europe seemed to be sinking into despair, the Marshall Plan offered the catalyst of hope. External resources were made available, contingent on the formulation of national plans for their use. Leaders and planning agencies sprang into action, entire societies were galvanized, and moribund economies were launched on the path to recovery and growth.

The Marshall Plan example has been rendered almost trivial through excessive use, but its crucial feature is frequently overlooked: External aid was made contingent on internal mobilization. As Ross Gittell noted in his study of U.S. urban recovery, "Outside resources may be necessary to local revitalization efforts. However, . . . the availability of outside resources alone is not sufficient. . . . Local organization of development activities appears to be fundamental."[27] Here is a point of direct relevance to contemporary rural development efforts: So far as possible, federal and state assistance to communities should be structured to encourage, perhaps even to require, local mobilization of energy and resources on behalf of a broadly supported course of action.[28] The Clinton/Gore administration's empowerment zone/enterprise community legislation is an important and promising example of this strategy.

Another important example for consideration is provided by Canada's "Community Futures Program," which offers local communities the opportunity to chart their own strategies and choose from a menu of subsidized development options. Alongside the local Futures Committee is a Business Development Center, which offers information and advice together with a limited amount of venture capital. While this program is just in its fifth year of operation and has yet to complete a full evaluation, more than 200 communities are already participating, and the effort is regarded as very promising.[29]

Once stimulated, the basic elements of effective local mobilization are reasonably straightforward conceptually, though challenging to carry into practice. The leadership must be assembled, the performance and assets of the community inventoried, the potential market researched, a vision of the future established, a strategy adopted, and institutional infrastructure and political support for the plan developed.[30]

As Gittell emphasizes, this process of mobilization can produce benefits transcending the simply economic. Channels of communication are opened between different sectors of the community, opportunities for mutual gain are identified, and the foundation is laid for long-term collaboration.[31] Perhaps most important, basic attitudes can be changed for the better. "New visions can alter negative perceptions and overcome community inertia in the face of economic decline."[32] As we have seen, this transformation—the replacement of despair and passivity with hope and a sense of control over destiny—can be the most important of all.

4. Even in the absence of external incentives, local mobilization sparked by the perceived importance of local communities and places can make a real difference. For example, Daniel Kemmis tells the story of the political struggle in Montana over public control of milk production and prices. Libertarians sought to overturn a long-standing state regulatory structure and eventually succeeded in placing their initiative on the ballot. During the election contest, they argued (and their foes did not deny) that deregulation would mean lower consumer prices. Nonetheless, the initiative failed. The majority of voters accepted the argument that deregulation would mean the disappearance of many family dairy farms and neighborhood grocery stores. They were willing to pay higher prices to avert this disruption, even though few of them were directly involved in dairying or milk retailing.[33]

This story illustrates a typical clash between abstract market and local place, and an atypical resolution of that clash. Two features of the outcome are crucial. First, individual inhabitants cared enough about the stability of local community structures to give continuity priority over other goals such as higher disposable incomes. Second, there was a public framework within which the alternatives could be explicitly discussed and a binding decision rendered.

The facts of this last case seem to point more generally toward the necessary conditions for a place-oriented economics capable of resisting national or global economic forces. If individuals do not really care about local continuity, then the calculus of producer efficiency and consumer costs is likely to prevail. But even if they do care, they cannot effectively register their preferences without a framework of collective action. Whenever individuals acting in isolation from one another produce a social result that they collectively regret, both market and politics have failed.[34]

Development: Overcoming Economic Obstacles

We have focused thus far on strategies designed to overcome institutional and cultural obstacles to rural development. But many other kinds of obstacles are of potential importance. We turn now to a brief survey.

Capital

From time to time, the shortage of capital is advanced as an obstacle to rural development. There is, however, little systematic evidence to support this as a general hypothesis. During the 1970s and early 1980s, in fact, rural credit ballooned, creating an overhang of debt that took years to work down to sustainable levels. It may well be that in some areas, conservative lending institutions are slow to consider new businesses on an equal footing with more traditional borrowers. In such circumstances, publicly sponsored venture capital efforts could act as a catalyst for the emergence of pools of resources for rural entrepreneurs.

Somewhat less speculative is the widening gap in information and transaction costs between rural and urban areas. As Kenneth Deavers notes, if the cost of obtaining information about investment opportunities in remote areas and small firms is high, capital markets may systematically underinvest in promising rural ventures. This is an example of the "market failure" that can be addressed through public efforts to reduce regional information and transactions costs. But it is not a valid basis for the general subsidy of rural credit.[35]

Human Resources

The gap between rural and urban education/training levels is frequently regarded as a source of rural disadvantage. But a recent comprehensive study has rejected the theses that low rural skills are a cause of rural economic misfortune and that increased rural education and training would serve as a cure. The reason is interregional leakage resulting from population mobility. In the context of the 1980s, higher rural education levels might well have increased rural out-migration. In sum, this report concludes that "While raising individual education levels improves individual opportunities, and raising the nation's education level should make us more competitive internationally, there is little evidence that raising local education levels is in itself a key to rural employment growth."[36]

In this connection, we note again that population mobility does not necessarily reduce interregional differences. Cross-national studies indicate that migrants "generally comprise a proportionately higher percentage of educated individuals and of those persons possessing characteristics associated with a high potential for economic improvement."[37]

The goal of population retention is more than a matter of family and community sentiment; it is essential for economic vitality and in some cases for community survival. But, to repeat, it is not a goal that can be achieved through increased rural investment in education and training.

Infrastructure

As we noted in the Introduction, a classic obstacle to rural development is distance, with all its attendant costs and disadvantages. During the New Deal era, investments in electrification, telephones, and road systems helped rural areas overcome isolation and move closer to the economic mainstream.

For economies heavily dependent on natural resources and routine manufacturing, the operation of equipment and movement of goods is critical, and New Deal-style infrastructure was well designed to serve these objectives. But in the economy of the 1990s and beyond, the emphasis is shifting: Access to, and transmission of, information is becoming central. The "highways" of the future will be made of fiber-optic cables as well as concrete.

This historic shift presents opportunities as well as dangers for rural America. On the one hand, as the development of new telecommunications systems surges forward, rural areas risk being left behind and shut out. In the worst case, these areas could once again become the backwaters of American life, as isolated from the sources of dynamism in the 1990s as were nonelectrified rural communities of the 1920s. On the other hand, advances in telecommunications hold out the possibility of weakening the link between geographic and economic distance. For example, if remote areas have instantaneous access to updated information, some traditional obstacles to economic development can be overcome. We do not suggest that modern telecommunications are sufficient for economic growth.[38] But they are quickly becoming a necessary condition.

Summarizing a large body of recent research, Edwin Parker and his coauthors show that the unfettered operation of market forces will produce suboptimal levels of telecommunications investment in rural areas: Because

much of the benefit comes in the form of externalities not captured in private
sector charges, additional public sector incentives are needed to evoke more
adequate levels of investment. This is especially true today because deregulation has largely eliminated the kinds of implicit cross-subsidies that made it
possible to provide average cost services to a wide range of users. These considerations suggest a major policy emphasis for rural development at the national level, one consistent with an orientation toward progressive rather than
preservationist strategies, and with positive-sum rather than redistributionist
outcomes.[39]

Diversification

The past decade has borne vivid witness to the perils of economic specialization. Areas heavily dependent on single sectors have been hit hard by increased mobility and by rapid shifts in competitive advantage. Rural communities were hardly alone in experiencing these effects. During the early 1980s,
urban centers of traditional manufacturing (autos, tires, steel) were deci-
mated. In the late 1980s, cities that had grown dependent on commercial
construction and finance suffered major losses in employment and revenue.

Still, the phenomenon of over-specialization is far more pervasive in rural
than urban areas. To some extent this is inevitable. Diversification is positively correlated with scale and density, while small scale and low density are
defining characteristics of rural areas. Considerations such as these have led
some observers to conclude that in contemporary economic circumstances,
the major obstacle to rural economic development is "rurality" itself.

This proposition clearly contains a significant measure of truth. Pushed to
the extreme, however, it is a counsel of despair. The problem may be posed as
follows: Given that efforts to diversify are to a considerable extent swimming
upstream, are there nonetheless strategies that offer hopeful prospects? The
following considerations seem relevant.

1. We have noted more than once that rural communities do better if they
   develop close ties to metropolitan regions. During the 1980s, geographical adjacency emerged as the surest route to such ties. For many
   imperiled communities, the question for the 1990s is whether effective
   alternatives to adjacency can be found. One possibility is that rural
   areas in which adequate telecommunications already exist might attempt to break into markets for business services now dominated by
   urban suppliers. Such efforts could spur diversification by increasing
   the economic options available to rural entrepreneurs. At the very least,
   updated telecommunications capacity can help improve the competitiveness of existing rural manufacturers by giving them improved

access to the types of advanced producer services available in metropolitan areas.

2. As Albert Hirschman has argued, diversification—and indeed development itself—is in part a function of linkages engendered by core economic activities.[40] A number of studies indicate that enterprises originating from within communities rather than from without have, on average, a far greater likelihood of generating productive linkages.[41] Thus the advantage of "homegrown" over "attraction" strategies is not limited to immediate job creation but rather ripples throughout the community, generating new possibilities not confined, for example, to consumer services dependent on wage income from branch plants.

3. During the 1980s, a key source of rural disadvantage was excessive concentration of employment and output in "routine" manufacturing, typically assembly of products at the mature end of product cycles. Standard explanations for this differentiation focus on urban "agglomeration economies," typically distance-related costs of transportation and communication. But more recent studies have emphasized "collaboration economies," close relations among firms engaged in overlapping activities. Among other advantages, these relations enable producers to respond quickly to changing specifications from potential customers. Specialized production can enable even high-cost firms in mature industries to survive and prosper.[42]

It may well prove possible for rural firms to reap the benefits of increasingly specialized production by occupying market niches, but only if they achieve collaborative economies. To do so, the locus of development will have to be redefined. Throughout rural North America, families now define their "community" as the range of activities that can be reached in drives of one hour or less—an "extended city" typically comprising a number of small communities.[43] If local residents and firms learn to think of such communities as neighborhoods sharing a common fate, the range of productive collaboration—and hence development opportunities—could be enhanced. Conversely, competition among declining communities along current lines of political jurisdiction will probably lead to suboptimal outcomes for all.[44]

As Tony Fuller points out, the areas under Canada's Community Futures Committees usually represent not isolated communities but rather collections of municipalities with a common (functional) identity. To qualify for assistance, these communities have to get together, sort out their differences, and develop a mutually beneficial strategic plan.[45] The results of this effort to provide external incentives for overcoming debilitating competition among local jurisdictions should be carefully examined for possible application to U.S. rural development. In the case of remote areas experiencing severe population outflows, such forms of economic collaboration could spill over into decisions affecting the consolidation of public services such as schools, hospitals, and social service agencies.

Conclusion

Throughout Part I of this study, we have emphasized the national and global context within which U.S. rural development must now take place. It is a new world of high mobility and accelerated change. Firms and communities that can cope with the pressures of constant change will prosper while those that cannot will wither. Successful organizations of the past ought to internalize, stabilize, and control change; the successful organizations of the future will respond flexibly to discontinuities they cannot control.

Rural development is no exception. In the 1990s and beyond, the rewards will be reaped by rural firms and communities that engage in constant learning and adaptation—that receive timely information, draw sound inferences from it, and respond with a unified sense of purpose.

Millennia of human experimentation have produced no better institutions for social learning than economic markets and political democracy. Each in its own way is a vital source of information about changed circumstances and feedback about the effectiveness of policy responses to those new circumstances. Neither the economics of sectoral protection nor the politics of interest-group domination can serve rural America well in the years to come. The task for the 1990s and beyond is to harness markets and democracy together in the service of rural renewal.

In carrying out this task, we have argued, it is important for communities to understand the basic direction of national and global economic change. Knowledge of the underlying economic "flow" will help communities assess the odds for and against specific strategies among which they may be called on to choose. This is not to say that strict inferences can be drawn from macrotrends to micropossibilities; individual communities can overcome even long odds. Still, as communities consider the merits of, say, routine manufacturing as an economic base, they should at least be aware of the global pressures now being exerted on this sector of the U.S. economy. In Part II of this study, therefore, we will examine in some detail the long-term economic prospects of various rural sectors, as well as their impact on the multidimensional conceptualization of development offered in Part I.

PART II

U.S. Rural Development: A Sectoral Analysis

In economic development, success often depends on building momentum. Growth begets more growth. Businesses follow other businesses. An existing employment base helps determine future job creation.

Perhaps the most striking fact about the U.S. rural economy in the 1980s was the shift in development momentum from the traditional economic base sectors (natural resources and manufacturing) to the new economic base sectors (tourism, retirement, and government). Many rural counties dependent on manufacturing or natural resources experienced significant declines in employment throughout the last decade—declines that cut across industries and sectors. At the same time, the majority of rural counties dominated by tourism, retirement-related goods and services, or government employment thrived; they picked up employment in all sectors, including those industries outside their areas of specialization.

In essence, rural America continued to shift from an economy based on exporting raw materials and manufactured goods to one based on importing people and public dollars. Some people and dollars came for short-term visits—tourists for example; others came to set up residency, as in the case of migrating retirees and government facilities.

Why the change in momentum? Theories about structural change in the rural economy abound, but five factors capture most of what has been going on at the macro level.

1. Rural areas over the past 40 years have been key participants in the natural, historical evolution of jobs and GNP from extraction of raw materials to production of manufactured goods and, more recently, out of manufacturing to services.

2. The high dollar and back-to-back recessions of the 1979–82 period dealt a particularly harsh blow to U.S. manufacturing employment and, in turn, to rural America, where more jobs depend on manufacturing than in urban America. Economic growth during the remainder of the 1980s barely brought rural manufacturing employment back to the levels of the previous decade.

3. All sectors of American business were exposed to stiff overseas competition, leading to a loss of market share in many industries. The resulting consolidations and modernizations took a toll on rural branch plants— the bottom of the organizational hierarchy in many corporations and the first place where many firms make cuts.

4. In the emerging global economy in which production has grown increasingly mobile, the traditional areas of U.S. rural comparative advantage— cheap land and low-wage labor—were gradually eroded by competition

from many Third World countries. Plants in maturing industries that once may have decentralized from urban to rural locations began decentralizing to lower-wage nations in Asia and Latin America.

5. While the more traditional rural countries were struggling to keep up with these forces of decline, some of their neighboring counties were enjoying large influxes of retirees as a result of general trends toward earlier retirement, greater mobility of the elderly, and generous public and private retirement benefits. At the same time, other rural areas with similar amenities were benefitting from rising American incomes and shifts in consumer preferences for travel and tourism.

The combined force of these and other factors may eventually be powerful enough to replace substantially the old sources of rural comparative advantage with the new rural drawing card—quality of life. Continuing analysis is needed to determine how thorough this transition will be.

The shift in comparative advantage brings both good news and bad news. The good news belongs to those communities endowed with the kinds of amenities sought by retirees and tourists, and even by certain high-tech and advanced services firms. Those areas can expect to enjoy high rates of employment, income, and population growth for many years to come. Rural communities with a solid existing base of industry and a strategy for improving the competitiveness of local firms may also look forward to more prosperous times.

The bad news falls on those communities where long histories of poverty and deprivation have left behind little in the way of either quality-of-life amenities or the foundations of a healthy industrial base. Survival for many of these communities will need to begin with the revival of collective action and public entrepreneurialism, whether through voluntary citizen groups, public–private development organizations, or innovative political leadership. Survival will depend on accepting the loss of old economic landmarks and the need for change in established social patterns. It may require forming new alliances with neighboring communities to create the scale needed for even the most basic economic and noneconomic activities—viable labor pools, consumer markets, schools, social services, and so on.

This shift in momentum also raises questions about the overall capacity of rural America to contribute to national wealth. While the "new" economic base sectors can prove extremely lucrative to individual rural communities, activities such as tourism, services for retirees, and government contribute very little to national economic growth. In economists' terms, they do not add value to their final products to the same extent that more traditional industries do, and, with the exception of foreign tourists, they do not increase U.S. exports. Instead, the new areas of strength in the rural economy draw on consumer demand, demographics, income growth, and, in the case of direct government employment, public policy.

These trends may well affect the future shape of public rural development policies. Americans are demanding strategies that expand the entire economic pie rather than strategies that redistribute growth more fairly across geographic regions. Therefore, rural communities interested in pursuing tourism or retirement-based development may need to rely almost entirely on their own resources with little or no help from Washington.

Rural America at this time is weakest in those areas of economic activity generally considered most vital to national competitiveness: product innovation, process innovation, management innovation, information development, high value-added services and production, and technical knowledge. However, other models of industrial progress may fuel growth in rural manufacturing and natural-resources-related employment and competitiveness. These include the emerging models of craft (rather than mass) production, flexible manufacturing, and regional production networks or complexes. To the extent that such strategies are successful in revitalizing primary and secondary industries, rural areas may begin to see more vigorous growth in tertiary industries—in particular, those portions of the service sector linked to business rather than consumer demand. Continued development along this trajectory would eventually create new rural growth regions and perhaps even new small cities.

The chapters in Part II take a sectoral approach to the rural economy. At the same time, however, we have emphasized the vital importance of building the strongest possible linkages between and among sectors to increase "value-added" or "upstream" enterprises (such as food processing) and improve competitiveness. The national economy is becoming more interdependent; rural areas, too, must participate in that trend. In some cases, stronger linkages will mean job creation in new kinds of industries (such as business services) on location in rural communities. In other cases, it will mean expanding access via telecommunications technology to the advanced services available only in large urban centers—the kinds of services that most rural areas can never dream of attracting but that hold the key to maintaining the competitive position of traditional rural firms.

Clearly, local rural officials must target more than those sectors conventionally thought of as wealth generators—manufacturing, raw materials, construction. At the same time, they must not abandon these traditional bases and become fixated on consumer-oriented sectors. With strong leadership and commitment from both private and public entrepreneurship, rural

America can pursue the full menu of old and new export industries and the linkages among productive activities that, in the end, will give its communities the best possible chances for success.

Each chapter in Part II is divided into five sections beginning with an introduction. The introduction provides a summary of the key points in the chapter as well as brief definitions of what each section includes.

The second section, "The Context: National and International Trends," describes how the sector in question has performed at the national and global levels over the past several decades. Rural development in the future will be determined by a combination of local community efforts to influence the location of individual firms and larger economic forces that shape overall industry trends. Thus, any discussion of rural development must include information about these larger forces.

The third section of each chapter, "The Rural Picture," uses both macroanalysis and microanalysis to describe aggregate trends in each rural economic sector, as well as experiences in individual communities or groups of communities that illustrate larger patterns.

The fourth section, "Economic Development Strategies," reviews the recommendations found in the literature for pursuing job creation and developing comparative advantage in each sector as well as pursuing linkages between sectors.

The fifth and final section, "The Quality of Development," evaluates what we know about development in each sector against the principles established in Chapter 2. Will these approaches fulfill the ideals of development? Will they attain the goals of relieving poverty, promoting community self-sufficiency, and providing adequate opportunities to stem the outflow of young people to cities? As the chapters show, these questions are often difficult to answer in the light of conflicting and often sparse research.

5

Natural Resources

Introduction

"Natural resources" is more than just another sector of the rural economy. The phrase describes what most people probably think of first when they think "rural": land, water, farms, forests. It also describes much of the social and economic history of rural America, which until recently was dominated by the cultivation and extraction of natural resources. Just four decades ago, 15 percent of all Americans and 40 percent of all rural Americans lived on farms, and agriculture engaged roughly one-third of the rural work force.[1]

The picture is very different today: Fewer than 2 percent of Americans live on farms, and the rural economy comprises a far more diverse set of industries and occupations, many unconnected to the primary products sector. Hence, books and articles written about rural development during the last 20 years often begin with a reminder that strategies for enhancing agriculture are no longer sufficient for improving the overall well-being of rural areas. The point is irrefutable. Farming and the other primary products industries have become increasingly marginal to the international, national, and rural economies.

Viewed in a larger economic and social context, however, natural resources industries have an important role to play in rural development. The main points of this chapter can be summarized as follows:

1. Although more than half of all natural-resources-related employment is located in urban areas, rural America depends heavily on income from this sector to fuel its economy.

2. Natural resources is a shrinking sector in the United States and many other industrialized nations in both employment and contributions to GNP. Much of the value once added by the primary goods industries is now captured in downstream activities such as processing and manufacturing, packaging, marketing and advertising, and retailing.

3. Rural areas find themselves at a disadvantage in attracting the downstream activities, particularly those that require close proximity to large

markets, access to sophisticated communications systems, or pools of specially skilled workers.

4. Still, strategies are available for rural communities interested in natural-resources-based development. These include creating entirely new agricultural, timber, or other commodity-based products; developing new uses for old products; upgrading production techniques to increase efficiency and quality; and applying emerging technology to production.

5. Traditional value-added strategies that focused on recruiting food processing, timber processing, and other natural-resources-related firms have brought mostly disappointment. New, more refined definitions of the value-added approach focus on improving the competitive position of existing secondary industries through technical and financial assistance, access to information, worker training, and other means. Although these activities have not been evaluated rigorously, they hold some promise for long-term benefits.

6. Institutions can play an important role in increasing the value added by existing primary and secondary producers in rural areas. Industry associations and cooperatives in agriculture or timber, for example, can serve as networks for exchange of information, provision of services such as technical assistance, and better coordination among growers, processors, shippers, marketers, and distributors.

7. Traditional natural resources industries have a reputation for creating dangerous, low-paying jobs. Some of the newer, value-added, competitiveness approaches to agriculture and timber development are expected to increase wages and skill levels for local workers, albeit with some loss of jobs due to higher productivity.

8. Even where communities face the dismal choice between low-wage jobs on the one hand and high unemployment and depopulation on the other, efforts can be made to compensate for and increase wages and to pressure employers for improvements in job quality.

9. Natural resources development also involves difficult tradeoffs between environmental conservation and economic growth. Examples of compromises struck during the past several years in the areas of farming practices and clean air illustrate how consensus can be developed and implemented at the policy level.

10. Decisions about tensions inherent in some natural resources development strategies should be based on public deliberation and choice.

Most analyses of natural resources focus on the five traditional industry groupings: agriculture, forestry, energy, nonenergy mining, and fishing.

These categories comprise the extractive side of the natural resources sector—activities that mine or harvest commodities in one place and sell them elsewhere. Recently, economists have begun paying more attention to what could be considered the amenities side of the natural resources sector—industries such as tourism, recreation, and retirement that create wealth by attracting people in to enjoy the natural endowments of rural areas rather than by shipping commodities and goods out. This chapter will discuss the performance of the traditional, extractive industry groups in the aggregate with special focus on agriculture, forestry, energy, and nonenergy mining. Chapters 8 and 9 will explore amenities.

Definitions

Definitions of the natural resources sector vary in their breadth. The authors of the OTA (Office of Technology Assessment) report, *Technology and the American Economic Transition,* include only the primary production of raw materials and energy in their natural resources category.[2] Weber, Castle, and Shriver, on the other hand, include some secondary and tertiary processing and services activities in their definitions of natural resources and agriculture.[3] Reimund and Petrulis use a very broad definition of agriculture that also includes distribution, wholesale, and retail activities.[4]

These definitions produce very different pictures of the size of the natural resources sector. By OTA's definition, natural resources account for about 4.5 percent of U.S. employment. The definition used by Weber et al. produces a comparable figure of about 9 percent. By Reimund and Petrulis' definition, agriculture alone (excluding the other natural resources industries included in the other two definitions) generates 18.5 percent of employment.

Agriculture is by far the largest of the five natural resources industry groups by any definition. Using Weber et al.'s calculations, it represented roughly 6 percent of total U.S. employment in 1985.[5] Forestry and wood products are the next largest category, with less than 2 percent of total employment. Energy industries provide only about 0.6 percent of employment, and nonenergy mining barely reaches 0.2 percent. Figures for earnings in these industry groups are similar.

Measured against national employment totals, these industries are relatively small. For residents of certain counties in the United States, however, they are pivotal. One in every nine U.S. counties qualifies as a natural resource county, which means that more than 20 percent of its annual income is derived from natural-resources-related enterprises. Not counting tourism and retirement communities,[6] roughly one quarter of all rural counties in the United States specialize in agriculture, and many others depend on one of the traditionally defined natural resource industries.[7]

Although natural-resources-related industries occupy a dominant position in the rural economy, the natural resources sector overall is an urban phe-nomenon.[8] This is because urban areas provide proximity to markets for ac-tivities such as agricultural services, food processing, and timber processing, and there is a tendency for cities to form around oil and gas wells. For these and other reasons, the majority of natural-resources-related jobs are located in urban counties. Still, as noted above, rural areas are more heavily depen-dent on natural resources for their prosperity.

The relative geographic concentration of different natural resource sectors varies widely.[9] In general, agricultural operations are spread the most evenly. Virtually every state has at least one county specializing in agriculture, except in New England. The Great Plains states contain the thickest concentration of counties dependent on agriculture. By contrast, other natural resources are more region- or place-specific. Forestry and wood products dominate the re-gional economies of the Pacific Northwest, upper Great Lakes, northern New England, and parts of the Southeast. Energy counties are concentrated in the Rocky Mountain region, Texas, Oklahoma, the Gulf Coast, and Appalachia. Mining activity is highly concentrated in a few western locations, with copper mostly in one state, Arizona. As a result of these geographic facts, nat-ural resources policies translate immediately into regional development poli-cies. Supporting one of these industries generally means favoring one or more geographic areas.

The Context: National and International Trends

The natural resources sector, taken as a whole, is changing in fundamental ways.

Shifting Income Share

The sector is shrinking relative to the other basic economic sectors. According to the U.S. Congress' Office of Technology Assessment (OTA), "one of the clearest structural trends in the U.S. economy has been the rela-tive decline of the Natural Resources sector."[10] The production of raw mate-rials and energy contributed 12 percent of U.S. GNP in 1950. But despite the quadrupling of oil and gas prices after 1973, which masked the true ex-tent of the structural shift, the sector's share of GNP dropped to 9 percent by 1984.[11] Agriculture accounted for most of the losses prior to 1972, according to OTA. After 1972, conservation and substitution of energy products led the sectoral decline. Both theory and experience suggest that this trend is likely to continue.

As we noted in Chapter 1, Peter Drucker provided the theoretical expla-nation for the shift away from natural resources in an influential article in

Foreign Affairs in 1986. He described a strange combination of events during the period from the late 1970s to the late 1980s that add up to a fundamental, probably irreversible, structural change that he calls the "uncoupling" of the primary products economy from the industrial economy.

During this period, while worldwide demand for most raw materials fell, output steadily increased as a result of productivity gains. The resulting surpluses caused a collapse of commodity prices other than oil beginning in 1977 and continuing for a decade. But in a total departure from the rules of classical economic theory, which hold that "a sharp and prolonged drop in raw material prices inevitably, and within 18 to 30 months, brings on a worldwide depression in the industrial economy," the world's industrial sector barely blinked.[12] Production continued to grow slowly but steadily throughout the 1980s.

Drucker explains the unexpected turn of events: "The only explanation is that for the developed countries—excepting only the Soviet Union—the primary-products sector has become marginal where before it had always been central."[13] He notes, for example, fundamental changes in the production recipes for goods and services. Today's manufactured goods are far less materials-intensive than the goods produced just 15 years ago.[14] Japan produced the same volume of goods in 1984 that it did in 1973 with only 60 percent of the raw materials used in the earlier period.

The change in materials usage extends to all types of industries. The prices of today's new high-technology products are based on the value of the skills, knowledge, research, and development that go into them far more than the value of the raw materials. The production cost of a computer chip includes 3 percent for raw materials; for a car, the portion is 40 percent. Even in traditional industries, the ingredients in the production recipe are shifting away from products made of traditional primary materials, like steel made from iron ore, to lighter, less energy-intensive materials such as plastic and fiberglass. As the amount of raw material needed to produce a dollar's worth of industrial output continues to drop, the markets for these commodities will continue to shrink.

According to Drucker, the uncoupling phenomenon is not likely to reverse itself anytime soon. He describes it as one of the basic realities of today's economy and predicts continued lower demand and lower prices for raw materials worldwide. By extension, any large economy that bases its economic development strategy on a recovery of natural resources jobs and income is fooling itself.

Two separate studies from the Congressional Office of Technology Assessment reach similar conclusions. The first study describes the uncoupling of economic growth and energy use over the past 15 years.[15] Between 1950 and 1971, growth in U.S. gross domestic product (GDP) moved in step with increases in energy use, both increasing at an average rate of 3.5 percent per year. In contrast, between 1972 and 1985, GDP grew at eight times the rate of energy consumption, an average of 2.5 percent annually, compared to 0.3 percent for energy. The amount of energy needed to produce a dollar's worth of goods and services remained steady between about World War II and just before the first oil crisis (1950–71), then dropped 2.4 percent each year from 1972 to 1985. After 1971, energy use seemed to lose its status as a key ingredient in economic growth. Although part of the drop in energy intensity can be explained by impressive gains in energy efficiency, OTA attributes as much as a third of the decline to "structural shifts in the economy," namely greater demand for services relative to manufactured goods and, confirming Drucker's point, substitution of less energy-intensive materials in production.

The second OTA study describes how GNP has steadily shifted away from the primary products sector into the other mostly nonextractive, nonmanufacturing sectors.[16] This analysis approaches the subject of economic transition from the perspective of "amenity networks," combinations of economic activities needed to furnish Americans with both basic and nonessential amenities as food, housing, and recreation.

Perhaps the most striking feature of these amenity networks is their declining reliance on inputs from the natural resources sectors. Of the eight amenity groups defined by OTA (food, health, housing, transportation, clothing and personal care, education, personal business and communication, and recreation and leisure), seven experienced declines in relative share of inputs obtained from the natural resources sector between 1972 and 1984. Transportation was the only exception. The trend was most pronounced in the food and housing networks.

Using OTA's illustration, the fraction of the price of a frozen pizza from the supermarket that goes to buy basic agricultural inputs (such as flour, oil, tomatoes, cheese) has declined over time. When we buy a pizza today, we are paying mostly for activities rather than goods: processing the tomatoes into tomato sauce; making the crust; assembling the pizza; packaging, freezing, shipping, and marketing; advertising; and retailing the product in the supermarket. A similar story can be told for other amenities, notably housing, where a rapidly increasing proportion of the value of the product is derived from the services provided by real estate agents, rather than the lumber and other primary goods needed for production.

The marginalization of the primary materials sector described by Drucker and OTA has profound implications for all economies dependent on natural resources industries for jobs and income, particularly many developing countries overseas and almost half of the rural counties here in the United States. Because these places export raw materials and import manufactured goods, they suffer greatly when the prices of raw materials drop relative to the prices of finished products.

The shift in value-added enterprises also has important consequences for the geography of future economic activity. If current patterns of business location continue, it means a shift of jobs and income toward urban areas, since value-added activities such as banking, finance, insurance, wholesaling, and retailing (the growth sectors) tend to favor urban locations. But it also suggests a range of opportunities for aggressive, forward-thinking rural companies and communities that can position themselves within these production and distribution networks. The keys to success will be state-of-the-art production and communications technology, up-to-date information on market conditions, and the ability to adapt to changing customer demands.

Shifting Employment Share

The shift to GNP away from primary products had predictable effects on employment in these industries. But other forces also have been contributing to the declining job prospects throughout the natural resources sector. During a period now famous among economists for its slow productivity growth (from 1973 through the early 1980s), certain natural resources industries were able to buck the overall trend. The result for these industries and the communities in which they operate was, on the one hand, a boost to overall competitiveness due to increased efficiency, but on the other, losses in employment, or at least in employment growth. And many of the jobs lost were in rural areas.

Agriculture provides the best example of the pattern. Between 1973 and 1987, when the service sector overall recorded annual labor productivity growth below 1 percent (0.69) and manufacturing sector productivity grew at less than 3 percent annually (2.61), the comparable figure for farming was more than 5 percent (5.22).[17] These advances are also reflected in the recent trend toward part-time farming.[18] Between 1974 and 1987, the proportion of all farmers whose principal occupation was not farming increased from 37 percent to 45 percent. Half of all farm household income now comes from off-farm activities.

Other natural-resources-related industries such as food processing, lumber and wood products, furniture, and paper and pulp also experienced high productivity growth and declining demand for workers during the late 1970s and 1980s.

OTA predicts continued productivity gains and employment losses in the primary and secondary food-related sectors of the economy.[19] Likewise, modernization in the timber and wood products industry should continue, but at a slower rate than during the 1980s because much of the fat has already been cut.[20]

Stronger Linkages

While the facts about natural resources decline are undeniable, Drucker's conclusion that the commodities sector is becoming marginal to the world economy does not adequately recognize the ways in which commodities production stimulates demand for other industrial products and services. The urban–rural geography of extraction and processing underlines the importance of understanding how networks form both within the natural resources sector and among different sectors.

OTA's report on the U.S. economic transition found that, while natural resources experienced probably the most dramatic decline of any sector in direct share of GNP between 1950 and 1984, it proved to be the biggest user, proportionately, of the products of other sectors.[21] Of every dollar of added value contributed to the economy by purchases from the natural resources sectors, 75 cents goes to pay for intermediate inputs of goods and services from other sectors (compared to 23 cents in social services and 57 cents in high-wage manufacturing). These trends intensified over the period, with the natural resources sector becoming more highly linked to its suppliers while the service-related sectors overall grew more insular.

Viewed in isolation, natural resources is clearly a more marginal segment of the world and national economy today than it was in earlier periods. But viewed in context, it remains an important source of demand for some of the economy's fastest growing industries. The natural resources sector continues to offer opportunities for economic development if rural areas can capture some of the dollars flowing out of natural resources to buy goods and services in other sectors.

The Rural Picture

A closer look at specific groups of industries within the natural resources sector illustrates these three trends—the natural resources sector's declining share of national income and of employment, and the strength of linkages between natural resources and other sectors.

Agriculture

The last 20 years have been a wild ride for American farmers. After a decade of exceptional growth and prosperity in the 1970s, farmers and others involved in the food and fiber network saw their fortunes reversed in the first half of the 1980s.

A variety of factors added up to one of the most dramatic industry shakeouts in recent memory. Worldwide recession in 1980–82 dampened demand for all kinds of products, including agricultural commodities. At the same time, U.S. policy makers' efforts to stop inflation—through substantial increases in both interest rates and the value of the dollar—dealt a double blow to American agriculture. High interest rates meant that the substantial debts accumulated by optimistic farmers during the 1970s ballooned out of control. The high dollar meant that foreign buyers looked elsewhere for their commodities purchases, dragging down U.S. exports. These forces combined to lower incomes across most of the farming sector and put many smaller producers out of business altogether. Farm-related industries, most notably farm inputs (implement manufacturers and dealers, seed, fertilizer and pesticide industries, and the like) lost jobs and income. As late as 1987, analysts were predicting continued hard times throughout the agriculture sector.[22]

Starting in 1987, however, the new, leaner farm sector bounced back, enjoying record high net income levels for four consecutive years. According to Federal Reserve analysts, "the farm recovery is proving to be one of the sharpest financial turn-arounds in U.S. agriculture's history."[23] By 1991, earnings were way up, led by livestock profits; farm asset values were up though not back to their previous 1981 peak; and farm debt was down with a debt–asset ratio as low as that of the mid-1970s. Since then, the sector has enjoyed a period of relative stability.

Although the aggregate performance indicators for agriculture have roughly returned to their 1970s levels, the sector is very different from that of 20 years ago. Four structural changes are particularly worthy of note.

First, while output is up, employment is down. Productivity increases across the board in growing, harvesting, and processing, have led to widescale substitutions of capital for labor. Improved mechanization, irrigation, and crop yields made the difference on the farm.[24] Advances in production engineering, packaging, and preservation techniques made the difference in food manufacturing and will continue to do so, according to OTA. The OTA authors predict, "With an appropriate research program in food process engineering, annual productivity increases of 2.5 to 3.5 percent are easily possible in food manufacturing during the next decade."[25]

Second, in both farming and food processing, consolidation has changed the structure of the industries dramatically. Fewer farms of greater size now produce most of the nation's output.[26] The number of farms declined sharply during the 1950s and 1960s, then stabilized during much of the 1970s and declined again between 1982 and 1987, probably due to recession-related financial stress.[27] Between 1974 and 1987, the proportion of farms in the largest class size (annual sales $500,000 or more in current dollars) doubled, and their share of total farm output rose from 25 to 40 percent. The proportion of very small farms (sales less than $10,000) remained steady throughout the period while the proportion in the small-to-medium-sized category ($10,000 to $99,000 in sales) sustained most of the losses, dropping from 43 percent of all farms in 1974 to 37 percent in 1987. Between 1950 and 1987, the total number of U.S. farms dropped from 5.6 million to 2.1 million and the average farm size more than doubled, from 213 to 462 acres.[28] Likewise, the number of food processing firms has declined on average 2.5 percent annually since 1947. These trends are continuing.

Third, crops are becoming more diversified. Changing consumer tastes are placing a premium on specialty items like raddichio, "broccoflower," and fresh herbs. While most past efforts to increase growing and harvesting efficiency focused on the bulk commodities, particularly those supported by government target prices, these and other more specialized industries offer opportunities for greater productivity growth.[29]

Finally, and perhaps most important for rural communities in search of economic development strategies, the action in agriculture is moving downstream to those activities that occur after harvesting, and even after processing. Between 1981 and 1984, rural areas in the United States experienced net job losses in every part of the agricultural sector (farming, input industries, processing, and marketing) except food and fiber wholesale and retail trade.[30] OTA points, in particular, to the growth in grocery stores, supermarkets, convenience stores, fast food operations, and other dining establishments, both commercial and institutional.[31] Thanks to a marked trend toward eating out, food service has become "an enormous enterprise in the United States, providing nearly 1 out of 13 U.S. jobs."[32]

More research is needed to determine the geographic distribution of jobs in the wholesale and retail portion of the agricultural sector, but available evidence suggests that the shift toward downstream activities means a shift in favor of urban areas. Reimund and Petrulis note that rural areas capture two-thirds of all farming jobs in the United States but only one-quarter of all jobs in the other agriculture-related industries such as inputs and wholesale and retail trade.[33]

Most of these trends are expected to continue. At the same time, new trends are developing. The Food, Agriculture, Conservation, and Trade Act of 1990, for example, was designed partly "to make farmers' planting decisions more responsive to market forces rather than to government subsidies."[34] It sought to accomplish this goal by freezing guaranteed prices at their 1990 levels and reducing the acreage base eligible for the government prices by at least 15 percent.[35] Farmers were allowed to grow whatever crops they chose that excluded 15 percent based on what they think the market will reward. One of the results has been a reversal of the rapid rise in government payments to farmers during the 1980s[36] and the establishment of more market-driven decision making.[37] While the precise shape of the 1995 farm bill is yet to be determined, its broad thrust is likely to accelerate these developments.

Forestry and Wood Products

Forestry is by far the largest of the nonagricultural natural resource industries in the United States, employing almost twice as many workers as energy, nonenergy mining, and fishing combined.[38] Timber products account for more than a quarter of all industrial raw materials consumed in the United States.[39]

The early 1980s was a difficult period for the forestry industry. The economy of the Pacific Northwest, a forestry hub, suffered particularly serious declines during this time. Between 1979 and 1985, income in the wood and paper industries in the Pacific Northwest fell by almost 25 percent.[40] Unemployment rates in counties dependent on forestry and wood products were above the national average every year between 1976 and 1985.[41] Production also fell, but not as dramatically, ending at about 13 percent below its pre-1979 level.

Several factors contributed to the trouble. High interest rates here at home during the 1980s dampened the housing and construction industry, major sources of demand for wood products. At the peak of the recession in 1982, housing starts reached their lowest level since 1946. At the same time, the high value of the dollar on world markets made U.S. timber exports less attractive to foreign buyers and paved the way for growth in imports.

In response to these hard times and the specter of international competition, the U.S. forestry industry began to invest heavily in new equipment, such as mechanized harvesting systems, to improve their competitiveness. The results can be seen in the impressive gains in productivity: "The wood products industry in 1985 produced more than 90 percent of its 1979 output with less than 80 percent of its 1979 employment."[42] Another result was the sharp drop in jobs and income that hit timber communities in the early 1980s.

Also in response to the new competitive pressures, companies moved production to Southeastern forests, where labor is cheaper and less of it is needed to produce output. The effect on once-thriving communities in the Pacific Northwest has been enormous.

With most of the labor-saving improvements completed, analysts do not expect forestry industry employment to continue declining as rapidly as it did in the 1980s. Harvests may drop off, however, particularly in the Northwest where old-growth forests are being depleted and the rate of removing trees exceeds the growth rate of newer plantings. Maintaining output levels in the coming years will depend on the ability to gain access to private, nonindustrial stands of timber in the Southeast as well as on the outcome of current conflicts between environmentalists and foresters over public policy on national forest lands. Demographic trends and rising long-term interest rates may well reduce demand for forest products by slowing new housing construction.[43]

Energy

The energy industry has been riding a roller coaster during the last few decades. The sudden price hike after the Arab oil embargo in 1973 was a boon to U.S. energy producers, while the subsequent drop in price in the 1980s, due to lower demand and instability in the OPEC cartel, dealt the oil fields a sharp blow. Unemployment rates in counties dependent on energy extraction were higher than the national average for 6 of the 10 years between 1976 and 1985.[44]

Coal, the most rural of the primary energy industries, benefitted from the higher energy prices in the 1970s and again in the 1980s as energy use patterns shifted away from oil and gas toward various sources of electricity, including coal-fired power plants, nuclear reactors, hydropower, and wind power.[45] Between 1972 and 1985, coal use increased 8 percent, more than any other form of energy, mostly as an indirect result of household purchases of more products and services made with electricity.

Most energy analysts forecast a fairly bright future for the global coal industry. World demand for coal expanded 30 percent over the last decade and rose almost 5 percent in 1988 alone.[46] With expectations for continuing healthy economic growth, rising oil prices, and mounting public discomfort with nuclear power, the OECD predicts a 26 percent rise in hard coal output by the year 2000, with production shifting from European to North American sources.[47]

Other factors, however, point to a less buoyant future for the domestic coal industry. Standard & Poor's describes consumption here at home as relatively flat, with no expectation for significant increases in the future.[48] Areas of uncertainty make accurate predictions difficult. These include the business cycle,[49] the acid rain regulations in the reauthorized Clean Air Act, and various local and regional battles between coal producers and environmental groups opposed to strip mining and long-wall mining practices.

Copper

Like the forest products industries, nonenergy mining industries tend to follow the ups and downs of the national business cycle, in part because of their dependence on markets in manufacturing and construction. Of the natural resources industry groups studied by Weber, Castle, and Shriver, oil and gas and metal-mining proved the most volatile between 1969 and 1985.[50] Over the period, mining experienced steady declines in employment of about 1.5 percent per year and unemployment rates above the national average in 9 out of 10 years.[51]

Copper, the third most widely used metal in the world, offers a case in point and follows the now-familiar pattern.[52] Copper producers enjoyed steady growth in demand from just after World War II until the oil shock of 1973. Then the bottom fell out of the market, sending prices down 40 to 50 percent. A huge proportion of the industry work force (42 percent) was laid off between 1981 and 1983 and the industry lost over $1 billion. Then, to the surprise of many analysts, copper rebounded: Prices almost doubled between 1986 and 1988, and companies once again became profitable.

Current good fortune for copper-dependent communities is the result of both increased demand in certain industries (building wire, plumbing, heating, and others) and significant productivity improvements put in motion by major capital investments since 1985.[53] Like timber producers, copper producers, jolted by international competition and generally bad times in the industry during the early 1980s, responded by significantly improving efficiency. They closed older mines, introduced new equipment, cut wages, and improved the quality of the ore.

As world copper capacity expands in response to better times, prices are likely to decline gradually in the 1990s, but with continued profitability for an increasingly competitive industry. Additional efficiency improvements and cost cuts in the near future are hard to imagine, short of an unanticipated technological breakthrough. Still, most analysts forecast an "extended period of strength" and profitability.[54] That is good news for some rural communities, mostly in Arizona, the heart of the U.S. copper mining industry.

From the shakeout of forestry, energy, and metals mining in the early 1980s, these industries have emerged leaner and generally more cautious about the future. The extent to which recent changes reflect ongoing cycles or fundamental, irreversible structural changes is still a matter for debate. But most analysts agree that employment levels in these industries will never return to their earlier highs; prices, too, are likely to remain below their peaks of the 1960s and 1970s even if demand continues to grow moderately. Raw materials are not the economic development growth poles that they once were.

Community Performance

In those counties most heavily dependent on natural resources income and employment, growth and decline parallels the general trend in the industries themselves—booming growth in the 1970s followed by upheaval and shrinkage in the 1980s. In an analysis that does not include a specific category for natural-resources-dependent counties, Drabenstott and Gibson have calculated the extent of overall decline in rural areas with a "traditional" economic base, which includes agriculture, mining, and manufacturing.[55] Between 1978 and 1985, these counties lost employment share virtually across the board.

The biggest losses for agriculture-dependent counties came in wholesale, retail, and services, a potentially ominous sign for farming communities hoping to take advantage of the growth in these activities' share of food and fiber value added.[56] Somewhat surprisingly, agriculture-based counties made significant gains in their share of manufacturing jobs. Whether or not these manufacturing jobs were in the food processing industries cannot be determined from the analysis. The other natural resources category, mining, lost jobs primarily in construction, manufacturing, and services. Mining counties gained a large number of local government jobs, however, and ended up with a net increase in employment share.

Economic declines were accompanied by declines in population growth.[57] According to the demographers at the Economic Research Service, agriculture-dependent counties experienced a downturn in population growth starting in 1982–83, eventually dropping into the negative range.[58] The 1986–88 period, however, brought an encouraging rise in growth, a trend that the analysts say "signals an end to losses caused by the earlier farm crisis."[59] Mining counties suffered the most dramatic population losses of any county group studied.

Economic Development Strategies

The previous section paints a gloomy picture of the natural resources sector's ability to function as a growth leader in rural economy. However, it is important to remember the diversity within this sector, not only across commodity groupings (farm, forestry, energy) but also across activities. The transformation of natural resources into GNP basically follows three steps, each of which contains the seeds of an economic development strategy. The three steps are harvesting and extracting, processing, and distribution.

Harvesting and Extracting

From a rural perspective, harvesting and extracting activities have the advantage of being captive: They must locate where the commodities are—in rural areas. Unfortunately, these activities also offer very few opportunities for jobs. The future profitability of logging, farming, drilling, and mining will depend on continued productivity increases and, therefore, continued declines in employment. If Peter Drucker is right and prices for primary products continue to fall, this group of activities will gradually lose its place of prominence in the rural economy, in both income and job creation. In some places, that change has already occurred.

Nonetheless, harvesting and extracting activities do generate export dollars. Thus, counties dependent on these activities should pursue strategies for improving their performance and strengthening their competitive position. The literature describes several such strategies.

In agriculture, for example, exchange rate adjustments create windows of opportunity for farmers to alter their crop mix and take advantage of both import substitution and export possibilities.[60] In 1987, for example, as the value of the dollar declined relative to the currencies of other industrialized nations, the prices paid by American consumers for imported products from Europe increased. This adjustment opened the door for American farmers to recapture domestic markets for imported items such as wine, beer, pork, cheese, olives, and fruit juice. At the same time, the value of the dollar rose relative to the currencies of many less developed countries, providing new opportunities for farmers in Latin America and other less developed regions to export their goods to the United States.

Beyond product shifting to take advantage of macroeconomic conditions, farmers can pursue more fundamental changes in their operations through innovation. Applications of new biotechnologies, no- and low-till farming, integrated pest management, irrigation and water conservation, and computerized information systems can increase efficiency and profitability while protecting the quality of the natural resource base.[61] Diversification of agricultural products can expand markets and create altogether new markets for local growers.[62] As Thomas points out, soybeans were considered an alternative product 30 years ago. Since then, researchers have invented scores of uses for soybeans and soybean oil in both food and nonfood products. Catfish farming, a relatively new innovation, has become an important industry in parts of the South. Aquaculture in general is "the fastest growing sector of agriculture in the United States today," increasing about 15 percent annually.[63] Growers of specialty products such as lentils, organic vegetables, nuts, grass seed, and nursery products have prospered in the Pacific Northwest.[64] Science also can develop new uses for most traditional commodities: Corn starch is a key ingredient in the production of the new generation of biodegradable plastic bags.

Similar innovations may be found in forest products. Daniel Kemmis describes how the residents and employers in the Missoula Valley of Montana could, if they chose to cooperate, simultaneously address their air pollution problem and increase the profitability of several small local sawmills.[65] The air pollution problem—the result of burning low-efficiency cord wood to heat homes in the area—could be reduced by creating a revolving loan fund to help homeowners buy clean-burning, wood pellet stoves on reasonable terms. At the same time, according to Kemmis' plan, local sawmills could take advantage of the shift in consumer demand toward wood pellets to improve their efficiency and increase their gradually eroding profit margins. By forming a supplier cooperative, the mill owners could build a facility that would process the sawdust from the mills (considered a waste problem) into pellets for sale to homes with the new clean-burning wood stoves.

Other examples of strategic thinking in the forest products industry include the use of waste wood from sawmills mixed with glue to produce items such as park benches and the collection of pine straw (the needles that fall from the longleaf pine tree) for sale to nurseries. Also, diversification into different tree species will meet rising demands for a wide variety of wood types.

Successful implementation of these strategies depends in part on access to reliable information about industry trends and economic conditions. Technical and/or financial assistance to primary producers seeking to modernize their operations, keep closer track of markets, develop alternative products, and strengthen their links with other parts of the natural resources network represent sound investments for rural communities.

Processing

Reports on rural development are full of exhortations to communities to pursue value-added upstream enterprises—the food processing, sawmilling, and copper refining components of the natural resources production cycle. The logic of this strategy is simple and attractive: Why not bring the cannery to the vegetables rather than the vegetables to the cannery? This way, the rural natural resources counties that produce the food and fiber capture more of those commodities' final value.

Despite the attractive logic, implementation of this approach has proven very difficult. Over the many years in which the value-added approach has been fashionable, only a relatively small number of rural areas have successfully attracted processing plants linked to their commodities base. Of 51 case studies of successful, local rural development initiatives analyzed by the Midwest Research Institute, only five involved the creation, attraction, or expansion of food processing or forest industry enterprises in or near natural resources production areas.[66] Three of the five involved industrial recruitment (of a peanut processing plant, an onion processing plant, and a lumber processing plant) and resulted in large numbers of new jobs (several hundred in each case) in the affected counties. The other two case studies described successes on a smaller scale: participation by five new farm families in a poultry house project in one case; leasing of farmland in an agricultural park to 30 farmers employing about 80 people in the other. These examples are encouraging and demonstrate what a community with strong leadership and an aggressive economic development strategy can accomplish. Unfortunately, considering the meager sampling, they may be exceptions to the rule.

The traditional model of value-added development in natural resources suffers fundamental problems. As Joe Cortright, staff member for the Trade and Economic Development Committee of the Oregon State Legislature, commented, it looks like little more than "old wine in new bottles."[67] Industrial attraction strategies that focus on adding value (through manufacturing) to local natural resources products are still just industrial attraction strategies—a zero-sum game in which communities spend precious resources chasing elusive industrial plants. This 30-year-old approach to economic development, frequently referred to as "smokestack chasing" or "buffalo hunting," fell out of favor with most development specialists in the 1980s for three reasons. First, it costs the participants dearly, particularly the winners of the bidding war who often have promised generous tax breaks and public expenditures for infrastructure improvements, free job training, and other inducements that cancel out at least some of the economic benefits of the newly created jobs. Second, this strategy trades long-term instability for a big employment payoff up front, because recruitable companies and plants are notoriously footloose: What's to keep the new plant in town from moving elsewhere in five years when a better incentive package comes along? Third, there simply are not enough mobile jobs to make this approach pay off for more than a handful of communities each year.

The case of agricultural processing confirms the third point. As noted above, while these industries have been making great strides toward modernization and increased competitiveness in recent years, they also have been losing employment. Some of the jobs have been mechanized, but many others are being moved to other countries where they can be filled more cheaply. The story of the Massachusetts garden nursery that set up a geranium growing operation in Mexico is just one example of a growing trend toward moving agricultural processing jobs to foreign locations.[68] According to Forbes, "Agro-maquilas now represent the fastest-growing segment of the $3-billion-a-year maquiladora industry."[69] Maquiladoras are the Mexican operations of American companies, mostly assembly plants for manufacturers, expected to proliferate as a result of the Mexican government's "newly relaxed attitude toward direct foreign investment" as well as the Mexican–American free trade agreement. As these trends continue, many rural areas in the United States simply will not be able, and may not want, to compete with wage levels in Mexico and other developing countries.

In the final analysis, the logic of value-added industrial attraction fails for agriculture and food processing. The evidence suggests that manufacturers gain little from locating near the harvest. In their study of states that concentrate in farming and states that concentrate in food processing, Barkema, Drabenstott, and Stanley (1990) found little overlap between the two groups. According to their calculations, farm production is concentrated in 10 states of the upper Midwest and Great Plains regions. Food processing activity, in contrast, is concentrated in the Sunbelt and the industrial Great Lakes and Northeast regions. Only one state falls into both categories—Wisconsin.[70]

Barkema et al. conclude that food processors seem to favor locations closer to major population centers.[71] They observe that the 10 top food processing states contain more than half of the entire U.S. population. Proximity to markets has several potential advantages for these industries. It cuts down on transportation costs of the final product, a potentially important consideration in certain cases (such as canned vegetables) where the final product weighs considerably more than the agricultural inputs. It may improve access to other inputs needed in the manufacturing process, such as other foods (for example, to assemble a frozen dinner), packaging materials, or laborers with specific skills. Finally, it may help ensure that managers are better attuned to changes in demand and market conditions. Assuming that most companies make rational location decisions, these economic considerations are likely to outweigh the advantages of proximity to raw materials in most cases.

Given the obstacles to food processing development, Barkema et al. recommend a more limited strategy, focused on states closer to the population centers (Iowa rather than Montana, for example) and states with an existing, viable base of food processing activity.[72] In these states, the authors argue, an economic development strategy focused on food processing may succeed so long as it targets food products that are in growing demand, that derive from locally supplied farm products, and that represent industries in easy-to-enter markets.[73] Barkema et al. also echo OTA's recommendation to pursue opportunities for technological improvements in weight-reducing processes, packaging, preservation techniques, and biotechnology.[74]

The research on food processing location points to a familiar pattern for rural development—adjacency. The apparent importance of access to markets and population centers at the state level may carry over to the community level, making rural areas adjacent to urban areas the best candidates for food-processing-related development strategies.

Traditional value-added development holds more promise in the other natural resources industries. It makes good economic sense to burn coal at the minehead when possible, to reduce transportation costs. Likewise, certain basic sawmilling processes typically are undertaken near the tree harvest areas. In the case of forestry and wood products, a general rule of thumb states that the more value added to the lumber, the more likely the enterprises are to concentrate near urban areas. Conversely, the more processes are driven by raw material inputs, the more likely the enterprises are to be dispersed among smaller logging communities.[75]

Still, the most promising basic strategies in wood products value added seem to follow the same general principles recommended by Barkema et al., OTA, and others for food processing. As David Harrison puts it, "Growing the number of secondary producers is not the answer."[76] Instead, states in the Pacific Northwest are using strategies to improve the competitiveness of their existing wood products manufacturers and spur the development of new products, new production processes, and new applications of emerging technology. The state of Washington, for example, is developing a network of lumber and wood products agents (modeled on the cooperative extension service in agriculture) who visit small lumber mills and other producers to provide needed technical assistance and information about national and international market trends.[77] On a slightly different track, Oregon is studying the feasibility of setting up flexible manufacturing systems in wood processing plants.

These recent trends in value-added development cut two ways. On the bright side, they bring creative, market-driven thinking to the problem of the marginalization of the natural resources sector. Some of the efforts now underway in Oregon and Washington State are sure to become models for realistic, successful, value-added economic development elsewhere in the country as other states and communities catch up. On the darker side, however, these competitiveness-based approaches offer very little hope to the most remote, most beleaguered natural resources communities that have no existing processing or manufacturing base on which to build. Some of these communities may choose to embrace the old industrial attraction strategies for lack of a better alternative.

Retail, Wholesale, and the Distribution Network

As noted in earlier sections, wholesale and retail distribution are the prime sources of growth in natural resources GNP and employment. Unfortunately, many of the activities generating that growth, most notably the "superstore" supermarkets and many dining establishments, are better suited to urban and suburban locations. Wholesale and transportation operations (warehousing, trucking, and so on) offer some possibilities for rural development. So do creative marketing ventures such as farmers markets and pick-your-own farms.[78]

In all of these cases, again, rural areas adjacent to population centers seem to have the advantage.

Some communities will never attract any of the jobs directly generated by agricultural retail, wholesale, and transportation. For these communities, the distribution network still offers valuable opportunities for improving the competitiveness of primary and secondary producers. Development of communications networks, for example, may allow small farms in remote locations to sell directly to superstores in the suburbs.[79] Stronger urban–rural communications linkages could also connect rural enterprises with valuable information about market trends and improve the quality of their decision making. Those who work directly with the primary products, whether farmers, loggers, or sawmill operators, are often thought to be out of touch with the demands of the downstream operators—manufacturers, marketers, and distributors. Better communications networks could help bring these worlds closer together.

Experience suggests that collective action can help individual communities take advantage of the linkage opportunities generated by market forces. One tool is the industry association, an institution that relies most heavily on cooperation among businesses but also may benefit from partnership with local government. Thomas describes ways in which local rural communities can come together to form regional food industry associations to encourage retention and expansion of food enterprises.[80] The functions of such associations may include referral services or clearinghouses to link member firms with free or low-cost assistance in areas such as marketing, management, financing, engineering, technology, and industry regulations; networks to link food businesses together in "product partnerships"; newsletters and/or workshops to disseminate technical and market-related information; shared promotional ventures such as food trade shows; and product directories to help member companies gain access to potential buyers.[81] Industry associations may also prove useful in timber regions. One of the more ambitious functions of industry associations may be establishing specialized industrial parks—property under coordinated management that brings together a variety of independent producers in a given industry, such as wood products or food.[82]

Quality of Development—Jobs

New job creation is an important goal of economic development (and one that is easily quantified), but it is not the ultimate goal. When economic developers assess their performance, they must remember that not all jobs are equally valuable or desirable and that not all industries make equally good neighbors.

Chapter 2 outlined the core values by which we can evaluate the content of an economic development strategy and the effect it will have on individual and social well-being. Three of these normative dimensions are of particular importance in analyzing the natural resources sector: relieving poverty, providing opportunities attractive to young people, and showing respectful concern for workers at the bottom of the economic hierarchy.

Poverty

Economic development must hold out the promise of relieving poverty. Yet conventional wisdom teaches that rural counties dependent on natural resources industries are more likely to be poor. What does this mean for the ability of natural-resources-based development to improve standards of living?

Statistical analysis generally confirms the conventional wisdom that poverty and natural resources are correlated. A 1983 study by Elo and Beale found somewhat higher poverty rates in natural-resources-based rural counties compared to counties with other types of economies. They conclude that, while "there is no major overall direct causal relationship between natural-resources activity and rural poverty," certain populations in certain regions and occupational groups do suffer substantially as a result of their ties with the natural resources economy.[83]

More recent analysis further describes the difficult conditions faced by rural residents dependent on the natural resources sector. Johnson, Kraybill, and Deaton compared various quality-of-life indicators in the natural-resources-dependent counties of Virginia—in particular, the coal field areas—and the rest of the state. Virtually across the board, the coal counties lagged behind their neighbors in real per capita income (68 percent that of the state), income distribution, income variability (18 percent greater in coal counties), percentage of families below the poverty line (more than 15 percent in coal counties, 9 percent statewide), unemployment, variability of unemployment, infant mortality, rates of high school graduation, levels of college education, dropout rates, and achievement test scores.[84] The authors conclude not only that the natural resources areas of Virginia suffer a far lower standard of living and quality of life, but also that the combination of unstable incomes, low levels of income, and low expected rates of return serves to discourage residents of these areas from making the kinds of human capital investments in education, health care, and housing that might improve their conditions in the future.

Establishing the connection between a natural-resources-based economy and low living standards is easier than explaining it. Part of the explanation can be found in the seasonal nature of much natural-resources-related work, particularly in agriculture. Farmers, farm laborers, and other farm-related workers move in and out of employment on a regular, predictable cycle. In addition, they generally work without the pension and health care benefits that workers in other sectors take for granted. Many of the jobs in the secondary natural resources industries are also known for being dirty and dangerous and for barely providing a subsistence income for a family. Although mechanization has improved some conditions, OTA reports that "food processing is still one of America's most dangerous industries, with the second highest rate of occupational injuries and illnesses per full-time worker."[85] The September 3, 1991 fire in a poultry plant in Hamlet, North Carolina focused national attention briefly on the problem of occupational safety enforcement in rural areas and small towns. After 25 workers died in that fire, state officials revealed that the plant had not been inspected for 11 years.[86]

Another part of the explanation is the economic structure of many natural resources counties. Contrary to the national trend toward greater economic diversification, the economic base of many natural resources counties has narrowed since the early 1970s.[87] Due in part to the loss of other types of enterprises, increased specialization in energy, agriculture, mining, and forestry has left these areas more vulnerable to the boom and bust cycles that characterize natural resources. In addition, labor-intensive processing activities in agriculture and other natural resources sectors provide a shaky foundation for any rural economy. These jobs are rapidly moving to developing countries where the wage rates fall far below those of even the poorest U.S. counties. Rural areas cannot and, many would say, should not try to compete for these jobs on the basis of wages.

A third explanatory variable is the simple fact that for many years, poverty has been a key element in rural America's comparative advantage, particularly in the South. As Donald Tomaskovic-Devey has explained, elite landowners throughout the South long have benefitted from the presence of a large pool of unskilled, surplus workers willing to do agricultural work at very low wages.[88] The shifting of timber production from the Pacific Northwest to the South during the 1980s provides evidence of how low wages (poverty-level wages in many cases) continue to serve the interests of southern rural producers.

If these explanations are correct, both structure and agency are at work in maintaining the link between poverty and the natural resources economy. Thus, efforts to break the link must address both factors.

While changing the structure of agricultural jobs may be an impossible task, policies can help compensate for the market's failure to provide a year-round living wage. These include the expanded earned income tax credit proposed by President Clinton and enacted into law in 1993. Promulgation and enforcement of more effective occupational safety regulations would help improve the nonwage quality of many natural-resources-related jobs.

Overcoming the vested interests of rural producers in maintaining low wages is an equally daunting task that requires collective action of many types. Creation of new institutions can make a difference, such as the industry associations described above that expand the reach and power of smaller producers and tend to have a greater stake in promoting innovation. Likewise, development of supplier and worker cooperatives may help shift the agenda for economic development toward the interests of the more vulnerable parties. Enlightened state and local development authorities can and should negotiate with potential employers to improve the prospects for workers. For example, in return for location inducements such as tax relief, employers might be expected to invest in ongoing worker training programs.

Ultimately, economic development strategies must be subjected to the scrutiny of the larger community via the political process. It is possible that residents of very remote areas with few prospects for industrial development will embrace a plan focused on food processing recruitment, for example. But such a choice should be made only after citizens are informed about factors such as low wage levels, hazards on the job, lack of opportunities for advancement, and the risk of losing plants to Third World locations. Citizens must then be given opportunities for public deliberation and consideration of alternatives.

Young People

Adequate development also requires the provision of suitable opportunities for the children of current adult members of the community. The development process must generate enough jobs of sufficient quality and diversity that young people who want to stay in the community can do so.

Rural development during the 1980s did not meet this criterion. Between 1988 and 1989, for example, rural areas lost better-educated residents to urban areas at an average annual rate of about 3 percent.[89] The outflow was greatest among young, college-educated adults aged 25–34. By contrast, rural residents with less education, especially high school dropouts, tended to stay in their communities. According to a recent study by the Economic Research Service (ERS), this "brain drain" in which the better-educated moved out leaving the less well-educated behind was large enough to "account for all of the relatively low growth in average education 1980–88 in nonmetro areas compared with metro areas."[90] The apparent 1980s trend runs contrary to that of the 1970s, a period when more highly educated people chose to move into rural areas than out.

Strange as it may sound, out-migration of educated residents is not a serious problem for communities whose comparative advantage lies in low-wage, low-skilled production. Thus, the findings of the ERS researchers should not come as a surprise: When differences in industrial structure are controlled, local economic growth rates do not correlate strongly with local educational achievement levels.[91] Clearly, despite the much-touted trend toward a more sophisticated economy, many U.S. employers still gravitated toward areas (both urban and rural) with surpluses of young, cheap labor during the 1970s and 1980s.[92] Many rural areas continued to grow in spite of, or perhaps because of, the low educational attainment of their labor force. Of course, while these employers brought welcome job creation, as Tomaskovic-Devey and others have argued, the jobs that they generated, particularly in the South, contributed far too little to improving living standards.[93] And, as the ERS data confirm, these job opportunities were not enough to keep young rural high school graduates and college-educated residents from moving to cities.

Out-migration of the better educated does become a serious problem in communities and larger regions seeking to shift their comparative advantage away from cheap labor toward innovation in products and processes. Where economic development strategies focus on adding value by improving the quality and diversity of products, increasing firms' responsiveness to market demands, and raising productivity, two employment effects are likely. First, some jobs will be lost, at least at first, as growers and manufacturers introduce more sophisticated, mechanized primary and secondary production processes. In the lumber industry much of that shift has already occurred; in agriculture there is still much room for improvement in productivity.[94] Second, the wages and skill requirements for many of the remaining jobs will increase, particularly for the workers who maintain and operate the more sophisticated equipment and the managers who keep the networks running.

Rural areas seeking to relieve poverty and retain their younger, better-educated residents have no choice but to pursue some type of value-added development. Such a strategy requires changes on many fronts. First, because "low-skilled workers seldom make high-valued products," as Cortright puts it,[95] upgrades in the quality of rural education at all levels are necessary: elementary school to make these communities more attractive places for adults to live and raise their families (and to improve the cognitive abilities of the future work force); high school to ensure that students are receiving the appropriate type of education to prepare them for local jobs or for college; community college to raise vocational skills; and 4-year college and university to generate a homegrown professional work force. (Most rural graduates will have to go away to college, but many could be induced to return.)[96]

The ERS research shows, however, that improvements in education and training alone do not affect the location of economic growth. Human capital policies must be part of comprehensive efforts to link rural areas with supply, production, and labor market networks via new institutional structures. These structures take the form of industry associations and cooperatives and new regional alliances, which the ERS authors call "larger territorial complexes."[97] Improvements in local educational opportunities must coincide with improvements in local and regional job opportunities in order to increase the returns to education and overcome the natural tendency of rural residents to underinvest in their own human capital.[98]

Respect

The work of Tomaskovic-Devey and other rural sociologists and historians focuses attention on how power structures in rural communities perpetuate economic systems that are fundamentally disrespectful of workers at the bottom of the hierarchy, particularly those who are female, black, or Hispanic.[99] These findings lend a note of caution to recommendations for shifting economic development strategies from those that seek outside investment to those that rely on "growth from within." If left in the hands of the existing economic leadership, internalized development processes may perpetuate the inequalities of the existing economic structure. As Tomaskovic-Devey notes, "There is a mutuality of interest between local and national and international capital in the maintenance of a low-wage nonunion economy. If economic growth creates uneven development outcomes it cannot be simply blamed on outside investment."[100]

This point does not lead to the conclusion that outside investment is preferable to internally generated development, even in areas where elites have a large stake in continued low-wage production. It does, however, underline the importance of broadening the base of local leadership in these areas as part of the process of adopting new economic development strategies.

Quality of Development—The Environment

As discussed in the introduction to Part I, economic development strategies also must be held accountable to the idea of rural place. And among the core values contained in the idea of rural place is a special human relation to, and regard for, nature. The survival of many rural communities depends on striking the correct balance between using and caring for natural resources— in other words, that feature of development called "sustainability" (see Chapter 2). Recent environmental policy developments at the national level illustrate how compromises can be struck that aid both market-based and place-based development.

Farms and the Environment

The last two farm bills produced by the U.S. Congress, the Food Security Act of 1985 and the Food, Agriculture, Conservation, and Trade Act of 1990, demonstrate the possibilities for innovation in resolving conflicts between economics and the environment. The most recent law represents an important, incremental step away from massive federal subsidization of unsustainable, purely production-driven farming practices and toward more responsible use of the land. The 1990 law contains the strongest conservation measures yet seen in agriculture.[101]

Farmers' interests are mixed. On the one hand, some farm groups pay lobbyists to fight hard to preserve their autonomy over land management decisions and to keep subsidies high. On the other hand, surveys show that farmers firmly support conservation planning (80 percent believe the approved conservation plans for their farms are reasonable) and the idea of government regulation to reduce agriculture-related pollution of streams and groundwater (61 percent in favor).[102] Experience shows that, with good management practices, committed farmers can reduce their use of pesticides and fertilizers and adopt conservation techniques without increasing production costs and without forfeiting production volume. In fact, costs should decline, at least in the long run, because of the high price of chemical inputs. Nonetheless, farmers shy away from many of the new, recommended (and in limited cases, required) techniques, fearing that they will reduce crop yields, increase input costs, and, in the worst scenario as agriculture becomes less profitable, cause land values to drop.[103]

Farmers themselves and their families are the most immediate beneficiaries of efforts to reduce human exposure to pesticides and keep toxic chemicals out of the rural drinking water supply.[104] Yet federal efforts to regulate use of agricultural chemicals have made little progress in Congress. Many farmers perceive an unattractive tradeoff between income on the one hand and health and safety on the other, and they intuitively oppose efforts by government to tell them what to do.

In the face of this stubborn opposition to controls, lawmakers have learned that the best way to promote environmental goals is to subsidize them via incentives.[105] The popular Conservation Reserve Program (CRP), established in the 1985 farm bill, pays farmers to take highly erodible land out of crop production. Under the 1985 law, it protected 34 million acres of land.[106] The 1990 law raised the target for the CRP to between 40 and 45 million acres and added a provision for setting aside wetlands, particularly those that provide habitat for birds and wildlife.[107] The law also introduced subsidies for farmers who undertake government-approved plans to reduce water pollution due to sediment runoff.[108] The only nod in the direction of traditional regulation was a requirement that farmers keep records of their use of certain very hazardous pesticides.

States, too, have taken an interest in conserving their soils and protecting the rural environment. All of the Great Plains states studied by the Center for Rural Affairs have active programs "to reduce the dependence of commercial agriculture on inputs that must be imported to the region," namely energy and chemicals derived from fossil fuels.[109] Programs include university-based research, field demonstration programs, and, in the case of Minnesota, a loan program for individual farmers seeking to reduce their inputs.

Federal and state farm policies have a long way to go before exhausting the environmentalists' agenda. Key proposals for the next round of negotiations at the federal level include, among other things, source reduction goals for agricultural pollutants;[110] extension of linkages between crop subsidy programs and conservation measures to include water quality and wildlife habitat programs; reforms of crop subsidy programs "to end discrimination against environmentally sound crop rotations and agrichemical source reduction"; efforts to promote markets for organic foods; and expansion of research and technical assistance programs that support the full range of conservation and environment concerns.[111] Prospects for these proposals will undoubtedly be influenced by the broad reaction against environment legislation and regulation that characterized the 103rd Congress and appears likely to intensify.

Forests: "The land has limits."

Although many regions of the country face ongoing conflicts between foresters and environmentalists, the controversy reached its most acute stage in the Pacific Northwest in the last several years. Here the central question becomes: How much wood should be cut, and where?

In the Pacific Northwest, the vast majority of logging occurs in two places: private lands owned by the logging companies (25 percent of the region's total commercial timberland); and federal lands managed by the U.S. Forest Service and the Bureau of Land Management (40 percent of the total).[112] After World War II, the region's companies began to clearcut their own private forests at an alarming pace in order to feed the baby boomers' insatiable demand for new housing. The rate of cutting peaked in 1952, dropped by half over the following 10 years, leveled off, and then slowed again in the

1970s and 1980s. The companies did not start replanting on a significant scale until the 1960s. That next generation of trees will take an average of 55 years (for Douglas-firs) to reach a size worth cutting down.

The results are shortages of timber on private lands and pressure to shift production to public lands.[113] To sustain current high rates of production nationwide, two options are available: (1) Public land managers in the Northwest can step up harvest volume to make up for the coming shortages on private lands, or (2) other regions, most notably the Southeast, can pick up the slack. As pointed out earlier in this chapter, a regional shift in timber production is already underway, with companies focusing more resources on the faster-growing southeastern forests where labor is cheaper and harvesting is easier.

Some powerful forces in the Northwest have dedicated themselves to pursuing the first option— increased production on public lands in the region. Backed by forest industry lobbyists, members of Congress from the region put considerable pressure on the U.S. Forest Service to build more logging roads and cut more trees during the 1980s in order to accelerate the region's economic recovery after the devastating recessions of 1979–82.[114] The Forest Service, a federal agency known for its traditional view of trees as commodities, obliged most of the Congress' requests. As a result, harvests on national forest lands in the region more than doubled between the recessionary low point in 1982 and the policy-induced peak in 1987.[115]

These policies kept people employed during the rough economic times of the early 1980s better than any local development strategy could. However, they also sowed the seeds of serious long-term problems for the very communities they were intended to serve. The first problem is sustainability. By repeating the mistakes made on private timberlands in the 1950s and 1960s— namely, overcutting beyond the forest's ability to regenerate and intensively managing second-growth forests (a practice that seems to produce a poorer quality of wood)—the forest service has been pursuing a course that could lead to future shortages of quality timber on public lands. The future of logging and milling jobs depends on responsible management of the land.

The second problem is environmental degradation. Soil eroded by clearcutting and road building has settled in lakes and streams all across the region, clogging salmon and trout runs and polluting local drinking water. The loss of habitat for various species, most famous among them the endangered northern spotted owl, threatens to reduce biological diversity in the region. In addition, the felling of hundreds of thousands of acres of national forest land takes a toll on recreation, an increasingly important component of the Pacific Northwest economy. Hikers, campers, cross-country skiers, and other outdoor enthusiasts are demanding ever more space for their activities and ever more pristine wilderness areas.

The third problem is economics. During the mid-1980s when the volume from federal harvests was reaching an all-time high, the average price for timber was dropping to an all-time low. The result was what is called below-cost timber sales on a massive scale—that is, sales of federal timber that didn't even cover the Forest Service's costs of cutting the trees. The controversy over below-cost timber sales reached a crescendo in the late 1980s. A wide range of interest groups, from the Sierra Club to the conservative National Taxpayers Union, registered their complaints about the sweetheart deals between the Forest Service and the private timber companies.[116] The Wilderness Society maintained that the Forest Service lost $2.4 billion in just five years, between 1982 and 1987, due to below-cost sales.[117] The agency's own calculations under a new bookkeeping system imposed by Congress in 1987 showed that about two-thirds of their sales that year lost money.[118]

The other sore point for timber critics is the issue of exports. In recent years, U.S. companies have increased their exports of raw, unmilled logs at a rapid rate (log exports rose 37 percent in 1988 alone), a practice that forfeits most of the value added that economic developers say we must capture.[119] Because, by law, logs obtained from federal lands cannot be sold for export before they are milled, U.S. companies have gotten in the habit of logging (overlogging) their own private land holdings to obtain raw logs for export while pushing for more access to timber from federal lands to satisfy domestic demands. Critics argue that not only are the lumber companies endangering U.S. sawmill jobs by exporting raw logs overseas, but also they are subsidizing this short-sighted practice by overharvesting the precious old-growth trees in the national forests.

The conflict over government timber sales is essentially a conflict between local and national, short-term and long-term interests. When asked to explain why they are willing to build roads and cut and sell trees at a loss,[120] agency officials cite their responsibility to, and long-term relationship with, local communities that depend on the forestry industry.[121] Viewed from the national perspective and with an eye to sustainability, the agency's practices seem wasteful and inefficient. The government is sacrificing conservation goals without reaping badly needed revenue through market-level sales. The Forest Service is not only propping up high profits in the private timber industry but also indirectly subsidizing the export of U.S. sawmill jobs. Viewed from the short-term survival perspective of struggling communities in the Pacific Northwest, however, these same policies can appear reasonable and humane. The benefits of government timber sales to local lumber towns are enormous in jobs and income as well as in proceeds from the "payments to counties" law which distributes 25 percent of the revenue from government timber sales to the counties where the national forests are located.

Public policy, however, must resist the temptation to favor the short-term view. As Savage observes, all of the possible scenarios for the Northwest forestry industry "have one thing in common—fewer jobs."[122] Continued overcutting on public lands will lead to timber shortages eventually and mill closures like those that occurred in earlier periods when the private lands began to run out of timber. Jobs and income will move to other regions. Injunctions against timber sales, too, like those authorized through the Endangered Species Act, will result in at least short-term job losses for loggers and millworkers. Other powerful forces within this industry, particularly the push for mechanization, guarantee continued reductions in employment levels. The tradeoff here is not between jobs and the environment, but between short-term profits and long-term sustainability. The 1993 forest summit chaired by President Clinton and Vice President Gore sought to strike a balance among these and other competing objectives. The policies flowing from that meeting are currently being litigated in federal courts.

Three strategies, joined together, offer strong possibilities for protecting the long-term interests of communities in a healthy timber industry and a healthy environment as well as the short-term interests in jobs and income. To begin with, the "New Forestry" is "a range of techniques designed to mimic or preserve natural processes in a forest stand while allowing commercial logging to occur."[123] It provides an alternative to the now villainized practice of clearcutting. While both environmentalists and logging companies have been slow to embrace these new techniques wholeheartedly, the continued development of these alternatives must be a critical piece of the region's long-term forest industry plan.

Alongside innovation in management and harvesting techniques, forest-dependent areas in the Northwest and elsewhere should pursue the types of competitiveness strategies described earlier in this chapter. The full range of value-added approaches is worth exploring, from quality control to new product development, advanced marketing techniques, and application of state-of-the-art processing technology. Any state or region interested in hanging on to its existing forestry and wood products industry base, and helping it grow, must facilitate modernization in all aspects of growing, harvesting, processing, and manufacturing.

Finally, policy makers need to consider possible mechanisms for compensating those communities that suffer most from sudden changes in policy toward federal timber harvesting. Clearly, the outcome of the federal debate over U.S. Forest Service policy will significantly affect the rural economy, particularly in the West, where most federal lands are located. Output from national forests accounts for roughly 15 percent of all U.S. timber production. Under current practices, much of this revenue is essentially redistributed through cheap timber sales from the federal budget to local timber-dependent rural communities. While this function is certainly not described in the agency's charter, it nonetheless performs an important economic development service. Should the policy change, federal, state, and local officials will be faced with the difficult challenge of how to make up for the jobs and income once supported by federal subsidies. Regardless of how the issue of logging on federal lands is eventually resolved, we will face the question of compensating the workers and communities left behind.

As the primary materials economy continues to uncouple from the industrial economy, the transition will be most painful for those local communities long dependent on the extraction and sale of natural resources. To the extent that domestic policies help speed the change—whether in forestry, mining, farming, or other sectors—government must find ways to help ease the transition for workers and proprietors. Trade Adjustment Assistance, a program designed specifically to help workers displaced by changes in America's international trade policy, provides a model. Further study is needed to apply the lessons learned there to the problems facing the natural resources work force.

Coal, Corn, and Clean Air

Another area of environmental policy with important implications for the rural economy is clean air. At the end of the 101st Congress, after years of struggle, members of Congress finally passed, and the president signed into law, a comprehensive reauthorization of the Clean Air Act. Analyses of this bill's potential impact on rural areas do not exist. However, with help from various national estimates of costs, we can begin to piece together a picture of good news for some rural regions and bad news for others.

Various models have sought to estimate the effects of the act's different provisions on jobs and employment around the country. However, two problems plague these ambitious efforts.[124] First, economists cannot accurately predict what types of technologies plants will employ to comply with the new standards. In the case of coal-fired utility plants in Appalachia that contribute to acid rain, for example, will these companies choose to retire the older, dirtier plants? Will they install scrubbers to reduce sulfur from the coal? Or will they switch, instead, to lower-sulfur coal mined in western states, leaving the eastern coal industry in a severe depression? No one can say for sure. Second, most models for predicting the costs of clean air are based on modifications of a model developed in the 1970s to predict changes in energy use. Some analysts question the ability of this particular tool to provide useful results.

As a result, cost projections vary widely. Some government estimates pin a $25–$35 billion business price tag on the new legislation.[125] A major study by the Business Roundtable, conducted prior to passage of the bill, forecasts anywhere between $14 billion and $104 billion a year depending on the particular scenario used ($54 billion is their middle estimate).[126]

The most important provisions of the revised Clean Air Act for rural communities are probably the acid rain standards. The new law calls for a 10-million-ton reduction in sulfur dioxide emissions, the pollutant that forms acid rain, by the year 2000.[127] Sulfur dioxide is produced mainly by utility plants that burn high-sulfur coal. The 111 dirtiest of these utility plants are targeted for the first phase of emission reductions. Plants have several options for complying with the new standards: They can use various types of "clean coal" technologies, the most common being scrubbers; they can switch from high-sulfur eastern coal to low-sulfur western coal; or they can switch to other types of fuel altogether—the most expensive and difficult option. The federal government has sought to provide some assistance for the development of new "clean coal" technologies over the last few years as part of their agreement with Canada to address the acid rain problem.

The effect of the acid rain standards on rural communities will depend largely on the decisions made by utilities about techniques for achieving reduced emissions. To the extent that the new standards actually put particular coal-fired plants out of business or motivate utilities to turn to other sources of power altogether, the drop in demand for coal will be dramatic.[128] At least one analyst argues that environmental problems related to coal are so serious and so difficult to mitigate that "coal may be best seen as a temporary cushion to ease the transition from oil to alternative, renewable energy sources" that are easier on the environment.[129] Industry analysts, however, as described earlier in this chapter, see a bright future for coal use worldwide.

The Bush administration predicted that up to 23,000 coal-mining jobs could be lost as a result of the acid rain provisions, many of these in rural areas, mostly in the Appalachian coal fields of Kentucky, West Virginia, Ohio, and Illinois. The United Mine Workers estimates are similar:[130] between 22,000 and 30,000 mining jobs lost by the year 2000.[131] Along with the job losses, according to this scenario, displaced miners in northern Appalachia and the Midwest would lose a total of more than $1 billion in direct income. The ripple effect on the local economies, many of which have already been experiencing long-term depression conditions, would cost more than $2.5 billion.[132] Losses in the eastern coal fields, however, may be offset by increased production and employment west of the Mississippi River, where low-sulfur, cleaner-burning coal is found.[133] We could not find any studies that quantify the possible employment gains for low-sulfur coal fields in the western states and western Kentucky.

While the acid rain standards are likely to cause suffering in many coal-dependent rural areas, another section of the new amendments, addressing reduction of smog and other motor-vehicle-related pollutants may actually provide a boost to a different part of the rural economy—farming counties. The new law mandates the sale of reformulated fuels in the nation's nine most polluted cities and establishes a pilot program requiring auto manufacturers to make clean-fueled cars available in California.[134] Clean fuel refers to gasoline blended with either methanol (a natural gas derivative) or ethanol (a form of alcohol made from corn, which has been used for several years to fuel some farm vehicles). A rise in the demand for ethanol produced by the recent government requirement for its use in reformulated fuels will mean a considerable boost for corn farmers and all the rural industries related to agricultural production.[135]

The likely redistributive effects of the Clean Air Act on the Midwest are significant and contradictory. While the acid rain standards will fall hardest on urban midwestern utilities (which tend to be older and dirtier) and the electricity-intensive industries that they support, the smog provisions will prove the greatest benefit to rural midwestern farmers, who produce most of the nation's corn.

6

Manufacturing

Introduction

The now-famous shift from farms to factories represents the single most dramatic structural change in the rural economy in this century—a change that generated tremendous wealth and boosted standards of living for millions of rural residents. Improvements in agricultural productivity during the 1950s and 1960s created a large pool of cheap, surplus labor that became the new source of comparative advantage for rural areas during the 1970s and 1980s. As factories moved from urban to rural locations, in part to take advantage of this surplus, economists began to speak of a "Rural Renaissance."

National and international trends in manufacturing today cast doubt on the continuing ability of the manufacturing sector to fuel rural economic growth on a large scale. Communities that can adapt to the new rules of manufacturing will prosper, but success will require substantial changes.

The literature on manufacturing-led development reveals patterns similar to those described in the Chapter 5, "Natural Resources." The basic conclusions are as follows:

1. Manufacturing no longer represents a steady source of job growth for rural areas. Rural America's historic position as low-wage employer has been usurped by even lower-wage developing countries. After a slide in the early and mid-1980s, overall rural manufacturing jobs have barely regained the levels of the late 1970s.

2. Nonetheless, so long as the sector's productivity growth remains high and industries keep up with the demands of rapidly changing technologies, processes, and markets, manufacturing will be an important generator of wealth and an important market for goods and services produced by other sectors.

3. There is ample room for improvement, or "slack," in rural manufacturing. Market forces have failed to generate adequate levels of investment in

production technology in rural factories; failed to provide access to advanced services such as marketing and finance that rural manufacturers need to compete; failed to develop collaborative networks of suppliers, producers, marketers, and distributors that could provide the base for stronger rural growth.

4. Rural manufacturing development strategies must strike a balance between competing activities: specialized recruiting of mobile plants (the traditional methods of "buffalo hunting" need to be altered and given less weight, but abandoning recruitment altogether is not necessarily wise); services to encourage continuous upgrading of both new and existing rural operations; efforts to strengthen the links within and among manufacturing and other rural industries. Each community or region's particular mix of activities should reflect its geography (in particular, its adjacency to or relative remoteness from metropolitan areas), its existing industrial base (starting from scratch is highly risky), and its leadership resources.

The Context: National and International Trends

Because rural growth in a particular industry or sector tends to parallel national growth in that industry or sector, we need to begin with the question: Is manufacturing a potential source of U.S. economic growth?

Some Facts about Growth

Economic history since World War II suggests three conclusions: Manufacturing employment is shrinking, output is rising, and the relative weight of manufacturing in the overall economy is declining.

Employment figures tell a story of gradual shrinkage over the past 30 years. Manufacturing industries employed 27 percent of all full-time equivalent workers in 1955 (the postwar high), but that share dropped steadily over the years to about 18 percent in 1985.[1] During most of this period, manufacturing's losses were relative; the actual number of manufacturing workers was growing steadily, but at a slower rate than other sectors. Then, between 1978 and 1986, relative manufacturing shrinkage turned into absolute losses as one to two million manufacturing jobs were eliminated from the economy. The recession of 1990–92 dealt a further blow to manufacturing jobs, and only a portion of that lost ground has been regained.

Output measures tell a slightly different story, depending on the choice of numbers. According to Department of Commerce figures, manufacturing's constant dollar share of GNP has remained remarkably steady since 1985, hovering around 21 to 22 percent.[2] Roughly speaking, this means that in spite of fluctuations in prices, demand, and conditions of trade, the volume of goods produced by American manufacturers has been rising at the pace of aggregate GNP during the past three decades. And, thanks to impressive gains in manufacturing productivity over the period, that volume has been produced with a steadily decreasing share of the work force.

At the same time, however, the current dollar share of GNP for manufacturing has fallen from about 30 percent in 1955 to below 20 percent in 1985.[3] In other words, actual dollar transactions for manufacturing goods have been shrinking as a proportion of total dollars for three decades. Lower relative prices of these products explains part of the decline: Because of higher productivity growth in manufacturing, the price of machine tools, for example, has not risen as fast as the price of health care or legal services. Other factors include constricting markets for durable goods, unfavorable exchange rates during much of the 1980s, and the recently reversed decline in the competitiveness of U.S. industry.

Within the manufacturing sector, some industries have been declining while others are growing or holding steady. OTA's study shows that all of the absolute job losses suffered during 1980–82 came from high-wage and low-wage manufacturing industries. Within these categories, petroleum refining, iron and steel, motor vehicles, footwear, jewelry, and toys reduced their share of total output. In contrast, medium-wage manufacturing increased its constant dollar share of GNP from 1972 to 1984, largely due to impressive performances in the high-tech industries. Office, computing, and accounting machine producers achieved an astounding sixfold increase in GNP share during the period. Within the low-wage category, lumber and wood products and apparel also grew in relative size.[4] Unfortunately for manufacturing as a whole, however, these high-growth subsectors were too small to offset the serious declines experienced in the other, larger industries within manufacturing. As a result, manufacturing has been a net job loser.

Short-term trends reflect the ups and downs of the business cycle. Manufacturing jobs eventually recovered almost completely from the ravages of the deep recession of 1979–82. By 1989, the falling dollar had helped bring back three quarters of the manufacturing jobs lost earlier in the decade.[5] The most recent recession, however, took a severe toll. Between January 1990 and April 1992, manufacturing lost one million jobs nationwide (seasonally adjusted figures from the Bureau of Labor statistics).

The declines in employment are attributable, in part, to increasing efficiency. Manufacturing's productivity growth rates during the 1980s were impressive—2.5 percent average annual growth between 1986 and 1991, compared to 0.2 percent for the total nonfarm business sector, and 2.3 percent average annual growth between 1979 and 1986 compared to 1.1 percent for the total nonfarm business sector during the same period (Bureau of Labor statistics). Some analysts claim that the competitive pressures of the 1980s closed down many inefficient plants and helped create a heightened awareness of the need to continually improve products and processes.

The short-term prospects for manufacturing are uncertain. It appears that the productivity increases of the 1980s are accelerating in the 1990s. A relatively cheap dollar, worldwide economic recovery, and significant global trade liberalization should contribute to expanded exports. On the other hand, high and rising real interest rates and intensifying global capital demands could choke off growth. Near-record factory utilization rates could produce production bottlenecks and spur inflation.

The structural transformation of the manufacturing sector in the long run seems easier to predict than the next swings of the business cycle. No evidence exists to suggest that the 40-year downward trend in manufacturing's employment share is likely to reverse itself. Manufacturers' unending quest for labor-saving productivity enhancements is spurred by competition for low-wage production and assembly jobs from developing countries. Coupled with that, the likely abandonment of certain low-wage, low-skill industries virtually ensures that manufacturing employment will continue to shrink relative to other sectors such as services. Production has become uncoupled from employment, and the change is here to stay.[6] Whether U.S. manufacturing industries improve their competitive position (largely through productivity gains) and perform well, or continuously lose market share and perform poorly, they will employ a decreasing share of the work force.

The Big Debate: Does Manufacturing Matter and How Much?

Does the shift in jobs and (to a lesser extent) GNP out of manufacturing mean good news or bad news for the U.S. economy as a whole? Economists have been arguing that question for a decade. A brief overview of the "deindustrialization" debate is a necessary prelude to understanding current issues in rural manufacturing.

During the early and mid-1980s, two opposing pictures emerged of a healthy modern market economy. Those who hold the first picture took a generally sanguine view of the steady decline in U.S. manufacturing's share of employment and GNP, explaining it as the inevitable result of industrial evolution. In the same way that agriculture lost jobs and GNP share throughout most of the twentieth century without causing the economy to crumble,[7] they argued, so manufacturing will recede in importance without severe losses in standards of living or economic power. Services will take up the slack.[8]

Economists who subscribed to this "post-industrial" view attribute the sharper declines in manufacturing of the early 1980s to adverse business cycles and bad macroeconomic policy. They asserted that U.S. firms lost market share in the early 1980s not because of laziness, greed, or poor management decisions, but rather because of larger economic forces beyond their control. Exchange rates made imports cheaper here and U.S. exports more expensive overseas; as a result, U.S. firms lost customers, particularly in many of the nondurable and low-wage industries so important to rural economies. At the same time, the recessions of 1979–82 reduced demand for durable goods and dealt a heavy blow to high-wage manufacturing. The uptick in manufacturing statistics for virtually all industries during the later part of the 1980s indicated that the sector was viable and would resume vigorous growth in the wake of the 1990–92 recession—so went the optimists' account.

In contrast, economists such as Bennett Harrison and Barry Bluestone viewed "deindustrialization" as a threat. In this second picture, the loss of manufacturing jobs and GNP was a signal of serious structural weakness in the U.S. economy. According to this view, the shrinking manufacturing sector is not a natural stage in economic development but a dangerous hollowing out of the nation's economic foundation. Other sectors such as transportation, banking, and business services exist to serve manufacturing and cannot perform well in the long run without a strong manufacturing base.[9]

The deterioration of goods production, according to these economists, is the result of a series of poor decisions on the part of both government and corporate management that must be corrected. The litany of complaints includes, among others:

- Excessive focus on short-term profits rather than investments in long-term growth

- Insufficient attention to the need for worker training and development

- Inability to develop new product innovations for the consumer market (the VCR, invented in the U.S. but produced exclusively by Asian companies, is the most infamous example)

- Stubborn reliance on old concepts of manufacturing such as mass production of standardized goods and reluctance to embrace new ideas of flexible manufacturing based on smaller batches of customized products

- Continued focus on volume output rather than quality control

These problems came home to roost in the 1980s under conditions of recession and unfavorable terms of trade. The result was loss of market share to more competitive producers in Japan, Germany, and other industrialized and newly industrializing countries.[10] At the same time, some U.S. companies were trying to cut their costs by shipping low-skill jobs to developing countries where they could pay rock-bottom wages. This loss of market share combined with the offshoring of plants added up to a significant structural loss of jobs and income here at home—wealth that could not be replaced by gains in a hollow, service-based economy.

Charting Change

More recent attempts to resolve the deindustrialization argument have reformulated the question altogether. According to Robert Reich, distinctions between manufacturing and services and debates over their relative capacities for generating wealth are increasingly artificial—vestiges of outdated thinking about how the economy works.

> The distinction that used to be drawn between "goods" and "services" is meaningless. So much of the value provided by the successful enterprise—in fact, the only value that cannot be replicated worldwide—entails services: the specialized research, engineering, and design services necessary to solve problems; the specialized sales, marketing, and consulting services necessary to identify problems; and the specialized strategic, financial, and management services for brokering the first two. Every high-value enterprise is in the business of providing such services.[11]

Reich describes an economy divided not into traditional industrial sectors (manufacturing versus services versus natural resources, and so on) that are dominated by large, monolithic corporations (General Motors, Citicorp, Weyerhaeuser) but into a collection of international, intersectoral webs of economic activity. In this view, horizontal connections among semiautonomous players (whether they be discrete firms, divisions within one firm, independent consultants, or brokers) are more important than vertical connections between a company's headquarters and its branch plants.

The patterns of ownership and geography for any given enterprise web are complex and hard to follow. Take a new product, X.[12] This product may have been conceived, design-engineered, fabricated, assembled, packaged, distributed, advertised, marketed, and financed by a stream of different groups located in a dozen different places across the country, even around the world, with various formal or informal ties to product X's "parent" company. Once the product is established, yet another stream of far-flung groups or companies may contract with the parent company to make, market, and sell X in other regions and countries. At each step, value is added and wealth created, but the flow of money is highly dispersed. Under such a regime, Reich points out, certain questions no longer make sense: Who makes product X? Is it an American company? Is it contributing to national economic competitiveness? Concepts of corporate coherence and nationality are being broken down in much the same way as concepts of regional and local identity.

While Reich's analysis offers valuable insights into the new global context for manufacturing, most of the evidence supporting his model is anecdotal. His radical rejection of conventional industrial categories precludes the possibility of proving his theories with existing data sets. Moreover, his rejection of national ownership as a significant variable has been strongly challenged by Robert Kuttner, Lester Thurow, Laura Tyson, and others.[13]

Other more mainstream inquiries, however, provide some statistical basis for the concept of the enterprise web. OTA's comprehensive analysis of the U.S. economic transition employs input–output analysis to trace the direct and indirect linkages between and among 10 different industry groupings.[14] These calculations show an overall increase in the interconnectedness of the U.S. economy between 1972 and 1980. Thanks largely to a higher volume of connections with business services—the brokers in transactions among other sectors—the lines between pure goods-producing and pure non-goods-producing enterprises are blurring.[15]

Some industry groups create more linkages than others, according to OTA's data. The natural resources and construction sectors had the greatest impact on other areas in generating both value added and jobs across sectors. A dollar's worth of sales in natural resources products stimulated 75 cents in value added in other areas, particularly manufacturing, transportation, and transactional services such as banking and information services. Natural resources production also made the largest relative contribution to employment in other sectors—almost 60 percent of the jobs stimulated by demand for natural resources products were in other sectors (24 percent in manufacturing and 35 percent in services).

Likewise, manufacturing's impact on other sectors was significant. Value added in other sectors accounted for 55 cents of every manufacturing sales dollar; and of the jobs stimulated by demand for manufactured products, 40 percent were in other sectors, mostly services. The service sector, on the other hand, "tends to be relatively insular" according to OTA.[16] Demand for services generated less than 35 cents of value added in other sectors for every dollar. Only 10 percent of the jobs generated by that same dollar benefit workers in other sectors.[17]

The OTA study shows services becoming a more critical ingredient in every other sector's activity, a trend that may persuade economists to rethink the traditional distinction between manufacturing and service activities. Transactions between firms and across sectors, rather than isolated decisions made inside firms and within sectors, are the defining characteristic of this new industrial regime.

Does manufacturing matter? Yes, according to the OTA findings, but it is not the chief engine of the economy. To the extent that certain industry groups must rely on performance elsewhere in the economy to stimulate their own output and employment, services are the most heavily dependent industry grouping. Manufacturing proves to be a far stronger generator of growth economywide, but not as strong as natural resources and construction. Based on this data, we may conclude that a healthy manufacturing sector is one of several key elements of a healthy economy.

Piore and Sabel, among others, have described other important patterns of change in manufacturing as well. Beginning in the late 1960s, they argue, the mass production paradigm that emerged to dominate the global industrial economy after World War II experienced a series of disruptions that added up to full-fledged crisis.[18] The resulting confusion created opportunities for reemergence of the smaller-scale craft paradigm of production—a model dependent on skilled rather than semi-skilled workers, broad rather than narrow job classifications, general-purpose rather than specialized tools, customized rather than generic products, constant technological breakthroughs followed by consolidation, and flexibility rather than rigidity. The reinvigorated craft system, whose roots stretch back hundreds of years, has been spreading more quickly and more extensively in some countries than in others.[19] It has provided the model for national development strategies in parts of Europe, for example, while Americans are just beginning to explore its possibilities. Examples of successful craft-based networks range from regional constellations of small, technologically sophisticated firms in places such as central and northwestern Italy that manufacture, among other products, ceramics, farm equipment, machine tools, textiles, and garments, to the construction trades industries in most U.S. cities.

Unlike Reich's description of a new, metanational economy, Piore and Sabel do not describe the evolution away from mass production toward flexible specialization as an accomplished fact. Instead, they argue that the United States stands at the second great industrial divide, faced with fundamental choices about technologies, systems of production, and forms of industrial organization. Although rural America fared well during the heyday of mass production when branch plants decentralized on a large scale to the countryside, experiences in some European countries and in parts of the United States suggest that future national prosperity will depend on our ability to adapt to production strategies that maximize innovation, flexibility, and responsiveness.

The central problem with the craft paradigm is the problem of scale.

Countries that have grown to dominate global manufacturing have done so through mass production of goods, not small-batch customized production. Japan has embraced some of the elements of the craft paradigm, such as flexibility, attention to quality, and continuous, incremental innovation, and applied them to routine manufacturing on a larger scale. This hybrid model may prove most useful for rural manufacturing areas.

From Macro to Micro

Before applying the enterprise web and flexible specialization models to rural development policy, two additional questions must be addressed. First, do the models help us understand industrial relationships at the local level as well as at the national and global levels emphasized by most economists? Second, is there a role for government and other nonmarket institutions in the process of network creation and development?

In the case of the first question, familiar spatial concepts such as decentralization (the manufacturing pattern of the 1970s) and agglomeration (the phenomenon in high-tech manufacturing in the 1980s) do not capture the geography of today's global, interdependent manufacturing/services economy. Reich says little about the location decisions of the various parts of the enterprise web, other than noting that they respect no boundaries and tend to cover the widest possible geographic spread. This may mean either good or bad news for certain rural areas.

The models of industrial evolution identified by Piore and Sabel similarly do not correspond directly to any particular location pattern. These authors describe four basic forms of flexible specialization: (1) regional conglomerations of small and medium-sized firms, otherwise known as specialized industrial districts; (2) federal enterprises that are more highly integrated than regional conglomerations but less hierarchical and more autonomous than the mass-production corporation; (3) "the solar system model" with one central firm and its "orbiting suppliers"; and (4) the factory organized as a collection of semi-independent workshops.[20]

The striking fact about all four models is their apparent reliance on the geographic proximity of members of the networks. At first glance, this feature seems to point to urban locations or, at most, to rural areas located adjacent to growing cities. But in theory, even remote rural areas could form flexible, specialized networks based on either a concentration of local craft skills or a small, existing cluster of related firms with the potential for growing into a larger, regional conglomeration. In the latter case, neighboring localities in rural regions could join together to encourage their small and medium-sized firms to exchange information, pool resources, and eventually form the kinds of networks that have fueled rural growth in other parts of the world. Such networks might resemble the industry associations discussed in the context of food and wood processing in Chapter 5, but they can take a variety of different forms.[21]

With regard to the question of government involvement, the models from Europe help provide some answers. In Italy, Denmark, Sweden, and other countries, governments have learned to play a constructive role in the formation and maintenance of industrial networks by providing groups of firms with "real services" such as brokering, coordination, and information dissemination.[22] Such services can leverage significant changes in the enterprise web. According to Italian economist Bianchi, "The inclusion of these services in the production process brings about structural changes, such as the restructuring of processes, product differentiation, or a change in the extent of the market."[23] Piore and Sabel describe a similar effort in the United States—the Footwear Revitalization Program of the late 1970s which, among other things, facilitated communication between shoe producers and retailers to help keep the U.S. industry in tune with fashions and the desires of customers.[24]

The Rural Picture

The rural economy has roughly paralleled national economic patterns for the past 30 years. Throughout the 1940s, 1950s, 1960s, and 1970s, as rural areas lost large numbers of natural-resources-related jobs (particularly agriculture) and replaced them with jobs in services, government, and manufacturing, the rural industrial mix came to resemble the urban mix more closely than ever before.[25]

Two exceptions to this trend, however, merit attention—the very good times of the 1970s and the very hard times of the 1980s. Starting in the 1960s, when mass production companies were seeking cheaper land and labor for their factories, rural America gained a decided comparative advantage. Lower land prices, taxes, and wage rates in the countryside persuaded many manufacturers to move their facilities and many of their jobs from urban to rural areas. Between 1969 and 1976, rural manufacturing increased at an average annual rate of 1.4 percent, compared to a 1.1 percent decline in urban manufacturing over the same period. By 1979, 44 percent of all rural residents lived in counties dominated by manufacturing.[26]

Unfortunately for rural dwellers, the tables turned after the late 1970s. Between 1976 and 1984, rural manufacturing employment rates stood still while urban areas expanded their goods-production jobs 0.7 percent per year.[27] The back-to-back recessions of the early 1980s, combined with large trade deficits, debilitated U.S. manufacturers everywhere, but especially those in rural areas. Overall unemployment rates rose two percentage points more in rural areas than in urban areas between 1979 and 1982. During the same period, while the national employment rate remained level, employment in rural manufacturing-dependent counties fell 5.6 percent.[28] Every state in the union except Nevada and Rhode Island lost rural manufacturing jobs in those recession years.[29] In the 1970s and 1980s the resemblance between rural and urban economies started to break down as rural areas, specializing in manufacturing, suffered the heaviest damages from recession, while a growing urban service sector helped insulate metropolitan residents from the worst of the business cycle.

Various studies have documented the dramatic decline in aggregate rural manufacturing during the 1980s. *Rural America in Transition* by the Federal Reserve Bank of Kansas City paints the starkest picture.[30] According to their analysis, not only did manufacturing-dependent areas lose manufacturing job share during the period 1978–85, they lost job share in construction, retail trade, services, and other industries as well. The entire momentum of rural economic growth made a decided shift away from "traditional" counties with economies focused on agriculture, natural resources, and manufacturing toward new, "emerging" counties where tourism, government, and retirement-related enterprises predominated. Viewed in this way, the shift appears to have been structural, not cyclical.

Two reports from the Southern Growth Policies Board, *After the Factories* and its sequel *Making Connections,* trace a similar path for manufacturing employment in the rural South from 1977 to 1984 and interpret it as a sign of structural change.[31] Despite a brief upswing between 1982 and 1984, many areas still had not fully recovered by 1984 and no net growth had occurred. In 1984, nearly half (45 percent) of southern rural counties remained behind their 1977 rates of manufacturing employment.

Performance in the late 1980s, however, casts some doubt on the structural interpretation of rural manufacturing losses. Many rural manufacturing areas were enjoying a healthy rebound by mid-decade. Rural unemployment declined steadily from 1986 through 1989 before turning upward in the 1990–92 recession. Rural manufacturing employment increased at a far more rapid pace than urban manufacturing employment (5.1 percent rural compared to 1.1 percent urban between 1987 and 1989).[32] Improvements were broadly spread among all regions and types of counties (except mining-based counties, which at least stopped declining), including counties with low educational levels and zero growth prior to 1986.[33] Between 1986 and 1988, rural manufacturing counties actually gained population. During the 1980s as a whole, the population of these counties grew by 1.5 percent.[34]

In the rural Tennessee Valley in 1989, analysts Robert Gilmer and Allan

Pulsipher estimated that manufacturing employment had not only recovered but actually surpassed its previous all-time high of 1979. The authors wrote, "There is little evidence of structural damage to the regional manufacturing base . . . and manufacturing provides a secure foundation for further growth and development in the Tennessee Valley."[35]

Based on these upswings, R.D. Norton in 1989 optimistically predicted a revival of all types of manufacturing in the 1990s. According to his analysis, areas of labor surplus, primarily rural counties, inland states farther from the coasts, and areas with heavy immigration, would attract most of the new manufacturing growth. McGranahan offered an equally optimistic view: As tight labor markets drive up urban wages, "rural areas may be able to attract new complex manufacturing firms and plants under conditions of full employment."[36]

Can rural America buck the national manufacturing trends? Based on the experience of 1986–89, the current slowly emerging recovery may expand the nonmetro share of new manufacturing jobs slightly, but no one anticipates a return to the levels enjoyed in the 1960s and 1970s. While some of the more aggressive, better placed rural counties could reap significant rewards in the form of jobs and income from 1990s manufacturing, the growth will not be enough to go around. Despite the short-term cycles of recovery, long-term manufacturing trends imply somewhat pessimistic predictions for the future health of rural America on the whole. Bluestone and Daberkow's 1985 projection proved true for the last half of the 1980s and may be an accurate description of the 1990s: "Because nonmetro areas still depend more on slow-growing nondurable manufacturing and national resource industries and less on fast-growing services than metro areas, nonmetro growth is expected to continue lagging behind metro growth."[37]

Some Exceptions to the Rule

The conclusion that manufacturing has passed its prime as an economic development strategy might surprise the residents of Crawford County, Missouri—which experienced 20 percent growth in employment, mostly in manufacturing, during the recession years 1979 to 1984—or Hoke County, North Carolina, where manufacturing jobs grew by more than 50 percent between 1977 and 1984. These success stories and others like them underline the importance of distinguishing between discussions of macrolevel national rural policy and microlevel development strategies suitable for specific local communities. Despite aggregate statistics showing manufacturing on the wane, individual rural communities may still make a good living from manufacturing for many years to come.

Two independent studies identified particular counties in the Farmbelt and the rural South that defied the averages for job growth during the late

1970s and early 1980s. The National Governors' Association study selected 16 unusually high-growth counties with greater than 20 percent growth in total employment from 1979 to 1984 in seven midwestern states and examined various factors that might account for their remarkable performance. On the subject of industrial mix, the list of the types of business contributing to growth seems to defy all of the national trends described above. The authors comment, "The most striking thing about this list is how traditional it is. It demonstrates that during this period all 16 counties relied heavily on 'plain vanilla' manufacturing (such as bending metal, making consumer products, or contributing to the ubiquitous motor vehicle industry)." The major national growth sectors at the time—business services and high tech—played only minor roles in the growth of these particular areas. While the results of this investigation should not be generalized too broadly, "The evidence from the high-growth counties suggests that traditional manufacturing may continue to be very important for some rural areas."[38]

A similar study from the Southern Growth Policies Board, mentioned earlier in this chapter, found 419 rural southern counties that enjoyed unusually high growth between 1977 and 1984; 49 of these actually registered better than 50 percent growth in manufacturing employment during the period.[39] These counties shared several notable characteristics: large minority populations; a surprising concentration in more remote rural locations; a large number of jobs in food processing industries; continued advantages based on low taxes and a low-skill, low-wage work force; and aggressive local leadership combined with a pro-growth attitude. The last factor, leadership, also figured prominently in the profiles of the 16 high-growth Farmbelt counties studied by NGA.

Another important aspect of the micro perspective relates to regional shares of manufacturing. Analysis by Leonard Bloomquist shows a clear shift of manufacturing share from the rural Northeast and Midwest to the rural South and West between 1969 and 1984. The West, in particular, experienced the highest rates of employment growth in both top-of-the-cycle and bottom-of-the-cycle manufacturing.[40] The South, on the other hand, significantly increased its share of top-of-the-cycle manufacturing while bottom-of-the-cycle jobs held steady. Based on these findings, Bloomquist notes an interesting shift not only in sectoral share but also specialization. Historically, the Northeast and Midwest have served as the center of more complex, sophisticated, better-paying production, due in large part to their ample supplies of highly-skilled, better-educated workers. Now, the West and South may be usurping that privileged position. Communities in these emerging regions, including rural communities, seem to have a better chance of capturing whatever new manufacturing jobs the economy can generate.

Economic Development Strategies

As the rules of manufacturing continue to change, communities interested in pursuing manufacturing-based growth will face new and bigger challenges. Rural areas, which used to rely on their comparative advantages in cheap land and labor, may find themselves at a disadvantage in the emerging manufacturing regime because of the particular set of market failures, government failures, and failures of voluntary action that characterize rural economies. An effective rural manufacturing-based economic development program would focus on overcoming each of these barriers to growth, as described below.

Linkages: The First Stage

As OTA has demonstrated, the U.S. economy is following a path of growing interconnectedness. Difficulties in the rural economy over the past 10 years, however, indicate that rural communities have not been able to take full advantage of the opportunities created by multiplier effects. Problems such as lack of access to information and communications, high transaction costs, and historic dependence on urban economies are probably to blame. Future strategies can seek to capture more of the benefits of economic integration for rural America in three ways:

1. Building on their traditional strength in natural resources, rural economies can try to promote the establishment of manufacturing enterprises that are linked to natural resources industries such as forestry, agriculture, and fishing. Examples include lumber and wood products, and food processing and packaging. The literature is full of exhortations to pursue these natural-resources-related value-added strategies. However, as the discussion in Chapter 5 shows, success in areas such as food processing development has been very limited. While areas with no existing base of value-added manufacturing are unlikely to be able to create one from scratch, areas with existing footholds in wood products or food processing should do what they can to improve the efficiency and competitiveness of these industries and build on this industrial base.

2. Localities and states can pursue "import substitution." This strategy proceeds in two steps: encouraging firms to buy inputs locally, and encouraging development of local businesses that can supply the needs of existing plants. While the theory behind import substitution is sound—local economies should reduce the leakage of dollars as much as possible—it runs into the hard reality of market forces. Assuming that the firms in question already make rational decisions about siting, it is not clear that communities can do much to influence the location of suppliers and service

providers short of lavish tax breaks and other incentives, an expensive use of precious resources.

Modest investments in local data gathering can help to ensure that suppliers are relying on the best possible information when making locational decisions. For example, economic development agencies can conduct surveys of the service and supply demands of local manufacturers and make the results available to aspiring entrepreneurs. Officials in Taylor County, Florida keep records of local firms' purchases from outside suppliers and then contact the outside firms, encouraging them to establish satellite offices closer to their Taylor County customers.[41] Examples such as this suggest that import substitution holds some promise as one very small part of a larger manufacturing development plan.

3. Development strategies can seek to facilitate the natural processes by which new manufacturing enterprises are born from old enterprises. A survey of 123 small manufacturing firms in rural New York State revealed strong connections between the strategies of stimulating expansion of large, existing firms and stimulating the birth of small, new firms.[42] The authors state, "The press has carried many stories of spinoffs from one or another large company. Our survey findings go beyond that; nearly all the new manufacturing firms had roots in another company, and many continued to survive as part of a network of companies."[43] More specifically, half of the company founders surveyed had developed or invented their own product when they were working at another firm and then spun it off. Many of the founders had partners who had been fellow workers at the parent firm.

The survey results emphasize the potential importance of local production networks—involving both small and large firms—for stimulating new jobs and retaining old jobs.[44] Of the firms surveyed by Young and Francis, two-thirds sold to other manufacturing firms in the area and four-fifths purchased parts or supplies from others; half subcontracted some of their work and half accepted subcontracts from other firms.

Local economic developers should do what they can to provide a favorable environment for such linkages. Ideas include services targeted to individuals interested in creating spinoffs and volunteer technical assistance programs in which larger companies lend expertise in engineering or other technical areas to small business.[45]

Linkages: The Next Stage

Finally, rural economic developers can help to ensure that local manufacturers take full advantage of larger interdependencies—those described by

Reich's enterprise web. This broader linkage approach recognizes that improving the competitiveness of a local community's employers may depend on actually helping a firm "leak" dollars to buy state-of-the-art goods and services from elsewhere. To take a fictional example, a rural development official in Iowa who spends her time persuading the local toy manufacturer to buy locally produced wood may not recognize an entirely different, but potentially more valuable, activity: helping the owners of that same firm connect with the leading toy designer in Los Angeles to improve their product line and, ultimately, their market share. This second approach, focused on long-term competitiveness rather than short-term creation, is alien to most economic developers, particularly those in rural areas traditionally focused on industrial recruitment.

The enterprise web and flexible specialization models push economic developers toward activities that involve cooperation between jurisdictions rather than competition, services to groups of firms rather than give-aways to individual firms,[46] and "brokering" rather than recruiting functions.[47] Such a strategy demands a high level of sophistication about existing industry networks and how to penetrate them. Researchers can help build the knowledge base for these activities by (1) mapping the natural supply, production, distribution, and marketing networks that form within particular industries; (2) identifying the barriers that prevent these networks from reaching full capacity;[48] and (3) determining whether rural firms suffer disadvantages in gaining access to these networks. States and the federal government can help by disseminating information about existing patterns of manufacturing supply, production, and service, and developing policies to address the barriers to entry. In partnership with the public sector or alone, interested private parties can organize institutions that will help bring suppliers, producers, marketers, distributors, and other key links together. These may include industry associations, such as those described in Chapter 5—unions, guilds, and "cooperatives for purchasing materials, marketing regional products, securing credit on favorable terms for members, and supplying semifinished products whose manufacture permits economies of scale."[49]

Some of the best examples of this linkage function come from Europe, where several countries have taken on the challenge of cultivating small business networks within specific industries and sectors.[50] Such networks may connect firms in the same line of business interested in pooling their resources for purchasing, research and development, access to market information, quality testing, or other expensive functions (horizontal linkage). Or they may connect firms at different points along the value-added chain (production/distribution/marketing). Finally, they may involve working relationships between producers and customers that generate valuable suggestions for improvements in products and service.

Applied Technology

Although good information about the state of manufacturing technology in rural America is hard to find, what little we know suggests that rural manufacturers are lagging behind in the drive to automate.

When the Southern Growth Policies Board set out to survey rural, automated plants about their practices, the researchers had problems identifying a large enough sample of even "partially automated" rural plants to survey. From this experience, they draw the tentative conclusion that "automation has not yet made major inroads into mass production of discrete goods" in the rural South.[51]

However, the SGPB survey also uncovered a growing awareness of the critical role of automation in productivity growth. As the authors of the SGPB study argue, "The South clearly needs new rural industrial development resources and strategies. Dramatic improvements in both productivity and quality within existing traditional industries are needed, and the likely path is the adoption of new process technologies." Three-quarters of the manufacturers who responded to the survey reported plans for significant investment in new process technology in the following two years; a majority of them also were considering management reforms, such as just-in-time inventory systems, to improve efficiency.

SGPB's report underlines the importance of modernizing the rural manufacturing base through application of new process technologies as well as new management techniques. Diffusion of information about the best practices is a key element of success here. Small firms in particular are falling behind in the adoption of new process technologies.[52] "Relying solely on the market mechanism to diffuse technology is detrimental to small business," according to Cortright, because small firms generally lack the capacity to monitor technological developments, let alone implement them.[53] In addition, the technology needs of small firms often differ from those of large firms.

During the 1980s, significant efforts were launched to close the manufacturing technology gap. By 1989, 40 states had economic development programs focused on the needs of small business for process innovation.[54] Two models seem particularly popular among state governments. The first employs the concept of "manufacturing extension services," modeled after the Department of Agriculture's cooperative extension service of outreach to farmers, in which experts employed by the state visit small goods producers one-by-one to discuss their engineering and other technical needs and provide information or assistance.[55] The second model involves information networks that link businesses with sources of technological expertise within universities, community colleges, research institutions, and elsewhere.[56]

These activities represent an important step forward. However, most of them suffer from a classic problem—not taking advantage of natural market processes. As Dertouzos et al. observe, "The vertical linkages in an economy, which connect a firm with its suppliers below and its customers above, can be conduits not only for incoming materials and finished products but also for technological innovations and other developments that enhance produc-tivity."[57] These authors' case studies of manufacturing, however, found that American firms lag behind their Japanese, German, and other competitors in developing close-knit cooperative relationships with suppliers to encourage innovation and improved quality, and in reaching out to end users for ideas about product and process improvements.

These ideas need further development, broader application, and, ac-cording to some recommendations, stronger participation from the federal level. Kelley and Brooks argue: "Instead of directing most of its energies to R & D (research and development) efforts on the frontiers of technology, . . . the U.S. government ought to be restoring some balance to its policies" through joint federal–state ventures to promote small business modernization.[58] Life on the R & D frontier may be glamorous and exciting, but what's needed most are the resources to take "well-known, scientifically uninteresting knowledge and assure that all firms in an industry can make use of it."[59]

Capital

The adequacy of the capital supply in rural areas is a matter of some contro-versy,[60] but one fact is clear: The new investments in production technology planned by respondents to the SGPB survey and needed to maintain the competitiveness of rural manufacturers, if actively pursued, would seriously strain existing capital resources. Who will fund the modernization of rural manufacturing?

In the recent past, a likely answer was foreign investors. The 1980s may be remembered, among other things, as the decade of foreign investment. Between 1984 and 1987, the foreign investment position in the United States nearly doubled, from $50.7 billion to $91 billion, after climbing from only $8.2 billion in 1973.[61] Other countries also saw increased flows of capital into their economies, but none on the scale of the United States. This devel-opment followed three decades in which U.S. investors had established large capital holdings in many regions of the world—primarily Canada, Europe, and Latin America. U.S. investments abroad still exceed foreign investments in the United States in both employment and assets, but the gap is narrowing rapidly.

Did all of this free-moving foreign capital offer significant opportunities for employment gains and production improvements in rural areas? The answer depends on three factors: the location of the investment (urban versus rural), the type of investment (new versus old facilities), and the likelihood of foreign owners investing in production technology.

Although foreign direct investment, despite the impressive $90 billion dollar figure, accounts for only a small proportion of total U.S. economic activity, most of it is concentrated in industries with special ties to rural America—natural-resources-intensive manufacturing, particularly chemicals; nonelectrical, electronic, and electrical machinery; transportation equipment; instruments; and rubber and plastic products.[62] By Glasmeier and Glickman's calculations, through 1987, rural counties garnered about 10 percent of all foreign investment in the United States, almost half of it concentrated in the South.

Furthermore, Glasmeier and Glickman have shown that rural areas received significantly more employment-creating foreign capital (38 percent) than do urban areas (17 percent). Viewed from a national perspective, the economic development potential of foreign investment appears to be dimmed by the fact that, as Schoenberger has pointed out, only a small fraction of these investment dollars (about 4 percent in 1986 and 1987)[63] created new facilities and new jobs: "The overwhelming share of new foreign investment . . . occurs in the form of acquisitions of already existing businesses. . . . The share of greenfield investments that are up for grabs is very small indeed."[64] While some of these acquisitions preserved jobs that were in danger, in other cases new management restructured the facility and eliminate jobs to increase productivity. It may even move some of the production of the newly acquired product, including jobs, back to its base production facilities in its home country. The fact that employment in foreign manufacturing affiliates in the United States grew only 1.3 percent between 1984 and 1986, a period when foreign investment in U.S. manufacturing increased 42 percent, casts some doubt on the idea of foreign capital as a significant source of new jobs nationally.[65] From a rural perspective, however, the picture is brighter. Foreign investment is more likely to support a new facility in rural America, "a pattern that can be viewed only as a positive sign for rural communities." According to Glasmeier and Glickman: "New plant construction signals prospects of expansions and, over time, linkages with local firms or stimulation of new suppliers."[66]

While Glasmeier and Glickman's conclusion is probably true—that in the short run at least, establishment of new businesses has a larger effect on the local economy than acquisition of existing operations—the potential benefits of acquisition should not be written off so quickly. To the extent that foreign buyers invest in new equipment for old plants and undertake modernization of management and the work force, they can make significant contributions to long-term rural development. The Department of Commerce recently reported that foreign affiliates spent far more on plant and equipment in 1988 than did their U.S. counterparts—$12,200 per worker in manufacturing operations compared to the national average of $8,400.[67] Foreign affiliates also invested somewhat more in research and development.[68] Rosenfeld, Milizia, and Dugan found that, on average, the Japanese firms responding to their survey used more extensive automation than other firms.[69] We do not know, however, what proportion of the Japanese firms were acquired rather than built on greenfield sites. And beyond such preliminary observations, we have scant information about the patterns of production technology investment by foreign-owned plants in the United States.

While economists argue about the relative contributions of foreign investment to U.S. national and rural economic growth, the opportunities for capturing those dollars appear to be shrinking. After rising sharply throughout the second half of the 1980s, foreign investment of all types fell dramatically in 1990 and 1991.[70] Department of Commerce figures for the first half of 1990 compared to the first half of 1989 revealed some striking trends:

- Direct foreign purchases of existing U.S. plants and companies and direct foreign investment in new facilities here fell 70 percent.

- Indirect foreign investment in U.S. company stocks fell more than 50 percent.

- Foreign purchases of U.S. Treasury securities (which finance our federal budget deficit) fell more than 75 percent.[71]

The rate of decline remained high in the second half of 1990 and the first half of 1991. Annual flows of foreign direct investment to the United States dropped by half between 1989 and 1990 and half again between 1990 and 1991. In 1991, the annual flow returned to its 1982 level.[72]

It seems clear that the competition for capital will grow more fierce in coming years. Japan and Germany, the sources of much of the increased cross-border capital flows during the 1980s, have important reasons for keeping more of their money at home in the 1990s—an ailing stock market in the case of Japan and the demands of East–West reunification in the case of Germany.[73] Elsewhere, developments such as the establishment of the unified European market in 1992, the breakup of the Soviet Union, Eastern Europe's turn away from central planning, the Chinese economic boom, and the liberalization of foreign investment regulations in much of Asia and Latin America mean that potential investors face a much longer menu of international investment opportunities than they did just a few years ago.[74] The sheer size of the U.S. domestic market ensures that significant amounts of foreign capital will continue to flow here for the foreseeable future, but that flow is unlikely to be enough to meet the economy's needs.

In light of these facts, what should a rural strategy for attracting foreign manufacturing investment look like? Many states and communities already have committed themselves to this development path, some with impressive results. The approach is fraught with danger, however, for rural areas that miscalculate the tradeoffs involved in wooing foreign investors. Glasmeier and Glickman describe the challenge this way: "As the competition for industry moves beyond the borders of the United States, and rural areas move into the global arena, they must remain wary of selling out their resources to settle for what may turn out to be a short-term layover in a multinational corporation's quest for the lowest-cost production location."[75]

This suggests two practical principles for soliciting rural foreign investment. First, rural communities should not be dazzled by the foreign source. Potential overseas investors may be just as footloose as domestic investors and should not be given richer incentive packages.[76] Second, rural communities should get something in return for what they give. In negotiating agreements with foreign firms, community leaders should push for commitments in areas such as technology investments, worker training, and longevity of operations.

Exports

Another area of potential "slack" in the rural economy is the area of exports. Industry experts tend to agree that U.S. producers, both rural and urban, have a lot to learn about fully exploiting the opportunities available in foreign markets. Government at both the federal and state levels recognized that simple fact during the 1980s and subsequently built an impressive network of services to help U.S. companies enter the world of export trade.

Exports probably represent the largest area of untapped potential for U.S. manufacturers, particularly small- and medium-sized firms. The U.S. Department of Commerce estimates that 75 percent of the nation's manufacturing firms produce items with potential for overseas sales, but only 10 percent are active in exporting.[77] A striking 80 percent of all U.S. manufactured exports are attributable to just 1 percent of the country's largest manufacturing firms.

Thanks to two separate surveys on the subject, experts have some ideas about why so many U.S. firms cling to the domestic market.[78] Common problems encountered in small business exporting include lack of information; regulations at home and abroad; expenses related to tariffs, shipping, marketing, and processing; and financing. In response to these problems, both the federal government and many state governments have devised three-pronged programs to assist businesses interested in exporting, through:

1. Information about markets and education services, including conferences, seminars, and publications, that help answer basic questions and expose business people to additional resources available through trade associations, universities, and government.

2. Technical assistance in areas such as market research, licensing, joint ventures, trade fairs and trade missions, referrals to shippers and distributors, and the like.

3. Financing, including help with applications to banks as well as direct financial assistance through underwriting of loans and other financial instruments.[79]

The National Association of State Development Agencies reported in 1986 that 48 states were operating at least some type of trade-related program, spending a total of $40 million on efforts to stimulate both exports and foreign investment.[80] The previous year, the federal government spent $232 million on export promotion, not including financial assistance.[81] Since then, the federal government has given an increasingly high priority to exports in both international economies and the conduct of U.S. foreign policy. Clearly, much is being done, but more is needed.

Suggested reforms in trade promotion focus on two problems: the need to better coordinate state and federal efforts to avoid redundancy and increase effectiveness, and the need for careful evaluation of the success or failure of various types of export promotion and assistance programs.[82]

Labor Force

Where rural communities want to alter their industrial mix and pursue both higher-wage industries and higher-wage auxiliary establishments of firms, the quality of the work force is a key element. Programs to improve the educational experience of young residents—the next generation of workers—as well as programs aimed at upgrading the skills of existing personnel show up on many recommendation lists. Others argue for the importance of additional education and training of managers to cope with the enormous organizational changes required to adopt and adapt to new production technologies, one of the keys to future manufacturing success.

A recent study by the Economic Research Service concludes, however, that education and training by themselves are unlikely to be effective in generating economic growth.[83] People, especially the better educated, are mobile. When they move out of rural counties, as so many did during the 1980s, they take with them the investments made by local schools and employers in their skills and knowledge. This is one of the most critical forms of "leakage" suffered by rural areas.[84]

For this reason, rural communities should seek to increase the opportunities available for better-educated workers at the same time that they improve the quality of education. Communities interested in flexible specialization and other more complex forms of manufacturing should pursue skills upgrading on two levels. First, the quality of local school systems must be maintained and, where possible, improved—not simply for the sake of producing the next generation of workers many of whom may move away, but also for the sake of retaining existing workers who care about their children's education. Schools must be seen as an amenity value as well as a labor force strategy. Second, localities must be responsive to the training needs of employers already in operation, particularly those firms interested in retooling, including small firms. Local development agencies, community colleges, or other institutions can become sources of information about state-of-the art management techniques in automated factories.

Here, in the complex area of "humanware," a rural community's human resources development strategy must join forces with its technology development and diffusion strategy. In all industrial modernization programs, special emphasis needs to be placed on the role of human resources in making new process technology succeed or fail. Programs that promote modernization of hardware only are likely to experience problems down the road. Human and technical issues must be considered in parallel.[85]

Quality of Development

Because aggregate economic growth is not the only thing that rural residents care about, other dimensions of development must be considered when thinking about manufacturing's role in the economy.

Jobs and Equity

Nationally, economists have focused their attention on manufacturing, in part because this sector has been seen as an important, perhaps even irreplaceable, source of "good" jobs. Closer examination shows that this reputation is deserved with regard to a particular subgroup of the work force—individuals with a high school education or less. Regardless of whether or not manufacturing is capable of generating new employment, it may be valued simply for its effect on the distribution of opportunity and income within a rural community. Manufacturing does not exactly satisfy the maximin principle (see Chapter 2), but by offering stable jobs at relatively good wages to individuals with low education levels, it gives a special boost to people at the lower end of the job ladder.

Two aspects of manufacturing employment have made it a highly sought prize over the years. The first is wages and income, and the second is stability. One characteristic of a "good" job is high pay. As the OTA categories described at the beginning of this chapter illustrate, not all manufacturing jobs are created equal with regard to pay. Most manufacturing jobs fall in the medium-wage category (roughly 9 percent of total employment), followed by high-wage (5 percent) and low-wage (4 percent).[86] Job losses during the early 1980s occurred at the high and low ends of the manufacturing wage spectrum, while medium-wage production jobs grew.

Historically, rural areas have attracted the lower end of manufacturing jobs. Rural communities tend to specialize in nondurable industries—such as textiles, apparel, shoes and leather, furniture and wood products—that pay lower wages.[87] In addition, rural facilities generally employ the bottom tier of workers within those industries.[88] In the mid-1980s, 22 percent of all manufacturing jobs were located in rural areas, but only 10 percent of all management positions and 8 percent of professional and technical positions. At the same time, a disproportionate number of lower-paying machine operator jobs were located in rural areas (29 percent of the national total) along with an even larger proportion of process labor jobs (35 percent).[89]

Low wages have been the blessing and the curse of rural communities for a long time. According to Steven Kale and Martin Lonsdale, "the availability of low-cost labor has probably been the most important attraction influencing industry to locate in nonmetropolitan America."[90] At the same time, due in part to low wages, rural residents have suffered higher poverty rates and significantly lower income levels than urban residents.

Perhaps the more significant characteristic of manufacturing employment is the premium that it pays, relative to other sectors, to workers with less education. Levy and Michel have shown that, between 1973 and 1987, the wages of young, less educated workers grew less (or declined more) than the earnings of all other groups.[91] Part of the explanation can be found in the decline of manufacturing jobs that began after 1979. Manufacturing jobs historically have been a valuable prize for younger workers with no college education. Manufacturing jobs, and blue-collar jobs in service industries like transportation, on average provide higher starting wages for high school graduates than do service jobs. When these production jobs are lost, younger workers suffer most, both because of the lost opportunities for jobseekers fresh out of high school and because union seniority rules generally ensure that younger workers will be laid off first in times of economic downturn. In rural areas, where a larger proportion of the labor force works in goods-producing industries, fewer people go on to college, and a larger share of young adults graduate from high school expecting to find good jobs at good wages in the manufacturing sector. Even the 3 percent shift out of manufacturing employment for young workers documented by O'Hare and Pauti could cause great distress.[92]

Significant gains in wages and income for rural areas will probably depend on two factors: attracting higher-wage industries and improving productivity. Chapter 7 discusses the feasibility of a rural boom in the upper-tier service industries, but in the case of high-wage manufacturing, the OTA report reminds us that it was the biggest job loser of all sectors during the last 30 years. While some rural communities may enjoy high-wage manufacturing growth, they will be the exception. In the case of medium-wage industries, most studies indicate that rural areas today cannot provide many of the amenities demanded by the emerging high-tech producers (see Chapter 10). Other medium-wage industries, such as some aspects of food processing, need to be carefully considered (see Chapter 5).

Another element of a "good" job is stability, or security. On the whole, despite its reputation for quality jobs, the manufacturing sector has a history of volatility. Durable goods producers, in particular, find themselves at the mercy of the business cycle. Demand for their products fluctuates with recession and recovery, interest rates, wages and income, and trade conditions. The heavy reliance of rural areas on manufacturing employment explains why the deep downturns of the 1979 to 1982 period were so much harder on rural areas than on urban areas. Most of the time, a local economy based on manufacturing can expect a regular cycle of layoffs and call-backs. Manufacturing-based economies tend to fall harder and faster during downturns and rebound faster during upturns than other types of economies.

Calculations from the Federal Reserve Bank of Chicago, however, indicate that manufacturing as a whole actually "looks more volatile than it is."[93] The study reveals that the U.S. Census Bureau's computations of employment levels and value added for manufacturing are skewed because they concentrate exclusively on activity in operating establishments. They overlook the important contributions to value added and employment that occur at "auxiliary" establishments such as corporate headquarters, research and development laboratories, data processing centers, and warehouses. The authors show that auxiliary employment as a share of total manufacturing employment is countercyclical. Auxiliary payrolls have steadily risen for the past 25 years in spite of ups and downs in business cycle.

These conclusions mean good news for regions that specialize in auxiliary sites, especially the mid-Atlantic Coast and New England. However, they mean bad news for rural areas where operating establishments have dominated.

Until rural areas can begin to attract auxiliary establishments, rural manufacturing jobs will continue to be the most unstable of all sectors.

Stability seems to come with diversity in rural economies. A study of various types of rural economies in 1984 showed the highest incomes in labor market areas (LMAs) that specialized in farming, wood products, or durable goods manufacturing.[94] The highest levels of income and job stability were found in LMAs with strong government sectors and in diversified LMAs. The authors identify a clear tradeoff between fast growth and high incomes on the one hand and stable growth and slightly below-average incomes on the other.[95]

Perhaps the most important job quality issue for rural America is the effects of modernization. As automation continues to transform rural factories, the distribution of job opportunities and wages is likely to change as well. Automation's impact on the work force is an important area of inquiry among researchers at the national level. Two related questions are critical.

First, to what extent will automation result in job loss? While most experts would agree that automation of an industry inevitably leads to some cutbacks in employment, they do not agree about the expected magnitude of the losses in the future. One surprising result of the SGPB survey of automated rural factories was the fact that very few manufacturers in this sample reported overall decreases in employment levels as a result of modernization. In 39 percent of the cases, in fact, overall employment actually increased because the new technologies accompanied expansion of the plant or construction of a new facility.

Part of the reason for this result, of course, is productivity. To the extent that automation improves a company's competitive position and profitability, it may open the door for net gains in employment or at least replacement of lost jobs in other areas of operations. Productivity offers the greatest possible hope for a rising standard of rural living in manufacturing-dependent communities. More than almost any other single factor, growth in output per worker has been responsible for wage and income gains in developed countries since World War II. In this regard, the manufacturing sector clearly outshines the service sector. Between 1970 and 1985, manufacturing productivity grew at a compound rate of 2.9 percent per year while service productivity dropped 0.2 percent per year. While service sector productivity has finally begun to improve in the 1990s, competitive pressures have forced manufacturers to accelerate already healthy rates of productivity gains.

The second question focuses on the nature of the qualitative changes that are occurring in occupations affected by new process technology. Here again, more research is needed to confidently predict future impacts. Clearly, some of the skills needed to monitor computers numerically controlling milling machines are different from those needed to manually operate traditional milling machines. But such simplistic descriptions of the complex changes underway understate the challenge for researchers. OTA explains the problem this way:

> The old debates over the links connecting technology and skill plainly need redefinition. The impact of complex production networks on jobs during the past few decades defies convenient characterization. It is not enough to ask whether technology degrades or upgrades a specific task (such as machining or typing). Rather, it is necessary to measure the effect of change on the entire network of employment that combines to deliver an amenity (such as food or housing). Jobs lost on the factory floor may be replaced by information-handling positions in other business sectors in other states.[96]

The confusion about new manufacturing technology, worker skills, compensation, and satisfaction is perpetuated by the difficulty of conducting definitive research on the subject. Several careful studies of changes in skill demands across the entire economy do exist.[97] However, these studies tend to focus on the shifts in job composition out of manufacturing into high- and low-skill service jobs and do not shed much light on the dynamics within manufacturing.

According to the ERS summary,[98] the "substantive complexity" of jobs overall has increased moderately since 1960, though at a declining rate. Half of the change has been due to shifts in employment to the service sector, where average skill levels are somewhat higher than in the goods-producing sector. The other half is attributable to the growth of professional, technical, and managerial occupations within industries, including manufacturing. Unfortunately, we do not have good data about the changing content of particular occupations within industries, largely because the only survey that tracks job content (the Dictionary of Occupational Titles, or DOT) has not been updated since 1977.[99]

Efforts to predict the future job mix suffer the same weaknesses. The best known projection, conducted by Johnston and Packer, shows that most of the largest-growing occupational groups require higher levels of education than in the past (beyond a high school diploma).[100] However, because many of these fastest-growing occupations—natural scientists and lawyers, for example—do not begin with a large base, even with high rates of growth, these occupations will not add large numbers of jobs. "In absolute numbers," Johnston and Packer write, "the biggest job creation categories will be service occupations, administrative support, and marketing and sales . . . [which]

require only modest levels of skills."[101] Thus, as the ERS authors point out, the average GED score (based on the general educational development test) of all jobs will increase only modestly in the future, from 3.1 in 1984 to 3.2 in the year 2000.[102] Teixeira and Mishel predict that skill demands during the 1990s will rise at about half the rate of the 1980–88 period. In rural areas, even under generous assumptions about economic growth rates, the demand for highly skilled workers will grow at a weaker pace than in the past and a weaker pace than in urban areas.[103]

Although the evidence is thin, a few observations can be made about the changing job mix in manufacturing. First, higher productivity due to automation has altered the occupational mix within the manufacturing sector.[104] While the proportion of managers and professionals has gone up (as in all sectors), the proportion of laborers and operatives has gone down. The middle-level category of precision craft and repair workers has held steady for almost 30 years. Future gains will likely come in the area of equipment maintenance. The OTA report states, "One undisputed trend is the increasing need for highly skilled individuals capable of designing, installing, and maintaining new automated equipment."[105] Many firms are facing shortages of equipment maintenance workers, and training focused on these occupations will become increasingly important.

Second, the nature and extent of change in the content of manufacturing jobs will depend on the adoption of "FMS" (flexible manufacturing systems). FMS, described as "a cluster of machines that can be reprogrammed without fuss to switch from making one product to making another,"[106] is an intermediate step on the path toward the fully automated, fully integrated factory. A successful FMS requires a different occupational mix than the conventional American production system—for example, double the engineers per unit of output—while placing a greater emphasis on teamwork, versatility of skills, and "intellectual flexibility."[107] In 1986, *The Economist* reported that about 300 flexible manufacturing systems were in operation around the world.[108] The United States has moved relatively slowly in adopting FMS, however.[109]

Finally, changes in the quantity and quality of manufacturing jobs will also depend on the ability of American industry to change its organizational and social structures. A 1986 study of American and Japanese automakers by M.I.T. concluded that much of the success[110]achieved by the Japanese auto industry was attributable to the degree and quality of interaction between hardware manufacturing and human resources in the Japanese plant, a relationship the authors call "humanware."[111] While Japanese "humanware" technology has been transferred successfully to a few Japanese-run and joint venture plants in the United States, so far, the ability to sustain this success and apply the humanware principles to American-owned and operated plants will depend on "how much the conventional American systems of production and industrial relations can accommodate change through modification of their internal power structure and reward system."[112]

The degree of change required seems enormous when viewed from the perspective of history. Henry Ford's legacy of the mass production factory and Frederick Taylor's conception of interchangeable workers performing highly specialized but mindless functions have defined the American system of manufacturing for nearly a century. The American production system and the American labor-management system have evolved together and depend on each other. A significant change in one area, such as flexible manufacturing systems, will require equally great changes in the other—human habits and mindsets. While anecdotal evidence offers some small success stories,[113] American industry's ability to overhaul its humanware technology has yet to be proven.

Self-sufficiency

Various approaches to manufacturing development also yield different outcomes for community leadership, the balance of power, and dependence and self-sufficiency. The older model of industrial recruitment focused on attracting branch plants with a combination of low wages, cheap land, and direct financial incentives. The problems with this approach are now well documented. Such plants tend to be footloose. The recruitment incentives force local communities to expend valuable resources through tax givebacks, promises for infrastructure improvements, free worker training, and the like. Recruitment is a zero-sum game—chasing a few mobile factories—that contributes to intercommunity competition rather than cooperation. Finally, an economy built on branch plants essentially embraces a culture of absentee ownership: Economic power becomes concentrated in the hands of a few outsiders and creates strong dependency relationships between local workers and managers and the chiefs back at headquarters.

Newer models of industrial development, in contrast, stress interdependence rather than dependence. Piore and Sabel, for example, take the concept of linkage to include not only ties among producers but also ties between an industry and its community. They argue that successful, small-scale, flexible manufacturing depends on the ability of the larger community to establish basic rules about how jobs are to be distributed, new workers are to be trained, and firms are to be prevented from exploiting their work force. The goal is a system that can innovate and adapt to market changes without sacrificing the quality and stability of jobs.[114] According to this model, the homogeneous, community-oriented, sometimes insular quality of rural areas—commonly viewed as a barrier to economic and technological development—could prove, instead, to be an invaluable asset for areas seeking to shift from the mass production to the craft paradigm of manufacturing.

At the same time, economic development strategists must not lose sight of the potential risks of homegrown growth. Tomaskivic-Devey (*Sundown on the Sunbelt?*) has described how elite landowners in rural North Carolina and other parts of the South have sought to control local development and channel it in the direction of low-wage, low-skill industries for private gain. Where such patterns of elite concentration exist, economic strategies based on growth from within may perpetuate existing inequities in industrial relations and fall short of the qualitative goals of development, such as relieving poverty, generating attractive occupational opportunities for young people, and building community self-sufficiency. Efforts to broaden the ranks of local leadership may eventually overcome traditional domination by elites.[115]

7

The Service Sector

Introduction

Traditional economic development practice, both urban and rural, paid little attention to the service sector. Services were viewed as the poor cousin of manufacturing, the real source of economic growth. Local cities and communities focused their energy on attracting the largest possible production plants and assumed that related service jobs would follow. Services were variously and disparagingly described as nontradable, nonbasic, residual, derivative.

Research over the last 10 years, however, has painted a different picture of the service sector. At the national level, we know that service industries have been a vital source of new jobs in virtually every state. We know that the economy's overall mix of value-added elements has been gradually shifting away from traditional activities such as natural resources extraction and manufacturing toward transactional services and some consumer services. We know that some service industries, particularly those such as advertising, finance, and software design that serve other businesses, do export their products and attract outside dollars to their communities. We know that these services can generate independent economic growth.

Some rural areas have benefitted from the services job machine, but more in the 1970s than in the 1980s. Prospects for the 1990s depend on various evolutionary forces. One of these forces is the apparent disintegration of the monolithic corporation, a trend that is, among other things, subcontracting what had been internal service activities to autonomous and semi-autonomous firms, and placing a higher premium on transactions between businesses. Historically, the phenomenon of decentralization has brought good fortune to rural areas. With the help of sophisticated information and communications technologies (see Chapter 11), some rural communities could benefit from the subcontracting trend.

At the same time, however, researchers are deepening their understanding of the forces that favor agglomeration. In certain types of industries, such as high-tech development and manufacturing and information services, firms tend to congregate in locations where ideas, a spirit of innovation, and

147

specially skilled workers are found in ample supply. Unfortunately for most of rural America, such locations tend to coincide with higher population densities in cities or adjacent areas.

Still, far more needs to be learned about the evolution of the service sector and its geography. Must producer services be located close to the producers? What value is added by face-to-face contacts between service providers and customers? Why do some service industries cluster together? Can they be persuaded to choose more remote locations?

As many analysts have pointed out, the source of much of the confusion about the service sector's contribution to economic development stems from problems of data, definition, and classification. Glasmeier and Howland review the various existing schemes to distinguish services from nonservices and to classify internal groupings of services. Divisions based on the nature of the product, the nature of the work, markets served, and international tradability are the most common. However, as Glasmeier has noted, these classification efforts still do not qualify as a clear definition of what we mean by a "service." Until researchers can agree on a rough understanding of what makes a service different from a good, progress in this area of study will be hindered.[1]

But despite the disagreements over definitions and the need for further study, a few tentative conclusions can be reached about the rural service sector:

1. Service industries have been and will continue to be an important source of new jobs in rural areas.

2. The rural mix of services has not favored those firms with the greatest potential for export and independent growth.

3. Efforts to cultivate producer services should build on the existing industrial base and its service needs and should focus on the regional, rather than the local, level. As part of an overall strategy to build regional conglomerations of industry, small localities can join together to develop strategies for recruiting or establishing new, homegrown services suited to the needs of nearby producers. The regional development strategy must address issues of manufacturing, services, technology, telecommunications, and work force skills together in a package.

4. Localities should recognize that such a regional approach might require a growth center model in which producers, suppliers, and manufacturing subcontractors spread out around the region but related service firms concentrate in a regional growth center with slightly higher population density.

5. Nascent agglomerations of services should be identified and supported, whether they be software designers or antique dealers.

6. Consumer services can play an important role in keeping local dollars circulating within the community or region. In areas with potential for tourism, consumer services such as hotels, restaurants, and shops can form a powerful economic base.

7. Rural economic developers must help new and existing businesses become smarter users of services in general, regardless of where those services and the jobs they represent are located. Investments in telecommunications and technical assistance to help local and regional industries obtain valuable information about markets, new products, and new technologies can help rural businesses overcome the problems of isolation and distance. If the new economy is characterized by larger numbers of transactions, rural areas must find ways to join those networks and keep their often higher transaction costs as low as possible.

The Context: National and International Trends

The growth of the U.S. service sector over the past quarter century is the flipside of the decline in manufacturing and natural resources and the debate over "deindustrialization" described in preceding chapters.

Growth, Growth, Growth

As *Fortune* magazine put it, "services have been the engine, chassis, and body of the great American job machine" for the past several decades.[2] Almost 95 percent of all net new jobs created in the United States since 1969 have been service jobs. Services have long been the dominant employer in this country. More than half of all U.S. workers held service jobs in 1955; today, more than 70 percent do.

As with goods-producing industries, however, these aggregate figures obscure important differences in performance among service subsectors. Despite the conventional wisdom that America is becoming a nation of hamburger flippers, most of the growth in service employment has come from producer and business services and the health care industry, not from fast food restaurants and other consumer services. More specifically, OTA's analysis finds the most dramatic source of economic growth between 1950 and 1984 to have been in the area of transactional activities, mostly from the business services such as computer repair, overnight delivery services, legal services and consulting, and real estate and rental industries.[3] The transactional activities sector increased its share of GNP (in constant dollars) from about 13 to 22 percent over that period.[4] Other service-related industry groups that increased GNP share were wholesale and retail trade (the country's largest industry overall), and some portions of the social services category,[5] particularly private health, education, and social services since 1972.

Personal services, on the other hand, have been "the exception to an otherwise dramatic shift toward a service-oriented economy."[6] As OTA's model shows, this category actually lost share of constant-dollar GNP between 1950 and 1972, then held a steady share until 1984.[7] Household and domestic services account for most of the decline, probably in response to the widespread adoption of labor-saving household appliances. Not surprisingly, some of the more traditional components of the service sector, such as rail transportation, also lost GNP share over the period.[8]

Why the Boom?

Thanks to studies such as OTA's, analysts now understand the scale and scope of the services boom, and they are beginning to get a better handle on the underlying causes. Several theories, in particular, have gained acceptance.

First, as mentioned earlier in the section on definitions, we know that some of the increase in service employment is simply the result of corporate decisions to buy from outside contractors certain services that were once provided internally. When manufacturing firms spin off or contract out these jobs, it looks like an increase in service jobs at the expense of manufacturing jobs, but the shift is illusory.

A second common notion suggests that employment growth in services is partly the result of inefficiencies in that sector. As Kirn states, ". . . it is generally acknowledged that the most significant cause of service employment growth has been a supply-side phenomenon—the relatively slow rate of increase in productivity, or output per worker, in services relative to goods."[9]

While "productivity gains are the key to improvements in output, wages, and national income," productivity gains in the service sector made a weak showing during the 1980s.[10] Each American worker employed in the service sector in 1985 produced output worth roughly $28,700, compared to $41,200 in output from each manufacturing worker the same year. Although service industries have always exhibited lower rates of productivity growth than either the natural resources or manufacturing sectors, the gap widened dramatically in the 1970s and 1980s. The post-1973 productivity slowdown hit services harder than any other sector. Average annual productivity growth rates in the service sector (measuring output per hour) fell more than two points (–2.07 percent) between the periods 1948–73 and 1973–87, compared to just one-third of a point (–0.30) in the manufacturing sector.[11]

Because of sluggish productivity growth, service industries, according to this theory, have been forced to add new workers at a faster rate than other industries in order to keep up with demand.[12] The ample supply of new workers created by the coming-of-age of the baby boom generation in the 1970s and the steady flow of women into the work force allowed service employers to grow by simply hiring more workers rather than improving the efficiency of their existing personnel.

This explanation probably accounts for some of the shift to service jobs, but it also encounters some technical problems. Most important, economists question the methods of measuring productivity in service industries, and therefore the magnitude of the recent slowdown in the service-producing industries. Repeated undercalculation of the true value added by industries such as health care, finance, education, and insurance to their intangible final products, along with an inability to account for differences in quality between various products and industries, may mean that current productivity figures for the service sector do not paint an accurate picture.[13] Actual service productivity and productivity growth may be higher than we think.[14]

Furthermore, as one analyst has noted, the conventional definition of productivity gain requires minimizing inputs, such as labor and capital, into the production process. But in the case of some services, which are defined by an exchange between a worker and a customer, greater labor intensity may actually "increase the perceived effectiveness of service delivery as customers could be given more individual attention."[15]

Will service productivity pick up in the coming years? One might suspect that changes in technology and demography would lead to future increases in service productivity and a slowing of growth in service employment. *Fortune* magazine, for example, describes the "enormous—and largely unremarked—boom in capital spending in the service sector," which promises to boost productivity growth in coming years.[16] According to the Hudson Institute, "Faced with a potential shortage of skilled workers willing to work for low wages, and responding to technological possibilities that are clearly within reach, many service industries are poised for a rebound in productivity."[17] However, as Baily and Gordon have pointed out, the investments in computer power have not shown a payoff yet in the white-collar service industries such as trade, finance, insurance, and real estate.[18] Still, there is mounting anecdotal and statistical evidence that as workers learn how to make better use of the machines on their desks and as official output data are revised to take account of quality improvements produced by computers, service productivity growth figures are in the process of rising more rapidly.

On the demand side, Kirn has described a third causal explanation for the service employment boom—rising personal income.[19] Economic theory predicts that as societies grow richer, they will spend increasing proportions of their total income first on manufactured goods, as opposed to food (one can only consume so much food), and then on services. In the language of economics, the elasticity of demand for services is greater than that for goods. According to Kirn ". . . this reflects a shift in emphasis from quantity to quality of life in consumer behavior in advanced economies."[20]

OTA's analysis of the forces behind the economy's sectoral shifts confirms this theory. Their report finds that roughly half of the shift in production from goods to services after 1972 was the result of changes in final demand for different products.[21] In particular, consumers turned their attention and their dollars toward the products of the real estate/rental and finance/insurance industries (transactional activities sector), eating and drinking places (transportation and trade sector), and health, education, and social services (social services sector).[22]

In OTA's model, changes in the "production recipe" (the inputs from different industries needed to produce all of our goods and services) for the U.S. economy accounted for the other half of the shift. In this case, American producers over time spent a steadily declining proportion of their overall budgets on raw materials and manufactured inputs. They shifted their purchases instead toward services, particularly business services such as advertising, legal services, and computer and data processing, as well as finance and insurance.[23] OTA explains the change by pointing to the increased complexity and specialization of the economy: "More complex business networks seem to require larger numbers of transactions, resulting in more demand for services like those provided by lawyers and consultants."[24]

Glasmeier uses a similar demand-side argument to explain how expanded world trade has stimulated service sector growth. "As the economy becomes increasingly globalized," she argues, "more and more intermediaries are needed to efficiently operate the complex system. Service growth is one result of this development."[25] OTA's analysis also confirms the importance of expanded trade, although it finds changes in domestic demand and production recipes to be larger factors.

Taking these notions a giant leap further, Reich paints a picture of the national and global economies in which the distinction between manufacturing and services is virtually meaningless.[26] He describes a process of disintegration and decentralization now underway in the modern corporation that could have enormous implications for the geography of economic activity:

> America's core corporation no longer plans and implements the production of a large volume of goods and services; it no longer owns or invests in a vast array of factories, machinery, laboratories, warehouses, and other tangible assets; it no longer employs armies of production workers and middle-level managers.... It is, increasingly, a facade, behind which teems an array of decentralized groups

and subgroups continuously contracting with similarly diffuse working units all over the world.

Many of those decentralized groups and subgroups engage in what traditionally would be called service enterprises: research, engineering, design, sales, marketing, consulting, strategic planning, finance, and management.[27] The real place to look for growth, according to Reich, is in the high-value-added, concept-oriented services whose business consists of identifying, solving, and brokering problems. In 1990, 40 percent of the cost of a car went to pay the "designers, engineers, stylists, planners, strategists, financial specialists, executive officers, lawyers, advertisers, marketers, and the like," compared to less than 15 percent in 1920.[28] Likewise, a large portion of the value added by specialty steel producers comes from the activities of steel service centers that help customers choose what they need and then prepare and deliver it.[29]

The high-value services that Reich describes are among the most attractive sources of job growth that a community could imagine. They even rival the high-tech manufacturing plants that economic developers dreamed of in the 1970s and 1980s. Before building them into yet another panacea for rural America, however, it is important to understand their geography. As noted in Chapter 5, Reich does not answer the location question for us except to make the point that, unlike the megacorporations they are replacing, the emerging enterprise webs extend around the globe and defy national identification. The challenge for geographers and rural analysts is to determine the extent to which this new form of decentralization might facilitate the diffusion of services to more remote locations.

The Rural Picture

The historic trend toward service jobs has been a universal phenomenon affecting all regions, all states, and all sizes of communities from the largest cities to the smallest rural towns. However, as research has shown, the momentum of service growth took a sharp turn in the last decade in the direction of urban America.

Shifting Momentum

Combining research results from both Kirn and Miller and Bluestone[30] allows us to paint a picture of the changes underway during three separate watershed periods in rural economic history.

The earlier period, defined as 1958–67 by Kirn, sets the stage for later, more dramatic changes. During this period, manufacturing industries experienced significant decentralization from urban to rural areas. Services on the

whole grew at a relatively uniform pace at different levels of the urban hierarchy, although a few categories of services—finance, insurance, and real estate; accounting; and engineering and architectural services—showed some
tendency to filter down to smaller communities and rural areas.[31]

In the 1970s, by contrast, nearly all indicators of growth pointed in the direction of rural America. During this period, dubbed the Rural Renaissance,
rural population growth rates exceeded those in urban areas for the first time
in more than half a century. Economic growth, too, concentrated in rural
areas. Between 1969 and 1976, rural employment expanded at nearly twice
the rate of urban employment—2.1 percent compared to 1.2 percent.[32] The
most striking difference between rural and urban performance came in the
goods-producing industries, which actually lost jobs in urban areas at an annual rate of 1.1 percent but gained jobs in rural areas at a 1.4 percent annual
rate. Despite this impressive performance in the rural goods-producing
sector, service jobs still dominated the economic growth picture, expanding
at an annual rate of 2.5 percent in rural areas, compared to 2.2 percent in
urban areas.[33]

According to Kirn, the decentralization of services that occurred during
the 1970s was the result of two separate developments. First, consumer service-related jobs followed the migration of people and personal income into
rural communities. As the population and wealth of rural counties rose, so
did demand for personal services. Once demand reached certain thresholds,
it became profitable to offer those services at lower levels on the urban hierarchy.[34] Second, producer services—particularly finance, insurance, real estate, banking, advertising, and miscellaneous services—also grew faster in
rural areas during the 1967–77 period.[35] Kirn suggests three explanations:
demand created by the decentralization of manufacturing in the 1960s and
1970s; availability of telecommunications, which allowed certain services to
be supplied at a greater distance from the customer; and, similar to the pattern followed by consumer services, overall growth in demand for producer
services, which allowed certain threshold market levels to be met at relatively
lower levels on the urban hierarchy.[36]

The convergence of many powerful forces in the late 1960s and early to
mid 1970s served rural America well. These included spectacular national
economic growth rates, rapidly rising demand for virtually all goods and services, a narrowing of the income gap between different economic classes and
geographic areas, renewed attention to the quality-of-life amenities offered by
rural communities, and industry's heightened interest in locations with
cheaper land and labor. Not only did manufacturing plants expand their rural
presence during this period, service industries, too, broke their traditional
pattern of urbanization and began to shift new jobs to the countryside.

Analysts viewing the landscape from the perspective of the late 1970s (and even later) predicted continued convergence of the urban and rural economies into the 1980s and continued rural prosperity.

These predictions, however, proved false. After 1976, the momentum of economic growth reversed itself, both in manufacturing and services. Miller and Bluestone compared the employment growth rates for the period 1976–84 to the earlier Rural Renaissance period. As they summarize, "Nonmetro employment growth in goods production came to a virtual halt after 1976, with the average annual growth rate declining by 1.3 percentage points from the 1969–79 rate. In service industries, the reduction in the growth rate was only half as large; nevertheless, that was almost 1 percentage point lower than the metro rate in service industries."[37] Clearly, the more recent shifts in U.S. employment toward services have favored urban areas at the expense of their rural neighbor.[38] Still, taking the 1980s as a whole, rural service employment expanded more rapidly than did any other sector of the rural economy and now accounts for more than half of all jobs in rural America. Not surprising, both earnings and population in service-dependent rural counties have risen significantly.

Residual Specialization

Because all services are not created equal, it is important to identify which service industries concentrate where. According to Miller and Bluestone's summary of the literature, we know that rural service industries are more likely to fall under the consumer/personal category than under the business category and are less likely to be specialized.[39] With advanced producer/business services concentrated in urban areas where they can be closer to corporate customers and more sophisticated labor markets, peripheral rural counties are left with "residual specialization" in consumer services and certain basic distributive functions such as warehousing and trucking.[40]

From many standpoints, the underrepresentation of producer/business services in rural areas is a bad omen. According to standard models, consumer services are locally bound and can only grow as fast as local population and incomes. Producer services, which are more mobile and more likely to attract export dollars from other regions, are the only potential source of real economic growth. As Kirn and others have shown, growth in producer services tends to occur in areas with previous concentrations of producer services.[41] Growth begets more growth. Hence, rural areas are expected to fall even farther behind the service employment race in the future.

As we will see in Chapters 8 and 9, however, certain rural communities with strong tourism and retirement industries have proven to be exceptions to this general rule. In these communities, consumer services—hotels, restaurants, recreation facilities, medical centers, and so on—have provided a strong foundation for real economic growth fueled by outside dollars from visiting tourists and by pension and Social Security checks to resident retirees.

Government

Another modest exception to the rule of rural comparative disadvantage in services is the area of government employment. Although government jobs are not strictly included in most definitions of the service sector, they bear more resemblance to services than to other sectors. They deserve brief mention for two reasons: (1) Government has been a relatively steady source of jobs on a national scale, and (2) rural areas with concentrations of government jobs have enjoyed significant growth in recent periods.

Not counting defense activities, the public sector in this country directly employs almost 10 percent of all workers: 3 percent in the federal government, 6 percent at the state or local level.[42] In some communities, the government's most significant economic contribution comes not through transfer payments or crop subsidies but directly via paychecks.

According to the Economic Research Service's (ERS) classifications, roughly 23 percent of the nation's 2400 rural counties depend on government-based employment as their primary industry. These counties may contain a military base, a prison, a power plant, or administrative facilities for state or federal agencies, or they may be dominated by public lands such as a national park or forest.

Recent studies have revealed two important facts about government-based rural economies. First and most striking is the tremendous growth enjoyed by these counties during the late 1970s and early 1980s. When most other rural communities were suffering serious declines in manufacturing, mining, farming, and even services (relative to urban areas), government-based counties were among an elite group of rural localities that continued to thrive.[43] Retirement-based and tourism-based counties were the only other rural areas that performed as well. Counties with predominantly public sector jobs not only benefitted from nationwide growth in government employment (particularly from state and local expansion, a trend that has since leveled off), they also gained shares of other types of jobs from other counties as well. Based on this observation, the analysts at the Federal Reserve Bank of Kansas City concluded that economic momentum in rural areas is shifting from traditional industrial and natural-resources-based counties to the "new" counties where government, tourists, and retirees are fueling a development boom.[44]

Second, government-dominated rural economies are enjoying not only stronger growth but also greater stability. A comparison of job turnover and cyclical unemployment among the various ERS rural county categories showed greatest stability in those areas with a diversified job base or heavy dependence on government.[45] Per capita income in government counties was lower than the average for all counties, but the countercyclical, anti-recession effects of these public sector jobs made up for at least part of the slightly lower wage rate.

Two primary disadvantages also accompany a government-dominated economic base. Although government employers use local services, they contribute less to the local tax base than private employers. In addition, although government jobs may hold steady in the face of economic downturns, they remain vulnerable to changes in political leadership and priorities. Note the effect on some local communities of federal workforce reductions, congressionally mandated military base closings, and recurrent fiscal crises in state governments.

Public sector employment clearly plays an increasingly important role in the lives of rural residents. But despite the growth over the past decade, Dubin and Reid have detected a strong preference on the part of the federal government for locating jobs in urban rather than rural areas.[46] Spending on federal salaries in 1985 was $548 per capita in urban counties compared to $287 per capita in rural counties. The distribution of indirect wages through procurement contracts was even more lopsided. In 1985, the federal government awarded contracts worth $898 per capita in urban areas and $243 per capita in rural areas. The uneven distribution of defense dollars to cities accounts for only a portion of this pattern. Metropolitan areas received not only the vast bulk of all defense procurement contracts (94 percent) but also a healthy share of all nondefense contracts (87 percent). Landing public sector jobs and contracts is a real feather in the cap of rural communities, but local officials pursuing government-based growth need to recognize that the prospects for substantial growth in government jobs are slim and the competition from urban centers is fierce.

Economic Development Strategies

Much of the research to date on the service sector has centered around a small group of conceptual questions about the capacity of service firms to export their products and generate economic growth independently, and about where such firms are likely to locate. These questions provide a useful framework in which to discuss what appear to be the most hopeful strategies for developing the rural service sector.

A False Dichotomy

One of the most intensively studied questions in this field is the question of the autonomy of the service sector. To what extent do service firms generate new wealth as opposed to recycling the income from other parts of the economy? Is service-led development possible? The evidence points in several directions.

Two studies operating on different scales arrive at the similar conclusion that service growth is not merely an artifact of growth in goods-producing sectors but is rather an active contributing force in overall economic development. Riddle's study used factor analysis to measure relationships among various determinants of economic activity in 80 different countries between 1977 and 1981.[47] While the results of the analysis show significant correlations between manufacturing's share of GDP and overall economic growth in the industrial countries, service's share of GDP also seems to be a significant factor in the growth equation for this sample, independent of manufacturing. Furthermore, in the case of the developing countries considered by Riddle, only the strength of the service sector distinguished between high-growth and low-growth economies. Manufacturing share did not register as an important factor. "The service sector, then," the author concludes, "is at least as important as the manufacturing sector in any growing economy. It would be more accurate to say that economic growth is a synergistic process, rather than manufacturing-dependent."[48]

Kirn obtained similar results from his analysis of randomly selected communities around the United States. During the period 1958–77, overall employment growth showed a high positive correlation with concentration of services, particularly producer services, in both urban and rural areas, and a negative correlation with manufacturing concentration.[49] According to Kirn's interpretation, "The findings ... provide support for the hypothesis that services play a significant role in the process of regional economic growth."[50]

Studies by the Federal Reserve Bank of Kansas City and the National Governors' Association,[51] mentioned in earlier chapters, reach similar results but do not offer exactly the same interpretation. Looking only at rural areas across the United States, these economists found that counties dependent on traditional industries such as agriculture, mining, and manufacturing have experienced the most severe losses in jobs and income over the past 15 years. During the same period, by contrast, rural counties with a strong service base in government, tourism, or retirement enjoyed booming growth in all sectors. These trends suggest an important and independent role for certain service industries in the economic growth process. Some services apparently can form a base industry.

A breakdown of service industries shows that some are natural leaders, others followers. According to the Federal Reserve and NGA studies, government, tourism, and retirement-based services attract the equivalent of export dollars and provide a solid economic base for some rural communities, although they do not contribute much to overall national economic growth. Personal services consumed primarily by local residents using income derived from local employment, however, do not have the same growth-inducing effect. They mostly follow local patterns of population and income growth or decline.[52] At the business end of the services market, the fortunes of producer and distributive service industries commonly found in rural areas (warehousing, trucking, banking, and real estate, for example) seem most closely tied to the ups and downs of the traditional rural export base—agriculture, manufacturing, and energy-related industries.[53]

Clearly, the conventional definition of services as derivative and residual covers only a portion of the rich diversity of economic activity contained in this sector. Recent descriptions of the evolving economy emphasize not only the importance of services as part of the growth process, but also the blurring of lines between goods and services in virtually all areas of production: design, engineering, and assembly; software and hardware; technology and technical assistance. As future research expands our understanding of the integrated economy, questions about which sectors operate independently and which do not will fade in importance. Until then, however, more research is needed to break down particular groups of service industries and determine which are active generators of wealth and which are passive.

These insights point to a general principle for rural areas interested in economic development: Service development must go hand-in-hand with manufacturing and natural resources development. The competitiveness of all local businesses depends on access to and knowledge of the enterprise web. How does this translate into practice?

Service Firms as Tools Rather Than Targets

Economic developers in the new, more tightly integrated economy must be informed users of services, not just aggressive pursuers of service jobs. Most development theories now recognize the importance of retaining and developing existing firms, not just attracting new firms. This means helping local employers improve their products, expand their markets, and add more value to their raw materials. Service providers are one vital tool for achieving those goals. Quinn and Gagnon state the proposition clearly: "The inescapable fact is that services have become a critical cost dimension of a nation's manufacturing competitiveness. Services can dramatically raise or lower the real cost of producing goods domestically—through differences in transportation, communications, financing, insurance, and health care costs. . . . Properly used, U.S. services offer our manufacturers unique international competitive advantages."[54]

Two sets of examples from Quinn and Gagnon's case studies help to illustrate the point. In the case of consumer items, the authors report that the advent of self-service retail outlets "can lower the real costs for manufactured goods as much as can savings in the production process itself."[55] Information services, likewise, are indispensable to highly competitive companies such as Exxon and Boeing: "These companies' profits can be made or devastated by how well they develop and deploy knowledge about supplier costs, new technologies, exchange rates, changing regulations, swap potentials, and political and market sensitivities."[56]

In this environment, the ideal economic development official begins to resemble Reich's description of the high-value-added worker in the new global economy:

> First are the problem-solving skills required to put things together in unique ways. . . . Next are the skills required to help customers understand their needs and how those needs can best be met by customized products. . . . Third are the skills needed to link problem-solvers and problem-identifiers . . . the role of the strategic broker.[57]

The people who run small business assistance programs in Europe embody these functions in their programs of "real services" to firms and groups of firms.[58] Such programs are designed to improve the overall competitiveness of industries by "increasing the know-how, the understanding, and the intelligence of firms."[59] Linking manufacturers with the designers, engineers, marketers, advertisers, financiers, and consultants who can help them grow their businesses is a critical part of the brokerage function of the new economic development official in either an urban or rural setting.

This analysis raises a particularly interesting set of questions for rural developers. Given the ample evidence of important linkages among the primary, secondary, and tertiary sectors, clearly, service jobs should not be viewed simply as substitutes for manufacturing jobs. Quinn and Gagnon make a convincing argument that, on a national scale, economic policy must promote a healthy, growing, innovative service sector for the sake of maintaining competitiveness throughout the economy. According to Kirn, this argument also applies to the individual rural community. He asserts that regional productivity depends on investments in service sector activities, including education, worker training, health care, and social services.[60] Would he include other productivity-enhancing service sector activities such as finance, business consulting, and information management in this list? If so, the message to rural areas is clear: To be productive, you must cultivate a vital producer service sector at the local level. If not, the message is very fuzzy indeed. Maybe it is enough for rural officials to provide telecommunications networks that allow their basic industries access to advanced producer services available in larger metropolitan areas.

If Quinn and Gagnon are right about the link between services and competitiveness, access to high-value services is a minimum requirement for all U.S. businesses. But beyond access, to what extent does local and regional competitiveness depend on the presence of producer service firms and their direct membership in the locality or region's business network? This question must be a central focus of future studies of the rural service sector.

Picking Plums

Rural economic development strategies that target the more sophisticated producer service firms as direct sources of new job creation face an uphill battle. Studies have found these types of services to be underrepresented in rural areas.[61]

Existing research tells us something about where producer services tend to locate and what they look for in a location:

- Most analysts agree that producer services, particularly the most complex and specialized, tend to concentrate in urban areas near other businesses that comprise their markets.[62] In particular, the better, higher-paid service jobs tend to be associated with specialization and larger metro areas.[63] Producer services tend to locate where the labor force is better educated and more highly skilled.[64]

- Some evidence indicates that producer services seek a "minimum threshold infrastructure," which includes convenient access to transportation, good education institutions, and high quality telecommunications networks.[65]

- Growth in producer services tends to occur in areas already blessed with a strong base of these enterprises, suggesting that existing producer services help create demand for more. In the same vein, Glasmeier and Howland review research that shows intra-industry transactions among service firms to be on a larger scale than intersectoral transactions.[66]

- At certain thresholds of population and economic activity, small urban and larger rural areas will see increases in producer service employment in industries where overall demand is growing. This phenomenon occurred during the 1970s when rural areas were attracting residents at the expense of larger cities.[67]

• Rural areas located adjacent to larger metro areas have higher concentrations of services compared to more remote areas.[68]

Based on these patterns of preference, rural areas on the whole do not appear well-positioned to compete for jobs in producer services, although adjacent and more densely populated rural areas may enjoy some advantage. The question remains whether or not more remote rural communities should bother trying to create a business climate that will attract producer services.

Clearly, a single, small, sparsely populated community cannot hope to build the infrastructure, work force, and overall environment needed to become a hub of high-value service firms. However, coalitions of small communities interested in building a regional economic base might have the capacity to include producer services in their overall plan for industrial modernization and development (see Chapter 6). As Glasmeier counsels: "Policies should couple the development of services with the upgrading of manufacturing."[69]

Just as some communities have persuaded business and industrial suppliers to come and set up branch offices near their major customers,[70] so emerging industrial districts might try encouraging the service firms that do business with the area's major employers to join the regional production network. Alternatively, development officials could try to identify local entrepreneurs interested in establishing new service firms to meet the demands of local industry.

This strategy receives mixed support from research findings. On the one hand, studies have shown that many service firms respond to export demand not by expanding on site but by setting up satellite offices near the customers or relocating.[71] Thus a strategy based on previously imported services makes the most sense.[72] On the other hand, Glasmeier and Howland also note that, while some analysts tend to assume geographic linkages between manufacturing and services, some evidence and "casual empiricism" suggest a weakening of the traditional producer–service linkages in this country and others. The links may be particularly eroded in rural areas where branch plants are known to form fewer connections with other local businesses. Finally, certain groupings of services, such as trade, banking, and finance, are strongly identified with city locations.[73] These industries probably cannot be expected to shift down the urban hierarchy on any large scale.

Given these potential problems, the growth center model of development might be best suited to the integrated, regional approach to manufacturing and service development. While small flexible manufacturers and workshop operators may be happy to locate in the countryside and the small towns, service firms may find larger population centers to be more attractive locations. The growth center model provides access for service firms to at least some of the amenities they demand, such as airports, advanced telecommunications, and skilled workers, while integrating them into the rural economy.

The Back-Office Strategy

Some analysts have predicted that certain types of service industries will follow the same life cycle as manufacturing—maturing, becoming more standardized, and, therefore, more decentralized.[74] Should this pattern prove true, rural areas may benefit in the same way that they benefitted when mature manufacturing operations decentralized to rural areas in the 1970s.

At this point, general data about the service sector do not support the decentralization theory.[75] Sophisticated services dependent on highly specialized information have shown very few signs of following the traditional product cycle. However, some have entertained the idea that entrepreneurs seeking relief from the congestion and fast pace of urban life may move their small consultancies and information-intensive service firms into the countryside.

In contrast to advanced corporate services, anecdotal evidence reveals that lower-value-added service functions are highly mobile and increasingly interested in cheap rural locations. Such operations include bill and check processing facilities, telemarketing offices, catalog sales offices, and data entry shops—the service sector equivalents of the manufacturing branch plants that specialized in routine, low-skill, mass production.

Some rural communities have reaped development benefits from such facilities.[76] However, the potential problems of the old branch plants—lack of security due to the "footloose" nature of the operation, low wages, boring and repetitive work, the sweatshop environment—also apply to back office service facilities. Glasmeier warns against large giveaways to lure these jobs: "If an operation's location hinges on tax incentives, it is in all likelihood a marginal facility to begin with. Past experience with branch plants of manufacturing firms indicate this type of employment is often ephemeral."[77]

Service Technologies

The key to decentralization of services in the future, of course, lies in the effect of telecommunications developments on the geographical patterns of the service sector.

As Kirn and others have noted, technological advances in information and communications push in opposite directions simultaneously.[78] A new marketing system, for example, that enjoys large economies of scale and requires very large markets to be profitable may force the consolidation of formerly local functions in a single, centralized place, like a large city. At the same time, other innovations that allow customers to be serviced at a greater distance may encourage certain producer service firms to decentralize to rural locations in order to escape urban congestion and take advantage of lower costs. The capacity of telecommunications to overcome the barrier of distance is not necessarily good news for rural areas. At this time, we can only speculate about whether the net effect of telecommunications advances will favor centralization or decentralization.

The role of deregulation is also uncertain. Some analysts have argued that the higher costs of telephone and data transmission services in rural areas after the switch to marginal cost pricing will discourage service decentralization.[79] Information- and communications-intensive firms may be forced to choose urban locations where the quality of equipment is higher and the costs of using it are lower.

As the discussion in Chapter 11 concludes, however, few rural areas can afford to utterly ignore the state of their communications and information infrastructures. They cannot wait to see whether telecommunications investment pays off in other rural communities. Here again, a regional approach, with support from the state, can seek to tap private and public resources for telecommunications development. Regardless of which service sector strategy a rural area chooses in order to attract and cultivate producer services on site or to help local industries tap services located elsewhere, that strategy must make provision for telecommunications upgrades.

Outside Dollars?

Some observers maintain that the ability of service industries to function as true engines of economic growth depends on their export potential. Traditional "economic base" theory defines economic development as a process that brings new dollars into circulation in a local economy. Those new dollars may come from government spending, transfer payments, or sales of products to consumers in another community, region, or country. Within the boundaries of this definition, the service sector qualifies as a source of economic development only to the extent that it attracts these outside, or export, dollars.

The evidence on the contribution of services to rural exports is mixed. Some studies have shown respectable levels of exporting by local service industries in the Puget Sound region of Washington State, in certain Wisconsin communities, and in Pennsylvania's 33 rural counties.[80] Other studies have reached the opposite conclusion, that services are thoroughly tied to manufacturing and to local markets.[81] Some evidence suggests that even where service firms do export, the benefits of service exports to the local economy don't last long.[82] In these cases, the service firms generally responded to their export market by shifting investment closer to the new customers either by relocating or setting up branch offices.

Not surprisingly, advanced corporate services seem to be the most active traders, particularly advertising, management, and computer services. Glasmeier and Howland's review of the literature shows this result to be remarkably consistent. However, as noted earlier, rural areas' share of these activities tends to be disproportionately small.

Another recent study on the subject concluded that most trade in rural services occurs within relatively confined regions.[83] Larger counties within a regional rural hierarchy tend to agglomerate service firms, which then sell their various products to smaller communities farther down the ladder. These larger rural counties function as important service centers for more sparsely populated, neighboring areas. In turn, the larger rural areas look up the hierarchy to urban areas for certain services that may not be available locally, such as air transportation, hotels, specialized medical care, legal services, and private education. Services rarely flow in the other direction, down the hierarchy. Service "exports" outside the boundaries of the region were also rare in this sample.

If these findings hold true, opportunities for service export growth in rural areas appear slim. Because smaller rural areas look to larger rural areas to meet many of their service needs, local efforts in small towns to foster homegrown service firms and reduce imports will simply shift jobs down the rural hierarchy rather than creating new jobs. In addition, the rural–urban gap in producer services casts doubt on the possibilities for significant expansions in these industries in the absence of regional collaboration.

Based on findings from Smith's most recent study of service exports, however, it is too early to write off rural producer services. In his sample of 639 service firms in rural Pennsylvania, almost one-quarter of the establishments surveyed made most of their sales (averaging 84 percent) in metropolitan areas.[84] Locally owned single-unit and headquarters firms were more likely to export services than were branch offices. Thus, exports up the urban hierarchy may be less rare than previously thought.

In addition, certain subsets of the service sector—government, tourism, and retirement—provide the equivalent of large-scale exports from rural areas. All three industries draw most of their dollars from outside the local economy—via state and federal funds for local government offices and activities, spending by tourists from outside the region, or fixed Social Security and pension payments to retirees. In addition, all three industries defy the notion that smaller places do not export services to larger places within a region.

For example, public agencies in the state capital of Springfield, Illinois serve constituents in Chicago; and ski resorts in Vail, Colorado cater to recreation-minded residents of Denver.

Strategies are available for strengthening these relationships. In particular, changes in policy could encourage a shift in new government jobs from urban to rural areas. Some policy makers have recommended that the federal government adopt plans for locating data processing and other administrative facilities in rural areas whenever possible. State governments could follow suit. Chapters 8 and 9 discuss ideas for developing the other promising rural service sectors—tourism and retirement.

Import Substitution

The flipside of export-based strategies, import substitution, is frequently touted as a promising approach. While retail and consumer services are usually written off by economists as nonbasic and, therefore, unimportant to local economic growth, Glasmeier and Howland argue that services can play a role in job creation when locally produced services are substituted for services previously obtained outside the community or region. They offer the example of a new local medical center that captures dollars for medical services that otherwise would flow out of the community.[85]

Unfortunately, studies show an increasing propensity not for import substitution but rather for more import consumption.[86] As transportation routes improve and costs of travel decline, rural residents are more likely to do their shopping, hairdressing, eating out, and so on in larger population centers, thus slowing growth in rural retail and consumer services. The problem is particularly acute in metro-adjacent rural areas, a fact suggesting that remote rural areas might have more success with import substitution strategies.

Quality of Development

Jobs and Equity

Perhaps the greatest source of public anxiety about the service sector is the issue of the quality of jobs. During the mid-1980s, several highly publicized articles and reports asserted that the shift of employment from manufacturing to services was polarizing the nation's work force between low-wage and high-wage jobs and knocking out the nation's middle class.[87] Americans began to picture a future of investment bankers and janitors with nothing in between. But is the growing service sector in fact making the rich richer and the poor poorer? For the most part, the answer is no. While inequality between income groups has increased somewhat over the past 15 years, the preponderance of evidence indicates that service employment has not been the primary cause.

Robert Z. Lawrence of the Brookings Institution has demonstrated that between 1969 and 1983, the national distribution of men's earnings became more unequal as a result of changes within sectors, not shifts between sectors.[88] In goods-producing as well as services-producing industries, his data show increasing proportions of workers in both the low-wage and high-wage categories and a shrinking proportion of workers in the medium-wage category over the 14-year period. Clearly, forces other than deindustrialization were chipping away at the middle class in all sectors of the economy.

Focusing on the rural experience, O'Hare and Pauti obtained similar results. They found the shifting industrial mix to be only a minor factor in the changing wage distribution of young rural workers between 1979 and 1987.[89] As the authors state, "The deterioration of wages for young workers in rural America was felt in every major sector of the economy."[90] While a higher percentage of young rural workers held jobs in service industries in 1987 than they did in 1979 (and a lower percentage in manufacturing industries), the shifts in employment across sectors were relatively small, according to this study.[91] Most of the growth in the proportion of low-wage jobs held by young rural workers occurred within industries and sectors; the decline was pervasive across all six industry groups studied, including the government category.

In addition, these trends must be considered in a broader historical context. As Levy points out, the trend toward service employment has been underway throughout the postwar period, but concern about a services-created two-tier economy only came alive in the past decade. In Levy's words, "The stagnation and chaotic conditions of the last decade had made the employment shift to services into an extremely painful process."[92] Prior to 1973, workers in all parts of the economy enjoyed several decades of luxuriously high income growth rates. Between 1947 and 1973, median family income in the United States more than doubled. Although manufacturing wages were 10–15 percent higher than service wages, everyone's paychecks were growing so rapidly that the difference largely went unnoticed. As Levy explains, "When your own situation is improving so fast, your neighbor's better situation is less of an irritant."[93]

After 1973, however, the story changed. Growth in median family income essentially came to a halt, growing less than one percent between 1973 and 1987.[94] While service industries continued to add workers during the early 1980s recession, manufacturing industries suffered absolute losses of more than one million jobs. Due to stagnant income growth, upward mobility became virtually a thing of the past for many workers, and large numbers of workers were displaced from manufacturing jobs and unable to find new jobs at similar wages. Under these conditions, the economy's historic trend toward service employment suddenly began to look more ominous.[95] Thus, while the shift to services has probably contributed somewhat to growing wage inequality over the past 40 years, its current reputation as our main economic culprit is more a matter of perception than reality. If and when productivity growth revives and median family incomes start to rise once again at a healthy rate, public anxiety over the wage gap between sectors may fade.

Two additional points of special significance to rural areas should be kept in mind. First, as discussed in Chapter 6, the shift from manufacturing to service jobs has had its most profound effect on the fortunes of younger, high-school educated workers with no college experience—a group disproportionately represented in rural areas. The loss of blue-collar jobs, both in manufacturing and in some of the more traditional service industries like transportation, has meant a loss of well-paying entry-level opportunities for these workers, opportunities that are harder to find in most service industries.

Second, as explained in earlier sections, the rural service sector is not an exact cross-section of the national service sector. Rural areas tend to depend more heavily on consumer services and those producer services most closely tied to traditional national resources and manufacturing industries than do urban areas. For this reason, we would expect the effect of the changing employment mix on rural areas to be different than the effect at the national level. Data analysis by Porterfield supports this conjecture. Between 1981 and 1986, the change in industrial structure from manufacturing to service employment cut average pay nationwide an average of two percent—in rural areas, an average of three percent.[96] The top four industries that gained jobs in rural America during the period were eating and drinking establishments, grocery stores, nursing and personal care facilities, and department stores—all industries paying average full-time wages of less than $10,000 per year.

One also might hypothesize that rural America's higher concentration of consumer service firms would mean a larger percentage of part-time jobs and involuntary part-time workers and, therefore, rising income inequality in rural areas. In their search for the causes of growing inequality in the wages of young rural workers, O'Hare and Pauti did not find evidence to support this thesis. According to their data, the share of young rural workers in part-time jobs actually decreased slightly over the period studied, from 54 to 52 percent.[97] In addition, they find wage deterioration across both job categories, full-time and part-time. More research is needed, however, to clarify the role of part-time work in particular and service jobs more generally in the rural income distribution.

Most of the tests employed to determine the worthiness of the service sector rest on traditional assumptions about the goals of economic development. To be worthwhile, according to this view, the service sector must generate new jobs, new wealth, and steadily rising productivity and income. But at least one analyst has questioned why every sector must be expected to demonstrate high productivity and wage growth.[98] Perhaps service jobs that absorb excess labor at the expense of somewhat lower efficiency and productivity perform an equally useful purpose—putting unemployed people to work, albeit at less pay. Riddle even suggests that an overall decline in average full-time wages due to service sector growth may not be all bad as long as it keeps inflation as low as possible.

Continuity and Mutuality

Service sector development provides perhaps the starkest example of how economic growth entails change. As Jane Jacobs would predict, a rural community or region that is able to create a viable producer services sector, particularly one linked to local primary and secondary production firms and based on import substitution, probably is moving beyond rural development to the first stages of urbanization (see Chapter 3). The phenomenon is not as uncommon as it sounds, particularly in certain parts of the South. As Berman has noted, "The South is in the midst of active—if not fully acknowledged—city *building* that continues to contribute disproportionately to the nation's roster of metropolitan centers and clearly shifts the national system of cities in a southerly direction."[99] The Commission on the Future of the South calls the trend "growth restructuring." Rural areas with an existing, strong industrial base and those located in some proximity to population areas are most likely to follow this development trajectory.

An alternative process would create the critical mass needed to sustain advanced services production by federating smaller rural communities into what the Economic Research Service calls "territorial complexes."[100] In theory, these regional markets could replicate some of the aspects of urban areas that promote growth—intersectoral and intrasectoral linkages, pools of skilled labor and management, and rapid diffusion of information and technology. They could function as growth poles.

A third services-based development process would rely not on the creation of new cities or rural growth poles but on stronger links between existing cities and rural areas. David Harrison and Jonathan Seib have outlined some of the possibilities for simultaneously expanding economic opportunities in rural areas and helping stem the decline of urban quality of life through urban–rural alliances that rechannel growth, increase value added in existing regional industries, and increase import substitution at the state or region level.[101]

Telecommunications and transportation have key roles to play in this process. Kenny Johnson has proposed expanding regional labor market areas through no-frills commuter networks that would allow unemployed and underemployed rural workers to travel to unfilled jobs in cities.[102] The basic equipment for such transportation systems already exists in some areas in the form of school buses and vans for transporting the elderly and disabled.

While these models of development are attractive in their capacity for generating jobs and increasing income, they may be unattractive to many rural residents because of the disruptions they cause in established social patterns. Given the needs of growing service firms, rural development led by the service sector on any significant scale is likely to violate the goal of social continuity described in Chapter 2. The fundamental, irreversible shift of employment out of agriculture into goods production and now into services is, by definition, destructive of old ways of life and creates uncertainty about what will replace them in the future.[103]

We do not know enough about services to know exactly what this sector's development pattern will look like, but we can define the upper and lower bounds of a scenario. At the most, rural service development will require a measure of urbanization or new city creation, a scenario that leaves the poorest, most remote communities entirely out of the picture. At the least, rural service development will require more intercourse with service providers in existing cities in order to enhance the competitiveness of rural producers or to recruit service branch offices, a scenario with more potential for remote areas. Either way, it will require both rural and urban citizens to adopt a broader geographic definition of community and a broader social vision of the "we" who share a common fate (see Chapter 4). Harrison and Seib describe the mutual interests of rural and urban areas as follows:

> Present programs targeted at "distressed" or "lagging" communities isolate these communities from their healthier neighbors. They perpetuate a "have versus have not" mentality that fragments state efforts and fails to build on the strengths of states as a whole. The programs are too small and narrow in scope to sustain long-term rural health. It seems unlikely that their scale will be significantly increased unless their benefits become much clearer. This itself is impossible unless rural–urban linkages are increased.
>
> Yet the stake of the Northwest's urban areas in strengthening less populated areas is certain as well. Urban dollars will ultimately sub-

sidize the rural poor. Urban growth, reflected in ever rising costs and congestion, threatens to decrease the quality of life for which our metropolitan areas are known. An increase in the number of economically strong rural communities could eventually alleviate pressures being placed on cities and their expanding suburbs.[104]

Economic development strategies should be expected to acknowledge and cultivate these shared interests among neighboring rural communities and between cities and rural areas. States and substate governmental entities (such as regional councils of governments) can help channel the natural competition between jurisdictions into mutual commitments to regionwide indigenous growth and change.

8

Tourism

Introduction

Tourism is one of the few areas where both macroanalysis and microanalysis point to good news for rural areas in need of economic growth. Not only is tourism activity expanding nationally and internationally, creating ever more opportunities for localities seeking their share, but it has already emerged as a leading factor in the success of numerous high-growth rural areas, particularly in the South. In this rare case, the flow of the market is in rural America's favor. Communities need only to tap into the existing growth momentum rather than fighting against the tide of decline, as in the cases of manufacturing and natural resources.

Embracing tourism as a development strategy, however, involves three fundamental challenges. The first is theoretical: Traditional theories of export-based development focus exclusively on the importance of exporting physical goods—commodities and manufactured products. Economists are now beginning to study how other types of activity that attract dollars from outside the economic region can serve as the functional equivalents of exports. In particular, transfer payments from governments to local residents, the permanent in-migration of individuals with outside income, and temporary visits from tourists looking to spend their travel dollars appear to be as effective as tangible exports for generating new local wealth.

The second challenge is research-related: Measuring the economic impact of tourism on rural areas overall is a difficult task. Most analyses do not isolate tourism as a separate sector within the urban or rural economies, and as a result, we do not know how many rural counties might be considered tourism dependent. Efforts to create a new analytical category of counties in which large proportions of income are generated from tourism would facilitate future evaluations of this sector's development potential.

The third and most important challenge to tourism development is that of equity. Much tourism-related rural development appears to create jobs and wealth in ways that do not adequately benefit the neediest and most vulnerable members of the community. Economic developers interested in tourism need to focus attention on improving the quality of jobs in these industries and developing tourism strategies that enhance rather than exploit local peoples and culture.

Despite the lack of aggregate rural tourism statistics, the existing literature does provide information about national and international industry trends as well as microanalyses of individual rural economies in which tourism has played a major role. From these studies, we can draw a few preliminary conclusions about tourism as a rural economic development strategy.

1. Tourism in the 1970s and 1980s proved to be a reliable source of economic growth both nationally and within rural communities and at all points in the business cycle. It is one of the few areas of economic activity where the national pie is growing, promising automatic spillover benefits for rural communities, and where rural America has some chance of increasing its share of the pie by upgrading tourism attractions.

2. Despite the positive trends, not all rural communities can count on tourism as a significant source of new jobs in the future. There is more growth to go around than in most other sectors, but the prospects are still limited. Some analysts expect national tourism growth to slow during the 1990s because of demographic and economic changes. As more and more communities, urban as well as rural, decide to pursue tourism, competition within the industry will grow more fierce. Eventually, as in so many other high-growth industries (computers, for example), this one may experience a shakeout.

3. Various case studies have illustrated the positive impact that tourism can have on local and regional development, including relatively large multiplier effects. However, some of this work has been criticized for overstating the benefits and understating the economic costs of tourism embedded in up-front investments and ongoing maintenance costs—burdens often borne primarily by local governments.

4. Strategies are available for better managing the public costs associated with tourism development. These include regional cooperative ventures among neighboring jurisdictions and public–private partnership models for financing new construction, renovation, and other tourism-related investment.

5. With some exceptions, such as large theme parks or resort complexes, tourism development strategies are mostly a variation on small business development strategies. Thus, tourism offers tremendous opportunities for developing a climate of entrepreneurship in a community or region and for expanding the local pool of entrepreneurs to include less advantaged populations.

6. While tourism clearly is a good source of new jobs, the quality of those jobs is often low in terms of wages, benefits, stability, continuity, opportunity for advancement, and dignity. Particularly where large-scale tourism development is planned, local leaders must find creative solutions for upgrading tourism-related employment and protecting workers during the off seasons. Planning processes for tourism development should become opportunities for broadening and deepening civic education and participation.

7. Tensions between and among conservationists, preservationists, and tourism development advocates also must be addressed in the early stages of planning. Models of consensus-building organizations and advisory boards can provide structures for resolving conflicts.

8. Tourism development is more than a job creation scheme; it involves conscious decisions about a community's way of life. More research is needed, both empirical and normative, to understand the economic, cultural, political, racial, and gender-related implications of this approach to economic development. Collective action is needed to prevent abuses against local populations and cultures.

Definitions

The Congressional Office of Technology Assessment (1988) has described recreation and leisure as one of the eight major "amenity groups" that American households expect their economy to provide.[1] This definition includes both goods (such as television sets, books, and tennis rackets) and services (such as campground, movie theaters, and video rental shops). While a broad definition is useful in understanding changes in consumer behavior in this category and their effects on various sectors of the economy, the definition of tourism used in this chapter will be considerably narrower. Following most other analysts, we shall use this category to denote strictly those services related to recreation and leisure outside of the home. The list of primary industries in this sector includes hotels and motels, restaurants, transportation, amusements, and recreational facilities such as parks.

The Context: National and International Trends

With so many U.S. industries from steel to semiconductors facing hard times during the 1980s, any industry enjoying steady growth in revenue and employment was bound to attract attention. The national travel and tourism industry, which reported 15 percent growth in sales between 1984 and 1986 alone, is a prime example.

Information about the size and scope of the national tourism and travel industry is readily available. From various sources, we know that tourism and travel-related enterprises account for between 6 and 7 percent of U.S. GNP. Americans took more than 1.1 billion "person trips" (at least 100 miles away from home, staying at least one night) in 1986. In the same year domestic and foreign travelers spent $269 billion in this country, making tourism the third largest U.S. retail industry (based on sales) and the second largest employer. That total rose to more than $300 billion by 1988. The U.S. Chamber of Commerce predicts that by the year 2000, tourism may capture the top retail position.

The vast majority of travel (66 percent of person trips in 1987) is vacation related; the rest is divided between personal travel (16 percent) and trips for business or to attend conferences and conventions (18 percent). This mix of different kinds of travel varies from location to location. The plurality of visitors to Cleveland (38 percent), for example, go to see friends and relatives, compared to 18 percent of those who visit Orlando. In contrast, over half of all visitors to Orlando (53 percent), the home of Disney World, fall in the sightseeing category, compared to 14 percent of all visitors to Cleveland.[2] Expenditure patterns differ markedly among groups with different purposes for traveling.

Federal, state, and local governments collected about $34 billion in taxes from tourism-related activity. In 1986, the industry supported 5.21 million jobs, which paid wages of $57.8 billion. More than half these jobs, 53 percent, are occupied by women, and 17 percent by minorities. Roughly 90 percent of all tourism-related businesses are "small businesses" by the federal government's definition (fewer than 500 workers).

The subset of the tourism industry of greatest interest to rural areas, outdoor recreation, also represents an important source of economic growth. According to the 1986 report of the President's Commission on American Outdoors, 90 percent of Americans surveyed "participate in some form of outdoor recreation," and fully 50 percent "describe themselves as 'outdoors people'." Participants in outdoor recreation activities spend more than $100 billion per year, supporting nine million jobs in the "private leisure/recreation industry." The government spends $5 billion per year on related "facilities and service."

Priority for Public Officials

The impressive performance of the tourism industry has not escaped the notice of economic developers, particularly at the state level. Almost every state (46 out of 50) counts tourism among its top three revenue-producing industries. Tourism promotion now ranks high on the priority lists of many state economic development officials. According to the U.S. Travel Data Center, states spent a total of $284 million on tourism development in 1987–88, an 80 percent increase from 1983–84. Some states have even granted cabinet-level status to their travel and tourism agencies.

Likewise, a growing number of localities are gearing up to attract visitors. In 1987, Illinois was home to 22 separate local convention and visitors' bureaus, with two in the planning stages, up from 10 a decade earlier. Even towns with populations as small as 10,000 are joining the competition.[3]

Many states have turned to tourism as an alternative to the old "smoke-stack chasing" and "buffalo hunting" strategies that dominated economic development in the 1960s and 1970s. New York started the trend toward state promotion in 1977, with their "I Love New York" campaign. Many states picked up on tourism's potential for attracting badly needed jobs and tax revenue and diversifying local economies, particularly during the early 1980s when manufacturing jobs were vanishing at a rapid rate. As Pennsylvania's Secretary of Commerce told Forbes magazine in 1984, "When you are transitioning out of heavy industry and trying to go after new technology, tourism fills in a lot of hills and valleys."[4]

The federal government, too, has focused increasing attention on the travel and tourism industry's critical role in job creation during both good economic times and bad. In 1980, for example, the travel industry picked up 300,000 new jobs while total U.S. payroll employment fell by 200,000.[5] Travel industry employment grew twice as fast as overall U.S. employment between 1958 and 1980. It took $200,000 in additional spending in 1981 to generate one new auto manufacturing job; hotels, airlines, restaurants, and other related establishments generated a new job for every $34,000 spent in the travel and tourism industry.[6]

Historically high trade deficits in the early 1980s focused attention on international tourism as an export equivalent or substitute. Each foreign visitor to the United States pumps outside cash into the economy and contributes to easing the trade deficit.[7] The currently low value of the dollar relative to other currencies makes travel within the United States a better bargain for both Americans and visitors from overseas. As a result, the flow of foreign tourists is expected to continue to increase, while more Americans are expected to take their vacations in the United States rather than traveling abroad. In recognition of these facts, the U.S. Travel and Tourism Administration (USTTA), an agency of the Department of Commerce, was established by Congress in 1981 for the primary purpose of coordinating efforts to market the United States to potential visitors overseas. Supporters of USTTA in Congress must struggle each budget session to maintain the agency's funding, but so far the federal presence in tourism development has survived.

Projections

Uel Blank may be right when she says, "Every community has a tourism industry; every community can have a better tourism industry."[8] But serious questions remain about tourism's ability to sustain high growth rates indefinitely.

Experts disagree about tourism's future. Demographic and social trends are pulling in opposite directions. On the one hand, Americans have more disposable income to spend on travel. New information and communication technologies are making it easier and more convenient to plan trips. With the baby boom generation aging, and people living longer and taking longer retirements, older travelers have come to represent a promising growth market for the tourism industry, particularly for packaged tour operators. On the other hand, time use studies show Americans with less leisure time on their hands. The number of busy, two-earner couples has grown while family size has diminished. At the same time, American workers have been earning fewer paid vacation days than their counterparts overseas.[9]

Despite the conflicting trends and methodological problems with predicting future behavior, a rough consensus has emerged among tourism experts. In a report issued in 1989, the USTTA projected a shrinking domestic travel market in the 1990s.[10] Most industry analysts expect increasingly tough competition for tourism dollars as population growth slows and more and more cities and rural areas join the tourism development race. Compared to annual industry growth rates as high as 20 percent during parts of the 1970s, future annual growth is expected to hover around the 3–5 percent range.[11] Fish quotes one tourism professional's forecast: "You will have to be good to simply maintain your market share and be exceptional to create successful new attractions."[12] Although there is room for growth, not everyone can succeed.

In the face of a shrinking domestic market, travel promoters must look more to the world market to generate growth in visitors, income, and jobs.

The Rural Picture

Despite tourism's impressive track record at the national level, solid information about rural tourism is hard to find. The Economic Research Service of the U.S. Department of Agriculture, a key source of data on rural trends, has no separate category for rural counties with tourism-dependent economies and does not calculate performance indicators for urban or rural tourism-related industries, most of which are offshoots of the traditional retail and services industry groups. Accordingly, it is difficult to say definitively how large a role tourism plays in the overall rural economy. The limited evidence available from two studies suggests that tourism was one of just a few significant contributors to rural growth during the late 1970s and early to mid 1980s.

The South Growth Policies Board's 1989 report, *Making Connections,* isolated tourism as one of the top three growth factors for rural areas in the South between 1977 and 1984.[13] The other top growth factors were status as a retirement community and presence of "special economic entities" such as military installations or nuclear plants. Of all the 816 rural counties in the South, those with more than 7.5 percent of their labor forces employed in tourism-related jobs (such as overnight accommodations, eating establishments, and auto service stations) experienced the highest rates of growth in overall employment and per capita income between 1977 and 1984. The cream of the crop, the 18 southern rural counties that experienced dramatic employment growth of more than 50 percent during the study period, all enjoyed either heavy tourism trade, "special economic entities," or spillover from nearby urban areas. These results led the authors to conclude, "Perhaps the most important ingredients of growth are the physical and recreational attractions a county can offer."

Similarly, the National Governors' Association's (NGA) recent report, *A Brighter Future for Rural America?*[14] examined economic trends in 16 high-growth rural counties in the Farmbelt between 1979 and 1984. Despite the fact that the Midwest is not generally known for mountains, seashore, or special natural attractions, growth in three of the 16 counties selected for study could be traced in part to tourism development. On a national level, the report shows that during the 1980s, rural counties with an employment base in government, recreation, and/or retirement experienced significantly higher growth rates than counties dependent on manufacturing, farming, mining, and/or trade. Because of structural declines in manufacturing employment and the tendency for most service firms to favor urban areas, the authors of this study concluded: "From a national perspective, neither services nor manufacturing is a particularly good long-term prospect for widespread employment growth in rural areas, *except for recreation and retirement communities*" (emphasis added).

In addition to studying the extent of tourism-led growth, researchers have begun to examine the net effects of tourism development on local economies through cost-benefit studies. So far, the evidence suggests that, while tourism will continue to play an important role in aggregate growth for rural America and in community-specific growth for certain areas of the country, it will not necessarily be a net plus for all communities that decide to embark on this strategy. As researchers develop more sophisticated methods for estimating benefits and costs, these preliminary results may need to be revised.

Many of the early studies of tourism's impact on local economies showed significant net benefits. For example, the Economic Development Administration of the U.S. Department of Commerce funded a study of tourism in the state of Delaware in 1977 which claimed to prove definitively that, based on travel-related tax revenues alone, tourism is a winning proposition for governments.[15] State tax receipts for nonresident motor fuel, hotel room taxes, hunting and fishing licenses, park user fees, visitor-based mercantile taxes, and related corporate income taxes (Delaware has no sales tax) amounted to more than $14 million in revenue in 1977. Related public expenditures for highways, police and fire protection, parks, and fishing and wildlife facilities came to less than $12 million according to this study, for a net return to the state of about $2.5 million. The authors of the study claim that the results can be projected nationally.

A 1984 analysis of the economic impact of North Dakota's state parks reached a similar conclusion.[16] One million annual visitors to the state's parks spent roughly $32 million directly on user fees, licenses, concessions, and related services, while costs to the park service for operation and maintenance of facilities ran about $2.8 million. When indirect economic impacts are included in the equation to account for circulation of the additional dollars in the local economies, the study shows that every dollar spent by a visitor to the parks generated a total of $2.22 in business activity.

A study of recreational spending in selected state parks in Georgia failed to include estimates of the costs of building and maintaining facilities and, therefore, did not arrive at a figure for overall net benefits.[17] However, the authors did calculate regional multipliers for recreational spending at the various parks in terms of total gross output, employee compensation, property income, total income, value added, and employment.[18] These multipliers ranged from 1.21 to 4.35, with most values falling roughly between 1.5 and 2.0.

The generalization of such results has been challenged, however. Myers notes that many of the "destination resorts" built in state parks around the country during the 1960s and 1970s generate positive cash flow, but these calculations often do not include the costs of raising capital (debt service on revenue bonds, for example), conducting advertising and promotional campaigns, or financing renovation and modernization, a particularly expensive undertaking.[19] A case study of tourism in four counties of Tennessee concluded that the hidden costs of tourism—in terms of impacts on roads, utilities, health care services, and the quality of life as well as the downward pull on local wages—make it a less attractive development option than the raw numbers suggest.[20] In the Tennessee case, the raw numbers indicated that local tax revenue from tourism exceeded the costs of providing police, fire, sanitation, and certain other public services to travelers by a multiple of two. Still, the auditors refrained from declaring it an unqualified success, expressing concerns about ill effects from tourism that cannot be quantified easily.

One of the most difficult areas of cost-benefit analysis is the projection of long-term effects. For example, tourism development has the potential eventually to affect larger migration patterns. Temporary visitors are not the only possible targets of tourism initiatives. Analysis of retirement communities has shown that many retirees end up settling permanently in areas where they vacationed during their younger years. More significantly, if quality of life factors come to have greater influence over business location decisions, areas endowed with recreational, cultural, historical sites, and other amenities are expected to advance in the competition for business attraction and retention. The same comparative advantages that apply in tourism may begin to apply in other potential growth sectors as well.

In addition tourism-related development may positively influence the spending patterns of existing residents in rural areas. To the extent that refurbished main streets attract the right kinds of retail establishments, they may help stem the flight of consumer dollars out of small communities into larger, regional malls. As Drabenstott and Gibson have shown, economic growth in one sector often helps spur economic growth in a variety of other sectors.[21] The enhancements needed to keep a community attractive to visitors also may serve to lure permanent residents and their investments, as well as winning back the consumption dollars of the community's own residents.

Economic Development Strategies

Although the natural market forces in tourism treated rural areas well in the 1970s and 1980s, future tourism-led growth may depend on more active intervention by economic developers and community leaders. As competition for tourist dollars intensifies, communities may need to develop more sophisticated strategies for expanding or even just maintaining their share of the market.

The literature on tourism is full of articles and reports intended to help local communities organize for tourism development.[22] While no precise formula exists for transforming a town or county into a popular travel destination, case studies of successful local tourism development programs point toward some of the prerequisites for attracting visitors. According to most of the sources noted above, the ingredients necessary for success include:

- Distinctive natural or historical attractions such as mountains, lakes, seashore, historical landmarks, or special subcultures such as Native Americans or Pennsylvania Dutch.

- Leadership from local individuals, including business people, public officials, economic development staff, and others willing to spearhead the tourism effort.

- Public support in the form of traffic control, road maintenance, police and fire protection, and favorable policies such as land development incentives.

- Cooperation among all local enterprises that benefit from or are somehow involved in tourism, including local businesses, development agencies, public lands managers, and cultural organizations.

- A carefully crafted tourism development plan that focuses on market differentiation.

Beyond a rough understanding of the ingredients for tourism success, however, many issues arising from this type of economic development strategy remain unresolved. The following discussions will explore some of these issues.

Creating Amenities

According to the "asset theory of tourism," successful tourism development depends on the availability of some immobile attraction that people want to visit, whether natural (lakes, mountains, seashore), historical, or cultural.[23] Some analysts claim that such assets are virtually infinite. According to Blank, "The benefits of a viable tourism industry are available to nearly all communities . . . potential for expansion is limited only by the vision and initiative of their people."[24] In other words, popular tourist attractions are made rather than discovered, and just about any locality can decide to become a tourist destination.

Some evidence supports this view, most notably examples of areas that have essentially created their own tourism assets from scratch. Danville, Illinois instituted an annual event, "Civil War Days," in which local residents reenact a relatively obscure Tennessee Civil War battle that involved many Danville men. In the event's third year, it attracted 12,000 visitors and generated $21.8 million for a town of only 42,000 people. Reflecting on this success, one economic development specialist said, "There are very few communities that don't have something unique or unusual to offer."[25]

Reading, Pennsylvania is an example of a small city that created a successful tourism development program out of nothing more than a few abandoned textile factory buildings.[26] Local developers converted the buildings into factory outlet stores and attracted 3.4 million patrons in 1984 (compared to one million in 1977 and almost no patrons in 1973 prior to the push). In addition to generating profits at the outlet stores, these shoppers also spend money at restaurants, hotels, gas stations, and other establishments. One analyst estimated that visitors to Reading spend about an additional $3 for every $10 purchase made in the outlets. For areas accessible to major population centers, "shopping" can qualify as a tourism asset.

These examples highlight the diversity of experiences that travelers seek. Clearly, rural tourism is not limited to outdoor activities such as canoeing, hunting, fishing, and hiking. It can also include industrial sites (such as the former mill town of Lowell, Massachusetts, centers that explain lumbering and mining, and simple tours of local factories),[27] ethnic and cultural attractions (such as Amish country in Lancaster County, Pennsylvania), historic features (such as Hannibal, Missouri, Mark Twain's birthplace),[28] specialty attractions (such as festivals, sports events, or theme parks),[29] shopping, and even religious attractions (such as Passion Plays or the Mormon Interpretive Center in rural Illinois).[30] "Ag-tourism" is one example of a thoroughly rural innovation in this field. The phrase describes the attraction of tourists to agriculture-related events and locations and efforts to sell agricultural products to visitors who may be in the vicinity for a variety of reason.[31] The components of ag-tourism are familiar to most travelers: farmers' markets, pick-your-own operations, harvest festivals, wineries/dairies, agricultural history museums, and recreational activities such as hunting and cross-country skiing on private farmland.

The list of potential tourist attractions, however, must not be interpreted as a sign that all rural communities can or should pursue tourism development. Most of the how-to literature in the field recommends that communities begin their tourism planning process by making inventories of their existing local assets and asking questions about what aspects of the communities might be attractive to visitors.[32] Fish places enormous weight on the existing physical setting for a would-be tourist destination: "The attractiveness of a place to visit is derived from the character of the place itself."[33] Attractiveness, however, cannot be faked: "The assets inventory must be based on a respect for authenticity, because attempts to fabricate tourist attractions are now much more difficult and less accepted by an increasingly sophisticated audience."[34]

Communities endowed with only marginal tourism assets must ask whether those assets are worth additional public and private investment. As one how-to manual put it, "Someone is interested in everything that has ever been developed, but whether or not people are interested enough to make it economical to develop and maintain will require some additional study."[35]

Communities can begin to answer questions about their own assets in two ways: (1) by trying to estimate the market potential for a given attraction and then conducting a rough cost-benefit analysis measuring expected revenues from tourism spending against maintenance costs and investments in new facilities;[36] and (2) by starting small—that is, seeking expanded visitation from local residents, then broadening the appeal to a wider geographic market.[37] In conducting their analysis, communities should consider whether their assets rate as "core" attractions or simply as secondary "supporting" attractions.[38]

Entrepreneurship

According to the Small Business Administration, almost 99 percent of all tourism-related establishments qualify as small businesses.[39] As with small businesses in other industries, the majority of these enterprises fail; according to Blank's calculations, "as few as one out of 15 develop beyond the 'ma and pa' stage."[40]

Thus, any community interested in tourism-based development must be prepared for the challenges associated with building an economy the hard, slow way, piece by piece, through small business development. While tourism may look like a glamorous way to create jobs, it requires the full range of hard work involved in cultivating and supporting an entrepreneurial economy in which local residents are willing to take the risks needed to start up a variety of service businesses to meet the needs of visitors. In areas with only a minimal tourism infrastructure, this means establishing new hotels, inns, or Bed and Breakfast lodgings; restaurants; retail shops; outdoor outfitters; gas and service stations; and so forth.

Alan Gregerman describes the challenge of establishing a small business economy:

Successful entrepreneur development is about the task of building relationships, developing new talents, creating spirit and excitement, knocking on doors, providing information, removing barriers, and inspiring people to take initiative. In creating an environment that encourages entrepreneurial behavior, we are actually creating the "human" infrastructure that will support risk-taking and minimize, or at least cushion, the entrepreneurial risks.[41]

Gregerman identifies the most important elements of an entrepreneurial environment: committed local leadership, a pool of entrepreneurial talent, knowledge about opportunities, sources of innovation, access to capital, and community spirit.[42] Business support systems that provide financial and technical assistance during the early phases of venture development are key components of any plan to cultivate new and small enterprises.

Case studies of successful rural tourism initiatives reflect many of the same lessons. The EDA (Economic Development Administration) -funded "Profiles in Rural Economic Development"[43] includes 65 case studies of promising development projects, almost 15 percent of which relate to tourism. Three common threads unite these rural tourism profiles:

1. Commitment by local officials to a cooperative effort which usually is embodied in some type of development organization—a chamber of commerce, ethnic heritage association, port district, or other nonprofit group.

2. The presence of a single individual or "sparkplug" who motivates others to join the effort and keeps things alive even in the face of major obstacles.

3. Renewal of civic pride, particularly in those communities where new tourism initiatives draw on the locality's historical, cultural, and/or ethnic heritage (New Glarus and Delavan, Wisconsin and Embarrass, Minnesota, for example).

By and large, the projects profiled by Thomas involved collaborative efforts by community business people and officials to develop a tourism plan, agree on a theme, and apply for outside grants and other forms of financial assistance.

Four additional case studies[44] illustrate the importance of financial and technical assistance for local businesses seeking to renovate historic buildings, expand operations, or start up new ventures. Services provided in these communities included assistance with market surveys, environmental assessments, land-use planning, grant writing, electronic data processing, local ordinances, tax increment financing plans, energy audits, state and local permitting, facility siting, and maintenance of working relationships with lending institutions and key players in local, state, and federal governments.

Within the tourism industry, one area of particularly dramatic small business growth has been Bed and Breakfast (B&B) operations. B&Bs—enterprises in which private homes or renovated historic sites are opened to provide lodging and limited meals for overnight guests—invariably qualify as very small businesses. In recent years, their popularity has risen rapidly. As a result, they have become the object of several research studies and technical assistance programs, mostly initiated by state tourism centers and cooperative extension agencies. At the state level, B&B operators have developed trade associations to pass legislation related to their interests, sponsored technical assistance workshops, and conducted joint promotional campaigns including development of state and regional directories of B&Bs. These efforts provide a possible model for collaborative activity among small business owners in other parts of the tourism industry as well.[45]

Partnerships

Most small rural communities with limited public resources cannot hope to handle the costs of tourism development alone. For this reason, tourism experts strongly recommend efforts to involve private investors and other local governments early in the planning process. A community with minimal tourism assets might benefit from joining together with neighboring communities to create a critical mass of secondary attractions or to piggyback on a major regional treasure.

Many of the case studies of successful rural tourism initiatives emphasize the importance of regional cooperation across jurisdictions.[46] In these cases, groups of towns can share planning responsibilities and infrastructure development costs and achieve economies of scale in advertising, promotion, and other related activities. Regional partnerships can provide the leadership needed to create greenways, riverways, rails-to-trails corridors in which old railroad beds are converted into biking and walking trails, and other conservation areas that appeal to the interests of outdoor enthusiasts.

The case studies also emphasize the role of public–private partnerships in raising the capital needed for major improvement. Several state parks have taken advantage of such opportunities to "joint venture" new construction and modernization of their older facilities, or at least to lay plans for doing so in the future.[47] According to Myers,[48] West Virginia has attracted private dollars to refurbish and expand state park campgrounds, recreational facilities, cabins, and lodges, and Maryland is encouraging private developers to build conference and recreational facilities, including a golf course, in its western state parks and forests.

Thomas' profiles[49] of rural tourism initiatives identify a variety of large and small public and private funding sources, including private donations, grass-roots fundraising, federal and state government grants, low-interest loans (from dozens of different agencies including Coastal Zone Development, Army Corps of Engineers, state fish and wildlife departments and library departments, as well as the more traditional economic development sources),[50] foundation grants, association membership fees, advertising revenues, local bonds, special taxes, and income from contractual services.

The State and Federal Roles

In addition to local programs, various technical and financial services also are available at the state and federal levels. More than 30 state-based tourism centers now operate around the country to foster interdisciplinary applied research and provide educational programs for policy makers, development officials, and tourism-related businesses.[51] Virtually all of these centers operate from a public university base; many are located in the cooperative extension unit. Federal programs exist throughout the cabinet agencies.[52] (Unfortunately, most eligible business owners don't know about these opportunities; obviously, there is a need for more outreach.)

Currently, the largest single contribution from states is in the area of tourism advertising. States spend roughly 43 percent of their tourism budgets on advertising, but what does this buy? According to the literature, the answer depends on the degree to which the advertising is part of a larger comprehensive marketing plan.

Marketing and Advertising

Recent tourism education materials emphasize the importance of the larger context of tourism marketing for localities as well as states. Simonson et al.,[53] for example, characterize marketing as identifying local attractions, developing facilities and services to meet the daily needs of visitors, identifying those segments of the tourism market with some interest in a specific community's attraction, and then pursuing various types of linkages with those market segments that keep the community in touch with the latest industry research findings. The last would include two-way communication links through advertising and other promotional activities as well as visitor feedback, transportation and informational links.

Blank emphasizes the importance of identifying a target market and selling to the most likely customers rather than trying to convince a wide array of people with vastly differing tastes to try something they won't necessarily like:

The marketing approach to tourism industry development is almost exactly the opposite of an advertising or selling approach. The philosophy of marketing is to fulfill client/customers' needs and wants. It determines these needs, develops products, facilities, and services to satisfy them, and then develops and executes appropriate sales programs. In contrast, the selling approach begins with an advertising program to sell what the community has. In its least effective form this approach is carried out without systematic analysis of what the community offers as a tourism experience, and without organized information on patterns of consumer needs in tourism–recreation.[54]

Most states, however, have not moved beyond the simple "selling" approach to embrace more comprehensive, systematic techniques for building tourist revenues.[55] Sizing up market potential requires more sophisticated data collection efforts than most small communities are familiar with, as well as consideration of a wide variety of complex factors: the distance of the community from major population centers, availability of good transportation, price and elasticity of demand for the particular product, and the degree of competition from other tourist destinations.

Various publications have been developed to help communities plan, execute, and evaluate marketing and advertising plans.[56] Despite the availability of such resources, rural development analysts still talk about the problem of "tourism illiteracy." According to one Texas tourism expert, "most communities are illiterate regarding tourism as a system. Individual businesses and agencies know a great deal about their separate enterprises but very little about how it all fits together—or perhaps, doesn't fit together. . . . Most areas have no information at all about markets, especially potential markets."[57]

Expanding Markets

In the light of shrinking domestic demand, some analysts recommend more aggressive efforts to promote the United States in overseas travel markets. Foreign visitors offer a potentially significant source of tourism growth.

The ability of rural areas to market to other countries, however, is probably limited. According to some industry experts, the federal government, through USTTA, should coordinate this marketing effort. Strategies might include advertising campaigns and sponsorship of local tourism development missions to countries with untapped travel markets. At the same time, supporters of this strategy call for reducing barriers to foreign travel—simplifying temporary travel permits for visitors from other countries, easing restrictions on foreign currency, and providing more information in foreign languages.

Quality of Development

From a distance, tourism looks like the ideal development strategy for rural America. It was a source of startling employment growth in many rural counties during the 1970s and 1980s. It tends to be recession-proof.[58] It doesn't pollute. It attracts the equivalent of export dollars. In theory, it can be tried anywhere.

Cost-benefit analyses, as described above, have begun to expose the weaknesses in this simple view by uncovering the hidden economic costs that accompany tourism-based development—stress on public infrastructure, demand for capital, and the costs of maintenance. These studies have not, however, proceeded to the next step to evaluate the impact of tourism on people and communities. Preliminary evidence suggests that, in the case of large-scale tourism development at least, these impacts have contributed significantly to the deterioration of quality of life, especially among women, minorities, and the poor. It appears that tourism development strategies will have to change substantially before they meet the criteria established in Chapter 2: relieving poverty, creating opportunities for young workers, preserving social continuity, promoting self sufficiency, treating people with respect.

Jobs and Equity

As noted above, tourism qualifies as a basic industry because, like trade, it brings new dollars into the economy from outside. Measuring the net contribution of those new dollars to overall economic vitality, however, is a difficult task. Various studies define and measure economic vitality in different ways. The most widely accepted indicators capture the broad goals of most economic development strategies: creating new jobs, raising incomes, and relieving poverty. Clearly, based on the results of studies such as *Making Connections* (Rosenfeld et al.) and *A Brighter Future for Rural America?* (DeWitt John et al.), an expanding local tourist trade is linked to improvements in these gross indicators—growth in jobs and per capita income as well as declining poverty rates. Counties with concentrations of tourism-related jobs performed better by these measures than other counties in the rural South and the Farmbelt.

These gross measures of prosperity, however, may not tell the full story. A study from the Southeast Women's Employment Coalition, for example, marshals evidence to support the claim that tourism development strategies

achieve economic growth at the expense of large numbers of poor, indigenous, rural people.[59] "Though the successful infusion of tourist dollars into a
local economy clearly helps spawn small business development and employment," the report states, "the vast majority of lasting jobs are the antithesis of
opportunity."

The study, *Behind the Glitter* (Michal Smith), compares quality of life
measures in 84 selected high-growth, tourism-dependent counties (using
jobs in the hotel industry as a proxy for tourism) in the rural South with national figures for the period 1970–84. Among their findings:

- Despite dramatic growth in overall job numbers in the study counties,
  unemployment rates rose steadily during the period and remained above
  the national average.

- Despite the fact that the hotel industry is dominated by female workers,
  women's unemployment rates remained higher than men's throughout
  the period. Women earned less than half of what men earned in 3/4 of
  the counties studied.

- The poverty rate for female-headed households in these counties increased, although not as dramatically as elsewhere in the country. Family
  median income remained below the national average.

- These counties experienced much higher than average population
  growth over the period, mostly among whites.

The study points out that jobs in the hotel industry tend to be low-wage,
seasonal, and part-time. They provide few if any employee benefits such as
health insurance and pensions, and virtually no opportunities for advancement. At the same time, tourism development often raises the local cost of
living, putting extra pressure on housekeepers, store clerks, and waitresses
who are trying to raise families on part-time, minimum-wage jobs.

In congressional testimony in 1982, Peter McCoy, Undersecretary of
Commerce for Travel and Tourism, expressed similar concerns about the seasonality of the tourism industry and suggested possible strategies for
spreading the benefits of tourism more evenly throughout the year and
around the country. In particular, he identified three negative consequences
of seasonality: lack of productivity gains in the lodging and related sectors,
deterioration in quality of the tourists' experience in overcrowded areas, and
seasonal unemployment.

These critiques identify serious problems with the quality of tourism-
based development and raise the specter of other problems so far undocu-
mented. For example, existing data are not adequate to determine how

tourism jobs are distributed. In some cases, owners of hotels, restaurants, and other establishments may choose to hire workers from outside the local area (or recent immigrants with higher skill levels) for the better-paying jobs. We do not know the extent of this practice. Existing data also fail to provide a full explanation for the growth in per capita incomes and declining poverty rates found by Rosenfeld et al. in their study of tourism counties. These changes may be attributed to improved prospects for local people (a result that contradicts Smith's findings) or to an influx of affluent people who skew the statistics. Further research is needed to determine the connection between improvement in gross indicators of economic vitality and real improvements in local standards of living.

The existing research also raises serious questions about the proper benchmarks for comparing development effects. Although the two studies shared a common database, *Behind the Glitter* compared quality of life measures for tourism counties with the national average while *Making Connections* compared overall economic indicators for tourism counties with other Southern rural counties. The use of national benchmarks for unemployment, poverty, and wages reflects the hope that rural areas eventually will catch up with urban areas in these measures of living standards. However, given that rural areas throughout most of their history have experienced greater unemployment and poverty and lower wages than urban areas, evaluations of performance based on national standards may be overly stringent. Instead, it may be sufficient to determine whether tourism-dependent rural counties perform better than rural counties in other economic categories. A new study that compared Smith's quality-of-life indicators for tourism counties against the same indicators for Rosenfeld et al.'s rural counties might yield a clearer picture of the relative impact of tourism on rural citizens and communities.

Beyond issues of research methods, there are affirmative steps that communities and public and private leaders at the state and national level can take to address the issues of indigenous jobs and distributional equity in tourism development. Four recommendations stand out:

1. *Provide more and better training for employees at all levels within the tourism industry.* Income gains for low-wage "hospitality" workers will depend, at least in part, on productivity gains, which depend in turn on enhancing workers' skills and providing better entry-level training. Increased productivity is a two-edged sword, of course. It raises wages but cuts demand for new workers. Achieving the goal of higher productivity and improved working conditions for tourism employees will require concerted joint efforts by private business owners and government officials.[60]

Some educators are calling attention to the problem of recruiting talented individuals into long-term careers in the travel and tourism field.[61] They note a general lack of prestige connected with the field and too few professional training programs at colleges, universities, and vocational schools. Some of the jobs in the tourism industry are attractive and lucrative, particularly those at the management level. Policy can boost this part of the employment equation by supporting management and professional training programs and encouraging the development of career ladders within tourism-related businesses.

2. *Draw entrepreneurs from a larger pool of local residents.* We know that most new ventures are started by local people where they live. Gregerman recommends various low-cost ways in which communities can encourage potential entrepreneurs to come forward. These include public relations campaigns to raise awareness of entrepreneurial careers, classes and workshops for individuals considering starting new businesses, and entrepreneur/small business appreciation days.[62]

Communities also might look for ways to distribute the benefits of growth more broadly. For example, the Corporation for Economic Development (CfED) has proposed models for states interested in using transfer dollars—particularly unemployment insurance funds (UI) and assistance for families with dependent children (AFDC) benefits—to create jobs. Ideas include: channeling transfer funds in the form of working capital to new and expanding firms willing to hire and train AFDC recipients; financing entrepreneurial ventures by UI and AFCD recipients who are interested in starting their own small businesses; and using transfers to capitalize community-based development programs that provide entrepreneurial assistance, sheltered workshops, and other services to transfer clients.[63]

3. *Increase demands by host communities on those businesses that benefit from expanding tourism.*[64] Such demands may include increased taxes on outside developers to help pay for the safety net services their workers must turn to in the off-season and to help finance housing, job training, child care, and health care programs for low-wage workers and the unemployed. Hotels, restaurants, and other businesses might be required to buy a certain percentage of supplies locally. Finally, proprietors can be encouraged to adopt more participatory management techniques, profit-sharing or worker ownership arrangements, and other practices that increase the quality of life for the average worker.

4. *Conduct further research on employment patterns in the rural tourism industry.* Microlevel analyses of employment patterns, population shifts (particularly in-migrants), and income and cost-of-living trends in selected tourism-dependent rural areas, for example, would make a significant contribution to the field. If data are available in a few selected areas, such studies could help refine the gross figures on increased job creation and per capita income in these areas. Who is being hired for the newly created jobs—including the managers, accountants, and supervisors as well as the housekeepers, retail clerks, and waitresses? To what extent is the higher per capita income and lower poverty rate in these counties a function of wealthy families moving in rather than local residents improving their standard of living? How does a growing tourism sector affect local cost of living?

A sequel to the work begun by the Southern Growth Policies Board and the Southeast Women's Employment Coalition should compare quality of life indicators in the selected high-growth, tourism-based counties with the rest of the rural South to see whether residents in these areas are faring worse than their neighbors. Similar techniques should be applied to other regions of the country to measure the economic impacts of tourism outside the South.

Growth, Conservation, and Preservation

Tourism-driven growth demands an ever-increasing volume of visitors to an area. In travel destinations known for their scenic beauty or indigenous cultures, steady growth in tourism threatens to degrade or consume the very assets that make the industry possible in the first place.

The problem of overcrowding in the most popular national parks illustrates this conflict. In congressional hearings from 1982 through 1987, witnesses mentioned the dilemma repeatedly, warning of future circumstances in which a park might have to shut down temporarily when it has reached its "carrying capacity." One park ranger in Yosemite described "the traffic jams you see in the valley . . . worse than anything you will find in Los Angeles at rush hour."[65]

One recommendation for addressing this problem would reduce the concentrations of tourists both geographically and seasonally. Specific ideas for accomplishing this goal include efforts to promote lesser-known travel destinations to reduce overcrowding in the most popular locations, higher user fees for crowded areas, and development and marketing of off-season attractions. A more radical solution to the problem of seasonality and overcrowding would follow the German model of staggering school and work holidays. In Germany, schools have a different summer recess schedule, summer vacations are shorter, and spring vacations longer. As a result, lodging, eating, and other businesses in popular family travel destinations find the flow of tourists more evenly spread throughout the year.

Conflicts between development and conservation are fundamental to virtually all tourism efforts. Various studies have concluded, for example, that highly developed tourist facilities such as resorts create the largest economic impacts.[66] Such facilities also take the heaviest toll on environmentally sensitive areas and radically change the character of an area. Myers describes a classic example of this tension in her profile of tourism development in Northern Berkshire County, Massachusetts.[67] Mount Greylock, the central feature of this scenic rural area, became a battleground for interest groups promoting at various times a summit tramway, resort and conference center, casino gambling, a golf course, "the largest ski area in the East," an artificial lake, and cross-country skiing and hiking trails. Some of these proposed projects were blocked by environmentalists and other concerned residents; others were begun but abandoned for lack of funds. Eventually, state officials and private interested parties from around the region formed a partnership to sort out the conflict. The partnership was able to build broad support for a compromise plan that allowed controlled development in some areas of the park but preserved other areas within the Mount Greylock state reservation.

Clearly, states, regions, and communities must be sensitive to the need for broad representation in all tourism planning processes. Public land managers and environmentalists must be included with investors, recreation groups, and other interests from the beginning, not as tokens but as active participants. Myers' description of the consensus-building process adopted to manage development in the northern Berkshires provides a model for other rural areas across the country.[68]

Culture and Community

"Tourism involves more than the simple addition of a few new businesses and jobs to the economic mix of a local community. It involves an entire way of life, which tends to transform the existing patterns of land ownership, indigenous culture, political relationships, and economic base."[69]

Problems such as traffic congestion and noise are just the tip of a large iceberg that represents the hidden effects of tourism on local people and communities. Experience in highly developed tourist destinations has uncovered a long list of disruptions to some of the most cherished aspects of rural life. For example, large-scale resort development inevitably causes property values to rise, leaving many long-time local residents unable to pay rapidly increasing property taxes and pushing them out of their homes. In addition, waterfront development often eliminates access to fishing areas for local people who rely on this activity for extra food and income. Developers moving into parts of the South have been known to dupe poor, long-time resident families out of their land, separate them from their cemeteries, and require them to carry passes to enter development areas. The history of certain southern resorts shows that successful tourism development can in short order eradicate an entire way of life.[70]

These are moral issues that do not lend themselves to easy policy recommendations. Some tradeoffs may be acceptable, but others simply may not, regardless of the potential economic payoff. Here, as in other areas of conflict over development, at least part of the solution must come through open, frank, inclusive community discussions. This does not mean a poorly publicized meeting sponsored by developers to inform citizens of a massive project already well under way. It means reaching out to a broad cross-section of the community to address potential problems early on in the development process. Local leaders should look within their own towns not only for entrepreneurs interested in starting new businesses, but also for people concerned about protecting indigenous cultures, integrating the poor into new job opportunities, providing assistance to individuals hit by skyrocketing property taxes, and educating local residents about tourism development. Community groups will need to play a key role in capturing the attention of local leaders in many cases. State and national policy, too, can create incentives or requirements for communities to open up their tourism planning processes and build in protections for the most vulnerable.

The impact of tourism on different rural areas will vary widely. In Guam, the Sea Islands, parts of New Hampshire, and other major tourism magnets where indigenous peoples enter the equation or overdevelopment threatens to go too far in changing people's way of life, the scale of conflict is enormous and the issues are those of controlling and channeling growth. In contrast, for residents of some small midwestern and southern towns where jobs have been scarce for decades, tourism promises little more than a modest boost for the local economy, not a full-scale transformation of cultures. Here, the issues are those of capitalizing on existing assets and trying to spark growth. In both cases, strong leadership and broad community input are essential, but the appropriate policies will be vastly different.

Similarly, there is a world of difference between an explicit decision by residents of a Wisconsin village to trade on the area's Swiss immigrant heritage to draw visitors[71] and an implicit decision by leaders in a South Carolina community to use an indigenous black population as a source of low-skilled labor for hotels and resorts and as a component of the local "ambiance."[72] The outcome in the first case may well be renewed civic pride and heightened sense of community; in the second, it is all too likely to be exploitation of the community's least well-off members.

9

The Elderly

Introduction

Alongside tourism, the other bright spot in the rural economy appears to be the network of industries that serve retirees. Gross economic indicators show that counties with economies dependent on retirement performed well during the 1970s and much of the 1980s. As with tourism, the outside dollars that retirees bring into the local economy via pensions, investments, and Social Security serve as the equivalent of exports. For this reason, we include a chapter on "The Elderly" in a sectoral analysis of the rural economy and, in fact, classify the elderly as an economic base for some communities.

Economic developers, constantly on the lookout for new avenues of job creation, have begun to view retirees the same way they viewed industrial plants and high technology firms in the 1960s and 1970s—as targets for recruitment. Though not yet in full swing, the competition for retirement developments and retirees is likely to accelerate during the 1990s.

Slowly but surely, states and localities are learning how to woo retirees and their money. A 1988 article in the *Wall Street Journal* mentioned a diverse set of rural communities—from Silver Bay, Minnesota in the economically depressed Iron Range, to Bennettsville, South Carolina in rolling countryside "ideal for golf." All are working hard to promote themselves as retirement meccas.[1] The state of South Carolina bought 3000 acres of land in 1986 with the intention of building roads and sewer hookups and then selling the improved site to a developer interested in erecting a retirement community. The Massachusetts government is getting involved in land acquisition with the same strategy in mind. According to the *Wall Street Journal,* these enterprises help state officials meet two policy goals simultaneously: overall development of the state's economy and allocation of jobs and income to the poorest counties within the state.

In some parts of rural America, particularly the West and South, retirement centers have long been an integral part of the economic base. Roughly one-quarter of all rural counties (481 out of a total of 2383) qualified as "retirement counties" in 1980 with at least 15 percent net in-migration of individuals 65 years and older. Based on the experiences of these communities, researchers have begun to establish a base of knowledge about the role of retirement-led development in rural areas:

1. Alongside tourism, retirees were one of the rare sources of economic growth for rural counties in the 1980s. Counties with elderly in-migration enjoyed rapid gains in employment and population relative to other rural counties throughout the 1970s and 1980s. During the 1980s, for example, population in retirement counties grew by 23 percent while employment grew by 32 percent. Along other economic dimensions, however, rural retirement counties have not performed well—in particular, income growth and overall stability.

2. Areas in the early stages of retirement-led development may face a rougher road and greater instability than areas long established as retirement destinations. The economies of the mature retirement areas, where retirees constitute a larger proportion of total population, outshine those of retirement counties (as a whole) on nearly every measure.

3. At this point in time, economic planners understand the advantages of retirement-led development better than the drawbacks. However, a few studies have begun to shed light on the problems that may accompany large influxes of elderly people. These include possible shifts toward low-wage, low-skill service jobs, and possible political pressure to resist tax increases and public spending on education, highways, and other services of less value to elderly residents.

4. As today's active, affluent seniors outlive their assets and age into tomorrow's frail elderly, they will come to demand more public services. These concerns suggest a hypothesis (as yet untested) that the local economic benefits of attracting retirees may tend to concentrate in the early years of these development efforts while the costs are postponed to later years.

5. For communities heavily dependent on transfer payments (Social Security, Medicare, private pensions) for their economic base, changes in federal social welfare policy can be devastating. Although the tremendous popularity of the Social Security system is sure to protect it from major budget raids in the near future, no program is ever entirely safe. Even small changes in COLA (cost-of-living adjustment) formulas would have a disproportionate effect on retirement communities.

6. Demographic analysis shows that the potential pool of affluent, mobile retirees is not as large as commonly thought, at least for the next several

decades. Thus, as the competition for retirees heats up, some developments are likely to fail. Local officials must be careful not to overextend
tax breaks, infrastructure subsidies, and other publicly financed incentives to marginal, high-risk retirement projects.

7. Even more than in other sectoral economic development strategies, long-
range planning is a critical component of retirement-based strategies.
Researchers can help here by creating models for calculating the costs
and benefits of elderly in-migration to local areas and developing guidelines to help distinguish among projects with more and less potential for
success.

8. Alongside efforts to attract the affluent elderly themselves, communities
must devise ways of capturing retirees' dollars within the local economy.
This means expanding opportunities for consumer spending on goods
and services as well as creating attractive investment opportunities.

9. Local economic development officials must beware of the tendency to
forget "the other" rural elderly population in the rush to create a new retirement mecca. Many rural areas have high concentrations of long-time
residents over age 65 whose interests may conflict directly with those of
the newer, more active elderly migrants. Many current residents are poor,
in poor health, and in need of a wide range of public services. Rural planning must focus renewed attention on improving the quality of life for
those individuals who, by choice or necessity, are "aging in place."

The Context: National Trends

The recent flood of interest in retirees and their incomes is based, in part, on
the perception of old people as a growth industry. The basic theme is well-
known by now, thanks to scores of articles and television reports about "the
graying of America" and the "geezer boom." Unfortunately, the flood of pub-
licity has perpetuated certain misconceptions about this phenomenon.

Timing of the Boom

The first misconception is that the aging explosion is already under way. The
facts, however, indicate that the growth in the elderly population will slow
down before it explodes. Two phenomena are at work here: changes in life expectancy and the effects of earlier fertility trends on the relative sizes of today's
birth cohorts—groups of individuals born during particular periods. The
most famous cohort is the baby boom, which includes all Americans born between 1946 and 1964.

Thanks to a steady increase in life expectancy, combined with long-term declines in fertility, the ranks of the elderly relative to the nonelderly have expanded steadily throughout this century. In 1900, 4.1 percent of the U.S. population was 65 years or older; by 1980, that figure rose to 11.3 percent. The gradual upward trend will continue during the 1990s.

At the same time, however, the birth cohort now approaching retirement age is small relative to the cohorts immediately preceding and following it— an unusual phenomenon, according to demographers. Those Americans now in their 60s were born during the Great Depression of the 1930s when fertility rates reached a historic low; at each stage in their life cycle, they have brought down the numbers in their age group. The admission of this generation to the over-65 group will actually slow the growth of America's elderly population for the next decade or so.

Following closely on the Great Depression cohort's heels is the famous baby boom cohort comprised of individuals born mostly during the fertile 1950s. These individuals are the source of the anticipated senior boom, which will commence officially around 2010 when the first baby boomers reach age 65.[2] According to current projections, at the peak of this group's influence (in 2030), almost one in every five Americans will be aged 65 or over, compared to one in 10 today.[3] The population of elderly (65 and over) will grow from about 25 million currently to possibly 59 million by 2030. Clearly, retirees will be a massive growth industry in this country, but not for another 15 years.

Migration

The second misconception follows from the rapid growth in recent decades of well-known retirement locations. This has led many people to think that the elderly are a particularly mobile group of Americans. Here again, the evidence suggests otherwise. Research shows that of all age groups, senior citizens are actually the least likely to move. Between 1975 and 1980, less than 5 percent of Americans over age 60 moved out of state, compared with 10 percent of the general population.[4] Between 1986 and 1987, less than 1 percent of the elderly (over 65) population moved out of state, compared to 3.1 percent of the nonelderly.[5]

Elderly migration rates have increased steadily in recent decades, however. The flow of 60-and-over migrants into the Sunbelt states of the South and Southwest, for example, doubled in the 20 years between 1960 and 1980.[6] Why the increasing mobility among older people? Possible answers include the weakening of family connections that link people to a home base, fewer Americans involved in agriculture and tied to farms, and portable financial resources such as Social Security and pension income that make moving possible.[7]

Americans who relocate after age 65 divide roughly into two groups: (1) "assistance seekers"—older old people (over 75) who need care and support either from a nursing home or other institution or from family members in another location; and (2) "amenity seekers"—younger, relatively affluent retirees who long for a milder climate, recreational opportunities, and other quality-of-life enhancements. Major life changes may trigger a move, such as retirement in the case of amenity seekers or the death of a spouse.[8]

The general trend for elderly migrants is from urban to rural areas. Between 1960 and 1980, the concentration of older Americans shifted from the Northeast and North Central regions to the South and West. Fully half of all retirees who move go to Florida, Texas, or Arkansas.[9] Retirees who migrate for part of each year, dubbed "snowbirds" and "sunbirds," favor Florida, Arizona, California, and Texas.[10] These states contain many of the counties identified by analysts as SARAs (specialized amenity retirement areas). Currently, 94 counties in 17 states qualify as SARAs.

Nonetheless, elderly migration flows in both directions. Data from 1975 to 1980 show an increasing trend toward "counterstream" migration in which elderly individuals return to their state of birth. Rates of return were higher in the mid-Atlantic, western Midwest, and eastern, noncoastal South. Those who return to their native areas are more likely to fall into the category of assistance seekers who move in order to be closer to their children, grandchildren, or other family caregivers.[11]

As Biggar has warned, these opposing currents of migration will have radically different effects on different regions and states around the country. In general, between 1975 and 1980, the Sunbelt gained large numbers of younger, wealthier, more independent elderly (many married couples) and lost older, poorer, more dependent, single elderly individuals to counterstream migration.[12] The Northeast, on the other hand, lost many of the elderly who contribute most to the economy and gained elderly populations that will place heavy burdens on health care, social services, and other public resources. Within the Sunbelt, Arizona and Florida attracted the most affluent of the older migrants while California and Texas attracted a far more dependent group.

Available research paints a clear picture of who among the elderly migrate and where they go. Why they decide to move in the first place and how they choose their destinations are more difficult questions. Elderly individuals who change their year-round residence give several common reasons for relocating (in order of priority): to be closer to relatives and friends; because they retired; for a more desirable climate. Seasonal migrants, on the other hand, reveal a slightly different mix of motivations (in order of priority): climate; visiting friends and relatives; recreation; cost of living; health-related reasons.[13] Some evidence indicates that those who move permanently tend to choose new communities that are familiar to them in some way; perhaps they owned a second home there or visited prior to retirement.[14]

Rich and Poor

A third category of misconceptions flows from dual stereotypes of the rich— the retired golfer and the dirt-poor, older widow. Although the problem of poverty among the elderly continues to demand attention, individuals over 65 actually have the lowest poverty rate of any age group in the United States. The steep drop in poverty rates among the elderly, from 30 percent in the 1960s to less than 13 percent in the second half of the 1980s, is widely considered to be the greatest and most abiding success of this nation's social welfare system, attributable largely to massive income transfers via the Social Security system.

Still, the average elderly resident is far from wealthy. According to calculations by Hoppe, almost 60 percent of all elderly individuals nationwide could be considered "comfortably retired" with annual incomes twice the poverty level (almost $15,000 for a two-person household) or more, while only 20 percent fit the highest income category, with incomes four or more times the poverty level.[15] Among the elderly, those more recently retired individuals between the ages of 65 and 75 (known as seniors) tend to enjoy higher incomes than those 75 and older (known as the aged). Nationally, the 9.0 percent poverty rate for seniors in 1983–84 was far below the 14.8 percent rate for the aged.[16]

The Golden Goose

The appeal of transfer payments as a local development strategy is based on both the size of the income transfer pot and its stability. The federal government spends more money on retirement-related transfer payments than on any other single activity, including defense.[17] Three-quarters of all income transfers in 1988 were retirement related, accounting for 11.3 percent of national personal income.[18] These dollars function both as transfers of income to individuals and as infusions of spending power into communities across the country. In terms of size, there is more than enough to go around.

The question of stability is less clear. In relation to the business cycle, transfer payments are highly stable. Unlike income from manufacturing, construction, and even certain types of services that ebb and flow with the overall performance of the economy, transfer payments remain level during periods of recession, recovery, and growth. Since the adoption of indexing, Social Security payments have even enjoyed insulation against inflation.

In relation to the policy cycle, however, transfer payments may be vulnerable to shifting political forces. On the one hand, Social Security is one of the most politically popular and fiercely protected government programs of all time. Even in the face of historically high budget deficits in the early and mid 1980s, members of Congress resisted the temptation to cut Social Security COLAs.

On the other hand, many economists and budget experts have raised serious concerns about the future solvency of this program. Today's surpluses in the Social Security Trust Fund are being used to offset deficits in the general fund and may not be available when the senior boom hits in the next century. While action to ensure the long-term solvency and affordability of social security will not occur in the near future, the strategy eventually selected will have important implications for local communities betting their economic future on retiree income.

Although the subject of less public attention, the current status of private pension funds should also be of interest to retirement community leaders. These funds have begun to feel pressure as worker-to-beneficiary ratios fall, prompting talk of a possible, large-scale federal pension bail-out sometime in the future.

Even assuming that the basic social insurance programs can be placed on solid footing, other areas of need are likely to increase demands for public spending targeted to the elderly. Long-term care is one such area. According to a study from the Urban Institute, the number of individuals over 65 who need help with basic functions such as dressing, eating, and bathing will more than double over the next 50 years, from 6 million today to 13.8 million by 2030.[19] The growth in nursing home beds is unlikely to keep up with the growing needs, leading to serious shortages down the road. But even if home-care providers and nursing homes can expand enough to meet all the needs, no one knows who will be able to pay the bills for these services. A year in a nursing home costs on average $23,000, and full-time home care can be even more expensive. Currently, Medicare does not cover either function except in rare cases, while few private insurance policies are available to fill in the gap. The burden falls largely on Medicaid for the elderly poor as well as for those previously independent individuals who are forced by overwhelming medical expenses to spend their assets down below the poverty line. While retirement communities may count on many older Americans choosing to move "back home" when these needs arise, surely some individuals will stay and demand services.

Uncertainty

Finally, despite efforts by analysts across the country to predict the effects of "the graying of America" on everything from the economy to the family, no one can say with certainty what life in a "gray" society will be like. At each stage of its life cycle, the baby boom generation has brought surprising patterns of behavior, from the political activism of the 1960s to the rise of yuppy lifestyles in the 1980s. Who can say how they will revolutionize old age? For example:

- Will baby boomers postpone retirement when the time comes? Labor shortages in certain regions of the country are already leading companies to encourage retirees to reenter the work force. In 2030, when the ratio of Social Security taxpayers (workers) to beneficiaries (retirees) drops to 2:1 (from 3:1 in 1990), the economic pressures for late retirement will be even greater.

- Once they do retire, will baby boomers be as mobile as their parents were? Economic pressures may slow the stream of elderly migrants to retirement locations in the Sunbelt and elsewhere. Or preferences may simply change. A generation of people who moved so often during their younger years may prefer to settle down as they get older.

- Assuming no dramatic change in fertility rates, the balance of political power will make a decided shift toward older Americans in the twenty-first century. What will such changes mean for public programs for the elderly? Will resources be shifted from services for younger people toward services for the elderly? Will new dollars be directed to increased cash payments or to new health-related programs such as long-term care insurance? Who will shoulder the burden for services targeting the elderly—the federal government or states and localities? Changes in social welfare funding patterns could have enormous implications for local retirement communities that rely heavily on a "mailbox economy."

The Rural Picture

Throughout much of the period after World War II, the 1960s most notably, rural areas suffered a "youth drain" as men and women between the ages of 20 and 34 sought their fortunes in the fast-growing urban job markets. When they left their home communities, they took with them important job skills, potential tax revenues, and a significant chunk of the local labor pool. As the less mobile residents of these communities soon learned, economic growth is hard to achieve with a population disproportionately represented by non-working dependents—in this case, the elderly. Compared to their counterparts in urban locations and in growing rural communities, the elderly in these areas are more likely to be poor or near-poor and chronically ill.

During the "Rural Renaissance" of the 1970s, the population of rural areas as a whole grew for the first time in half a century. The net out-migration of young adults slowed while older Americans at or near retirement age increased their rate of flow into many rural communities. This group of newcomers projected a profile distinctly different from that of the majority of their elderly neighbors who were long-time residents. The new arrivals were healthier, more affluent, and better educated. They brought with them valuable economic assets: Social Security checks, private pension payments, accumulated bank savings, capital gains from sales of their houses, and other forms of income. While it is still too early to determine the long-term net effect of in-migrating retirees on rural America, their contribution to short-term growth in the host communities is without question.

Profiling the Rural Elderly

Thanks to the efforts of John A. Krout and other social scientists and demographers, a rich body of material now exists describing the general elderly population in rural areas.[20]

While most Americans over 65 live in or near cities, rural areas are home to more than their share of this age cohort. In 1980, 13 percent of the rural population was elderly, compared to 10.7 percent of the urban population. Compared to urban areas, rural areas have experienced more rapid growth in the relative size of their elderly populations over the past four decades. Some of the growth is attributable to outflow of younger people (agricultural areas, for example) and some to inflow (retirement areas). The smaller the community, the more likely it is to have a high concentration of elderly. Proportionately more rural elderly live in small towns, fewer in the suburbs.

Concentrations of rural elderly vary significantly from state to state and region to region. The South houses the largest number of rural elderly of any region (43 percent of the total) followed by the North Central region.

Rural elderly are more likely to be white, female, married, and employed than are their urban counterparts. Although the economic status of the rural elderly has improved since the 1960s, they still suffer higher rates of poverty than the urban elderly as well as more chronic health problems. Most at risk of poverty are older rural residents who are female, members of minorities, not married, unemployed, living alone, and totally dependent on Social Security.[21]

These objective measures seem to reveal a lower standard of living for those elderly individuals who find themselves "stuck" in rural areas. However, Krout has raised the question whether factors such as a lower cost of living, services provided by family members and friends, nonmonetary resources such as homegrown food, and higher rates of home ownership may actually bring the standard of living for rural elderly closer in line with urban standards.[22] In addition, the results of various psychological surveys of this population point to possible advantages for the rural elderly in terms of quality of life. These data show greater personal satisfaction and emotional well-being among the rural elderly than among urban dwellers in the same age group.

Needs of the Rural Elderly

According to sociological literature, older rural Americans face a "service gap." Fewer social services are available both in number and scope in rural areas, including health care, mental health care, home care, adult day care, educational and recreational activities, transportation, and housing assistance.[23] What is available tends to be less accessible and of poorer quality. Even where services are available, data show lower rates of utilization by rural elderly.[24]

Although the rural elderly enjoy higher rates of home ownership than the urban elderly, they also suffer more housing problems.[25] Inadequate plumbing was a problem in 5 percent of rural households containing residents 60 years and older in 1980, more than twice the urban rate. Rural elderly living in the South and rural elderly who rent rather than own their homes faced particularly high rates of plumbing deficiencies.

Transportation and communication problems are also more pronounced among the rural elderly, who are twice as likely as older urban dwellers not to have a phone and less likely to have access to public transportation.[26] The greater distances to medical, shopping, and other services in rural areas increase the importance of communication and transportation for older people living in small towns and the countryside.

According to self reporting, chronic health conditions that limit activity plague the rural elderly and middle-aged (particularly those living in the South) at a higher rate than their urban counterparts.[27] Elderly in rural areas visit physicians less frequently but experience more hospital admissions.

Several studies, including hearings before Congress, have explored the special needs of the rural elderly. Here, emphasis has been placed on the high rates of uninsured and underinsured among this population; problems related to lower payments to rural hospitals for Medicare; inadequate information about those services that are available; and an absence of linkages among service providers who deal with the elderly, leading to fragmented care.[28]

The New Rural Elderly

During the 1970s, many older Americans moved to rural areas, creating a net inflow of 275,000 in the latter half of that decade alone.[29] The 1990 census shows continued population growth in areas that attract retirees. Areas of in-migration tended to cluster around retirement and recreation areas in Florida, the Southwest, New England, the South Atlantic Coast, the Ozarks, the Texas hill country, California, Hawaii, and the Pacific Northwest.[30]

The Sunbelt still captures most of the interstate migration of elderly, but some evidence suggests that traditional retirement centers may be losing their appeal for today's retirees, in part because of overconcentrations of elderly. As one sociologist put it in the Washington Post, "When they think Florida, they think of condos full of old people driving around in Cadillacs with white hair."[31] For this reason, more "unconventional communities, ranging from Cape Cod, Massachusetts to rural Georgia, the Upper Great Lakes, and the remote Rocky Mountains" are gaining in popularity among mobile seniors.[32] These early signs suggest possible changes in the geographic patterns of elderly migration. However, these newer patterns still involve mostly rural area.

The characteristics of elderly Americans who migrate differ in important ways from those who age "in place." Calvin Beale and others have noted that the vast majority of older migrants to rural areas are between the ages of 60 and 74—in the category of seniors rather than aged.[33] Those who move from urban to rural areas are more affluent than either nonmigrants or those who move between rural areas. They are more often married couples with previously established connections to their new homes. They tend to settle in the open countryside rather than in small towns.

Performance Indicators

Economic developers have long believed that recently retired migrants bring important sources of economic growth to their new home communities, at least in the short run. Several studies conducted over the past decade confirm this conjecture.

Making Connections, published by the Southern Growth Policies Board,[34] identified three outstanding factors that accounted for increasing employment and income in the rural South in the late 1970s and early 1980s: tourism, retirement communities, and presence of a military base or other large government installation. *A Brighter Future for Rural America?*, published by the National Governors' Association,[35] studied a smaller sample of high-growth counties in the rural Farmbelt. Here again, retirement communities ranked high on the list of industries contributing to local prosperity. Finally, the Federal Reserve Bank of Kansas City completed a report in 1986 that identifies retirees as a critical factor in rural growth. *Rural America in Transition* points out that retirement-based counties were the only rural counties that actually improved their overall income picture relative to urban counties between 1973 and 1984, a period when the overall gap between urban and rural prosperity was expanding.[36]

Retirement-based counties enjoyed the highest levels of population growth of any rural counties for close to two decades (1970 to 1987).[37] However, as recent analysis has pointed out, annual average population growth rates for these counties in the 1980s were not able to match the extraordinary performance of the 1970s. Retirement-based counties grew more slowly during the recessionary period 1980–83 and then more slowly still in the post-recession period. The long-term implications of these trends will depend on whether they represent a lagged response to the economic downturns of the early 1980s, a more enduring structural change in migration patterns, or a shift in preferences of retirees away from rural locations.[38]

Reeder and Glasgow also point out that, while employment in rural retirement counties grew at almost four times the total rural average between 1980 and 1986, the per capita income in these areas made little progress during that period. On average, per capita incomes remained lower in retirement-based counties than rural counties overall. The gap narrowed only slightly during the 1980s, from $360 in 1977 to $320 in 1986. By the close of the 1980s, earnings per job in retirement counties averaged only $17,600 versus $18,400 for all of rural America.

Reeder and Glasgow have also identified differences in performance among the nation's 481 rural retirement counties, roughly one-quarter of all rural counties. Most notably, they found that "mature retirement counties with a relatively high (one-sixth or more) proportion of population that is elderly performed much better economically than retirement counties in general."[39] Compared to retirement counties in general and all rural counties in the 1980s, these mature retirement destinations enjoyed more rapid population and employment growth; they also enjoyed lower unemployment and income growth at a consistent rate fast enough to eventually catch up with urban income levels. The economies of mature retirement counties also proved to be more stable than those of retirement counties in general, suggesting that "some of the benefits of attracting retirees may be realized only over the long run."[40]

Economic Development Strategies

As in the case of tourism, a central question is whether retirees represent an opportunity for real, sustained economic growth in rural areas. A city councilman from Seneca City, South Carolina, a retirement boomtown, told the *Wall Street Journal:* "We ought to be looking at retirement communities as a whole new form of light industry." Is this a wise or foolish strategy?

At this point, the economic advantages to a community of an influx of re-tirees are better understood than the drawbacks. Elderly migrants often bring with them accumulated capital assets that can be put to work in the local economy to help finance business start-ups and expansions and create jobs. Retiree income provides a hedge against the ups and downs of the business cycle, at least within mature retirement communities. Pension checks are extremely stable; setting aside rare corporate bankruptcies and defaults, neither local nor national downturns will affect these payments significantly. Given the overwhelming number of members of Congress committed to protecting Social Security, this source of income is unlikely to shrink, at least in the near future.

Finally, as Glasgow has noted, retirees often bring other valuable, if less tangible resources such as high educational levels, professional skills, and a willingness to volunteer for community activities.[41] Together, these factors help explain at least some of the success of retirement counties over the past several decades.

The studies cited above demonstrate a clear link between retirees and overall growth in employment and population in rural counties in the short run. However, assurance of continuing on this trajectory may be limited by several factors.

First is the potential market. As Hoppe has shown, communities interested in attracting well-to-do older Americans must compete for the attention of more than 5 million individuals nationwide,[42] the vast majority of whom (probably well over 90 percent) will never move out of state. If the mid-1980s trends away from migration to rural retirement destinations continue, this market may shrink even further, increasing the level of competition among localities for this economic development plum.[43] Repeating earlier patterns of behavior, states and counties competing for retirement-based development may end up spending far more on publicly financed incentives for retirement projects than they receive back on their investments.

Second is the long-term economic impact once the wealthy, spry, 65-year-old newcomers enter their declining years and begin to require more services. As Hoppe puts it, "Although most elderly are in good health, both physically and financially, as they age, they can become frail, and they may outlive their assets. They, too, may need help in the future."[44]

It is very difficult to predict the level of demands that today's retirees will place on state and local governments a decade or two in the future. The calculation depends on how many elderly will return to their original locations once they experience the death of a spouse or a serious illness (that is, once they are no longer amenity seekers but have become assistance seekers). The calculation also depends on possible changes in federal policy. Passage of a federal long-term care insurance program, for example, would take the heat off states, some of which have begun to experiment with ways of funding and delivering home and community-based long-term care services.[45] However, the shift of Medicaid costs from the federal to the state governments would have the opposite effect, increasing the heat on states. While Medicare, an exclusively federal program, combined with private health insurance pays for most medical care for the nation's elderly, Medicaid, a joint federal–state program, covers the poor elderly and those who must spend their resources down to the poverty level in order to qualify for nursing home benefits that are not covered by Medicare. More than half of all nursing home bills are now paid by Medicaid, with states picking up about 45 percent of that tab—a significant portion of their overall budgets.[46]

Third is the very long-term outlook for retirement-based communities when the senior boom begins in earnest. While this demographic phenomenon will expand the potential market for retirement communities, it will also put enormous pressure on social services at all levels of government and among private providers. Analysts are predicting stiff competition for public and private resources as health care costs continue to consume larger and larger portions of the nation's GNP and as the bulge in the U.S. population curve enters old age. Forty years from now, communities dependent on retirees for their jobs and income may find themselves wishing for a more lucrative, less burdensome economic base.

At this point, the pluses and minuses seem to balance out roughly in favor of pursuing retirement-led economic development, at least for some communities. In these cases, the near-certain short-term gains outweigh highly uncertain, heavily discounted long-term risks. Beyond this general if tentative conclusion, however, a number of more specific questions need to be addressed.

Which Rural Communities Should Compete?

The literature reviewed for this chapter contained no guidelines for communities considering a plunge into retirement development. Analysts know that locations with scenic and cultural attractions generally have the best chances of attracting retirees. Beyond that vague idea, however, research is needed to determine what other factors translate into comparative advantage in the retirement center market.

In addition, local officials need to know how to go about developing and marketing their communities as potential retirement development sites, as well as what kinds of returns to expect on up-front investments in social services and recreational amenities. One study of nursing home beds and adult day care costs in rural areas concluded that "services tend to follow rather than draw migrants."[47] But the story might be different for golf courses and movie houses. Further study is also needed to learn about the relationships, if any, between tourism-based and retirement-based development.

Planning Models

Once a community has decided it is a strong candidate for retirement development, planning is essential. Virtually all of the literature on rural elderly as an economic development tool includes a note of caution for local officials: This is not a panacea. Communities need to anticipate the long-term costs and monitor closely the income sources of their elderly residents. Unfortunately, no models exist at this time for determining the net costs or benefits to communities that wish to attract retirees. Even a simple workbook to help community leaders make rough estimations of costs and benefits would make an important contribution to the field.

Capturing the "Old Money"

Once the retirees arrive, communities still face the challenge of keeping the newcomers' dollars in the local economy. One article provides useful recommendations for implementing the equivalent of an import substitution strategy in retirement communities.[48] The authors suggest applying standard market analysis techniques to determine what types of goods and services local elderly residents need and want, then encouraging entrepreneurs to provide them. Innovative products for the elderly market include home delivery of a variety of services from grocery shopping to hairdressing, retail shopping via mass communication such as special radio and television programs, and housing developments that combine a variety of services under one roof. In addition, local business owners with a particularly promising product may seek to enlarge their markets to include elderly consumers throughout the region or state, or even nationwide. If successful, these businesses would reach beyond import substitution to bring valuable export dollars home.

Transfers versus Investments

Despite all of the enthusiasm for the "mailbox economy," analysts do not agree entirely on the development power of transfer payments—funds made available from incoming retirees. On the one hand, Dubin and Reid[49] argue that transfer payments are one of the less valuable forms of federal largesse for local communities because they have no long-term impact on development. According to this argument, transfer payments provide little more than a "short-term income boost" to the local economy, possibly creating some immediate jobs but contributing nothing to the community's capacity for sustained growth. These analysts recognize some multiplier effects as the transfer dollars circulate through the local economy but conclude that, in most cases, the multiplier will be no larger than 1.0 to 1.5. Rural areas in particular, they warn, must be careful not to overstate multiplier effects because most rural income quickly "leaks out" of the local economy to purchase goods and services available only in urban areas.

Finer-grained analysis of the transfer payment question yields a somewhat different view. Plotnick and Hoppe, for example, argue that retirement transfers in particular (mostly Social Security benefits and Medicare) can have substantial development effects.[50] The elderly have a greater proclivity than others for "buying local" so long as a basic selection of goods and services is available locally. Thus, more diversified rural areas with large elderly populations and a broader range of products can benefit from higher transfer multipliers. In addition, as mentioned previously, retirement payments are one of the most stable forms of local income possible. Unlike volatile jobs in manufacturing, mining, and even some service industries, Social Security checks do not fluctuate with the business cycle and can cushion the effects of recession on local merchants.

According to traditional economic development theory, transfer payments such as Social Security and pensions are as good as income from exports for expanding employment, possibly even better. One study provides evidence that retirement incomes are "more effective and efficient in creating jobs than traditional industries."[51] In Kentucky, Smith determined that it takes about $40,000 of Social Security income to create one new job, compared with roughly $90,000 in manufacturing payroll or more than $60,000 in agricultural sales.[52] The reason, according to this analysis, is "less leakage." Not only do the rural elderly tend to keep their money in the community by purchasing mostly local goods and services, but also they lose less of their total income to taxes.

Local planners interested in hedging against the multiplier question must seek to tap not only the power of household spending generated by transfer payments but also the capital assets that many retirees hold in the form of personal savings, stock and bond holdings, proceeds from the sale of a home, and the like. With the right opportunities, these assets can be used to expand the local capital base.

Summers and Hirschl recommend creating homegrown capital funds to encourage both new and established community residents to invest locally.[53] "Capital shortages and insufficient capital formation are myths," these authors argue. "The problem is the distribution of capital between geographic areas and sectors of the economy." As an example, they cite the trust fund formed in 1980 by the American Association of Retired Persons (AARP), which accumulated $4.1 billion in just two years from 650,000 of AARP's members around the country. "These investment dollars are siphoned out of local economies," the article points out, and rarely returned in the form of new loans, except at higher borrowing rates. Efforts by local bankers and economic developers to form competitive local capital funds can help stem the flow of investments out of the community and direct those dollars toward productive enterprises closer to home. The authors also call attention to a growing interest on the part of pension fund managers in small-scale community economic development projects. The enormous wealth accumulated in pension funds represents an exciting opportunity for rural development programs in need of capital.

Social Services

Although policy analysts are just beginning to catch up with this new wave in economic development strategy—wooing retirees—policy recommendations oriented toward the less advantaged rural elderly have been available for many years. Many recommendations focus on the need to improve services for older Americans living in rural areas.

One innovative recommendation calls for greater efforts to reward and sustain family caregivers who devote time and energy to looking after their elderly relatives. Particularly in rural areas, these valuable individuals shoulder much of the burden that would normally fall on social service agencies. Through support groups, provision of respite care, training, and financial incentives for caregivers who are unpaid, policy makers can help keep this informal network of elder care in business.[54]

Other ideas include (1) raising the quality of services provided by rural Area Agencies on Aging (local offices established by the Older Americans Act) through establishment of minimum standards and increased funding; (2) bringing neighboring communities together to pool services and coordinate programs; and (3) developing continuing education programs for seniors.

The Center on Rural Elderly, established by the University of Missouri-Kansas City in 1987, has collected and reviewed information on hundreds of programs related to issues of caregiving, health promotion, and intergenerational relations in rural areas. Likewise, the Washington, D.C.-based National Center on Rural Aging, a subsidiary of the National Council on the Aging, Inc., seeks to bring together rural service providers, educators, researchers, advocates, volunteers, and policy makers to share strategies for addressing the special needs of the elderly living in rural areas.

Quality of Development

Many of the concerns raised about the effects of tourism development on local people and communities apply as well to retirement-based development. While the short-term, gross economic indicators make retirees look like an attractive economic base, the hidden economic, social, and cultural costs of this strategy have yet to be thoroughly examined. What kinds of changes do retirees bring to a rural community? Preliminary evidence suggests three possible qualitative effects that give cause for concern.

Jobs and Equity

First, as with all segments of the service sector, questions arise about the quality of retirement-related employment. Many of the positions associated with a retirement-based economy (waitresses, groundskeepers, housekeepers, bus and van drivers, retail clerks, home aides, and recreation facility attendants, to name a few) may be menial and low-paying, offering few benefits and little job security. If so, proliferation of such jobs could perpetuate and even enlarge the economic and social gulf that separates the community's disadvantaged residents from the more affluent. (For more information on the quality of jobs, see Chapters 7 and 8.)

As far as we know, researchers have made few efforts to examine employment patterns in retirement-based economies. A recent study by Reeder and Glasgow found a somewhat more pronounced shift toward service-based employment in retirement counties than in rural counties in general.[55] By the end of their study period (1986), 65 percent of workers in retirement counties held service sector jobs, compared to 62 percent in all rural counties. This shift toward labor-intensive services may help explain why retirement counties enjoyed such rapid employment growth during the 1980s but only very modest income growth.

In addition, Hirschl has identified different factors that might cause local wages to decrease or increase as a result of growth in the retiree population.[56] Two factors would cause local wages to decline: (1) increased demand from retirees for the goods and services of low-wage industries, such as retail trade; and (2) an increased level of volunteerism, which might depress the demand for paid labor in public sector service jobs and other areas of the economy. Two different factors would cause local wages to rise: (1) increased demand from retirees for the goods and services of high-wage industries, such as health care; and (2) increased overall labor demand (due to increased total consumption of local goods and services), which might cause labor shortages and, as a result, rising wage rates across industries. Hirschl's statistical analysis of the effects of retiree income on local wage rates produces varying results in different time periods and contributes little to our understanding of the relationship. Clearly, further work is needed to understand the employment dynamics of retirement-based economies.

New versus Old Elderly

The effects of retirement-based development on current elderly residents of a community are particularly difficult to predict. On the one hand, by augmenting local resources and generating more interest on the part of local officials in the population over 65, retirement development might produce a kind of trickle-down effect for those residents who are "aging in place." The overall quality of local social services such as health care might improve, and along with it, the quality of life of the more vulnerable elderly.

On the other hand, assuming somewhat different needs and interests between the two groups, influxes of retirees might generate a competition for resources between the new, younger, better educated, more affluent elderly and the older, needier resident elderly. If the drain on resources to meet the demands of new retirees is great enough, long-time older residents may actually see their standard of living decline. And if, at the same time, accelerated development increases local property values, property taxes, and other cost-of-living factors, the long-time elderly may ultimately be pushed out of the community—turned into assistance-seeking migrants involuntarily.

This second scenario violates even the minimum moral condition for acceptable development: The absolute well-being of the worst-off members of the community cannot be allowed to decrease (see Chapter 2 for a discussion of the "no-harm" principle). In addition, it violates the goals of protecting social continuity and treating all community members with respect. Even under a less extreme scenario where development benefits everyone at least on a small scale, the relative differences in standard of living between the affluent elderly and poor or near-poor elderly might grow more stark. Communities must decide for themselves, consciously and deliberately, whether they are willing to accept retirement-based growth on those terms.

Depending on how political power is distributed and used and how local officials respond to the needs of various populations, retirement-led development may take different forms and produce different effects. Through collective action by both government and the voluntary sector, including efforts to broaden the base of civic participation, community leaders and residents can push for more equitable distribution of the benefits of local retirement growth. Tax policies, provision of social services for the disadvantaged, education and training for low-skilled workers, and demands on retirement industry employers for better working conditions are some of the means available for compensating the people left behind by this approach to development.

Schools, Infrastructure, and Political Culture

Other questions have arisen about the impact of elderly in-migrants on the social, political, and cultural life of rural communities. To what extent do these newcomers get involved in community issues? Do they turn out to vote? Do they volunteer? What effect do they have on local allocation decisions?

While the information base for addressing these questions is limited, anec-
dotes are plentiful. For example, one retirement village in Southbury,
Connecticut made a name for itself locally when the residents mobilized solid
blocs of elderly voters to defeat proposed tax increases for the schools four
times in a row.[57] Is this experience typical?

Reeder and Glasgow found some evidence to support the hypothesis that
elderly in-migrants "influence their local governments to restrain expenditures on education."[58] Their data show that retirement counties spent 6 percent less per pupil than rural counties in general in 1982. Retirement counties in the South, where education spending levels tend to be lower, spent 8
percent less per capita on schools than all rural counties in the South.[59]
Mature retirement counties spent even less on education.

According to Reeder and Glasgow, roads, highways, and public health services also received lower levels of local funding in retirement counties than in
other rural counties. Infrastructure spending was 28 percent lower for retirement counties than all rural counties (18 percent lower in the South). The
spending gap between retirement and all rural counties for public health was
11 percent.

Why do rural elderly oppose these services? On the subject of education,
Reeder and Glasgow note:

> The elderly do not benefit directly from most forms of public edu-
> cation, and many retirees have no family in the area who would
> benefit directly from local education expenditures. The elderly also
> tend to be property owners and property taxpayers, and they may
> bear a disproportionate share of local taxes. Many retirees have rel-
> atively fixed incomes, and higher taxes would mean lower living
> standards. If they were to act in their own interest, they would tend
> to be less supportive of public spending on education than the gen-
> eral public.[60]

Similar arguments might be applied to public taxation for roads and highways—long-term investment projects from which older people may not expect to benefit, particularly if they do not drive. The finding of lower
spending on public health is more surprising until one considers the fact that
most retirees depend entirely on nonlocal sources (Medicare/Medicaid and
private health insurance) to cover medical costs.[61]

As the authors of this study point out, "One advantage of spending less on
local government services is that such places will have lower tax rates, a plus
for some businesses and individuals seeking lower costs."[62] Retirement counties, particularly mature retirement counties, did tax at a lower rate than other

rural counties in 1982—3.1 percent compared to 3.7 percent for all rural counties.

These findings may be cause for some alarm. To the extent that public investments in education and infrastructure fuel future economic growth, retirement communities that skimp in these areasx may see their development options narrowing down the road. On the other hand, the low tax rates in these counties leave room for significant revenue increases in the future. Such revenue may be needed to pay for public transportation, Meals on Wheels, increased police and fire protection, adult day care, at-home care, nursing home care, and other services demanded by a more vulnerable aging population.

10

High Technology

Introduction

The economist's classical production function states that economic growth or GNP is the result of the interaction of land (including all raw materials), labor, and capital. This function has come under increasing scrutiny over the past 50 years. In particular, economists such as Robert Solow have added another factor of importance to the equation (of greatest importance, according to Solow): technical knowledge. If Peter Drucker is correct and raw materials have become an increasingly marginal concern for those interested in economic growth (see Chapters 2 and 5), then "information" in all its many forms is the factor that has taken their place.

According to more recent formulations of this idea, which can be found in dozens of "agendas" for U.S. competitiveness, future success in the world marketplace will depend on the ability of nations , industries, and regions to innovate—that is, to mobilize their intellectual resources. They will have to develop, apply, and diffuse new technologies and manipulate vast quantities of information about market conditions, consumer tastes, prices, and the like.

Where does rural America fit into this prescription? While many issues remain unresolved, recent research has clarified at least part of the answer to this question.

1. High-tech industries have performed remarkably well for several decades, with growth rates among the highest of any industry group.

2. That growth has occurred on top of a relatively small employment base, however, creating misleading impressions of the absolute number of jobs that high-tech industries can generate. The high-tech sector simply is not large enough to make up for losses in the very large but declining sectors such as traditional manufacturing and natural resources.

3. Most high-tech operations locate in urban areas. Rural high-tech enterprises are concentrated in the more mature, less sophisticated (and unfortunately, slower growing) parts of these industries such as

chemicals and machinery. The star high-tech performers nationally (computers and communications systems) are rarely found outside metropolitan areas. Likewise, defense-related high tech has a history of shunning rural locations.

4. High-tech operations with higher levels of research and development (R&D) tend to be the most attractive targets for development. They offer better jobs and generate larger economic multipliers than other types of facilities.

5. High-tech firms have strong agglomeration tendencies. A handful of rural counties have been identified where agglomeration appears to have begun. Local communities should be on the lookout for early signs that certain types of firms are favoring their areas and provide whatever supports are needed to encourage these firms.

6. Given the relatively small number of overall new jobs generated by high tech and the location preferences of these firms, most rural communities cannot hope to participate in this phenomenon on any significant scale. Rural areas adjacent to cities probably have a comparative advantage, although this has not been proven.

7. Rural areas should not assume that R&D-intensive, high-tech firms will eventually mature and decentralize, following the same path as traditional manufacturing in the 1970s. However, a strategy based on attracting industries undergoing decentralization may work for those rural communities willing to settle for firms in the less glamorous parts of the high-tech sector.

8. In areas with emerging high-tech agglomerations or other good reasons for joining the race for high tech, experience suggests that government can play a limited role in spurring this type of development. The latest wave of state economic development strategies has emphasized the kinds of principles that will be most useful in encouraging high tech: focusing on business retention and expansion rather than recruitment; eliminating barriers to private initiative rather than substituting for it; leveraging resources (states as wholesalers rather than direct goods and service providers); actively involving business, labor, and the university community in all planning efforts; winning support for these efforts at the highest levels of public leadership, including the governor.

9. States have already invested large amounts of public money in the pursuit of high tech, but evaluations of those programs have not revealed the extent to which rural areas have benefitted. Future research should examine

the geographical distribution of both money and technical assistance within states.

10. Although American businesses have made massive investments in applied technology over the past 10–15 years, they lag behind their counterparts in other industrialized nations. It is not clear whether or to what extent rural firms may suffer an even greater deficit in high-tech inputs.

11. States and the federal government are beginning to invest in strategies for technology diffusion. However, far more research is needed to better understand the process by which advances in technology are spread within and across industries. Based on the results of this research, states will want to reevaluate their current practices.

Definitions

Of all the sectors and activities discussed in Part II, high tech may be the most difficult to define. Analysts have not yet reached agreement on what makes a particular product, business activity, company, or industry part of the high-tech sector. Even if and when they do, the definition probably will not stand up for long under the pressure of relentless change in product descriptions and industrial structure. Two main obstacles stand in the way of consensus on definitions.

First, analysts do not agree on the distinguishing characteristics of a high-tech company. Suggested criteria include a high growth rate, a high value-added product, geographically large markets, and continuing innovation.[1] However, some of these characteristics, such as the propensity to innovate, are very hard to quantify, while others, such as high growth rate, are a moving target. Will the computer industry cease being a high-tech industry if its growth rate slows?

Second, analysts must function within the constraints of available data. Most studies construct their "high-tech sectors" from industries listed under Standard Industrial Classification (SIC) codes, a limited system that can assign only one classification to even the largest, most diversified companies. As a result, each category even at the four-digit level includes a hodge-podge of different kinds of products, processes, and companies.

Malecki, however, argues that the "most meaningful" definition of the high-tech sector must distinguish between different types of activities and product lines within a corporation.[2] He is most interested in capturing non-routine, innovative activities such as R&D, prototype production, and small-batch manufacturing of highly sophisticated products such as cruise missiles or diagnostic machines. Standardized, mass production that can be easily shipped offshore to low-wage countries should not qualify as high tech, according to Malecki, although many current definitions of the sector include such routine functions as semiconductor manufacturing and computer assembly. Other researchers may agree with Malecki's critique, but unfortunately his definition of high tech does not fit existing data sources.

Given these methodological problems, the most common definitions of the high-tech sector in recent years have focused on the peculiar features of labor and/or investment input in high-tech industries. Glasmeier, OTA, and Armington, to name a few, focus on industries with a higher than average concentration of technical and professional workers such as scientists, engineers, and mathematicians.[3] Malecki, Armington, and others look for industries with high proportions of overall spending dedicated to R&D.[4] Some studies consider only high-tech manufacturing,[5] while others include certain services such as computer programming, data processing, and research and testing labs.[6]

Ultimately, the question of how to define the high-tech sector relates to the more fundamental question of how to stimulate technological change in the economy. Most definitions of high-tech currently in use imply that technology is embodied in people—the industry's human capital mix—who, given adequate investment in R&D-related activities, push out the frontiers of knowledge. Does this particular conception of the high-tech sector then lead to the conclusion that higher proportions of technical and professional workers, generously funded, will stimulate stronger economic growth through more rapid technological change? Different economists would give different answers, but the question serves to illustrate the intimate relationship between definitions and results.

High tech is not just a sector unto itself, however; it is also a key source of inputs for virtually all other sectors. These inputs—pieces of equipment, most of them computerized, along with the software that makes them run and the networks that link them—are known as process technology or advanced manufacturing technology (AMT).[7] Robots and computer numerically controlled machines; computer-aided drafting, design, engineering, and manufacturing systems; automated materials handling systems; flexible manufacturing cells; and even computers for accounting, invoicing, and inventory are among the best known examples of process technology.[8]

While the distinction between product and process technologies seems plain at first, viewed on a macro level, the line between the two becomes far less distinct. For example, a spray-painting robot on an auto assembly line clearly qualifies as process technology. The robot manufacturer, however, views robotics as a product technology. As U.S. manufacturers increasingly must turn to foreign firms to find state-of-the-art process innovations, such as robots or computer numerically controlled machine tools from Japan, the link between new product technology and applied technology in the United States becomes even more vital.

The Context: National and International Trends

The reason for all the local, national, and international fuss about high technology is simply growth. While traditional manufacturing has been losing employment worldwide, sectors that appear capable of adding new jobs have been attracting lavish attention.

Producing Technology

The cluster of industries generally characterized as high-tech producers has expanded at a startling pace over the last two decades, adding jobs and building new facilities even during the deep recessions of the early 1980s. Because estimates of growth rates for high tech depend on one's definition of the sector, they vary widely. But virtually all estimates point to an impressive performance. Focusing exclusively on high-tech manufacturing, Glasmeier found growth of 28 percent in jobs between 1972 and 1982, compared to job growth of 21 percent across all sectors.[9] During the period, high tech became a more significant piece of the nation's manufacturing base, according to the same study, expanding its share of total manufacturing jobs from 24 to 29 percent. Using a broader definition that includes some service industries, Armington found growth in high-tech jobs of 20 percent between 1976 and 1980, compared to 15 percent for all private industry.[10]

Despite these figures, however, high tech falls short of being the answer to America's economic prayers on three grounds. First, the boom did not last. Between 1982 and 1987, national employment in high-tech industries actually declined by 3 percent as a result of overcapacity, supply gluts, foreign competition, and automation.[11]

Second, the high growth rates of the 1970s and early 1980s ultimately did not add up to very many new jobs because the sector simply does not employ enough people to make a significant impact on overall national employment figures. Even fabulously high rates of growth applied to a relatively small base yield only marginal gains.

The size of the high-tech base depends, again, on the industry definition being used. But by any definition, the number of jobs is not enormous. Armington counted 6.7 million workers in high-tech manufacturing and services in 1980, which represents less than 6.5 percent of total jobs.[12] Glasmeier counted 5.6 million in high-tech manufacturing in 1982, which accounted for less than 5.5 percent of total jobs.[13] Malecki says that, using the Department of Labor definition of high tech (based on proportion of engineers and scientists), the sector's share of national employment is unlikely to exceed 10 percent.[14] According to one estimate, only 3 percent of all new jobs created since 1970 came from high-tech industries.[15]

Third, the high-tech boom did not touch every industry under the high-tech umbrella. Armington, Harris, and Odle have shown that small high-tech firms grew much faster than larger firms between 1976 and 1980.[16] Even more important from a rural perspective, Glasmeier has shown that within certain high-tech industry groupings, dramatic growth was the exception rather than the rule.[17] While categories such as computers and electronic components more than doubled employment between 1972 and 1982, large portions of the chemicals and machinery industries actually lost jobs.[18] In fact, well over half of the 94 high-tech industries considered in Glasmeier's study grew at less than the average national job growth rate during the period, and a full one-third of them sustained absolute employment losses.[19]

Applying Technology

High technology also has attracted attention on the input side, as a potential solution to the problem of declining American competitiveness and a remedy for the productivity slowdown. Although measuring the deployment of process technology is an even more dubious undertaking than counting high-tech jobs and firms, some information is available about technology application and its effectiveness.

We know that huge gains in automation of factories and offices have been achieved over the last 10 years. Between 1983 and 1989, increased spending on computers and office equipment accounted for virtually all of the growth in U.S. capital investment.[20] As a result, "Most white-collar workers now have computers on their desks."[21] But we do not know how much more is yet to come.

On the one hand, it may appear that "the most obvious savings and productivity improvements [from computer-related technologies] for the most part already have occurred." On the other hand, plenty of evidence exists to show that the process of fulfilling business demand for computer-related technology is far from complete. In the banking industry, for example, Automated Teller Machines (ATMs) and electronic fund transfers have improved productivity. Direct-debit machines have become commonplace at supermarkets and gas stations. Still, huge additional capital investments will be needed to hook up all retail establishments.

In the case of manufacturing, firms have a long way to go before exhausting the potential of even yesterday's technological advances. For example, computer-controlled machine tools, often seen as a symbol of modernization in manufacturing, have been around since midcentury but have penetrated only about half of all metal-working plants in the United States and account for only 11 percent of all machine tools in operation today.[22] Adoption rates for other key process technologies were even lower. Computer-aided design was used in less than a third of the roughly 4000 manufacturing plants surveyed by Rees, Briggs, and Oakey.[23] Computer-aided manufacturing was somewhat more widespread with a user rate of almost 45 percent. Computerized materials handling systems were rare, showing up in less than 10 percent of the firms responding. Of the six machinery industries considered in the survey, aircraft—the one with the highest urban concentration—proved to be the most sophisticated in terms of advanced process technology. Farm machinery, on average, had the lowest adoption rate.

America's foreign competitors have embraced automation much more quickly and enthusiastically. According to Rosenfeld et al., manufacturing industries in Germany, Japan, Belgium, and Sweden have higher ratios of automated machines to workers than their counterpart industries in the United States.[24] Japan, the world's biggest user of robots, has three times as many robot installations as the United States, despite having only half the U.S. population.[25] Manufacturing affiliates of foreign companies operating in the United States outspend their domestic counterparts on plant and equipment by almost 50 percent.[26]

The Rural Picture

Analysis of rural America's high-tech economy is frustrated by generally out-of-date figures. Nonetheless, the existing research paints a useful picture.

Location, Location, Location

Description of the rural high-tech sector must begin with the fact that high-tech industry is overwhelmingly not rural. In 1982, 90 percent of all high-tech jobs were in urban areas, with particular concentrations in major cities of over one million population.[27] In more recent years, high-tech momentum has shifted somewhat toward slightly smaller cities of between 200,000 and one million population. Rural areas have picked up a few high-tech jobs, but the shift has not been dramatic.

Those high-tech manufacturers that do locate in rural areas tend to favor counties adjacent to major metropolitan areas, but the differential is not particularly striking. In 1982, adjacent rural counties were home to 51 percent of the nation's total rural population but boasted 59 percent of all rural high-tech employment.[28]

Perhaps most important of all, we now know that the preponderance of rural high tech represents only a narrow slice of the national high-tech universe. According to Glasmeier, most rural high-tech industries tend to be slower growing, more mature, and less technically oriented than the sector overall.[29] A striking one-third of the 25 high-tech industries with employment concentrations in rural areas manufacture chemicals. Glasmeier has found that large numbers of rural high-tech industries have strong links to traditional rural industries such as agriculture and forestry. Examples of high-tech products commonly produced in rural areas include organic chemicals used as pesticides and fertilizers; gum and wood chemicals used in the production of wood products; synthetic organic fibers used in textiles; and construction, farm, and mining equipment.

The fastest growing national industries classified as high tech—computers, electronics, communications, and defense-related production—are clearly underrepresented in rural America.[30] In 1982, 22 percent of national high-tech jobs were attributable to the CEC sectors (computers, electronics, and communications) compared to only 9 percent in rural areas. And the trend is downward; rural counties captured a smaller share of all CEC jobs in the United States in 1982 than it did 10 years earlier. While population in rural areas was increasing during the 1970s, the share of high-tech jobs showed little change.

The other jewel in the nation's high-tech crown during the 1970s and 1980s—the rapidly growing defense-dependent sectors (DDS)—also failed to share its wealth with the rural economy.[31] Despite a whopping 50 percent growth rate in rural DDS jobs between 1972 and 1982, by the end of that period rural America still hosted only 7 percent of total U.S. DDS employment compared to its population share of 25 percent. This is a scant one percent gain in share over the 10-year period. The defense high-tech sector plays a smaller role in rural economies than in the national economy,[32] a pattern that is unlikely to change in the near future given the expected path of military spending.

Spillover?

Researchers are still examining the question of whether high tech operates as a seedbed for economy-wide growth. Based on what we know about location patterns for different types of high-tech activity, this question must be answered differently for urban and rural economies. Larger and smaller urban areas with the good fortune to attract high-tech clusters are likely to experience some multiplier effects. Predicting the degree of local spillover is difficult, however, because so many factors enter the equation. Various analysts have identified variables that help explain the process of forming local linkages and generating spinoff enterprises in high-tech manufacturing. These include the type of product produced, levels of R&D spending, plant size, nature of the production process, ownership and organizational structure of the firm.[33] Glasmeier finds that corporate policies and attitudes also play an important role. She writes, "Insufficient attention has been paid to the fact that high-tech industries, and firms within them, shape the type of development that unfolds around them and are not passive agents in the process of high-tech industrialization."[34] A corporation's decisions regarding personnel development, local purchasing, subcontracting, and other aspects of the business can stimulate entrepreneurship and job creation in the local economy or stifle it. Even within budding high-tech complexes, large economic multiplier effects are not guaranteed.

Other evidence indicates that rural high-tech establishments are the least likely to stimulate local economic development. In Smith and Barkley's study, the high-tech plants purchased only one-third of their inputs (other than labor) in the county where they were located, compared to 42 percent of inputs purchased locally by the low-tech plants.[35] Rural areas with high-tech plants will enjoy some spillover development, but probably not enough to turn many communities around.

Technology Applied

Information about the extent of rural deployment of technology is spotty and restricted to the manufacturing sector. Thanks to the Southern Growth Policy Board's (SGPB) survey of southern rural manufacturers, we know that large rural manufacturing plants embarked on major modernization efforts.[36] Three-quarters of the respondents to the SGPB survey (which sampled mostly branch plants with an average of 400 employees) indicated plans for significant new investments in process technology over the following two years.[37] However, the authors of that study report that they had great difficulty locating a large enough sample of "even partially automated rural plants to survey," a fact which suggests that "automation has not yet made major inroads into mass production of discrete goods" in the rural South.[38]

Rees, Briggs, and Oakey also looked briefly at adoption rates of manufacturing technologies by urban and rural locations of plants.[39] Their data suggest that machinery-related firms in the larger Standard Metropolitan Statistical Areas (SMSAs) enjoy the highest levels of technological sophistication, but not by a wide margin. Given their rather inconclusive results, the authors downplay any significant advantage for large urban areas, claiming that "smaller SMSAs and, to a large extent, the more urbanized of the nonmetropolitan counties are also conducive environments for the adoption of these new production technologies."[40]

Economic Development Strategies

We know that high-tech industries, despite stunning growth rates, do not generate large numbers of jobs in the final analysis. We also know that most of the innovative, high-growth high-tech jobs have strong incentives to locate in major urban areas. Finally, we know that competition is fierce among states and localities to build the next Silicon Valley. For some analysts, the combination of these facts leads to the conclusion that rural areas should not waste too much time or too many development resources in the pursuit of high-tech dreams.

Vaughan and Pollard warn that even at the state and regional level, many high-tech development initiatives inevitably will fail.[41] There simply "are not enough marketable ideas, scientists, entrepreneurs, and venture capital to go around."[42] Edward Malecki points to the extremely long time horizon of most high-tech projects.[43] Even plans that succeed will not generate significant changes in economic growth for many years. Silicon Valley, Route 128 in Boston, and North Carolina's Research Triangle all took 20 years or more to develop into recognizable high-tech hubs. The most attractive pieces of the high-tech sector, the innovative, R&D-intensive establishments, are least likely to disperse from their current locations in certain core regions.[44] Therefore, he concludes, "the implications for most regions must be, on balance, pessimistic."[45] Even analysts with generally hopeful predictions for the rural high-tech sector caution rural officials not to put too many eggs in this basket, at the expense of other promising development strategies.[46]

More positive strategies for promoting high-tech establishments in rural areas are linked to different theories about why high-tech industries locate where they do—mostly in urban areas.

Wait and See

The first school of thought views high tech as not so different from other types of manufacturing. Barkley, for example, uses traditional product cycle theory to argue that certain high-tech industries have moved into the mature, standardized phase of the product life cycle and, as a result, are decentralizing to locations where routine production is cheaper.[47] Examples include industries in the chemicals, petroleum, and machinery sectors.[48] He anticipates further benefits for rural areas as the maturation of the high-tech sector continues.

Certain high-tech industries clearly have been decentralizing for some time, both to rural areas within the United States and to cheap-labor countries overseas. Both Barkley and Glasmeier have demonstrated that high-tech industries found in rural America tend to be less innovative, less likely to be operating on the front end of the product cycle, and less likely to show high growth rates.[49] In addition, certain routine high-tech functions such as computer assembly and semiconductor manufacturing have moved to sites in Asia, Latin America, and elsewhere to take advantage of low Third World wage rates.

This perspective on high-tech location points to a strategy of waiting for decentralization, combined with doing whatever is possible to create an attractive climate for these plants once they reach maturity and decide to decentralize. The product cycle theory supports applications of traditional economic development practice to the world of high-tech industry: keeping labor costs low, and providing land-based and tax-based incentives to mobile plants.

However, the decentralization model probably paints a misleading picture of the high-tech sector as a whole. Edward Malecki has argued that the best definition of this sector would not include the types of routine manufacturing activities that are most likely to decentralize or move offshore.[50] These ordinary production and assembly plants do not fit any of the key characteristics of high tech—a high proportion of the work force composed of engineers and scientists, a high proportion of spending devoted to R&D, a fast growth rate, innovativeness—but they show up in most calculations partly because of data limitations.

In addition, with the exception of chemicals, machinery, and a few others, most high-tech industries show no sign of moving into the later stages of the theoretical product cycle. Competitive pressures, in fact, have been shortening the product cycle in many industries. Today's high-tech products appear at shorter intervals and are phased out or overhauled before production ever becomes truly standardized. Under these circumstances, the chances for widescale decentralization of high-tech jobs seem slim.

Invest Strategically

A rival school of thought emphasizes the ways in which the behavior of high-tech firms appears to differ from that of traditional manufacturing firms. Traditional location theory assumes that a firm will locate in the place where it can best maximize profits. This generally translates into the place with the lowest costs—including, most important, costs for labor, land, transportation of inputs and outputs, and utilities.[51] According to this theory, industries like autos, for example, originally located in the Great Lakes region in order to be close to suppliers of steel, glass, and other heavy materials and to minimize the distances between the plants and their markets around the country. Shipping costs were a primary concern.

High-tech producers, however, defy traditional location theory in very basic ways. They tend to locate in areas where the major factors of production—labor and land—are unusually expensive, and markets (and sometimes suppliers) are very far away. High-tech firms seem to demand an entirely different type of business climate than that identified for traditional manufacturing. Analysts generally agree on the main components of the typical high-tech firm's shopping list:[52]

- Access to a large pool of highly skilled workers (availability and quality are more important than prevailing wage rates)

- Proximity to one or more top-notch universities, which can provide both trained personnel and new product and process ideas

- Convenient air travel (transport of managers and customers is more important than transport of materials and goods)

- A quality of life that appeals to professional and technical workers (Analysts disagree on the relative importance here of recreational versus cultural opportunities: Do engineers want national parks or world-class museums?)

Another potentially important factor is the flow of government research dollars. Ann Markusen hypothesizes that defense-related manufacturing, much of which qualifies as high tech, has played a significant role in the development of this country's high growth, high-tech complexes in California, Massachusetts, Florida, Texas, and a few other states. In a study of 266 metropolitan areas around the nation, she finds that "[d]efense spending per capita was the single most important variable explaining high-tech dependence . . . and was also important and significant in explaining variation in high-tech job growth rates across metropolitan areas from 1972 to 1977."[53] The power of the federal government to influence high-tech development should come as no surprise given that, prior to 1976, the federal government purchased more than half of all microprocessors produced in the United States.[54]

Clearly, these location determinants do not fit the conventional interpretation of location theory. Several recent studies, however, have reconfigured the theory to accommodate high tech, with some success. Oakey and Cooper point out that profit maximization does not always depend on cost minimization.[55] In the case of high tech, for example, hiring crack professional and technical staff may require locating in areas where salaries are relatively extravagant. To the extent that these top-quality workers contribute to the development and production of higher value-added goods or services, however, the firm's steeper labor costs can be more than recaptured by charging premium prices for the new and improved products.

Unlike Oakey and Cooper, Satterthwaite sticks with the least-cost version of location theory and sheds light on the ways in which industry clustering may actually reduce certain hidden costs for high-tech firms.[56] These costs, which do not show up in ordinary accounting reports, relate to the critically important and time-consuming activities of recruiting highly skilled personnel and searching for specialized supplies and services. According to Satterthwaite, the development of intra-industry agglomerations in places like Silicon Valley or Boston's Route 128 ensures a large, readily available pool of workers with industry-specific skills and specialized suppliers and contractors, as well as an environment that stimulates invention and innovation. Under these circumstances, each firm's costs of recruiting and searching can fall while their standards rise. The result is higher profits.

This perspective on high-tech location also suggests a strategy of developing the right climate for these firms, but the definition of climate is a new one. While high tech clearly should not be viewed as the answer to the economic developer's prayers, even the pessimists agree that certain well-designed, carefully targeted strategies can help to stimulate high-tech growth. Vaughan, Pollard, and Malecki all concede that while high tech will not benefit every local community, government has a role to play in promoting this sector.

Most state governments clearly feel the same way. In only two years, 1983–85, the number of states operating technology promotion programs grew from 22 to 40.[57] By 1987, more than 250 separate state programs were in place in 45 states, all seeking to win a slice of the coveted high-tech pie.[58] While many of the programs are still too new to evaluate, recent experiences are beginning to point to certain basic principles of success.

First, technology development programs should focus on retaining existing high-tech firms and growing new ones locally, not on recruiting footloose firms from other communities. The problem, as stated by Atkinson, is that "recruitment is a zero-sum activity, where states compete for a fixed level of business (and federal) investment."[59] In addition, we know that most new job growth is the result of expansions of existing plants and brand new start-ups; plant closings and relocations account for only a small share of employment shifts.[60] Therefore, policies that focus on recruitment at the expense of helping local firms expand and helping local entrepreneurs set up new ventures will not be cost effective.

Second, because the private sector will always be the major force in high-tech development, "[t]he most effective role for government is to eliminate barriers that inhibit incentives in the private sector, and to supply those resources and services that the private sector cannot supply efficiently or at all."[61] Researchers simply do not know enough about why particular regions have turned into high-tech hubs or what role government plays in the process. The nation's early high-tech centers in California and Massachusetts were not the result of state or local government plans, although they did rely heavily on federal grants and contracts. States must walk a fine line between allowing the competitive market to operate and intervening where the market needs to be strengthened.

Third, where government does not need to intervene, the proper role is as wholesaler, not retailer.[62] In 1985, states contributed only one percent of all national expenditures on research and development.[63] Clearly, states on their own cannot effect dramatic changes in the distribution of high-tech activities. They can, however, "use public resources and leverage to change private sector behavior—to get banks and other private investors to provide more venture capital, for instance, or to nudge businesses to broaden their research relationships with academia."[64]

Fourth, according to Malecki, "far-sighted industrial recruitment encourages firms to establish mainly R&D facilities rather than manufacturing plants."[65] Not only do R&D labs provide better jobs and create more spin-offs, they also provide a buffer against swings in the business cycle.[66] As noted in Chapter 6, auxiliary facilities are less likely to lose employment during recessions than production facilities. While no form of employment should be turned away, states should favor strategies that target R&D.

Fifth, active support and involvement from business, labor unions, universities, and other affected interests are key to the success of any technology-related effort.[67] These key players must function as long-term, institutional partners (not just consulted on a temporary basis or viewed as obstacles to be overcome) in both the planning and implementation phases of technology policy making. A hands-on role for business in particular activities is also critical. In the case of state-sponsored research and development projects, for example, business involvement is critical to ensure that project results will be commercialized and marketed.[68]

Finally, based on experiences in states such as Michigan and Pennsylvania, "active stewardship" on the part of the state government, particularly the governor and the executive branch, appears to be a key element in getting ideas enacted, funded, and implemented.[69]

The list of state technology programs that spring from these basic principles is long and varied. It includes technology research centers, science parks, applied R&D matching grant programs, industrial extension and modernization services, entrepreneurial assistance and training, business incubators, venture capital funds, and product commercialization assistance, among many others. Clearly, a lot is happening.

But what does all of this assisting, training, granting, loaning, and investing mean for rural areas interested in building a stronger high-tech base? No one seems to know for sure. To date, the literature contains no hard data about what proportion of the half million dollars states spend annually on technology-related programs flows to rural communities. According to the Center for Rural Affairs, many of the public–private development groups, technology centers, and other organizations that serve as conduits for state funds disclose little or no information about the businesses they serve.[70] As state development strategies, including research funds and other technology programs, have become more dynamic, "It is increasingly difficult to determine where the money comes from, where it goes, and how much good it does."[71]

Some anecdotal evidence suggests that rural areas generally find themselves shut out of state technology promotion efforts. In their recent study of economic development policy in six Great Plains states, the Center for Rural Affairs found that the vast majority of state-sponsored venture capital and technology-related investments concentrated on "high-glamour, high risk" enterprises located in those states' largest metropolitan areas.[72]

Given states' dominance in the area of technology promotion programs, any boost to the rural high-tech base is most likely to come from state resources. Two recommendations flow from this fact. First, as part of the ongoing evaluation of the new wave of state development strategies, analysts need to examine the distribution of grants, loans, and other forms of assistance from technology programs to urban, suburban, and rural areas within each state. To the extent that promising rural investment opportunities are going unnoticed and underfunded, policy reforms should be developed and implemented.

Second, the Center for Rural Affairs calls for greater accountability on the part of the quasi-public organizations that carry out state governments' newfound role as "investor, innovator, and technology commercializer."[73] They suggest statutory standards of performance, reporting requirements, and ongoing monitoring to ensure that these programs are serving public goals and making wise use of public resources.[74]

Build on a Base

High-tech firms prefer larger urban areas. They tend to cluster together with other firms in the same industry to form complexes that eventually adopt names like Silicon Valley (the San Francisco Bay area), Silicon Beach (San Diego), Silicon Prairie (Dallas-Fort Worth), Tech Island (Long Island), and Satellite Alley (Montgomery County, Maryland). These complexes then become self-perpetuating as new spinoffs created from the existing firms decide to locate nearby. On the one hand, such a pattern seems to leave little hope for high-tech employment creation in rural areas. On the other hand, we can use this pattern to make clearer distinctions about which rural communities should pursue high-tech development and which should put it toward the bottom of their lists.

Mark Satterthwaite offers a model for making these determinations.[75] He says that local economic development policy must recognize the reality of intra-industry high-tech clustering rather than trying to fight against it. First, local economic development officials should be on the lookout for emerging high-tech industry concentrations within their local areas. Once a particular industry shows early signs of favoring a locale, efforts should be made to help build linkages among the firms, to publicize the trend so that other firms and relevant personnel will be encouraged to locate there, to direct more resources toward local assets of use to the industry (for example, a particular university program or department), and to support the potential agglomeration in whatever ways are effective.

This strategy acknowledges that for most locales, urban or rural, building a high-tech economic base from scratch is a difficult if not impossible task. But it also leaves room for the possibility that effective, carefully targeted development strategies can help a small emerging cluster of firms become a successful seedbed for local economic growth.

In the case of nonroutine functions such as R&D, testing, prototype manufacturing, and central management, urban agglomerations of high tech are likely to thrive well into the future. The need for a continuing supply of quality labor and access to universities, airports, suppliers, and specialty service providers will fuel the growth of existing high-tech complexes and stimulate new ones. This prediction does not mean the death of rural high tech, however. Although Satterthwaite's recommendations were addressed mostly to urban areas, some clustering seems to be underway in the countryside as well as in the big cities. Smith and Barkley found that rural high-tech employment is heavily concentrated in a relatively small number of counties (82), all of which are adjacent to urban areas.[76] Follow-up studies should examine the industry mix in these areas of concentration and evaluate their potential for developing into full-blown high-tech complexes.

Applied Technology

Just as strategies for developing high-tech industries depend on sound theories about why high-tech firms locate where they do, strategies for promoting the diffusion of applied technology depend on a clear understanding of how new technologies spread.

Debates about the spread of technology and innovation take both theoretical and empirical forms. Rees and Stafford have summarized the main theoretical models related to industrial technology and consumer products.[77] The diffusion theory of greatest interest to rural analysts, however, comes from an even larger body of work concerned with the learning curve.

According to Gregory A. Daneke and others, the process of economic development may be viewed fundamentally as a learning process.[78] Just as individual firms improve their efficiency and performance with the more experience they get in their particular area of production (the economist's "learning curve"), so, too, individual regional economies will gradually develop and grow as they build their base of institutional knowledge and technological capacity. Under this evolutionary model of economic development, the growth process requires a long time horizon, a willingness to experiment with new ideas and new forms of organization, a strong capacity to adapt to change, and investments in institutions—for example, building up university research faculties. The slow but steady emergence of innovation centers like Silicon Valley and Route 128 —areas now characterized by a constant cycle of creating, diffusing, and refining new ideas—lends credence to the picture of economic development as a process of learning and adapting.

If the learning theorists are correct, then the process of technology transfer becomes a central ingredient in economic development, at least as important as the invention of new technologies. Satterthwaite points to the example of the chemical industry where "learning has not been kept proprietary within a company, but has diffused throughout the industry. Whenever learning does diffuse among all firms within an industry, it becomes an intra-industry externality. The faster competitors grow and produce, the further all firms' costs fall."[79] Clarke makes a similar point on a general level: "The major benefits of technology development will be experienced when new discoveries are introduced into the existing business sector."[80]

Economic development officials interested in putting these theories to work need more than theory, however. They need to know how learning— technology transfer—occurs within an industry and how they can influence it. Existing empirical studies provide a few clues to this puzzle in the area of process technology. Surveys of manufacturers by SGPB and Rees, Briggs, and Oakey,[81] for example, found that large branch plants of multiplant firms were by far the most sophisticated in terms of advanced manufacturing technologies like computer-controlled machines and robots.[82] This finding suggests that information about new process technology spreads quickly and effectively within a particular corporate structure, even to those branches of the corporation that may be located in remote rural areas. The two studies disagreed, however, as to the effects of the age of the plant on its decision to invest in new production equipment. The SGPB study, which focused exclusively on rural plants, suggests that new and expanding facilities are more likely to introduce advanced technologies,[83] while Rees, Briggs, and Oakey find greater process innovation among older plants in their sample of both urban and rural establishments.[84] The most common reasons for investing in new technology among the surveyed firms included a desire to increase productivity, improve competitive position, reduce costs, and improve the quality of products.[85]

Another route for technology diffusion seems to exist between large corporations and their suppliers in one direction and between large corporations and the vendors of their products in the other direction. Although more research is needed on these relationships, several states have reported anecdotal evidence of the powerful influence exerted by large producers on smaller firms within their network to modernize and improve quality and efficiency.[86]

Finally, evidence also exists to support the idea that leading-edge technologies spread geographically, beginning near the source of the innovation and then diffusing out to more distant locations. Rees, Briggs, and Oakey found higher deployment rates for computer-controlled machines among independent plants in the industrialized Midwest, for example, the region that originally spawned this innovation.[87] Likewise, they discovered higher rates of use of microprocessors in the products of firms in Massachusetts and California, where this technology was first developed. In regions farther away from the technology's birthplace, rates of use declined. Other studies have looked more closely at whether innovations travel first between large cities, or from a large city down through its urban hierarchy to smaller towns and the countryside. As yet, there is no clear consensus.[88]

More research is needed to explain the variety of mechanisms by which good ideas diffuse throughout an industry. Two issues in particular are worth watching. First is the role of foreign plants and equipment. Rosenfeld et al. report that, in their sample, the Japanese-owned firms were more highly automated on average than the domestically owned firms.[89] In addition, much of the automation equipment in use in the rural South was made outside of the United States, mostly in Japan and Europe.[90] These authors note the important relationship between America's lower rates of manufacturing automation and our declining position in world production of automation equipment such as robots and computer-controlled machine tools.[91]

A second issue concerns relations between users and producers of technology. Shapira notes that one of the most disappointing aspects of existing industrial extension programs in the United States is the absence of a feedback mechanism that allows users of manufacturing equipment (especially small firms) to have adequate input into the development of new process technologies.[92] United States manufacturing equipment makers need better two-way communication in the market in order to learn about potential customers' needs and wants as well as to inform small manufacturers about currently available technology.

According to analysis by James Orr of the Federal Reserve Bank of New York, these two issues are also closely related.[93] Compared to U.S. plants, affiliates of foreign companies operating in the United States are known to buy more of their inputs, including capital goods as well as supplies and parts, from overseas. As the affiliates become more established, however, Orr predicts that they will shift away from importing inputs to buying locally, generating significant improvements in the overall U.S. trade balance. Statistics from the 1980s confirm the trend: Between 1982 and 1987, the ratio of imports per worker to exports per worker for foreign affiliates in the United States fell from 2.0 to 1.6.[94] This shift in demand suggests potentially enormous opportunities for U.S. makers of production technology.

Technology diffusion has begun to move up on the economic development priority lists in some areas. According to one survey, states spent about $46 million on technology transfer programs in 1988, more than four times the level of spending just two years earlier.[95] Despite the impressive growth, however, the problem of bringing existing mature manufacturers up to speed on process technology still takes a back seat to more high-profile activities such as research on new technologies, new product development, and investment in new start-up ventures. The vast majority of the states' technology-related expenditures in 1988 supported these research, development, and firm start-up functions; outlays for technology transfer represented only 8 percent of the state technology pie.

State technology transfer programs take a variety of forms. Loosely patterned on the well-known Agricultural Extension Service partnership between the U.S. Department of Agriculture, states, and counties, there are industrial extension services that provide individualized consultations, technical assistance, and even financial support for firms interested in modernizing their operations. Also available are exchange networks that link developers and users of technology via interactive databases.[96] Most such programs focus on small- to medium-sized manufacturing firms. Some operate out of universities or nonprofit organizations; others directly out of state agencies. All programs provide assistance to firms interested in simply applying existing, "off-the-shelf" process technologies (like numerically controlled machine tools), while others can respond to requests about more advanced, state-of-the-art systems (robotics and flexible manufacturing systems).[97]

The federal government also plays a role in the transfer of automated manufacturing technology. The U.S. Congress' 1988 Trade Bill instructed the Department of Commerce's National Institute of Standards and Technology (NIST, the old National Bureau of Standards with a new name) to establish regional centers whose mission is to aid in the transfer of modern manufacturing technology to U.S. firms.[98] Recent efforts have focused on defense conversion, dual-use technologies, and strategic investment.

Of all the innovative technology development programs percolating within state governments (and the federal government to a lesser extent), industrial extension and technology transfer probably hold the most potential for strengthening rural economies. As Chapters 5 and 6 demonstrated, the rural economy continues to depend heavily on some of the most traditional, most mature sectors in the U.S. economy: manufacturing, natural resources, and agriculture. Even the high-tech firms that do concentrate in rural areas are among the older, less dynamic members of the high-tech club, such as chemicals and machinery. Programs that help such mature industries modernize could stimulate rural economies in two ways.

First, deployment of new process technologies would improve the efficiency of rural industries and the quality of products, thereby strengthening much of rural America's economic base. The authors of the SGPB report lay out these assumptions clearly: "that automation and innovation are necessary to maintain and improve the viability of southern industries, and that effective policies and programs would improve the abilities of southern manufacturers to compete in world markets."[99]

Second, as Shapira has pointed out, government-sponsored industrial extension activities may go even one step further, helping "to change the way smaller firms interrelate and to encourage them to form their own networks that can disseminate information, share and advance technology, and develop products and markets."[100] Just as horizontal relationships among firms have created seedbeds for growth in high-tech complexes like Silicon Valley and Route 128 in Boston, they may also stimulate local and regional economic development in areas with concentrations of more mature industries. Shapira mentions a few examples of efforts to increase collaboration and develop production networks among smaller firms within traditional manufacturing: New York in textiles and metalworking and Michigan in auto suppliers.[101]

Recommendations for improving the nation's technology transfer capacity target both state and federal efforts. Most analysts would probably agree that states should continue to experiment with and refine different approaches to technology transfer that suit different economic conditions and industrial configurations. However, states face an information transfer problem of their own—how to disseminate the lessons learned in pioneering states to other states that may be just initiating technology transfer activities. Shapira suggests a possible role for NIST in helping build an interstate network to share ideas about what works.[102] He also recommends closer state/federal partnerships in industrial extension, and higher levels of federal funding for technology transfer in general, possibly through matching grants to states in block form.[103]

Rosenfeld et al. call for increased efforts by states to make sure that technology transfer reaches the smaller manufacturers in rural areas who suffer the greatest isolation.[104] According to their analysis, even the most sophisticated state technology transfer programs do not have sufficient resources to penetrate rural manufacturing and effect meaningful change. Their ideas for reaching rural manufacturers include databases, newsletters, and public information services. Most important is the need for frequent, personalized meetings that bring small firm owners and managers together with equipment vendors to discuss applications of technology within particular industries. In addition, rural community colleges could perform a useful function by serving as intermediaries between remote, far-flung engineering centers in state capitals or on state university campuses and local industries back home.

Both Shapira and Rosenfeld et al. emphasize the importance of integrating work force training with technological modernization.[105] The introduction of new process technologies often is, and almost always should be, combined with changes in the organization of work. In many cases, automation demands new skills from workers as well as new ways of relating to both machines and fellow workers. Training can help ensure a smoother transition to new forms of "humanware" (see Chapter 6). Rosenfeld et al. recommend a series of activities designed to improve workers' skills and strengthen management's capabilities in these areas.[106]

Finally, both studies describe a need for states to actively encourage the development of intra-industry networks. Rosenfeld et al. offer specific ideas, which include programs to strengthen relationships between regional producers and suppliers as well as programs that encourage collaborative efforts among small firms in tasks such as process technology research and development, technical training, market information services, and even joint bids on supplier contracts.[107] The latter idea assumes that if small firms within an industry can overcome some of their competitive and proprietary instincts, they can make more progress working together than they can working separately.

Quality of Development

Questions of jobs and equity come up less often in discussions of the high-tech sector than in discussions of natural resources, services, and other areas of the economy. Many analysts automatically equate high-tech jobs with "good" jobs.

Smith and Barkley's survey research support this view to some extent.[108] Among rural single unit plants and headquarters plants, they found larger percentages of employees in the highest skill occupations (namely professional/technical and skilled production workers) and smaller percentages of laborers within high-tech operations. High-tech plants in these categories boasted nearly twice the percentage of professionals (15.1 percent) of low-tech plants (7.9 percent). The statistically significant difference did not hold for branch plants, however, where high- and low-tech plants exhibited roughly similar job profiles.

Looking at opportunities for rural women, however, a tradeoff emerges between quantity and quality of jobs. According to Smith and Barkley, "while high-tech plants employed a higher percentage of women overall, the female employees were concentrated in branch plants and in the lower-skilled production occupations. Low-tech plants, on the other hand, provided considerably higher percentages of jobs for women in the professional/technical occupations."[109]

Obviously, not all high-tech jobs are created equal. To the extent that a rural community can come up with enough professionally and technically trained employees to keep a company in business, it should pursue the upper end of the high-tech field where skill levels and wage rates are higher—the research and development functions, the headquarters operations, and the single-unit plants where production is not totally routine. For communities where those skills are in short supply, high-tech branch plants offer just as many opportunities as the traditional manufacturing branch plants so coveted in the 1970s.

As in every other instance of industrial recruitment and business development, local citizens should have some idea of what they are getting before the decision is made. What kinds of jobs will be generated, at what salaries, with what benefits and what safety concerns? How many net jobs will accrue to current residents? How secure will the jobs be in a potentially footloose plant? These and other questions should be the subject of explicit public deliberation among residents and local leaders. With some exceptions, high tech is likely to pass the test of job quality with relatively high marks.

The issue of labor effects becomes more complicated when we turn to applied technology. The literature on this subject is extensive. As Rosenfeld, Malizia, and Dugan have described it, the debate ranges from those who see automation as the panacea for improving the quality of work life to those who see it as a new tool for exploiting and oppressing those at the bottom of the job ladder.[110] These researchers found support for the ideas that automa-

tion neither upgrades nor degrades the level of skills required in manufacturing but rather requires "reskilling" of the work force; that autonomy and
responsibility increase in the automated work place (though some of the
work may be more tedious); that total employment usually increases rather
than decreases following investments in technology; and that automation
generally provides equal opportunities for women and minorities.[111]

The challenge for manufacturers everywhere, but particularly in rural areas
where the knowledge and experience base is often narrower, is to marry new
investment in technology with new thinking about management and organization. As researchers learn more about the possible downsides of applied
production technology, community leaders must respond with innovative
ideas for restructuring the human side of the automation equation to increase
the net benefits. The alternative—resisting technological change—is likely to
accelerate local job loss and further diminish long-term economic prospects,
particularly for well-trained and educated young people.

11

Telecommunications

Introduction

Telecommunications functions in two ways: as an "economic base" industry—a firm that directly generates new wealth through development and sales of communications products and information services—and as a piece of the collective infrastructure that all other industries need in order to do business. This is not a new phenomenon. The U.S. economy has depended on the telephone for decades. Recent advances in economic development theory and practice, however, place a special premium on activities made possible through telecommunications.

The latest wave of economic development theory emphasizes the importance of leveraging investment by building partnerships within industrial sectors, among sectors, and between business and government. For small businesses in particular, networks that provide information, services, and opportunities to achieve greater economies of scale can make the difference between success and failure; access to communications is the basic prerequisite for activities.

Consider the strategies for development described in earlier chapters of Part II. They emphasize linkage in the form of production, distribution, marketing, and sales networks; shared purchasing and brokering; diffusion of technology; promotion of export trade; streamlining of processes; and civic education—improvements in the flow of information about economic development choices within communities. Virtually all of these activities rely to some extent on the transmission of voices and data over distance. The link between telecommunications and contemporary economic development seems plain.

The argument, however, must not be overstated. Telecommunications is but one tool, albeit a critical one, that firms and communities can use to restructure the ways they do business. Yet the mere presence of a modern telecommunications system is not enough to improve competitiveness. Entrepreneurs in the private and public sectors must learn how to apply these capabilities. They must stay in touch with developments elsewhere and come up with their own innovative ways of building networks and using information technologies. They must learn to think differently about both space and time.

This chapter reviews what we know about telecommunications and its impact on rural development. In summary:

1. Telecommunications is a boom industry nationally and internationally. New products, both goods and services, enter the market constantly. Competition is fierce, but the opportunities for innovation and for development of new markets seem almost limitless.

2. Rural areas probably do not see many of the jobs produced by this production boom. As shown in Chapter 10, even those rural areas with a high-tech industry base tend to concentrate in the slower growing, less sophisticated parts of the sector.

3. Some rural areas have been successful in attracting telecommunications-intensive services known as back-office functions. These include telemarketing, catalog sales, bill and check processing, and other routine service activities—the nongoods equivalent of manufacturing branch plants. While some communities have benefitted from this type of development, analysts are still sorting out its cost-benefit balance sheet.

4. In the final analysis, the indirect effects of telecommunications on the rural economy are more important than the direct effects. High-quality communications capabilities allow existing rural businesses to improve their competitiveness, reach new markets, and in some cases expand capacity.

5. To take advantage of the opportunities presented by telecommunications, rural areas must overcome significant barriers. The deregulation of the industry in the 1980s created certain disadvantages for rural communities, particularly those in more remote locations, in both access and price. Overcoming these barriers—upgrading the rural telecommunications infrastructure without pushing rates too high—will require cooperative efforts on the part of both the public and private sectors.

6. Demand-side approaches to rural telecommunications development are probably more effective than supply-side approaches. Instead of paying directly out of the public treasury for the improvements in infrastructure needed to bring rural areas up to standards, government should invest in certain public activities, particularly health care and education, that will stimulate market demand for better communications capacity.[1]

7. Analysis of rural telecommunication development issues raises fundamental questions about the nature of rural development itself. To the extent that rural areas are defined by their geographic isolation—a characteristic that protects cultural identity—advances in telecommunications, which seek to eliminate the barriers of space and time, may be said to transform the rural way of life. Both empirical research and normative analysis are needed to assess the effects of telecommunications development on culture, community, and politics in rural areas.

Definitions

The term "telecommunications" encounters some of the same definitional problems encountered in Chapter 10. Sometimes telecommunications refers to a group of industries, mostly the telephone carriers. Sometimes it refers to a group of products that include goods such as telephones, answering machines, and fax machines, and services such as linked networks and voice mail. Sometimes it refers to the total inventory of physical infrastructure—the wires, cables, and switches that make instant communication possible across great distances. Telecommunications is just one segment of the high-tech universe, a segment that functions both as its own industrial sector—generating products, income, and jobs—and as a critical tool for all other sectors, allowing buyers and sellers to come together. Telecommunications facilitates coordination within and across production and distribution networks. This chapter will look at telecommunications as a separate sector, but will focus on what is being learned about it in its role as part of the economy's basic infrastructure.

The Context: National and International Trends

The multibillion dollar telecommunications industry is both a manufacturer and a service provider. Companies such as AT&T, MCI, Sprint, and others provide long-distance telephone service around the country and overseas, while the "Baby Bells" and a handful of small, independent firms provide local service as well as feeders to the long-distance lines. Independent companies, many of them operated as cooperatives, are most common in remote areas where the old Bell system never got around to staking claims. AT&T, Northern Telecom, and a few other smaller companies manufacture the equipment (switches, satellites, fiber-optic cable, amplifiers, modems, telephone sets, and the like) that make possible the transmission of voices and data.

The massive size and scope of today's telecommunications industries is due in part to a series of regulatory decisions during the 1970s and early 1980s that introduced competition into what had been a government-sponsored monopoly. Communications deregulation began with the manufacturing end of the business, allowing Bell system customers to use non-AT&T telephones and other equipment, and culminated in 1984 with the breakup of AT&T and the opening of competition in long-distance service markets. But oddly enough, as Edward Carr argues in *The Economist,* deregulation's greatest impact probably will not occur in either the manufacturing of basic equipment or the simple carrying of long-distance telephone signals, but instead in the brand new, virtually unlimited arena of information services.[2] Here, telephone companies, computer companies, software companies, and management consultants have begun to battle over highly profitable activities such as designing, building, and managing computer networks, and selling technical services like electronic mail, paging, and on-line information databases. The $25 billion a year information services market has been growing faster than almost any other high technology industry, at an annual rate of 30 percent.[3] As Carr describes the new information services industry, "Competition has proved riotously fertile. It is pushing the industry along at a breathless pace."[4] The market's appetite for new products seems insatiable.

Competition also has proved to be a source of intense pressure for U.S. telecommunications firms. Private networks using satellites and transmission lines leased from the public switched system, for example, are threatening to channel large amounts of voice and data traffic through systems that yield little or no revenue for conventional service providers like AT&T, MCI, or the regional Bell companies.[5] IBM has spent more than 20 years building a global communications system that now connects the corporation's 400,000 employees in 145 countries around the world through electronic mail and transmission of data such as payroll and sales records.[6] Now, IBM has begun to sell time shares on its network to other companies and raises the strong possibility of the phone companies' largest customers in the past becoming their fiercest competitors in the future.[7]

A second source of pressure, this time from overseas, focuses on U.S. equipment makers. Along with deregulation came the lifting of barriers to imported telecommunications equipment and a rapid loss of market share to foreign manufacturers.[8] While the United States does control one-third of the world market for telecommunications equipment (Europe holds another third and Japan one-eighth),[9] it has gone from a position of trade surplus in telecommunications equipment prior to the breakup of AT&T to substantial trade deficit.[10] With too many producers in the global equipment market now, Carr anticipates an international price war over switches—the central component of every local telephone exchange—and a shaking out of the industry.[11]

The future of the telecommunications industries, both manufacturing and services, will depend on a multitude of factors: the pace of deregulation and trade liberalization in Europe, Japan, and other foreign economies; domestic companies' decisions to make what could be a $250 billion to $500 billion investment in bringing fiber-optic technology to individual homes and businesses across the country;[12] potential lifting of the ban on U.S. telecommunications firms in the area of video transmission;[13] and other elements in the race to upgrade equipment and provide new and enhanced services to customers.

The Rural Picture

What does the national and international whirlwind of telecommunications activity mean for rural communities? The question has two parts: (1) Will rural areas share in the new jobs and income created by this booming new industrial sector? (2) Will the state-of-the-art products of this sector—the equipment and services—penetrate the countryside and improve the economic competitiveness and quality of life there as they have elsewhere?

Telejobs: New Technology, Same Old Story

Glasmeier's analysis of the geographic distribution of high-tech manufacturing enterprises suggests that most sophisticated telecommunications equipment probably is produced in larger urban areas (see Chapter 10). Likewise, Malecki's work indicates that the research and development that goes into new high-tech products also occurs largely in urban America. Neither of these trends is likely to reverse itself anytime soon.[14]

In the area of communications services, Williams has noted the tendency for telephone companies to move out of smaller, more remote communities once the new, low-maintenance, easy-to-operate switches and transmission equipment are installed.[15] The new technology reduces the need for personnel on site. Communications consultants and information services entrepreneurs also seem to favor larger population centers. Observations such as these suggest that rural areas should not count on the telecommunications boom to create large numbers of new manufacturing or services jobs directly.

One family of jobs *indirectly* related to telecommunications, however, may hold some promise for more remote areas—the family of back-office and telemarketing jobs made possible by the new information technologies. Telemarketing is one of the better known members of this business group. It includes operations that receive calls via toll-free 800 numbers and fee-based 900 numbers from customers seeking information or ordering products and services by phone from catalogs, direct mail advertisements, and so on. It also includes those businesses that place calls, usually via WATS services, such as telephone solicitations for fundraising and advertising of products. Tele-marketing "has been touted as a way to diversify those rural economies hit hard by setbacks in the agricultural, energy, and manufacturing industries in the 1980s."[16] According to Strover and Williams, the traditional pattern of urban-oriented telemarketing development has shifted somewhat in recent years, with more and more operations moving to smaller communities in order to lower costs, particularly in the Midwest.

More than any other state, Nebraska made a decision to pursue telemar-keting jobs aggressively during the 1980s by deregulating telecommunica-tions entirely. The effect on rural parts of the state has been mixed. While some telemarketing jobs have spilled over from the cities to smaller, more re-mote communities, rural areas also have suffered rate increases without no-table improvements in the quality of service.[17]

Despite the ultramodern sound of these jobs and their reliance on sophisti-cated communications technology, the economic development strategies em-ployed to attract them harken back to the old days of industrial recruitment. Plans to lure mail order warehouses away from Seattle to struggling agricul-tural communities in the eastern part of Washington, for example, will not generate net new jobs for the state. Likewise, Nebraska's relatively successful effort to establish its own telemarketing empire appears to have come at the ex-pense of control over its communications network. And most of the jobs rein-forced traditional development patterns favoring urban locations over rural.

Although back office attraction strategies may serve some communities well, perhaps the more important telecommunications opportunity for rural America is not in the short term through landing new jobs, but in the long term by using the new products to expand capacity and improve competi-tiveness in existing rural industries. Telemarketing's biggest contribution to rural development may be the stimulation of demand needed to generate in-frastructure investments, which, in turn, may increase opportunities for other businesses and other sectors.

Application and Innovation

Telecommunications is important to the countryside for a simple reason. These networks hold out the promise of overcoming the drawbacks of those very qualities that make rural areas rural, of ending "the tyranny of rural space."[18] As Williams puts it:

> In many ways, telecommunications addresses the two interrelated aspects of the "rural disadvantage," namely distance and low popu-lation density. For some services and needs, telecommunications can make distance irrelevant; and by aggregating markets, telecom-munications can create new economies of scale.[19]

While the potential is enormous, some observers have voiced doubts concerning the overall effects of telecommunications on rural America. As Dillman, Beck, and Allen have pointed out,[20] the "elimination" of distance is a two-edged sword. In some cases, it may mean that enterprising rural companies will be able to serve customers in large cities and other far-off places and compete more successfully in regional, national, and global markets. But in other cases, it may mean that large, sophisticated urban firms will take over rural markets once served by local operations. As the authors put it, "Information technologies provide as much potential to pull business out of the community as to bring it in." Telecommunications may prove to be the high-tech, service-sector equivalent of the regional shopping malls that put many small-town retailers out of business in the 1970s and 1980s.

The most recent evidence points toward a more optimistic view. In Nebraska, for example, some 6700 miles of fiberoptic cable have been laid in recent years. All but five of the state's county seats are now linked to the fiberoptic network and many of them are participating in experiments such as telemedicine and distance learning.

While causal attributions are hard to prove, the change in Nebraska is vivid. During the 1980s, 83 of the state's 93 counties lost population. Since 1990, however, all but 20 counties are either gaining population or have stabilized, a positive development that many state and local officials trace to expanded opportunities flowing from the telecommunications revolution.

In a similar vein, the Denver-based Center for the New West has been tracking the contribution of telecommunications to the growth of small towns throughout the Rocky Mountain states. "Lone Eagles"—individual entrepreneurs whose work is knowledge-based—have been flocking to these communities, drawn by their unique combination of lifestyle amenities and technological linkage to urban centers.[21]

Fulfilling the promise of rural telecommunications has three prerequisites. (1) Rural areas must have access to the new services. (2) The costs to rural customers of the new services must be "reasonable." (3) Rural businesses must figure out how to use the new services to their advantage. Unfortunately, each of these prerequisites comes with its own set of barriers to success.

Access

While rural telecommunications services have improved steadily over the past several decades, they still have a long way to go to catch up with the state-of-the-art networks now in place in many metropolitan areas.

But before cataloging the inadequacies of the rural communications infrastructure, it is important to note one of the central achievements of federal rural policy over the past 40 years—the provision of basic voice telephone service to almost every rural household in the country. Thanks to the efforts of the Rural Electrification Administration, whose charter was expanded to include low-cost loans to rural telephone companies in 1946, 96 percent of all farms today have telephones, compared to 35 percent after World War II.[22] Most of the remaining 4 percent lack service because they can't afford it, not because it is unavailable. According to Parker et al., "Income is a far better predictor of whether a household will have telephone service than urban/rural location."[23] Of the 6.8 million households in America without telephone service, only about 3 percent (183,000 households) lack access because of geographic isolation.[24] Even in remote locations where installation of copper wire is prohibitively expensive, radio and satellite technologies can provide basic voice transmission.

Now that basic *telephone* transmission is available virtually everywhere, the concept of universal service must be expanded to include "*gateway* service," the infrastructure that allows information to flow through the system as well as voices. Information technology indisputably has become a basic tool of doing business in the United States—at the least, the capacity to communicate between computers by modem, send and receive faxes, and upgrade telephone services to include multiple lines, call waiting, and the like. Therefore, by definition, this service has become a necessity for economic development everywhere.

Deciding in principle that universal gateway service must be the new cornerstone of the nation's telecommunications policy, however, would not solve all of the rural telecommunications riddles. Which advanced services should the new concept of "universal" cover? Who should bear the responsibility for ensuring access to the next generation of universal services? The answers to these questions will shape the evolution of rural telecommunications through the rest of the century.

Beyond "plain old telephone service" (called POTS), the rural telecommunications system remains several steps behind the rest of the nation. The inadequacies take two basic forms: (1) reliance on old equipment that needs to be upgraded to improve the quality of signals and allow for transmission of data as well as voices; and (2) lack of access to the new value-added services that are becoming a necessary ingredient in many industries' competitiveness. Parker et al. survey the major problems with the existing rural telecommunications infrastructure:[25]

- Too many multiparty, shared telephone lines
- Slow progress in updating local switches from the old analog technology to the newer, more efficient, higher capacity digital technology[26]
- Unacceptably high levels of circuit loss and circuit noise in 10–12 percent of local transmission loops[27]

- Lack of access to cellular phone service in sparser rural markets

- Higher long-distance rates because of lack of choice among long-distance carriers (many rural areas don't have equal access)

- Lack of toll-free access to data networks

- Lack of availability of other advanced services like voice mail and video-conferencing

- Greater vulnerability to line damage where no parallel lines are in place (many urban systems are disaster-proofed by installing parallel lines that can be used in case original lines are knocked down or fail)

Some of these problems are well on their way to solution. The vast majority of multiparty lines, for example, were upgraded to single party lines by 1993.[28] In addition, all rural areas will soon be licensed for cellular; the majority of rural residents either have, or are on the verge of gaining, access to this service.[29]

Even assuming higher rates of rural investment by private companies and the government, however, other inadequacies will not be eliminated for another 20–25 years in certain locales. And while the rural communications systems are playing catch-up with existing technologies, other innovations are sure to be developed that will leave rural areas even farther behind. The danger in delay, of course, is that well-wired urban areas will siphon off all of the available information-related business opportunities before rural areas can even begin to compete.

The rural–urban access gap has a long history. The original bargain struck with AT&T in 1934 offered a government-protected monopoly over local and long-distance telephone service in return for a commitment to provide access to those services for every household in the United States.[30] Over the following 50 years, virtually all American businesses and households gained not only access to basic service but also affordability. This came about through a combination of capital investment in wires, cables, and switches; cross subsidies that kept local phone rates low by charging more for long-distance calls; and national averaging of phone rates that kept more expensive service areas from having to pay their true costs of calling. By the time deregulation came along, the original goal of universal telephone service, using the old definition of service as simple access to a dial tone, was complete.

Now the landscape looks different. One side of the original bargain has been dissolved: The 1982 consent decree that broke up AT&T replaced monopoly with competition, at least in the long-distance markets.[31] Competition is attractive as a means of forcing greater efficiency, innovation, and consumer choice in telecommunications. But what about its distributive effects?

Economic theory tells us that businesses will invest in markets where enough demand exists to ensure a reasonable rate of return. In the case of installing and upgrading communications technology, this means high-density urban areas where every new mile of cable or state-of-the-art switch will serve large numbers of customers and pay for itself quickly.[32] Historically, telephone companies and other utilities made their capital investments first in the cities and then eventually expanded to more and more remote locations.

In the current competitive environment, the pressure for "cities first" policies is even greater. As several analysts have noted, big corporate users are flexing their muscles when it comes to development and deployment of new telecommunications services.[33] Some of the nation's largest corporations like IBM and GM are choosing to bypass the public system and build their own private networks for electronic mail, data transmission, and other advanced forms of communication; established phone companies are feeling heavy pressure to give their large customers everything they want.[34] The result is a strong market incentive for the phone companies to concentrate on serving places like New York, Los Angeles, and Chicago, where the big corporate headquarters are found, and to introduce quickly the most advanced, state-of-the-art communications technologies, some of which only the giant corporate customers are equipped and staffed to use.[35]

The issue of large business users bypassing the public network is not limited to urban areas and huge, multinational companies. Strover and Williams[36] found examples of bypass in rural areas as well, when local firms outgrew the capacities of their local telephone exchange companies and lost patience with the peculiarities of the new semi-deregulated public system.

Price

The debate over competition versus universal service also bears on the second prerequisite for rural telecommunications development—affordable prices.

In addition to ensuring nationwide access, the old monopoly system kept rural and urban telephone bills on roughly even footing through national averaging of rates and cross subsidies between different parts of the operation such as local and long-distance services. Once again, however, the new commitment to competition clashes with the old goal of uniform pricing. Where competition exists, for example, in long-distance calling and equipment manufacturing, the struggle for market share (along with technological advances) has caused prices to fall.[37] In contrast, where the old sources of cross subsidies have disappeared but monopoly structure has remained (as in local service), rates have gone up.[38]

When it comes to price, rural telephone users clearly suffer from several disadvantages. First, large capital investments are required to provide equal access to the competitive long-distance companies, and local exchanges need up-to-date switching technology to allow different households to automatically hook up with different carriers. Consequently, some rural areas have not enjoyed all the benefits of the new national system of competition and consumer choice.[39] Second, to the extent that regulators embrace the idea of cost-based pricing—that each customer should pay the true cost of receiving a service—rural areas where economies of scale don't exist and costs per line are higher will see their phone bills grow.[40]

The new "competitive paradigm" poses the greatest threat to the small, independent telephone companies and cooperatives not owned by the Bell System, GTE, United, or other large companies. These small companies generally serve the sparsest, remotest rural areas and depend most heavily on subsidies from urban operations and intrastate long distance. As Williams has reported, "If you talk in depth with small telcos or go to their association meetings or workshops, the greatest fear is that they will lose access to outside funds that support their high-cost operations." One solution for some small independents, according to Williams,[41] has been diversification—branching out into other ventures such as cellular franchises, cable TV, and equipment sales—to capture new revenue sources. The improvements in modern equipment also provide some hope for these small companies. The new switches and transmission technologies require less maintenance and cost less to operate.

Does the government's historical commitment to universal services mean a commitment to continued low prices in rural areas? On the one hand, rural residents might argue that access to new and improved services is relatively meaningless if sky-high prices prevent customers from plugging in. On the other hand, their opponents might argue that continued subsidies to rural users create inefficiencies in service provision and distort the telecommunications market in negative ways. Current pricing policy seems to be pursuing a moderate course between the extremes, moving toward greater price competition while protecting the most vulnerable customers from sudden changes. Parker et al., among others, generally endorse this approach.[42] They continually emphasize the need for transition policies that cushion rural areas from the full force of change as federal and state telecommunications policies proceed down the path of deregulation.

Necessity and Creativity

In telecommunications as in other technologies, the infrastructure and the hardware are only as "smart" as the people who use them. Unfortunately, rural isolation, the very quality that telecommunications investments aim to overcome, presents a serious obstacle to the proper application of telecommunications in business and the public sector.

Orders from above may not be the economic developer's ideal avenue to innovation, but they seem to work. Almost one quarter of the businesses surveyed in a 1987 study of three small rural communities in Washington State reported that their company headquarters or suppliers pressured them to install computers and dedicated telecommunications systems.[43]

In the absence of outside pressure, however, some analysts have suggested that the culture of rural communities makes them slower to "accept new ways of doing things."[44] Case studies conducted by Strover and Williams reveal this to be true among many of the Bell Operating Companies and affiliates of other larger corporations that serve local rural exchanges.[45] During the 1980s, several growing businesses in Kearney, Nebraska—both telemarketers and branch production plants—complained about the local phone company's failure to keep up with their increasing demands for advanced services. Although the local companies were cooperative and actively supportive of local economic development efforts, they simply did not have the resources and the knowledge—and perhaps the future-oriented mindset—needed. They were unable to beef up their capabilities, work with local users to assess their problems, develop customized services to meet particular needs, and market their services more aggressively.[46]

In Glendive, Montana the local Bell Company was described as complacent, far from a mover and shaker in local telecommunications development.[47] In Eagle Pass, Texas the Bell affiliate was a genuine obstacle in the path of progress toward transborder communications, due to regulations against operating across international lines.[48] Also, smaller communities find themselves at a disadvantage when it comes to seeking out communications consultants to help them design better systems—or even phone company representatives, most of whom have become concentrated in larger urban markets since deregulation.

The case studies also provide evidence in support of the other side of the argument, that many rural areas can and do embrace change. Strover and Williams' stories illustrate a high level of creativity among many rural businesses eager for improved telecommunications capacity. Examples include the simple use of microwave and radio technology among cattle farmers and maquiladoras plant operators to circumvent the local telephone providers along the Texas–Mexico border. This approach tends to be disorganized (too many vendors) and technologically backward—due, in part, to complex regulations governing international connections.[49] On a more sophisticated level, a large catalog sales company in Kearney, Nebraska applied creative

problem-solving to ensure access to certain advanced services not available locally—automatic call distribution, call overflow, data collection functions,
and the like. They accomplished this by partially bypassing the local exchange, purchasing their own digital switch, and hooking directly into a
portable, long-distance hub provided by AT&T.[50] The arrangement was the
first of its kind and has since been tapped by other large telemarketing outfits
in Kearney seeking to upgrade their telephone operations.

Among small businesses, several case studies demonstrate innovative
telecommunications applications for computer hookups.[51] A real estate agent
can gain access to amortization tables and property financial statements via
computer. Employees in a building supply store use computers to call up information about products, place orders, monitor inventory, bill customers,
and balance accounts. Rural residents who operate businesses out of their
homes, such as the desktop publisher who operates via home computer and
modem, often rely heavily on the quality of voice and data transmission.

Public institutions clearly emerge as leaders in telecommunications in
some rural areas. High schools, community colleges, and universities around
the country have used fiber-optic, satellite, and microwave technologies to
provide "distance learning" via one-way or two-way audio and/or video. This
technique allows smaller educational institutions to enrich their curricula by
offering specialized courses well beyond their local capabilities, such as
Japanese language or advanced mathematics. Schools in neighboring remote
communities, particularly in areas where population is shrinking, are learning
to share educational resources through video hookups, thereby saving
teaching positions that might otherwise be eliminated. Some pilot projects
are making it possible for students with home computers to log into electronic mail networks and special databases. Hudson has identified education-
related rural telecommunications projects in at least a dozen states.[52] Parallel
examples can be found in the health care field.

Economic Development Strategies

The new economic realities of telecommunications investment provoke different reactions. At one end of the spectrum, advocates of government intervention argue that the market is distorted. According to this view, many of
the benefits attached to rural telecommunications investment accrue to the
economy and society at large but have little impact on the private investor's
revenues.[53] These benefits include improved productivity and outreach for
existing firms, attraction of new business, and increased efficiencies in social
service delivery. Left to its own devices, therefore, the private sector will underinvest in rural telecommunications.[54] Government must step in to ensure

rural businesses and households "access to telecommunications and information services comparable to those available in urban areas."[55] The consequences of not connecting rural America with the latest communications technologies are akin to the consequences of not maintaining and upgrading rural highways, waterways, and railroads. The basic defining feature of rural life—distance—makes transportation and communications even more critical to socioeconomic development in the countryside than in the city.[56]

Various studies support the idea that telecommunications investment yields significant social and economic payoffs. Hudson, Parker, et al. cite a "pioneering" 1980 study that showed not only that economic development makes increased investment in telecommunications possible, but also that telecommunications investment directly contributes to the rate of economic development.[57] The relationship holds for investments in both business and residential service. Three years later, a study of REA borrowers demonstrated that loans to rural telephone companies and cooperatives generated expanded economic growth valued at six to seven times the original costs of the government's interest subsidies.[58] Studies of the benefits from telecommunications for developing countries reach similar conclusions.[59] More recently, researchers have demonstrated links between quality of telephone service and income and unemployment levels in communities in Washington and Oregon. Care must be taken in interpreting findings from studies such as these, however, because it is not always clear in which direction the causation runs.

As Hills summarizes the relationship: "Telecommunications is the node that links production activities with exchange activities involving the circulation of goods and with information activities that coordinate the economic system."[60] Businesses with access to telecommunications benefit from better price information, reduced need for inventory, timely delivery of goods to market, lower travel costs, enhanced responsiveness to market demands, reduced downtime due to machinery failure, and a variety of other improvements in efficiency and quality.[61] In other areas of rural life—transportation, health care, education, social services, civic participation, and cultural activities—improved communication also translates into a higher quality of life.[62] Although many of these benefits are difficult to measure, advocates of telecommunications-led development both here and overseas argue that they far outweigh the costs.

At the other end of the spectrum, advocates of a free market approach in the United States assert that no further collective investments in telecommunications are needed; the market is working very well and will get the job done. According to this view, America's basic telecommunications infrastructure—the fiber-optic trunk lines between local exchanges—is already in place and accessible for long-distance use just about everywhere. This is the equivalent of the interstate highway system. "What is left to be constructed then is not the national fiber backbone," says Gail Garfield Schwartz, "but the local arterials and feeder roads: the arterials being the loops to large commercial and nonprofit entities such as universities, and the feeder roads being fiber-optic subscriber loops linking individual small customers (residential and business) to the installed trunk system."[63] In the free market model, these remaining pieces eventually will be put in place by private firms once they have completed the network in the more profitable areas of the country.

In support of this argument, analysts warn of two potential problems with government intervention in telecommunications investment decisions. The first danger comes from weakening the publicly switched network. Rules that require only certain firms (AT&T, for example, bound by Judge Harold Greene's rulings, or the Bell companies) to upgrade services and deploy new technologies in low-density markets may put undue pressure on these firms and erode their competitive position.[64] The unintended results of such a policy could include further defections from the publicly switched network by large companies dissatisfied with their service and, eventually, creation of a two-tiered communications system: "one system for residential consumers and businesses unable to build their own systems, and a second, superior, privately owned system."[65]

The second danger of government intervention is waste. James Bennet claims that most of the telephone companies that borrow from the Rural Electrification Administration's existing telephone lending programs don't need public subsidies.[66] Net operating profit margins of REA lenders doubled between 1980 and 1988, and "a 1989 Kidder Peabody analysis showed that the average telephone borrower could easily attract lenders on the private market."[67] He goes so far as to say that recent government subsidies have actually tilted the system in favor of rural dwellers: "Not only does the government pay part of the bills of rural users regardless of their income, while offering the urban poor no such breaks—it taxes the urban poor to pay those rural bills."[68]

Those concerned about waste must also ask whether federally subsidized rural telecommunications upgrades would be fully utilized, since no one knows exactly what the demand is. Although utilization tests do not exist, the question requires careful consideration.

Government as Investor and Regulator: The Supply Approach

Parker et al. recommend 10 changes in federal and state policy that would expand the supply of telecommunications services in rural areas. The proper role for government, they argue, is not to control microlevel decisions but rather to encourage the private sector to "provide affordable access to telecommunications and information services comparable to those available in urban areas."[69] The specific recommendations encompass both (1) increased infusions of public capital to help upgrade and rebuild the rural system and (2) changes in the rules of the game to make private companies focus more attention on supplying rural customers. These recommendations include the following:

- Expand REA's mission "to include fostering affordable rural access to the basic communications tools of the Information Age" and raise their lending authority by 30 percent, roughly $150 million a year, to provide capital for rural carriers to update their equipment and services.[70] (Requires Congressional action.)

- Protect current distributional equity in rural/urban phone rates by continuing to average long-distance rates across the country, maintaining the "lifeline" and "universal service" subsidies for low-income customers, and facilitating equal access to competitive long-distance carriers in rural exchanges.[71] (Requires FCC action.)

- Provide incentives for the Bell operating companies and other large carriers "to prepare and implement plans to upgrade completely their rural facilities by the year 2000," including both overall infrastructure and provision of specific voice and information services on a par with urban areas.[72] (Such incentives would require action by the FCC and the U.S. Justice Department via the AT&T consent decree.)

- Remove barriers at the state level that inhibit rural telecommunications development.[73] These barriers include accounting procedures that stretch out the period over which old investment costs for now-obsolete equipment can be recovered, thereby discouraging new investment in modern equipment. (Requires action by state Public Utility Commissions.)

- All federal and state government agencies with connections to rural development, including economic development, social services, agriculture, and others, should include telecommunications issues in their planning processes and, where possible, help fund relevant telecommunications services through their budgets.[74] State governments should coordinate the making of telecommunications policy across agencies. (Requires action by a wide range of state and federal agencies.)

Government as Customer: The Demand Approach

Gail Garfield Schwartz offers an alternative form of government intervention in rural telecommunications. Her general thesis boils down to this: "Any economic development policies should be focused on generating and augmenting demand for [telecommunications] services, not on generating infrastructure per se."[75] More specifically, she recommends that government make a high priority commitment to expanding telecommunications capacity in two areas of vital public interest—(1) the provision of health care and (2) education. By following this scheme, government takes the lead in directly stimulating rural demand for telecommunications without trying to significantly alter the natural workings of the private telephone and information services markets.[76]

The "superwiring" of rural public health care providers, public schools, and training programs has two clear advantages.[77] First, it starts small. Instead of mandating large investments in universal access to technologies that may or may not prove useful to customers, it tests the market in rural areas for the types of high-cost, state-of-the-art services that Parker, Hudson, et al. consider vital to all communities in the Information Age. This approach assumes that where demand is great enough to cover costs of infrastructure improvements as well as the costs of providing services, private companies will expand.[78] But demand for the latest technologies in any market is highly uncertain. Neither public nor private officials know whether the rewards from investment in advanced telecommunications will cover the up-front costs. Thus, when the public sector makes a commitment to help generate large-scale demand for advanced technologies (in this case, medical imaging, interactive information services, video classrooms, and other applications), it paves the way for long-term, sustainable, market-driven development of rural telecommunications. Second, this approach spreads the risk around by leaving decisions about financing up to locally determined configurations of the regulated telephone companies, competing firms, information suppliers, and government partners rather than placing the entire burden of investment on the regulated companies or the public treasury.[79]

By subsidizing state-of-the-art health and education technologies for rural providers, government not only improves the quality and efficiency of critical social services, it also accomplishes the goal of expanding rural telecommunications capacity. And it does that without having to coerce or bribe private companies to do something that they don't perceive to be in their interests. Schwartz's proposal, while not cheap, merits serious further study.

Leveraging through the Private Sector

The philosophy behind telemarketing-led development is not so different from Schwartz's demand-side recommendation. Some communities have successfully used traditional incentive schemes to recruit back-office firms that, in turn, attract the attention of telecommunications firms and lead to upgrades in the local communications infrastructure. Kearney, Nebraska, for example, provided free rent for a year and other benefits to its initial telemarketing firms[80] and ended up with a local AT&T hub, one of only four in the state.

Of course, this is a high-risk strategy; a community never knows whether a new corporate resident will succeed or how the firm's presence will influence the larger business climate. But anecdotal evidence suggests that a telemarketing-based strategy can work in a limited number of locations. The industry is a national growth sector in which some rural areas enjoy comparative advantage.

In some cases, leadership for a demand-side strategy may even come from the local telephone companies themselves rather than from government investments in education and health or an up-and-coming telemarketer. The case of Glendive, Montana provides the model. There, Strover and Williams report, a particularly far-sighted telephone cooperative made a commitment to create an extensive fiber-optic network and invited four rural schools to participate in a pilot project using interactive television in the classroom.[81] Plans are now in place to expand the distance-learning network to include the local high school and community college.

Quality of Development

Telecommunications development has the potential to make large and lasting changes, not only in the ways rural residents do business, but also in how they conduct their community affairs.

Jobs and Equity

The issue of job quality depends on how the economic developer chooses to view telecommunications development. Under the traditional industrial attraction approach to local growth, a community may decide to offer incentives to lure telemarketing or other back-office operations to boost local employment roles. In these cases, the issue of job quality is bound to arise.

On the one hand, it can be argued that phone answering and other basic transaction-processing jobs offer a community very little. They generally pay low wages, hire part-time workers, provide minimal worker benefits, and involve low-skilled, tedious, repetitive work with little room for advancement. Oversight may be oppressive, often conducted through computer counts of keyboard strokes or calls answered. As with the branch plants that moved to the countryside in the 1970s, today's back-office operations may be seen as exploiting cheap, rural labor.[82]

On the other hand, telemarketing jobs have the advantage of being clean and relatively safe. While they may not provide a living wage for a family, they can help supplement other household income. These businesses helped many Midwestern farm communities weather the agricultural downturns of the 1980s. As with other sectors, the debate over whether to pursue back-office jobs must be resolved by local people themselves, through deliberation based on accurate, widely distributed information about the types of jobs in question.

Under the alternative approach to telecommunications development, the nature of the jobs debate is less clear. The economic developer who views telecommunications as an infrastructure strategy intends to stimulate job creation across local sectors, not in a single type of industry such as telemarketing. What will such change do to the quality of local jobs? Unfortunately, we do not know the answer because we do not fully understand the impact of telecommunications development on local economies. Researchers are only beginning to ask the question. Case studies like those by Strover and Williams help deepen our understanding of the dynamics of telecommunications development in a few locations but fall short of revealing general trends.

Will enhanced telecommunications capacity primarily allow existing firms to increase the number of existing jobs, or will the nature of the jobs change, too? As productivity growth increases, thanks to better communications and information, how many jobs will be eliminated? What kinds of jobs will they be? Will other types of jobs be created elsewhere—to manage and coordinate the new, highly touted industrial networks, for example? What kinds of jobs will they be? Researchers are beginning to find answers to these questions in the context of factory automation, but far more work is needed to understand the effects of technology on labor markets in other parts of the economy.

Community

The study of telecommunications development in rural areas reveals pockets of inspiration, places where innovation and creativity are being brought to bear on community needs. But study also has exposed huge expanses of unfulfilled potential. Four areas of opportunity are worth noting: (1) telecommunications as a rallying point for economic development planning; (2) joint activities by business, education, and health groups to press for innovations in communications and information; (3) contributions of small local telecommunications companies to community development; and (4) consolidation of small rural communities to overcome barriers to growth.

First, analysts have begun to examine how telecommunications has functioned as a catalyst for organizing state and local leaders to address long-term economic development issues. People naturally get excited about new technologies and new ways to communicate and gather information. Local officials can take advantage of this excitement by making telecommunications the centerpiece of a community planning process.

Second, efforts are underway to take advantage of opportunities to aggregate telecommunications demand across business, education, health, and other institutions. In some locales, partnerships have formed among employers, community colleges, and other educational institutions to provide worker training. Commenting on the case study of Demopolis, Alabama, for example, Strover and Williams note, "It was intriguing for us to see at this research site the growing complementarity of school officials and local plant personnel regarding the challenges of educating the work force."[83]

This example, however, is the exception to the rule. Far more could be done. In areas where telecommunications development is well on its way, local leaders should encourage business, education, and health leaders to explore opportunities for developing new applications achieving economies of scale through joint action. In areas where telecommunications capacities are still primitive, cooperative efforts could provide the critical spark needed to spur upgrading.

Third, the case studies of Strover and Williams provide valuable information about which telecommunications providers tend to make the greatest contributions to their communities. This research points to small, independent companies as the most promising actors in rural development. These companies have a greater stake in the performance of the local economy because their revenues are solely dependent on local sales. For this reason, they may tend to pursue system upgrades and service innovations more aggressively. They may pay closer attention to the needs of basic local institutions like schools and medical facilities that affect quality of life and, indirectly, economic growth. They may take bigger risks. With sufficient access to capital, these companies have the potential to be key leaders in rural development across the country. Therefore, a community-oriented rural policy should seek to strengthen the small independents and cooperatives, or at least be careful not to weaken them.

At the other end of the continuum, local exchange operators owned by large companies like the Bell system companies have far fewer incentives to invest time, energy, and money in the rural communities they serve. The new competitive paradigm for U.S. telecommunications places a premium on larger markets; deregulation makes rural areas more of a nuisance. This reality is reflected in the case studies, in which the Bell affiliates tended to define their mission in rural areas as providing basic dial tone service and nothing more. Cable operators, too, generally seem to demonstrate only weak community ties. Although the larger incentive structure for phone companies is difficult to change, community leaders may get results by putting pressure on their local phone company and its regional affiliate to get more involved in telecommunications planning.

Fourth and finally, telecommunications may also be influential in helping some of the most remote, sparsely populated rural communities make the difficult decision to merge with their neighbors rather than to pursue separate growth strategies. Expanded capacities would make small-town consolidation far easier and more effective in areas where few alternatives exist. Video hookups would allow school districts to share teachers; information technologies would allow social service agencies to consolidate files; networks would allow local elected officials to keep in touch across distance. The problem with this strategy, of course, is finding the capital needed to invest in upgraded telecommunications capacity in isolated places. Here again, more research is needed to identify the opportunities and obstacles.

Culture

Finally, the question of telecommunications development comes back to the definition of "rural." Some analysts already say that the concept of rural has lost its descriptive power as borders between cities, towns, and countryside have grown fuzzier. If telecommunications-based strategies succeed in creating adjacency where it does not exist spatially, and if these strategies succeed in neutralizing the effects of isolation, remoteness, and distance, then the decay of boundaries will be hastened.

Economic developers generally welcome such changes, which contribute to the goal of connecting rural America to the rest of the national and world economy. But after the jobs have been counted, what becomes of the character of rural America? Does distinctiveness decay along with economic backwardness? Do rural communities want to become just like everywhere else in order to prosper?

The answers to these questions are not self-evident. However, one fact does seem clear. Telecommunications is a necessary, though not sufficient, ingredient in rural survival. To the extent that small communities want to protect their heritage and culture, they must find ways of doing it that do not require shutting out the larger world. Telecommunications must be perceived as an opportunity in rural America rather than as a threat. It can serve as a rallying point for citizens to discuss the full range of long-term planning issues. Whatever its risks, it cannot be stopped. Here, as elsewhere, accepting telecommunications change is a key precondition for maintaining whatever measure of social continuity may be possible in contemporary economies.

Conclusion

Toward the Next Millennium

Our analysis of development in rural America leads us to restate, with emphasis, the principal conclusions reached.

The crucial first step is to acknowledge the concept of what we have called *embeddedness*. We mean simply that it is impossible to understand the current problems or future prospects of rural America in isolation from national and global trends. At the global level, the increasingly rapid and unfettered mobility of capital, information, and technology is unlikely to be reversed any time soon; consequently, the intensifying international economic competition it has engendered will continue.

This competition, in turn, will also continue to exert pressure on economic sectors such as natural resources and routine manufacturing, with two key results. What we term the *inexorable logic of productivity*—in particular, increased output with diminished labor input—will continue to squeeze jobs out of these sectors, and many of the jobs that remain in them will experience continued downward pressure on wages. A recently released Census Bureau report documents a sharp rise in low-wage jobs from 12 percent to 18 percent of the full-time work force over the past decade, a phenomenon many analysts trace to increased global competition among workers performing relatively low-skill jobs.[1]

This is not to say that global pressures are entirely outside the control of national or international political decisions. Another factor of production that has witnessed increased mobility in both the United States and Europe—namely, labor—could come under renewed control through stricter immigration policies. The difficulties encountered during the Uruguay round of GATT negotiations signal, at the least, a slowed movement toward a global regime of freer trade that could give impetus to the formation of restrictive regional trading blocs. Still, it is difficult to imagine that the genie of factor mobility and global competition can be forced back into the bottle.

The implication for rural America is straightforward: the "decoupling" (Drucker's term) of output from employment in traditional economic sectors is likely to continue. Major sources of new rural jobs will be found, if at all, in sectors less exposed to global pressures and more responsive to emerging forms of rural comparative advantage. This logic leads us to focus on services—in particular those related to tourism and retirement, which are both labor-intensive and attracted to the beauty, tranquility, and security that many rural areas can offer. This logic also directs our attention to technological changes, especially in telecommunications, that might over time reduce the impact of key rural disadvantages such as isolation and distance.

To repeat once again: this macroanalysis does not mean that every local effort to develop through manufacturing and natural resources is doomed to fail. We have identified a basic "flow" of economic events, which enables us to say that in the aggregate, certain strategies have better odds of success than others. But these aggregates conceal a wide variety of local circumstances and histories. Our point is only that in addition to assessing such local knowledge, each community ought to understand the broader tendencies that affect its fate.

Throughout this book we have suggested that change is the price of community survival in rural America. In most cases, adequate levels of employment and income cannot be expected from traditional sectors; the real choice is between decline and forms of economic innovation that will leave neither individual lives nor the structure of social relations unaltered. Some, perhaps many, rural residents will regret these changes, but they cannot be avoided. Every way of life requires some kind of economic basis; a commitment to preserving a total way of life in the face of profound economic shifts cannot hope to succeed. Individuals who are devoted to continuity of place, who want generations to have the opportunity of following one another in place, must therefore accept some *dis*continuities of economic and social life.[2]

To be effective, efforts to preserve rural places must rest on genuine local preferences. For example, if individuals care more about personal convenience and disposable income than they do about the maintenance of their community, patterns of consumption are likely to favor regional hubs at the expense of local merchants. This is not to say that individual preferences, however supportive of locality, will be automatically translated into community preservation. Coordinated collective action—political deliberation and decision—is needed to transform such priorities into effective public structures.

A community's political structures cannot be immunized from change any more than can its economic and social activities. To survive and flourish, previously separate local jurisdictions may have to learn the art of collaboration in education, public services, and economic planning; political authority must to some extent mold itself to the contours of emerging economic and social regionalization.

Another form of political and institutional change involves new relationships between rural and urban areas. As we have seen, recent research indicates that during the 1980s rural counties closely linked to metropolitan areas on average fared better than did the more remote counties, a finding at least consistent with Jane Jacobs' thesis that cities provide the focus and stimulus for rural economic activity.[3] Building on Jacobs' work, Dan Kemmis argues that the historic quasi-Jeffersonian rural mistrust of urban America has been outrun by events:

> As rural life is threatened more and more severely by international markets, by technological dislocations and corporate domination, it may be time for a reassessment of the relationship between cities and their rural environs. It may well be that neither towns nor farms can thrive in the way they would prefer until they turn their attention more directly to each other, realizing that they are mutually complementary parts of the enterprise of inhabiting a particular place. . . .[4]

As Jacobs observes, however, the economic contours of the "city-state" do not conform to the political jurisdictions of American federalism, let alone the centuries-old identification of the "nation" as the basic unit of economic life. At this juncture, forging effective new links between cities and hinterlands is a problem to be addressed, not yet an agenda to be implemented. During the 1820s, the construction of the Erie Canal helped realize a bold vision of new relationships between eastern seaboard cities and western rural hinterlands.[5] The equivalent vision for the 1990s has yet to be developed. At most, we can say that it is more likely to involve the electronic transfer of information than the physical transport of goods.

While an effective concern for place must begin in local communities, it does not end there. We have argued that the states and the federal government can help spur local mobilization for development as well as movement toward regional cooperation. In addition, these larger jurisdictions can significantly affect the context of market decisions—for example, through regulation or deregulation of such activities as transportation, communication, and financial services. Decisions in these and similar areas represent an implicit weighing of partially conflicting values such as economic efficiency versus equal consumer costs regardless of location.

Underlying these decisions is some understanding of what individuals, considered simply as citizens, are thought to deserve. Beginning in the 1930s, the United States made a political determination that all citizens, wherever they happened to live, were entitled to electricity, decent roads, and adequate water/wastewater facilities. The question in the 1990s is whether access to (for example) air travel, credit, and fiber optics will be similarly defined as elements of social citizenship. The question is on the table, and the viability of many rural areas hangs in the balance.

The challenge of place is hardly confined to rural America. During the past generation, we have moved toward mobility-centered policies for urban areas as well. The results have been positive for individuals able to make good use of opportunities for advancement, many of whom have left central cities for the suburbs. But for those left behind, economic opportunity, social cohesion, and physical security have plummeted. The dilemma now before us is whether the strategy of mobility must now be supplemented by an urban strategy of development-in-place.

Although from a moral and philosophical point of view an affirmative answer might seem to lend support to comparable rural needs, from a practical standpoint the reverse is likely to be the case. Rural decline is more dispersed than urban, and its consequences are far less visible and dramatic. In an era of $200 billion annual federal budget deficits, a nation struggling to respond to urban-based threats to the constitutional goal of domestic tranquility is unlikely to embark on major new initiatives targeting rural places. Under these circumstances, policies focused on class rather than place—for example, assistance to the working poor through increases in the Earned Income Tax Credit —may actually hold greater promise.[6]

Place and poverty are not the only respects in which the federal government can supplement the market. Throughout this study we have focused on the choices local communities must make and on the institutions and strategies they can use to render their choices effective. But we have also argued that the classic analysis of market failure points toward important areas of broader-scale public action. To the extent that local communities (like firms) cannot fully internalize the benefits of education and training, they may not have adequate incentives to supply optimal quantities of these goods. Therefore, states and the federal government have compelling reasons to upgrade their efforts. These larger jurisdictions, moreover, can play important roles in reducing costs of information and transactions in rural areas and accelerating the transfer of technology to them.

More generally, as Alice Rivlin and others have recently suggested, it is time to rethink, from the ground up, relations among the different levels of our federal system. The logic of public goods and market failure can help us understand which problems are truly national and which are local, state, or regional. For example, it may well be that the most appropriate federal role in health care is to establish a general framework that frees states to make choices for themselves within broad limits.[7] Similarly, the federal government would do better to help states act as innovators to community-level rural development rather than, as at present, channeling local efforts into the well-worn grooves of categorical grant programs.

The relation between state and economy is hardly a one-way street. As government compensates for market failures, it must change the way it operates to correct its own characteristic failures. Two shifts are critical. First, top-down New Deal-style bureaucratic mechanisms best suited to resource-based and mass-production industrial economies must give way to entrepreneurial mechanisms that can serve grass-roots needs in economies driven increasingly by information and innovation. Recent controversies concerning hundreds of USDA offices in which the number of employees exceeds the number of local clients is but one example of how outdated bureaucratic institutions come to serve their own interests at the expense of public goals.

As the second step, public programs must be redesigned to minimize the probability of capture by special interests. For example, public choice theorists have shown how government efforts to restrict the supply of desired goods (for example, through licensing and protectionism) not only generate individual "rent-seeking" behavior but also spur the formation of narrow groups to pursue special interests. The artful use of market mechanisms within legal and regulatory regimes can help rechannel self-interested behavior toward larger public purposes. Standard examples include the use of tradable emissions rights in environmental policy and the preference for tariffs over quotas in trade policy. Judged from this standpoint, most existing rural programs at the federal level would have to be judged as failures.

Development without deliberation is virtually certain to generate distortion, unfairness, and unpleasant surprises. Political jurisdictions must assess the ways in which partly conflicting goals such as growth, equity, continuity, sustainability, and participation are to be ranked and balanced. Clearly "development" is far more than simply an economic process.

Notes

Part I Introductory Text

1. On these points see "An Argument for Diversity" in *What are People For? Essays by Wendell Berry* (San Francisco: North Point Press, 1990), 109–122.
2. See especially Daniel Kemmis, *Community and the Politics of Place* (Norman: University of Oklahoma Press, 1990).
3. "The Work of Local Culture," in *What Are People For?*, 154–169.
4. Wallace Stegner, *Where The Bluebird Sings to the Lemonade Springs: Living and Writing in the West* (New York: Random House, 1992), 12.
5. Ibid., 33.
6. Ibid., 71–72.
7. Peter A. Morrison, *A Taste of the Country: A Collection of Calvin Beale's Writings* (University Park: The Pennsylvania State University Press, 1990), 18.

Chapter 1

1. For fuller discussion, see Kenneth L. Deavers, "Rural Development in the 1990s: Data and Research Needs," paper prepared for the Rural Social Science Symposium, AAEA, Baton Rouge, Louisiana, July 28–29, 1989.
2. Ibid., 12–13.
3. Scott Barancik, "The Rural Disadvantage: Growing Income Disparities Between Rural and Urban Areas" (Washington, D.C.: Center on Budget and Policy Priorities, 1990), 9.
4. Lucy Gorham and Bennett Harrison, "Working Below the Poverty Line: The Growing Problem of Low Earnings in Rural and Urban Regions across the United States" (Washington, D.C.: The Aspen Institute, 1990), 16.
5. Isaac Shapiro and Robert Greenstein, "Fulfilling Work's Promise: Policies to Increase Incomes of the Working Poor" (Washington, D.C.: Center on Budget and Policy Priorities, 1990), 3.

    The interaction of poverty and the relative scarcity of critical services such as health care has devastating consequences for many rural residents: "Maternal and infant mortality rates are substantially higher than those in urban areas and are rising at a faster rate. Rural Americans have disproportionately high rates of serious chronic illness, accidents, and disability. But the health care system is not equipped to adequately serve these needs." *Searching for "The Way That Works": An Analysis of FmHA Rural Development Policy and Implementation* (Washington, D.C: The Aspen Institute, 1990), 3.

    For the best recent research on rural poverty, see generally Cynthia M.

Duncan, ed., *Rural Poverty in America* (New York: Auburn House, 1992).

6. Deavers, "Rural Development in the 1990s," 11. Unless otherwise attributed, the figures cited in the foregoing summary of rural trends are drawn from this paper.

7. Calvin L. Beale and Glenn V. Fuguitt, "Decade of Pessimistic Nonmetro Population Trends Ends on Optimistic Note," *Rural Development Perspectives* 6, 3 (June–September 1990), 1418.

8. David Shribman, "Iowa Towns Shrivel as the Young People Head for the Cities," *Wall Street Journal,* April 24, 1991, A1.

9. Deavers, "Rural Development," 7.

10. Peter F. Drucker, *The New Realities* (New York: Harper & Row, 1989), 122.

11. Drucker, "The Changed World Economy," *Foreign Affairs* 64:4 (Spring 1986), 773.

12. Gavin Wright, "The Origins of American Industrial Success, 1979–1940," *American Economic Review* 80:4 (September 1990), 651–668.

13. Drucker, "The Changed World Economy," 775–777.

14. Lester C. Thurow, *The Zero-Sum Solution* (New York: Simon and Schuster, 1985), 84.

15. Thurow, "The Big Lie That Caused the Budget Catastrophe," *Washington Post,* October 7, 1990, D5.

16. Ibid.

17. For a useful summary of the early warning signs, see John Burgess, "Flood of Money into U.S. Slows to a Trickle," *Washington Post,* October 7, 1990, H1.

18. David Osborne and Ted Gaebler, *Reinventing Government* (Reading, MA: Addison-Wesley, 1992).

19. Deavers, "Rural Development," 11, 17.

20. Ibid., 9. For a detailed analysis of this issue, see Amy K Glasmeier and Michael E. Conroy, *Global Squeeze on Rural America: Opportunities, Threats, and Challenges from NAFTA, GATT, and Processes of Globalization* (Institute for Policy Research and Evaluation. The Pennsylvania State University, 1995).

21. For a good summary discussion, see Graham S. Toft, "Urban Development: Radical Perspectives on a Perennial Problem," *The Entrepreneurial Economy Review* 8:4 (January/February 1990), 13–19.

22. Emery Castle, "Policy Options for Rural Development in a Restructured Rural Economy: An International Perspective," in Gene F. Summers et al., *Agriculture and Beyond: Rural Economic Development* (Madison: University of Wisconsin College of Agricultural and Life Sciences, 1987), 16–17.

23. For a similar account, see Charles E. Lindblom, *Politics and Markets* (New York: Basic Books, 1977), chapter 2.

24. For a more recent theoretical look at civic action not dependent on centralized institutions, see Robert N. Bellah et al., *Habits of the Heart* (New York: Harper & Row, 1985).

25. For a multifaceted exploration of these themes, see Dieter Helm, ed., *The Economic Borders of the State* (Oxford: Oxford University Press, 1989).

26. See especially *Democracy in America,* Volume Two, Part II, chapters 2–8.1.

27. For the best discussion of the decline in civil society in contemporary America, see Robert D. Putnam, "Bowling Alone: America's Declining Social Capital," *Journal of Democracy* 6:1 (January 1995) 65–78.

28. Anne O. Krueger, "Government Failures in Development," *The Journal of Economic Perspectives* 4:3 (Summer 1990), 11, 13.

29. Ibid., 17–18. She goes on to observe that this is so regardless of whether the policies were initially adopted because of special interest lobbying or out of genuine concern for the public interest. Government action can trigger the mobilization of interest groups.

30. James T. Bonnen, "U.S. Perspective on the Interest Group Base of Rural Policy: People, Agriculture, the Environment," paper prepared for the International Symposium on Economic Change, Policies, Strategies, and Research issues, Aspen, Colorado, July 4–7 1990.

31. Albert Hirschman, *Exit, Voice, and Loyalty* (Cambridge, MA: Harvard University Press, 1970), chapter 3.

32. For some encouraging recent evidence of the positive impact of telecommunications on rural America, see "Many Rural Regions Are Growing Again; A Reason: Technology," *Wall Street Journal,* November 21, 1991, Al.

33. On the points covered in this paragraph, see generally *Education and Rural Economic Development: Strategies for the 1990s.* Agriculture and Rural Economy Division, Economic Research Service, U.S. Department of Agriculture. ERS Staff Report No. AGES 9153, September 1991.

Chapter 2

1. For this episode and the quotations, see H. W. Arndt, *Economic Development: The History of an Idea* (Chicago: University of Chicago Press, 1987), 104–105. For more extended discussion of basic needs in development, see Danny M. Leipziger, ed., *Basic Needs and Development* (Cambridge, MA: Oelgeschlager, Gunn, and Hain, 1981); and Bruce F. Johnston and William C. Clark, *Redesigning Rural Development: A Strategic Perspective* (Baltimore: Johns Hopkins, 1982), chapter 4.

2. Arndt, *Economic Development,* 106.

3. Quoted in Mark Sagoff, "The Humanities and Sustainable Development" (Institute for Philosophy and Public Policy, University of Maryland at College Park, unpublished).

4. Arndt, *Economic Development,* 165.

5. The economist Frank Levy also argues that, if widely shared, rapid growth in a country's overall income can reduce social conflict by reducing the salience of inequalities in the distribution of that income: "When your own situation is improving so fast, your neighbor's better situation is less of an irritant." *Dollars and Dreams: The Changing American Income Distribution* (New York: Norton, 1988), 80.

6. Wolfgang Sacks, "On the Archaeology of the Development Idea," Essay Two

(English translation by Science, Technology, and Society Program, Pennsylvania State University, unpublished).

7. Robert Chambers, *Rural Development: Putting the Last First* (New York: Longman, 1983), chapter 5.

8. For a useful survey within the U.S. context, see Ann R. Tickamyer and Cynthia M. Duncan, "Poverty and Opportunity Structure in Rural America," *Annual Review of Sociology* 16 (1990), 67–86.

9. This represents only a rough first approximation. A more complete specification would have to reflect the distinction, so fundamental to migration theory, between "push" and "pull" factors. Within a vigorously growing economy, opportunities in one growth sector may be superior to those in another *that is also growing*. If substantial numbers of individuals are pulled from the latter into the former, this is hardly evidence of policy failure with regard to the latter. This is to be distinguished from cases in which certain sectors or regions can simply no longer sustain their populations and employment bases, portions of which are then pushed out. This is what counts, at least prima facie, as inadequate development. For a discussion in a Third World context, see John Connell et al., *Migration from Rural Areas: The Evidence from Village Studies* (Delhi: Oxford University Press, 1976), chapter 1.

10. Jane Jacobs, *Cities and the Wealth of Nations* (New York: Vintage, 1985), 72, 224.

11. This risk-based argument for diversity is largely unrelated to the long-standing debate over "balanced development," which (depending on the point of view adopted) may well lead to an endorsement of economic diversity as a critical element of development strategy. For a useful review of the issues and literature, see Amitava Krishna Dutt, "Sectoral Balance in Development: A Survey," *World Development* 18:6 (June 1990), 915–930. See also Joel A. Thompson and Mark W. Lanier, "Measuring Economic Development: Economic Diversification as an Alternative to Standard Indicators," *Policy Studies Review* 7:1 (Autumn 1987), 77–90.

12. Similar possibilities exist (indeed, perhaps to a greater extent) within the Third World. In India, for example, "The social position of the migrant in the village vis-a-vis other social groups can affect the decision to migrate. Where the migrants have an inferior social position in the village society, they may well lose their distinctive (and usually repressive) social characteristics on migration." Connell et al., *Migration from Rural Areas*, 49.

13. Quoted in James H. Street, "The Institutionalist Theory of Economic Development," *Journal of Economic Issues* 21:4 (December 1987), 1871. We are indebted to Street as well for the overall account of institutionalism offered in the text.

14. James Fallows, *More Like Us* (Boston: Houghton Mifflin, 1989).

15. The new centrality of sustainability in discussions of development is urged in Jessica Mathews, "The New Dogma of Environmentalism," *Washington Post*, January 3, 1991, A21. Book-length explorations of key issues include Michael Redclift, *Sustainable Development: Exploring the Contradiction* (London:

Methuen, 1987); and F. Archibugi and P. Nijkamp, eds., *Economy and Ecology: Towards Sustainable Development* (Dordrecht: Kluwer, 1989). For a particularly forceful summary of the skeptical view, see Mark Sagoff, "The Concept of Overlapping Consensus as an Organizing Principle for International Regime Formation and Environmental Management" (Institute for Philosophy and Public Policy, University of Maryland at College Park, unpublished), 5-7.

16. This is not to say that developing strategies taking nonrenewable resources as their point of departure are necessarily self-defeating, but only that their exhaustibility must be given due weight from the outset. At the very least, this requires more attention to nonmarket planning and to technological substitution over time than is typically forthcoming. For one discussion, see Charles W. Howe, "On the Theory of Optimal Regional Development Based on an Exhaustible Resource," *Growth and Change* 18:2 (Spring 1987), 53-68.

17. For a well-known discussion, see Arthur Okun, *Equity and Efficiency: The Big Tradeoff* (Washington, D.C.: The Brookings Institution, 1975). For reflections within the genre of development theory, see Amartya Sen, "Development: Which Way Now?" in *Resources, Values, and Development* (Cambridge, MA: Harvard University Press, 1984), 495-496. For a summary of recent research indicating a substantial degree of mutual reinforcement rather than conflict, see Jan Hogendorn, *Economic Development* (New York: Harper and Row, 1987), 12-13.

18. Joyce Appleby, "Commercial Farming and the 'Agrarian Myth' in the Early Republic," *The Journal of American History* 68 (March 1982), 833-849.

19. Jane Jacobs contends that this phenomenon—the absence of useful feedback to places being abandoned—is global rather than peculiar to the United States: "The most striking fact is that abandonment has no effect upon stagnant communities, other than to shrink them." See Jacobs, *Cities and the Wealth of Nations*, 73. All of Chapter 4 is worth reading in this connection.

20. See Robert Caro, *The Power Broker* (New York: Vintage, 1975); and Robert Dahl, *Who Governs?* (New Haven: Yale University Press, 1961).

21. For an account of the debate over this issue in the Third World context, see Martin Staniland, *What Is Political Economy?* (New Haven: Yale University Press, 1985), 82-83.

Chapter 3

1. Mrinal Datta-Chauduri, "Market Failure and Government Failure," *Journal of Economic Perspectives* 4:3 (Summer 1990), 26.

2. For an excellent summary and discussion, see Nicholas Stern, "The Economics of Development: A Survey," *The Economic Journal* 99 (September 1989), 614-622.

3. For presentations of, and reflections on, these views by many of their originators, see Gerald M. Meier and Dudley Seers, eds., *Pioneers in Development* (New York: Oxford University Press, 1984). A good brief discussion is in Datta-Chauduri, "Market Failure," 26-27. Lengthier treatments of this period

include P. F. Leeson, "Development economics and the study of development," in Leeson and M.M. Minogue, eds. *Perspectives on development: Cross-disciplinary themes in development studies* (Manchester: Manchester University Press, 1988), chapter 1; H.W. Arndt, *Economic Development: The History of an Idea* (Chicago: University of Chicago: University of Chicago Press, 1987), chapter 3; Gerald M. Meier, *Emerging from Poverty: The Economics That Really Matters* (New York: Oxford University Press, 1984), chapter 6.

4. Arndt, *Economic Development*, 61–62. This is *not* to say that capital is trivial. For a revisionist view (one, that is, that restores a portion of the intellectual status quo ante), see Amartya Sen, *Resources, Values, and Development* (Cambridge, Mass.: Harvard University Press, 1984), 489–493.

5. See, for example, Albert Hirschman, *The Strategy of Economic Development* (New Haven: Yale University Press, 1958), 51; and *Essays in Trespassing: Economics to Politics and Beyond* (Cambridge: Cambridge University Press, 1981), 9.

6. Hirschman, *Strategy of Economic Development*, chapter 6; *Rival Views of Market Society* (New York: Viking, 1986), chapter 3.

7. Amartya Sen has done perhaps the most important theoretical work on the relation between GNP, distribution, and basic needs. He argued that traditional development economics goes wrong in its concentration on income rather than on "entitlements" of people and the "capabilities" these entitlements generate. Ultimately, the process of economic development has to be concerned with what people can or cannot do—for example, whether they can live long, escape avoidable morbidity, be well nourished, be able to read and write and communicate, take part in literary and scientific pursuits, and so forth. See *Resources, Values, and Development*, 496–497; *Commodities and Capabilities* (Amsterdam: Elsevier, 1985); *The Standard of Living* (Cambridge: Cambridge University Press, 1987).

8. The relation between the perception of rising inequality and the facts of the matter are by no means simple, however. For a good summary of the standard view, see Jan Hogendorn, *Economic Development* (New York: Harper and Row, 1987), 20–30. For dissents, see Jeffrey G. Williamson, "Comments on 'Reflections on Development'," in Gustav Ranis and T. Paul Schultz, *The State of Development Economics: Progress and Perspectives* (New York: Basil Blackwell, 1988), 25–26; and Jagdish N. Bhagwati, "Development Economics: What Have We Learnt?" in Krishna Ahooja-Patel et al., eds., *World Economy in Transition* (Oxford: Pergamon Press, 1986), 20–23.

9. For a good example, see R. P. Misra, "Development or Disruption: The Challenge of Culture-Neutral Development Planning," in Misra and M. Honjo, *Changing Perceptions of Development Problems* (Hong Kong: Maruzen Asia, 1981), 71–121. Misra goes so far as to endorse a definition of development as the "increasing attainment of one's own values."

10. For a presentation and discussion, see Hirschman, *Essays in Trespassing*, chapter 5.

11. Hirschman, *Essays in Trespassing*, chapter 1.
12. The "declining terms of trade" thesis is controversial. For a good summary of the contending theories and evidentiary bases, see Jan Hogendorn, *Economic Development*, 344–358. His measured conclusion is that what is certainly true for specific primary products is not nearly as valid for a general index of such products. This suggests that countries heavily and inflexibly dependent on a single primary product may well experience the difficulties trade pessimists predict. For other important surveys of trade issues, see Jose Antonio Ocampo, "New Developments in Trade Theory and LDCs," *Journal of Development Economics* 22:1 (June 1986), 129–170; and David Jaffee, "Export Dependence and Economic Growth: A Reformulation and Respecification," *Social Forces* 64, 1 (September 1985), 102–118.
13. For a summary, see Arndt, *Economic Development*, 72–76.
14. Ibid., 78–84.
15. Anne O. Krueger, "Government Failures in Development," *Journal of Economic Perspectives* 4:3 (Summer 1990), 13–15.
16. Datta-Chauduri, "Market Failure," 30.
17. Krueger, "Government Failures," 18, n. 17.
18. Adapted from Nicholas H. Stern, "The Economics of Development: A Survey" *The Economic Journal* 99 (September 1989), 616.
19. Krueger, "Government Failures," 17–21. Other important contributions to the neoclassical revival include Jagdish N. Bhagwati, "Directly Unproductive, Profit-Seeking (DUP) Activities," *Journal of Political Economy* 90 (October 1982), 988–1002; and P.T. Bauer, *Dissent on Development* (London: Weidenfeld and Nicolson, 1972). For survey discussions of this revival, see Stern, "The Economics of Development", 597–685; Wing Thye Woo, "The Art of Economic Development: Markets, Politics, and Externalities," *International Organization* 44:3 (Summer 1990), 403–429; Albert Fishlow, "Review of *Handbook of Development Economics*," *Journal of Economic Literature* 29 (December 1991), 1728–1737; Helen Shapiro and Lance Taylor, "The State of Industrial Strategy," *World Development* 18:6 (June 1990), 863–865.
20. Larry E. Westphal, "Industrial Policy in an Export-Propelled Economy: Lessons from South Korea's Experience," *Journal of Economic Perspectives* 4,3 (Summer 1990), 54.
21. Ibid., 55–56. For a useful survey of the theoretical issues raised by technology acquisition in developing countries, see Tom Ganiatsos, "Transfer of Technology: Theory and Policy," in Ahooja-Patel et al., *World Economy in Transition*, 229–251.
22. Datta-Chauduri, "Market Failure," 32–33.
23. For discussions of the complexities of export-led growth, see Shapiro and Taylor, "The State and Industrial Strategy," 866, 868–871; and Ronald Findlay, "Trade, Development, and the State," in Ranis and Schultz, *State of Development Economics*, chapter 4.
24. Albert Fishlow, "The Latin American State," *Journal of Economic Perspectives*

4:3 (Summer 1990), 65.

25. Ibid., 66, 73. As Pranab Bardham puts it, "The key issue ... is the ability of the state to insulate economic management from the pressures of short-run rent-seeking by powerful interest groups." Taiwan and South Korea were able to do so; Latin American governments were not. "Comments on 'Development Economics: What Next?'" in Ranis and Schultz, *State of Development Economics*, 137–138. For a measured if unadmiring examination of the neoclassical revival, see John Toye, *Dilemmas of Development: Reflections of the Counter-Revolution in Development Theory and Policy* (Oxford: Basil Blackwell, 1987); and in a similar vein, if with a broader sweep, P.F. Leeson and F.I. Nixson, "Development Economics and the State," in Leeson and Minogue, eds., *Perspectives on Development*, chapter 2. The debate between P.T. Bauer and Nicholas H. Stern is also instructive. See Stern, "Professor Bauer on Development," *Journal of Development Economics* 1, 3 (1974), 191–211; and Bauer, "N.H. Stern on Substance and Method in Development Economics," *Journal of Development Economics* 2:4 (1975), 387–405.

26. Shapiro and Taylor, "The State and Industrial Strategy," 866.

27. Ibid., 872–873.

28. Paul Cook and David Hulme, "The Compatibility of Market Liberalization and Local Economic Development Strategies," *Regional Studies* 22:3 (June 1988), 224.

29. Hirschman, *Strategy of Economic Development*, 196.

30. Jacobs, *Cities and the Wealth of Nations* (New York: Vintage, 1985), 161–162.

31. Hirschman, *Strategy of Economic Development*, 187–190.

32. Ibid., 199–200.

33. Peter F. Drucker, *The New Realities*, (New York: Harper and Row, 1989), 116.

34. Jacobs, *Cities and Wealth of Nations*, 31–32.

35. Michael J. Piore and Charles F. Sabel, *The Second Industrial Divide: Possibilities for Prosperity* (New York: Basic Books, 1984); C. Richard Hatch, "Flexible Manufacturing Networks: Cooperation for Competitiveness in a Global Economy" (Washington, D.C.: The Corporation for Enterprise Development, 1988).

36. Robert B. Reich, "Who Is Us?" *Harvard Business Review*, January–February 1990, 58–59; "The Real Economy," *The Atlantic*, February 1991, 35–52; *The Work of Nations: Preparing Ourselves for 21st-Century Capitalism* (New York: Knopf, 1991).

37. For a good discussion, see Hogendorn, *Economic Development*, 239–243.

38. For a provocative set of prescriptions for managers in a knowledge-intensive global economy, see Drucker, *The New Realities*, chapter 15.

39. As we shall see in Chapter 6, there is also a connection (at least at the level of theory) between education and the emergence of entrepreneurs in local economies.

40. One of the best is Martin Neil Baily and Alok K. Chakrabati, *Innovation and the Productivity Crisis* (Washington, D.C.: Brookings, 1988). For a spirited popular treatment, see Walt W. Rostow, "Economic Growth and the Diffusion

of Power," *Challenge* 29, 4 (September–October 1986), 29–37. As Rostow sums up his case: "Economists will have to deal with large discontinuous changes in production functions and their impact on employment and productivity growth. Specialization of function and economies of scale with all their refinements are no longer enough. ... In short, neoclassical economists— the neo-Newtonians—don't know how to deal with the generation and diffusion of technologies as an integral part of mainstream economics. . . . Yet we can't understand the processes of growth and development until we do." Drucker offers a parallel argument: "There is no room in contemporary economic theory for technology, for innovation, for change altogether. Like their predecessors, the neoclassicists, economists postulate an unchanging economy, an economy in equilibrium. Technology, innovation, and change are external. Economists [to be sure have] made several attempts to bring technology and change into their model. These have all failed, and for the same reason: There is very little, if any, correlation between monetary policy, credit, and interest rates on the one hand and entrepreneurship, invention, and innovation on the other." (*The New Realities*, p. 163). For an important review of entrepreneurship in theory and practice, see Richard R. Nelson, "Incentives for Entrepreneurship and Supporting Institutions," in Bela Balassa and Herbert Giersch, *Economic Incentives*, (New York: St. Martin's Press, 1986), 173–187.

41. Baily and Chakrabati, *Innovation*, chapter 6.
42. Jacobs, *Cities and Wealth of Nations*, 39–42, 59–71.
43. For a particularly clear account of the shift from static to dynamic comparative advantage, see Hogendorn, *Economic Development*, 330–337.
44. Thirty years ago, Hirschman had already captured a portion of this idea in his distinction between "creative" and "cooperative" entrepreneurship. See *Strategy of Economic Development*, 16–20.
45. Kenneth L. Deavers, "Rural Development in the 1990s: Data and Research Needs" (paper prepared for Rural Social Science Symposium, AAEA, Baton Rouge, LA, July 28–29, 1989), 13–14.
46. Brian J. L. Berry, "Strategies, Models, and Economic Theories of Development in Rural Regions," Agricultural Economic Report No. 127, ERS-USDA, December 1967.
47. Steven R. Kale, "Theoretical Contributions to the Understanding of U.S. Nonmetropolitan Economic Change," *Economic Development Quarterly* 3:1 (February 1989), 58–69.
48. William J. Coffey and Mario Polese, "Local Development: Conceptual Bases and Policy Implications," *Regional Studies* 19:2 (April 1985), 87; Paul Cook and David Hulme, "The Compatibility of Market Liberalization and Local Economic Development Strategies," *Regional Studies* 22:3 (June 1988), 224; Hogendorn, *Economic Development*, 278–279; E.A.G. Robinson, ed., *Backward Areas in Advanced Countries* (London: Macmillan, 1969), xiv.
49. Jacobs, *Cities*, chapter 5. A curious mirror-image of this gulf between theory and practice arose in the case of the celebrated Samuelson analysis of interna-

tional trade. Making exactly the opposite assumption—*no* mobility of production factors—Samuelson argued that free trade would tend to equalize
absolute factor prices, including incomes, on a global basis. This analysis was
published just as consciousness of international income disparities was rising
sharply. As Hirschman comments, with some asperity: "While in Kuhn's scientific revolution sequence, the accumulating facts are supposed to gradually
contradict the paradigm, here the theory contributed to the contradiction by
resolutely walking away from the facts." *Essays in Trespassing,* p. 60.

50. Deavers, "Rural Development," 19.
51. A recent article suggests that West Virginia communities as far as 80 miles
    from the Washington, D.C. metropolitan area are now benefitting from func-
    tional adjacency, polarizing that traditionally depressed state into areas of
    growth in the east and vast bypassed areas to the west. Barbara Vobejda, "In
    West Virginia, the Great Divide," *Washington Post,* January 7, 1991, A1.
52. For some dated but intriguing perspectives, see Robinson, *Backward Areas,*
    xv–xviii. It has recently been suggested that certain rural regions may benefit
    from forming political alliances with no-growth or limited-growth forces that
    have been building in congested urban (and even suburban) areas—that is, to
    the extent that public policy can induce urban/suburban growth to spill over
    to a greater extent into adjacent or near-adjacent rural counties. See David
    Harrison and Jonathan Seib, "Toward 'One Region': Strengthening
    Rural–Urban Economic Linkages," in Northwest Policy Center, *A Northwest
    Reader: Options for Rural Communities* (Seattle: University of Washington,
    1988), chapter 6.
53. Jacobs, *Cities,* 178.
54. Douglass North, "Location Theory and Regional Economic Growth," *Journal
    of Political Economy* 63 (1955), 243–258.
55. For example, the proportion of nonmetro manufacturing jobs classified as rou-
    tine production is far higher than for metro areas. Deavers, "Rural
    Development," figure 4.
56. Some analysts have predicted that service industries will follow the same
    product cycle evolution, hence will eventually decentralize. To date, however,
    available evidence provides little if any support for this conjecture. For a fuller
    exposition, see Chapter 7.
57. Kale, "Theoretical Contributions," 63.
58. Edgar M. Hoover, "Some Old and New Issues in Regional Development," in
    Robinson, *Backward Areas in Advanced Countries,* 345–346.
59. Peter B. Doeringer and David G. Terkla, "Turning Around Local Economies:
    Managerial Strategies and Community Assets," *Journal of Policy Analysis and
    Management* 9:4 (1990), 488–489.
60. Robinson, *Backward Areas,* 3–4.
61. Ibid., 4.
62. Ibid., 462–463.

Chapter 4

1. For discussion, see Kenneth L. Deavers, "Rural Development in the 1990s" (1989), 15–18, 20–21.

2. Ross Gittell, "Managing the Development Process: Community Strategies in Economic Revitalization," *Journal of Policy Analysis and Management* 9:4 (1990), 520. There is a wonderful story of two salesmen sent to a poor country by a shoe company. The first cabled back: NO PROSPECTS HERE. NO ONE WEARS SHOES. The second sent a very different message: IMMENSE PROSPECTS HERE. MILLIONS WITHOUT SHOES. See Jan S. Hogendorn, *Economic Development* (New York: Harper and Row, 1987), 489. Our suggestion is that rural development needs more people like the second shoe salesman—particularly at the local community level.

3. Center for Community Change, *Searching for "The Way That Works,"* chapter 14.

4. For a fuller description of the state role in this new federalism, see DeWitt John and Kim Norris, "Rural Communities: State Governments Can Help," *Choices* 4:2 (second quarter 1989), 12–15. As the authors emphasize, substantial movement in this direction has already occurred.

5. See Doug Ross, "Thinking about Rural Economic Development in the 1990s," paper prepared for the CSPA Rural Development Academy, Spring 1990, 13.

6. Emil E. Malizia, "Economic Development in Smaller Cities and Rural Areas," *Journal of the American Planning Association* 52:4 (Autumn 1986), 489–99.

7. The State Policy Program, undertaken by the Aspen Institute in collaboration with the Ford Foundation, represents the most systematic effort to pull together the subnational experiences of the 1980s and to draw policy-relevant conclusions from them.

8. Peter Drucker, *The New Realities*, (New York: Harper and Row, 1989), 212.

9. Ibid., 62–66.

10. John and Norris, "Rural Communities," 13.

11. For this "three waves" analysis, see Ross, "Thinking about Rural Economic Development," 6–16.

12. Osborne, "Reinventing D.C.: How Sharon Pratt Dixon Can Turn the City Around," *The Washington Post Magazine*, December 9, 1990, 43. For a useful survey of various approaches to public entrepreneurship, see Susan E. Clarke and Gary L. Gaile, "Moving Toward Entrepreneurial Economic Development Policies: Opportunities and Barriers," *Policy Studies Journal* 17, 3 (Spring 1989) 574–598.

13. Ross, "Thinking about Rural Development," 16.

14. John and Norris, "Rural Communities," 13.

15. Peter B. Doeringer and David G. Terkla, "Turning Around Local Economies: Managerial Strategies and Community Assets," *Journal of Policy Analysis and Management* 9:4 (1990), 487–506.

16. William J. Coffey and Mario Polese, "Local Development: Conceptual Bases

and Policy Implications," *Regional Studies* 19:2 (April 1985), 86. A similar
conclusion is reached by Paul Cook and David Hulme, "The Compatibility of
Market Liberalization and Local Economic Development Strategies," *Regional
Studies* 22:3 (June 1988), 224.

17. Deavers, "Rural Development," 33–35.
18. Helen F. Ladd, "Introduction to Symposium on Managing Local
    Development," *Journal of Policy Analysis and Management* 9:4 (1990), 485.
19. John and Norris, "Rural Communities," 13–14.
20. Cornelia B. Flora and Jan L. Flora, "Developing Entrepreneurial Rural
    Communities," *Sociological Practice* 8 (1990), 197–207. The theme of disper-
    sion of economic and political leadership is emphasized by Ron Shaffer and
    Gene F. Summers, "Community Economic Development," in James A.
    Christenson and Jerry W. Robinson Jr., eds., *Community Development in
    Perspective* (Ames, AI: Iowa State University Press, 1989), chapter 9. For a dis-
    cussion of cultural diversity among U.S. rural communities, see Thomas L.
    Daniels, "The Goals and Values of Local Economic Development Strategies in
    Rural America, *Agriculture and Human Values* 8:3 (Summer 1991), 4–5.
21. Ross Gittell, "Managing the Development Process: Community Strategies in
    Economic Revitalization," *Journal of Policy Analysis and Management* 9:4
    (1990), 507–531.
22. Michael Hibbard, "Community Beliefs and the Failure of Community
    Economic Development," *Social Service Review* 60:2 (June 1986), 195.
23. Ibid., 196; James Fallows, *More Like Us* (Boston: Houghton Mifflin, 1989),
    25–27.
24. Mancur Olson Jr., *The Logic of Collective Action: Public Goods and the Theory
    of Groups* (Cambridge, MA: Harvard University Press, 1965), chapter 1. For a
    more detailed analysis of the leadership issue, see Norman Frohlich and Joe A.
    Oppenheimer, *Political Leadership and Collective Goods* (Princeton: Princeton
    University Press, 1971).
25. Coffey and Polese, "Local Development," 89. For the importance of trust, co-
    operation, and general "social capital" for community development, see Robert
    D. Putnam, "The Prosperous Community, Social Capital and Public Life,"
    The American Prospect 13 (Spring 1993), 35–42.
26. Fallows, *More Like Us*, 21.
27. Gittell, "Managing the Development Process," 521–522.
28. To the extent that resources are scarce, the differential willingness of commu-
    nities to organize could serve as the basis of a kind of triage policy, but one
    that is (so to speak) self-administered.
29. See Tony Fuller, "Local Development Strategies: A Canadian Perspective,"
    paper prepared for the International Symposium on Economic Change,
    Policies, Strategies, and Research Issues, Aspen Colorado, July 4–7, 1990,
    12–15; and Philip Ehrensaft and David Freshwater, "Direct and Indirect Rural
    Development Policy in a Neo-Conservative North America" (unpublished: on
    file with the authors), 61–63.
30. Ross, "Thinking about Rural Development," 27–39.

31. Gittell, "Managing the Development Process," 521.
32. Ibid., 520.
33. Daniel Kemmis, *Community and the Politics of Place* (Norman: University of Oklahoma Press, 1990), 92–94.
34. For a broad discussion of choices between integration into the national/global economy and strategies of local resistance, see Peter B. Meyer and Michael Burayidi, "Is Value Conflict Inherent in Rural Economic Development? An Exploratory Examination of Unrecognized Choices." *Agriculture and Human Value* 8:3 (Summer 1991), 10–18.
35. Deavers, "Rural Development," 18.
36. David A. McGranahan, "Introduction" to *Education and Rural Economic Development: Strategies for the 1990s.* Agriculture and Rural Economy Division, Economic Research Service, U.S. Department of Agriculture. ERS Staff Report No. AGES 9153, 8.
37. Coffey and Polese, "Local Development," 87; see also Cook and Hulme, "The Compatibility of Market Liberalization," 224.
38. For some expressions of skepticism, see Ehrensaft and Freshwater, "Direct and Indirect Development Policy," 14. They emphasize that telecommunications can make possible siting of routine services such as data entry in lower-cost locations outside rural North America, and they suggest that face-to-face contacts characteristic of metropolitan regions are a necessary condition for innovation and growth in contemporary economies. We may add that eliminating the distance penalty is a two-edged sword. Along with decentralization, it can also lead to greater centralization of certain services in urban areas, with clients from far-off places linked together through telecommunications.
39. For a clear and persuasive treatment of themes, see Edwin B. Parker, Heather E. Hudson, Don A. Dillman, and Andrew D. Roscoe, *Rural America in the Information Age: Telecommunications Policy for Rural Development* (Lanham, MD: Aspen Institute/University Press of America, 1989).
40. See especially Hirschman, "A Generalized Linkage Approach to Development, with Special Reference to Staples," in *Essays in Trespassing: Economics to Politics and Beyond* (New York: Cambridge University Press, 1981), chapter 4.
41. For a summary, see Cook and Hulme, "The Compatibility of Market Liberalization," 224.
42. For general theory and description, see Michael J. Piore and Charles F. Sabel, *The Second Industrial Divide: Possibilities for Prosperity* (New York: Basic Books, 1984). For case studies, see Doeringer and Terkla, "Turning Around Local Economies."
43. Ehrensaft and Freshwater, "Direct and Indirect Development Policy," 15–16; Fuller, "Local Development Strategies," 8–12. In 1967, Brian Berry (1967) was already discussing a conception of functional regions defined by the travel behavior of consumers.
44. Deavers, "Rural America: Lagging Growth and High Poverty ... Do We Care?" *Choices* 4:2 (Second Quarter 1989) 7.

45. Fuller, "Local Development Strategies," 14.

Chapter 5

1. David L. Brown and Kenneth L. Deavers, "Rural Change and the Rural Economic Policy Agenda for the 1980s," in David L. Brown et al., eds., *Rural Economic Development in the 1980s: Prospects for the Future,* RDRR-69, Economic Research Service, U.S. Department of Agriculture (Washington, D.C.: U.S. Government Printing Office, Sept. 1988), 1–28.
2. U.S. Congress, Office of Technology Assessment (OTA) report (1988), 149.
3. Bruce A. Weber et al., "Performance of Natural Resource Industries," in Brown et al., eds., *Rural Economic Development,* 104.
4. Donn Reimund and Mindy Petrulis, "Performance of the Agricultural Sector," in Brown et al., eds., *Rural Economic Development in the 1980s: Prospects for the Future,* RDRR-69, ERS, USDA (Washington, D.C.: U.S. Government Printing Office, Sept. 1988), 92–93.
5. This includes farming as well as food processing and agricultural services. The farming category alone, including farm proprietors and farm wage workers, accounts for about 4 percent of total employment. See Weber et al., "Performance of Natural Resource Industries," 106.
6. See Chapters 8 and 9.
7. "The Status of the Rural Economy," Economic Research Service, U.S. Department of Agriculture, 1994.
8. Ibid.
9. See the maps on pages 108–109 in Weber et al., "Performance of Natural Resource Industries," for a graphic illustration of natural resources concentrations.
10. OTA 1988, 170.
11. According to Mark Drabenstott and Lynn Gibson (*Rural America in Transition,* 1988), farm income alone generated one-fifth of GNP at the turn of the century.
12. Peter Drucker, "The Changed World Economy," *Foreign Affairs,* 64:4 (Spring 1986), 770.
13. Ibid.
14. Ibid., 773–774.
15. OTA 1990.
16. OTA 1988.
17. See Martin N. Baily and Alok K. Chakrabati, *Innovation and the Productivity Crisis* (Washington, D.C.: The Brookings Institution, 1988) for a careful examination of the productivity slowdown in nonfarm industries. See also Baily and Robert J. Gordon, "The Productivity Slowdown, Measurement Issues, and the Explosion of Computer Power," Brookings Papers on Economic Activity, 2:1988, Washington, D.C., 347–420.
18. Donn Reimund and Fred Gale 1992, 1–9.

19. OTA 1988, 395–396.

20. When a lumber mill retools, employment drops an estimated 20–25 percent, on average (J.A. Savage 1990, 47).

21. OTA 1988, 154–157.

22. Reimund and Petrulis, "Performance of the Agricultural Sector," 98–99.

23. Drabenstott and Alan D. Barkema, "A Turning Point in the Farm Recovery?" *Economic Review*, 76:1, Jan.-Feb. 1991, 18.

24. Between the late 1950s and the early 1980s, the labor hours required to produce a bale of cotton fell from 75 to 5, and the labor hours required to produce 100 bushels of soybeans fell from 23 to 12. Between 1950 and 1984, the amount of acreage needed to meet America's domestic food and fiber demands dropped from 295 million to 237 million, despite a 56 percent increase in national population (Reimund and Petrulis, "Performance of Agricultural Sector," 85).

25. Note current efforts to develop new products such as artificial citrus juice and calorie-free deserts (OTA 1988, 206-207).

26. For an excellent description of how a wide variety of U.S. government policies, from price supports and tax rules to research agendas and immigration laws, favor large, commercial farms over small and medium-sized family farms, see Alain de Janvry et al., "Toward a Rural Development Program for the United States: A Proposal" (1989), 56–59.

27. Reimund and Fred Gale, *Structural Change in the U.S. Farm Sector, 1974–87: 13th Annual Family Farm Report to Congress,* Agriculture and Rural Economy Division, ERS, USDA, Agriculture Information Bulletin No 647, May 1992, 3–6.

28. Weber et al., "Performance of Natural Resource Industries," 81; and Reimund and Gale, *Structural Change,* 7.

29. OTA 1988, 40.

30. Weber et al., "Performance of Natural Resource Industries," table 11 on p. 97.

31. OTA 1988, 41, 209–210.

32. OTA 1988. p. 210.

33. Reimund and Petrulis, "Performance of the Agricultural Sector," 93.

34. Drabenstott and Barkema, "A Turning Point," 24.

35. Also see Gene D. Sullivan ("FYI: The 1990 Farm Bill," *Economic Review,* 76:1, Jan.–Feb. 1991).

36. Direct government payments to farmers totaled $1.3 billion in 1980 and peaked in 1987 at $16.7 billion.

37. Commodity price support and supply control programs have shielded agriculture from market forces since the 1930s.

38. Weber et al., "Performance of Natural Resources Industries," 105.

39. William E. Nothdurft, *Renewing America* (Washington, D.C.: Council of State Planning Agencies, 1984), 68.

40. Charles E. Keegan, III and Paul E. Polzin, "Trends in the Wood and Paper Products Industry: Their Impact on the Pacific Northwest Economy, *Journal of*

Forestry, 85:11, Nov. 1987, 34.

41. Weber at al., "Performance of Natural Resources Industries," 126–127.
42. Keegan and Polzin, "Trends in Wood and Paper," 34.
43. Standard and Poor's 1989, B84.
44. Weber et al., "Performance of Natural Resources Industries," 129.
45. OTA 1990.
46. Stanley Tucker, "Bright Future for Coal," *Petroleum Economist,* 16:10, Oct. 1989, 315.
47. Ibid., 316–317.
48. Standard and Poor's 1989, R27.
49. OTA 1990 notes that the effects of economic slowdowns on energy consumption are complex (pp. 3–4). Conventional wisdom suggests that energy use simply would drop in hard economic times due to lower production. However, OTA notes other offsetting factors: (1) slow economic growth tends to slow down efforts to innovate and improve energy efficiency; (2) the mix of spending during downturns tends to shift toward more basic, energy-intensive products and more energy-intensive inputs into the production process.

      See Chapter 7 for a discussion of how consumers spend an increasing share of their income on services that are relatively less energy-intensive than manufactured goods as their incomes go up.
50. Weber et al., "Performance of Natural Resources Industries," 124.
51. Ibid., 123, 129.
52. OTA 1988; Andrew Smith 1989.
53. OTA 1988, 40–42.
54. Andrew Smith 1989, p. 320.
55. Drabenstott and Gibson, *Rural America in Transition,* 41–44.
56. Ibid., table 3.2 on p. 44.
57. Rural counties in general grew more slowly during the 1980s than during the 1970s.
58. Calvin L. Beale and Glenn V. Fuguitt, "Decade of Pessimistic Nonmetro Population Trends Ends on Optimistic Note," *Rural Development Perspectives,* 6:3, June-Sept. 1990, 15–16.
59. Ibid., 15.
60. de Janvry et al., "Toward a Rural Development Program," 67–68.
61. Margaret G. Thomas, "A Guide to Rural Economic Development through Tourism and Wildlife-based Recreation," chapter VI in *Recouples: Natural Resource Strategies for Rural Economic Development* (Kansas City, MO: Midwest Research Institute, 1990), IV–7.
62. Ibid., IV–12.
63. Ibid., IV–20.
64. Chris Leman, "A Natural Resources Strategy for the 1990s," in *Northwest Region Watch,* Northwest Policy Center, Seattle, WA, 1990, 4.
65. Daniel Kemmis, *Community and the Politics of Place,* (Norman, OK: University of Oklahoma Press, 1990), 104–108.
66. Thomas, "A Guide to Rural Economic Development."

67. Phone interview, July 3, 1991.
68. Joel Millman, "There's Your Solution," *Forbes*, January 7, 1991, 72.
69. Ibid.
70. Barkema et al., "Processing Food in Farm States: An Economic Development Strategy for the 1990s," *Economic Review*, Federal Reserve Bank of Kansas, July/Aug. 1990, map on p. 9. It is important to note, however, that food processing is a relatively important part of the economies of the larger, more diversified farm states (p. 7).
71. Ibid., 9,11.
72. Ibid., 11.
73. Ibid., 14–17.
74. Ibid., 15–16; OTA 1988, 206–208. OTA cites a serious obstacle to achieving this goal: the low proportion of sales (0.4 percent) that today's food processing industry spends on research and development.
75. Phone interview with Joe Cortright, July 3, 1991.
76. Phone interview with David Harrison, Executive Director, Northwest Policy Center in Seattle, Washington, July 3, 1991.
77. In the area of primary production, Margaret Thomas describes a similar service provided by the College of Southern Idaho that helps farm operators improve their farm business management techniques. The program "has strengthened the financial position of approximately 68 farm operations since its inception" (Thomas, "A Guide," IV–4).
78. These activities are also considered tourism development strategies in some cases. See Chapter 8.
79. OTA 1988, 212. Unfortunately, experience suggests that day has not yet come. According to William E. Nothdurft and Mark Popovich ("Bucking the System: Lessons from One Foundation's Investments in Agricultural Diversification," Report to the Northwest Area Foundation, St. Paul, MN, 1991), one of the most important rules of thumb for on-farm and near-farm entrepreneurs is: Match the scale of the business with the size of the targeted market (p. 9). These authors tell the sad story of Shakopee Farms Meats, a small producer of premium quality pork (pp. 20–21). This company enjoyed some success selling to premium retailers at a higher price but then dissipated its energies trying to break into the discount supermarket chains and eventually went out of business. One lesson to be drawn here is not to try to compete on the basis of price if you don't have the scale and volume to back it up.
80. Thomas, "A Guide," IV–12.
81. Ibid., IV-16–18.
82. Ibid., II-13–28.
83. Irma T. Elo and Calvin Beale, *Natural Resources and Rural Poverty: An Overview* (Washington, D.C.: Resources for the Future Inc., c.1983). They focus attention on agricultural laborers, residents of the coal-mining and agricultural areas of Southern Appalachia, rural blacks in the Southern Coastal Plain and the Mississippi Delta, and Native American communities in the Great Plains and the West.

84. Thomas G. Johnson et al., "Improvements in Well-Being in Virginia Coalfields Hampered by Low and Unstable Income," *Rural Development Perspectives,* 6:1, Oct. 1989, 38–39.

85. OTA 1988, 396–397.

86. U.S. Labor Secretary Lynn Martin threatened a federal takeover of the state's job safety and health enforcement operations if they did not rectify their problems in 90 days. See *The New York Times,* January 9, 1992, A-17.

87. Weber et al., "Performance of Natural Resource Industries," 111–112.

88. The study by Donald Tomaskovic-Devey (*Sundown on the Sunbelt? Growth Without Development in the Rural South,* Raleigh, NC: North Carolina State University, Oct. 1991) also shows how southern elites have worked to maintain the low living standards of this surplus labor force, most of which is black, in order to attract branch plant manufacturing while at the same time reserving the existing social relations of production.

89. David A. McGranahan and Linda M. Ghelfi, "The Education Crisis and Rural Stagnation in the 1980s," in *Education and Rural Economic Development: Strategies for the 1990s,* ERS, USDA, Staff Report AGES 9153, Sept. 1991, 63.

90. Ibid.

91. Molly S. Killian and Timothy S. Parker, "Education and Local Employment Growth in a Changing Economy,"in *Education and Rural Economic Development: Strategies for the 1990s,* ERS, USDA, Staff Report AGES 9153, Sept. 1991, 95.

92. Ibid., 106.

93. See study by Tomaskovic-Devey and Rosemary Ritzman, *Back to the Future? Human Resources and Economic Development Policy for North Carolina* (Raleigh, NC: North Carolina State University, Dept. of Sociology, Spring 1990).

94. OTA notes that the continuing demand for seasonal farm laborers is "the most glaring exception to cheerful estimates showing how machinery has substituted for difficult and dangerous work" (p. 396).

95. Joseph Cortright, "Old World, New Ideas: Business Assistance Lessons from Europe," *Report to the Legislative Committee on Trade and Economic Development,* Oregon Legislature, April 1990, 25.

96. A complete agenda for rural education and training policy is described by Paul L. Swaim and Ruy A. Teixeira, "Education and Training Policy: Skill Upgrading Options for the Rural Workforce," in *Education and Rural Economic Development: Strategies for the 1990s,* ERS, USDA, Staff Report AGES 9153, Sept. 1991.

97. McGranahan, "Introduction" to *Education and Rural Economic Development: Strategies for the 1990s,* ERS, USDA, Staff Report AGES 9153, Sept. 1991, 8–9.

98. Even in the absence of local improvements in job quality, the ERS authors stress the importance of equipping rural young people with the best possible education. Such policies make it easier for local workers to migrate to where

job opportunities are better, thus alleviating local unemployment (McGranahan, "Introduction," 9).

99. See Tomaskovic-Devey, *Sundown on the Sunbelt?* chapter 2, for a summary of research on the subject of elite control over economic development.

100. Ibid., 9.

101. David S. Cloud, "Conferees Forced to Seek New Ideas in Farm Bill," *Congressional Quarterly,* Oct. 20, 1990, 3491.

102. See Center for Resource Economics, *Farm Bill 1990: Agenda for the Environment and Consumers* (Washington, D.C.: Island Press, 1990), 7, 21.

103. "Good times are back on the farm for a bit," *The Economist,* March 10, 1990, 26.

104. See Center for Resource Economics, *Farm Bill 1990,* 15.

105. "Good times are back," *The Economist,* 26.

106. See the study by Center for Resource Economics, *Farm Bill 1990,* 14.

107. Cloud, "Conferees Forced to Seek New Ideas," 3493.

108. Experts have estimated the cost of sediment damage to waterways at $2.2 billion a year (Center for Resource Economics, *Farm Bill 1990,* 9).

109. See Center for Rural Affairs, *Half a Glass of Water: State Economic Development Policies and the Small Agricultural Communities of the Middle Border* (Walthill, NE: Center for Rural Affairs, March 1990), 84.

110. It is interesting to note certain tradeoffs that will occur if and when farmers begin to make truly significant changes in their pesticide consumption rates. If pesticide demand drops, chemical companies will feel the blow. As noted in Chapter 10, the chemical industry is one of the largest high-tech employers in rural America. Many of the jobs lost to sustainable agriculture practices will still be rural jobs.

111. See Center for Resource Economics, *Farm Bill 1990,* 5.

112. Durbin and Koberstein, "Northwest Forests: Day of Reckoning," a special section of *The Oregonian,* Oct. 15, 1990, 3. The rest of the commercial timberland in the Pacific Northwest is owned by states and individuals.

113. Ibid., 3.

114. Oregon Representative Less AuCoin and Senator Mark Hatfield have used their positions on the respective House and Senate Appropriations Committees to direct the U.S. Forest Service to increase sales of Northwest timber. For a chronology of the legislative battles, see Durbin and Koberstein 1990, p. 11.

115. Kathie Durbin and Paul Koberstein, "Northwest Forests: Day of Reckoning," a special section of *The Oregonian,* Oct. 15, 1990, chart, p.8.

116. Karen Franklin, "Timber! The Forest Disservice," *The New Republic,* Jan. 2, 1989, 12.

177. Ibid.

118. Margaret E. Kriz, "Last Stand on Timber. A Bush Administration plan to restrict money-losing sales in national forests fans a conflict between timber interests and environmental groups over the future of the forest system," *National Journal,* March 3, 1990, 510.

119. Standard and Poor's 1989, B81.

120. One unstated reasons, of course, is that it allows the Forest Service's budget to grow at a healthy annual clip. Forest managers get more money for building logging roads than for other conservation-minded activities. ("The Forest Service: Time for a Little Perestroika," *The Economist*, March 10, 1990, 28.)

121. Franklin, "Timber!" 13.

122. J.A. Savage, "Timber Companies Can't See the Forest for the Trees," *Business and Society Review* 74, Summer 1990, 47.

123. This approach includes practices such as leaving dead and decaying trees and other material on the forest floor to cycle nutrients back into the soil, cutting selected trees and removing them by helicopter, and harvesting only trees around the perimeter of largely pristine areas (Durbin and Koberstein 1990, 21–22).

124. Paul Starobin, "Foggy Forecasts. So, how much is the new clean air legislation going to cost?" *National Journal*, May 19, 1990.

125. Alyson Pytte, "A Decade's Acrimony Lifted in the Glow of Clean Air," *Congressional Quarterly*, Oct. 27, 1990, 3587. That comes on top of the $33 billion business already spends each year on air pollution control (Barbara Rosewicz and Rose Gutfeld, "Clean Air Legislation Will Cost Americans $21.5 Billion a Year," *Wall Street Journal*, March 28, 1990, Al).

126. Robert W. Hahn and Wilbur A. Steger, *An Analysis of Jobs-at-Risk and Job Losses Resulting from the Proposed Clean Air Act Amendments* (Pittsburgh: CONSAD Research Corporation for the Business roundtable, Feb. 20, 1990).

127. Pytte, "A Decade's Acrimony," 3592.

128. In one survey of electric utilities prior to the passage of the new Clean Air Act amendments, 42 percent of the companies indicated that they would switch to lower-sulfur coal to comply with tougher emissions standards (Standard and Poor's 1989, R29).

129. Nothdurft, *Renewing America* (Washington: D.C.: Council of State Planning Agencies, 1984), 32.

130. Kriz, "Dunning the Midwest," *National Journal*, April 14, 1990, 893.

131. Richard L. Trumka, Statement on Acid Rain Control Legislation before the Subcommittee on Energy and Power, U.S. House of Representatives, Sept. 7, 1989 (Washington D.C.: United Mine Workers of America), 4.

132. Ibid., 5.

133. Standard & Poor's 1989, R29.

134. Pytte, "A Decade's Acrimony," 3590

135. As of 1990, development of ethanol-based products was the second largest economic development initiative (in terms of dedicated state resources) underway in Nebraska (Center for Rural Affairs, *Half a Glass of Water*, 88–89).

Chapter 6

1. U.S. Congress, Office of Technology Assessment (OTA) 1988, 166.

2. Ibid.

3. Ibid., 167.

4. Ibid., 170.

5. R.D. Norton, "Reindustrialization and Economic Development Strategy," *Economic Development Quarterly,* 3:3, August 1989, 188–202.

6. Peter Drucker, "The Changed World Economy," *Foreign Affairs,* 64:4, Spring 1986, 773.

7. Agriculture today produces less than 10 percent of total GNP with about 2.5 percent of the work force. In 1900, the majority of U.S. workers were employed on farms that produced 20 percent of GNP (Mark Drabenstott and Lynn Gibson, *Rural America in Transition,* Kansas City: Federal Reserve Bank of Kansas City, April 1988, 2).

8. William B. Johnson and Arnold E. Packer, *Workforce 2000: Work and Workers for the Twenty-first Century* (Indianapolis, Indiana: Hudson Institute, June 1987).

9. Bennett Harrison and Barry Bluestone, *The Deindustrialization of America* (Boston, MA: Basic Books, 1982).

10. Note that the United States lost market share not only in traditional manufactured products such as machine tools and steel but also in high-tech products. The U.S. Department of Commerce looked at 10 high-tech products between 1970 and 1980 (pharmaceuticals, business machines, electrical and electronic machines, telecommunication equipment, electronic components, consumer electronics, jet engines, aircraft, and scientific instruments) and found that the U.S. lost market share in eight: Japanese producers gained share in all 10 (OTA, 322).

11. Robert B. Reich, *The Work of Nations: Preparing Ourselves for 21st-Century Capitalism* (New York: Alfred A. Knopf, 1991), 85.

12. Ibid., 100–101.

13. See Laura D'Andrea Tyson ("They Are Not Us: Why American Ownership Still Matters," *The American Prospect,* Winter 1991, 37–49) for a careful description of how U.S. economic vitality is still closely tied to the fortunes of American firms.

14. OTA 1988, 154–158; 346–348.

15. These transactions occur within production networks which may include, in the case of a clothing manufacturer for example, the textile mill that weaves the fabric, the machine tool manufacturer that supplies the mill, the chemical plant that produces the synthetic fiber, the department stores and boutiques that retail the finished product, the advertising companies that handle the retailers' accounts, the banks that finance the various transactions, and so on. The relationships generated by intermediate and final demand for products from different sectors are the subject of much of OTA's analysis of changing "production recipes" in the U.S. economy.

16. OTA, 346.

17. It is important to note, however, that given the significantly larger absolute size of the service sector, growth in services actually generates the same number of jobs in manufacturing as manufacturing growth generates in services. Only the

proportional rates of contribution are dramatically different, not the absolute numbers (OTA 1988, 348).

18. Michael J. Piore and Charles F. Sabel, *The Second Industrial Divide: Possibilities for Prosperity* (New York: Basic Books, 1984), 165. Also see Stephen S. Cohen and John Zysman, *Manufacturing Matters: The Myth of the Post-Industrial Economy,* New York: Basic Books, 1987.

19. Piore and Sabel, 1984, 221–250.

20. Ibid., 265–267.

21. It is important to note the value of including larger firms in these networks in some cases, as the New York survey found (Ruth C. Young and Joe D. Francis, "Who Helps Small Manufacturing Firms Get Started?" *Rural Development Perspectives* 6:1, Oct. 1989).

22. Joseph Cortright, "Old World, New Ideas: Business Assistance Lessons from Europe," *Report to the Legislative Committee on Trade and Economic Development* (Oregon Legislature, April 1990), 10–22.

23. Ibid., 10.

24. Piore and Sabel, *The Second Industrial Divide,* 303–304.

25. Herman Bluestone and Stan G. Daberkow, "Employment Growth in Nonmetro America: Past Trends and Prospects to 1990," *Rural Development Perspectives,* 1:3, June 1985, 20+.

26. Thomas A. Carlin, "Rural Areas Weaning Themselves from Farming," *Rural Development Perspectives,* 4:1, October 1987.

27. James P. Miller and Herman Bluestone, "Prospects for Service Sector Employment Growth in Nonmetro America," in David L. Brown et al., eds., *Rural Economic Development in the 1980s: Prospects for the Future,* RDRR-69, Economic Research Service, U.S. Department of Agriculture (Washington, D.C.: Government Printing Office, Sept. 1988), 135–158.

28. Bluestone and Paul R. Myer, "Rural Manufacturing Counties on Upswing Again," *Rural Development Perspectives,* 4:1, Oct. 1987.

29. Steven R. Kale and Richard E. Lonsdale, "Recent Trends in U.S. and Canadian Nonmetro Manufacturing," *Journal of Rural Studies* 3:1, 1987, 1–13.

30. Mark Drabenstott and Lynn Gibson, *Rural America in Transition* (Kansas City: The Federal Reserve Bank of Kansas City, Research Division, April 1988).

31. Stuart A. Rosenfeld et al., *Reviving the Rural Factory: Automation and Work in the South,* (Research Triangle Park, NC: Southern Growth Policies Board, May 1988); and *Making Connections: "After the Factories" Revisited* (Research Triangle Park, NC: Southern Growth Policies Board, May 1989).

32. Based on data provided by telephone, Economic Research Service, 1990.

33. David A. McGranahan, "Recent Rural Employment Gains," *Rural Development Perspectives,* 5:1, Oct. 1988, 44–45.

34. See Calvin L. Beale and Glenn V. Fuguitt, "Decade of Pessimistic Nonmetro Population Trends Ends on Optimistic Note," *Rural Development Perspectives,* 6:3, June–Sept. 1990, 15; and "The Status of the Rural Economy" (Economic Research Service, U.S. Department of Agriculture, 1994), 8.

35. See Robert W. Gilmer and Allan G. Pulsipher, "Structural Change in Southern Manufacturing: Expansion in the Tennessee Valley," *Growth and Change,* 20:2, Spring 1989, 62–70.

36. McGranahan, "Recent Rural Employment Gains," 1988. The effects of labor market trends on rural manufacturing growth are difficult to sort out. Kale and Lonsdale note various theories suggesting that differentials between rural and urban wages are shrinking thanks to urban workers' greater willingness to negotiate wage cuts to save jobs. To the extent that new immigrants, who compete for lower-wage jobs, choose to settle in urban areas, this trend will also work against rural job growth (Kale and Lonsdale, "Recent Trends in U.S. and Canadian Nonmetro Manufacturing").

37. See Bluestone and Daberkow, "Employment Growth in Nonmetro America."

38. DeWitt John et al., *A Brighter Future for Rural America?* (Washington, D.C.: National Governors' Association, Center for Policy Research, 1988).

39. See Rosenfeld et al., *Making Connections.*

40. See Leonard E. Bloomquist, "Performance of the Rural Manufacturing Sector," *Rural Economic Development in the 1980s: Prospects for the Future,* RDRR-69, ERS, USDA (Washington, D.C.: U.S. Government Printing Office, Sept. 1988), 49–75.

41. Margaret G. Thomas, *Profiles in Rural Economic Development: A Guidebook of Selected Successful Rural Area Initiatives.* (Midwest Research Institute: Kansas City, MO, April 1988), 31.

42. Ruth C. Young and Joe D. Francis, "Who Helps Small Manufacturing Firms Get Started?" *Rural Development Perspectives,* 6:1, Oct. 1989, 21–25.

43. Ibid., 22.

44. The commonly held view that rural areas should shift their focus entirely from wooing large employers to midwifing small businesses is thus oversimplified.

45. An example of the latter can be found in Albert Lea, Minnesota. See Matt Kane and Peggy Sand, *Economic Development: What Works at the Local Level* (Washington, D.C.: National League of Cities, 1988), 37.

46. Michael L. Dertouzos et al. (*Made in America: Regaining the Productive Edge,* Cambridge, MA: M.I.T. Press, 1988) describe a similar difference at the national level between policies focused on collaboration in which "government facilitates the cooperation of many potentially different interests in projects from which all parties can benefit," and traditional industrial policies in which "government action characteristically selects one firm or a few firms to receive subsidies and protection" (p. 112).

47. Cortright, "Old World, New Ideas."

48. Dertouzos et al. (*Made in America*) have argued that the collective goods generated by vertical and horizontal interfirm networks are undersupplied in the United States (pp. 94–107). Harrison and Kelley (1991) have argued that the American preference for economic transactions that are "competitive, one-time, 'price auction' events," and therefore supposedly more efficient, has prevented large American firms from developing the kinds of long-term cooperative relationships with their supplier that have been so successful in Japan and

elsewhere (pp. 57–58).

49. Piore and Sabel, *The Second Industrial Divide,* 265.

50. Cortright, "Old World, New Ideas," 10–12.

51. Rosenfeld et al., *Reviving the Rural Factory,* 40.

52. Kelley and Harvey Brooks, "From Breakthrough to Followthrough," *Issues in Science and Technology,* 5:3, Spring 1989, 42–47.

53. Cortright, "Old World, New Ideas," 13.

54. Kelley and Brooks, "From Breakthrough to Followthrough."

55. Marianne K. Clarke, *Revitalizing State Economies* (Washington, D.C.: National Governors' Association, 1986), 65.

56. Ibid., 68.

57. Dertouzos et al., *Made in America,* 1988, 99–100.

58. Kelley and Brooks, "From Breakthrough to Followthrough," 47.

59. Cortright, "Old World, New Ideas," 13.

60. Although most rural banks have high reserves of capital, they were lending money at a slower growth rate in the 1980s than they did in the 1970s while urban lending rates maintained steady growth over the two decades. Explanations for the rural lag range from the savings and loan crisis to changing demographics. Various research studies have examined perceived problems such as imperfect information about lending opportunities, high transaction costs, and the effects of policy changes such as banking deregulation and interstate banking. Based on her review of the findings, however, Deborah Markley (1988) states: "Concluding that the supply of rural capital is adequate or inadequate or is affected positively or negatively by structural and regulatory changes is not yet possible" (p. 8). Rural lending practices did not follow any clear patterns during the past decade, but were characterized by wide variation across different kinds of communities and different kinds of institutions.

    Despite the general lack of clarity, most analysts seem to agree that rural areas do need more equity-based financing than is currently available to help start-up ventures get on their feet (Charles Morris and Drabenstott, "Rethinking the Rural Credit Gap," *Rural Development Perspectives* 7:1, Oct.-Jan. 1991, 25; Peter S. Fisher, "Risk Capital and Rural Development," in *Toward Rural Development Policy for the 1990s: Enhancing Income and Employment Opportunities,* 101st Congress, first session, Senate Print 101-50, 1989, 138–141).

61. Erica Shoenberger, "Foreign Manufacturing Investment in the United States," *Commentary,* National Council for Urban Economic Development, 13:3, Fall 1989, 20. These figures describe only those cases in which a foreign individual, partnership, group, or organization owns or controls 10 percent or more of the voting securities of a U.S. manufacturing enterprise (considered a "U.S. affiliate" of the forgoing investor). The investment position adds up the book value of the equity held by foreign investors in these U.S. affiliates.

62. William J. Kahley, "U.S. and Foreign Direct Investment Patterns," *Economic Review,* Federal Reserve Bank of Atlanta, 74:6, Nov./Dec. 1989, 46. In 1987,

only 3.6 percent of all U.S. jobs in nonbank businesses were in U.S. affiliates of foreign firms; the share for manufacturing jobs was 7 percent (p. 45).

63. Using slightly different methods of counting, Amy Glasmeier and Norman Glickman ("Foreign Investment Boosts Rural Economies," *Rural Development Perspectives* 6:3, June/Sept. 1990) estimate this figure to be roughly 7 percent (p. 19).

64. Ibid., 22. Prior to 1985, Japanese direct investment established new ventures. Beginning in 1986, it shifted toward takeovers of existing firms. The trend toward foreign takeovers of U.S. firms in general (which continued in 1990) lasted beyond the boom in domestic mergers and acquisitions (which peaked in 1988) (Edward M. Graham, "Foreign Direct Investment in the United States and U.S. Interests," *Science* 254:5039, Dec. 20, 1991, 1741).

65. Ibid., 23.

66. Ibid., 22.

67. Gene Koretz, "Will Direct Foreign Investment Help on the Trade Front?" *Business Week*, December 16, 1991, 20.

68. Ibid.; Graham, "Foreign Direct Investment in the United States," 1743.

69. Rosenfeld et al., *Reviving the Rural Factory,* vii. Although many Americans believe that the bulk of foreign direct investment comes from Japan, in fact, the British are the biggest investors in the U.S., followed by Europe (excluding the Netherlands) (Graham, "Foreign Direct Investment," 1741).

70. John Burgess, "Flood of Money into U.S. Slows to a Trickle," *The Washington Post,* Oct. 7, 1990, H1; Graham, "Foreign Direct Investment," 1740.

71. Ibid.

72. Graham, "Foreign Direct Investment," 1740.

73. Burgess, "Flood of Money," H5.

74. Kahley, "U.S. and Foreign Direct Investment Patterns," 54.

75. Glasmeier and Glickman, "Foreign Investment," 25.

76. Ibid.

77. Clarke, *Revitalizing State Economies,* 75.

78. See Committee on Small Business, United States Senate, "Survey of Findings on Obstacles to Exporting Faced by Small Business," July 30, 1982, 7; and Mark Weaver, *Small Business Export Markets,* National Federation of Independent Business Research and Education Foundation, Washington, D.C., February 1985, 29 (cited in DeWitt John, *Shifting Responsibilities: Federalism in Economic Development* (Washington, D.C.: National Governors' Association, 1987, 27–28).

79. DeWitt John, *Shifting Responsibilities: Federalism in Economic Development* (Washington, D.C.: National Governors' Association, 1987), 28–32.

80. Ibid., 30–33.

81. Ibid., 32.

82. Ibid., 36–40; Clarke, *Revitalizing State Economies,* 87–88

83. ERS 1991.

84. Piore and Sabel (*Second Industrial Divide*) note that the prosperous European industrial districts have been able to slow that leakage of talent. Their success

"derives largely from their capacity to draw the younger generation back into their parents' industries" (p. 293).

85. Dertouzos et al., *Made in America*, 96.

86. See OTA 1988, graph on p. 349.

87. Kale and Lonsdale, "Recent Trends."

88. Nonmetro manufacturing facilities are typically limited to production and oversight of production. Metro facilities serve other, higher-order functions, such as coordination of firm-wide production, marketing, product development, and firm finance (Blackley, "Urban-Rural Variations," 1986).

89. U.S. Congress, Economic Research Service.

90. See Bloomquist, "Performance of Rural Manufacturing Sector," 52.

91. Frank S. Levy and Richard C. Michel, *The Economic Future of American Families: Income and Wealth Trends* (Washington, D.C.: Urban Institute Press, 1991), 16.

92. William O'Hare and Anne Pauti, "Declining Wages of Young Workers in Rural America," staff working papers (Washington, D.C.: Population Reference Bureau, May 1990), 14–15.

93. Philip R. Israilevich and William A. Testa, "The Geography of Value Added," *Economic Perspectives,* Federal Reserve Bank of Chicago, 13:5, Sept./Oct. 1989, 2+.

94. Molly S. Killian and Thomas F. Hady, "What Is the Payoff for Diversifying Rural Economies?" *Rural Development Perspectives,* 4:2, Feb. 1988, 2–7.

95. One study sheds a slightly different light on the question of stability with regard to "footloose" manufacturing facilities. James P. Miller ("Rethinking Small Business as the Best Way to Create Rural Jobs," *Rural Development Perspectives* 1:2, Feb. 1985) studied job stability relative to types of plants rather than industry mix. He concluded that branch plants of large corporations tend to provide more stable jobs than new small firms. Branch plants accounted for "proportionally fewer losses from plant closings and employment cutbacks," and therefore generated the majority of net new jobs in rural areas. Most of the net new jobs created by these corporate affiliates were in the manufacturing sector; the largest proportion of net new jobs in all sectors (except construction) came from this source. A repetition of this study using more recent data would determine whether these patterns continued during the 1980s.

96. OTA 1988, 368.

97. See ERS 1991, chapter 2, for an excellent summary of findings.

98. Ibid.

99. Ibid.

100. Johnston and Packer, *Workforce 2000,* 95–101.

101. Ibid., 99.

102. ERS 1991, 21.

103. Ruy A. Teixeira and Lawrence Mishel, "Upgrading Workers' Skills Not Sufficient to Jump-Start Rural Economy," *Rural Development Perspectives,* 7:3, June-Sept. 1991, 20–21

104.OTA 1988, 419.

105.Ibid., 421.

106."The Factory of the Future," *The Economist*, April 5, 1986, 98.

107.OTA 1988, 420. The ERS study describes three trends that may contribute to future upgrading in job content: technological change, flexible automation, and international competitive pressures. These trends may require workers to have higher levels of cognitive skills, greater adaptability, and better problem-solving abilities (p. 23).

108."The Factory of the Future," 99.

109.OTA 1988, 420.

110.Success refers to high productivity, low costs, superior quality products, and "peaceful and productive labor–management relations" (Haruo Shimada and John Paul MacDuffie, "Industrial Relations and 'Humanware': Japanese Investments in Automobile Manufacturing in the United States," Sloan School of Management, M.I.T., Dec. 1986, p. 3).

111.Ibid., 4.

112.Ibid., 85.

113.See John Holusha, "Beating Japan at Its Own game: A 'quiet revolution' is changing America's factory floors," *The New York Times*, Sunday, July 16, 1989, section 3.

114. *The Second Industrial Divide: Possibilities for Prosperity* (New York: Basic Books, 1984). The authors show that many existing regional industries are held together by ethnic ties (as in the New York City garment industry), religious and political affiliations (like the "Third Italy"), and kinship structures (like France's *systeme Motte*). They conclude: "To judge by these cases, it is doubtful whether regional conglomerations can survive without community ties, be they ethnic, political, or religious" (p. 266).

115.Dillman, Beck, and Allen (1988) describe many rural people and communities as being stuck in the "community control era mindset," defined by its highest standard: "What will the neighbors think?" (p. 68). These authors argue that such communities are at a disadvantage in developing information age businesses:

> Associating with the same people or at least the same families over several generations tends to encourage spending a greater amount of time on the creation and consumption of local knowledge and less seeking, sorting, and using information about distant places and ideas. Information needed for entrepreneurialism . . . is that information that will come predominantly from outside the community rather than over the backyard fence or from lifelong friends (p. 77).

Chapter 7

1. Amy Glasmeier, *Bypassing America's Outlands: Rural America and High Technology* (Austin: The University of Texas at Austin, Graduate Program in Community and Regional Planning, October 1988), 8.

2. Richard I. Kirkland, Jr., "Are Service Jobs Good Jobs?" *Fortune,* 111:12, June 10, 1985, 39.

3. OTA 1988, 171.

4. Ibid., 169.

5. Ibid., 171. Note that social services' impressive gain in GNP share was in current dollars only. This sector's constant dollar share grew at the same rate as the rest of the economy. The discrepancy, according to OTA, is due to low productivity growth in this part of the economy and rising prices of inputs. Costs for social services rose significantly faster than output over the period (p. 171).

6. Ibid., 171.

7. Ibid., 169. It is important to note, however, that certain consumer-oriented industry groups included in OTA's other sectoral categories (other than personal services) showed impressive growth over the period. These included eating and drinking places (transportation and trade sector), real estate and rental (transactional activities sector), and health and education (social services sector). Although the lion's share of service growth in the postwar period has been generated by producer and business services, consumer services have also contributed to the boom. Changes in OTA's personal services category do not fully describe the evolution of consumer services industries.

8. Ibid., 171. Growth in air transportation enterprises made up for this loss.

9. Thomas J. Kirn, "Growth and Change in the Service Sector of the U.S.: A Spatial Perspective," *Annals of the Association of American Geographers,* 77:3, 1987, 354.

10. William B. Johnston and Arnold E. Packer, *Workforce 2000: Work and Workers for the Twenty-first Century* (Indianapolis, IN: Hudson Institute, June 1987), 37.

11. Martin N. Baily and Robert J. Gordon, "The Productivity Slowdown, Measurement Issues, and the Explosion of Computer Power," *Brookings Papers on Economic Activity,* 2:1988, Table 1.

12. Glasmeier, *Bypassing America's Outlands,* 14; James P. Miller and Herman Bluestone, "Prospects for Service Sector Employment Growth in Nonmetro America," *Rural Economic Development in the 1980s* RDRR-69, ERS, USDA (Washington, D.C.: U.S. Government Printing Office, Sept. 1988, 138).

13. Baily and Margaret M. Blair, "Productivity and American Management," in Robert E. Litan et al., eds., *American Living Standards: Threats and Challenges* (Washington, D.C.: The Brookings Institution, 1988), 186.

14. According to Baily and Blair, productivity figures for four sectors in particular, three of them service sectors, are fraught with problems: construction; transportation; finance, insurance, and real estate; and business and personal services (ibid., p. 186).

15. Dorothy I. Riddle, *Service-led Growth: The Role of the Service Sector in World Development* (New York: Praeger Publishers, 1986), 71.

16. Kirkland, "Are Service Jobs Good Jobs?" 35. OTA (1988) reports that, in recent years, the service sector has been responsible for 77 percent of all expen-

ditures on office, computing, and accounting machines and 93 percent of all expenditures on communication equipment (p. 153). According to James Quinn and Christopher Gagnon ("Will Services Follow Manufacturing into Decline?" *Harvard Business Review,* Nov./Dec. 1986), new technology investment per service worker increased 97 percent between 1975 and 1982 (p. 97).

17. Johnston and Packer, *Workforce 2000,* 43.
18. Baily and Gordon, "The Productivity Slowdown," 389.
19. Kirn, "Growth and Change," 353.
20. Ibid.
21. OTA, 172.
22. Ibid., 174–175.
23. Ibid., 176.
24. Ibid.
25. Glasmeier, *Bypassing America's Outlands,* 12.
26. Robert B. Reich, *The Work of Nations: Preparing Ourselves for 21st-Century Capitalism* (New York: Knopf, 1991), 85.
27. Ibid.
28. Ibid., 104.
29. Ibid., 85.
30. See Kirn, "Growth and Change"; also see Miller and Bluestone, "Prospects for Service Sector Growth."
31. Ibid., 362.
32. Miller and Bluestone, "Prospects for Service Sector Growth," 144. Total U.S. employment grew 1.4 percent during the period.
33. Ibid.
34. Kirn, "Growth and Change," 269. One recent study contradicts this assumption. Jack C. Stabler ("Nonmetropolitan Population Growth and the Evolution of Rural Service Centers in the Canadian Prairie Region," *Regional Studies* 21:1, Feb. 1987) found that, despite significant population growth in the rural areas of the Canadian Prairie Region during the 1960s and 1970s, the "trade center role" of many of the region's small communities continued to decline. He attributes this surprising finding to shifts in consumer preferences of rural dwellers toward the goods and services available in more distant, urban centers. Improvements in roads during the study period "extended the range over which [the rural dweller] traveled to purchase both consumer and producer goods." (p. 45).
35. Ibid., 362.
36. Ibid., 369.
37. Miller and Bluestone, "Prospects for Service Sector Growth," 145.
38. Ibid., 147. It is interesting to note the possible role played by deregulation in the 1980s pattern of slower rural services growth. Glasmeier and Marie Howland (in press) discuss the thesis that direct and indirect subsidies to rural transportation and communications industries fueled the decentralization of services in the 1970s. When these subsidies were removed in the 1980s and rural airfares, trucking costs, and telephone rates rose, investment naturally

moved backed to the cities, where transaction costs were lower.

39. Ibid. These authors provide examples of less specialized services: "repair shops run by jacks-of-all-trades or offices that offer a combination of real estate, insurance, and financial services" (p. 140).

40. Ibid., 139.

41. Kirn, "Growth and Change," 369–370.

42. OTA 1988, 454.

43. Mark Drabenstott and Lynn Gibson, *Rural America in Transition* (Kansas City: The Federal Reserve Bank of Kansas City, Research Division, April 1988); DeWitt John et al., *A Brighter Future for Rural America?* (Washington, D.C.: National Governors' Association, Center for Policy Research, 1988).

44. Ibid.

45. Molly S. Killian and Thomas F. Hardy, "What Is the Payoff for Diversifying Rural Economies?" *Rural Development Perspectives,* 4:2, Feb. 1988.

46. Elliott Dubin and Norman J. Reid, "Federal Funds to Rural Areas: Fair Share? Right Mix?" background paper submitted to the Task Force on Rural Development (Washington, D.C.: National Governors' Association, 1988).

47. Riddle, *Service-led Growth.* Her definition of development included factors such as literacy rates, life expectancy, per capita GNP, per capita and total GDP, inflation, domestic investment and savings, external debt, exports and imports of goods and services, and sectoral percentage of GDP. This is obviously a much richer and more complex view of economic development than that projected by the usual proxy measures of employment and income growth.

48. Ibid., 90–91.

49. Kirn, "Growth and Change," 368. The correlation in rural areas was stronger in the later part of the period, 1967–77.

50. Ibid., 370.

51. Drabenstott and Gibson, *Rural America*; John et al., *A Brighter Future.*

52. Kirn, "Growth and Change," 369. Note that "export" services such as those related to tourism and retirement centers also depend on trends in population and income, but on a larger geographic scale—regional and national, rather than local.

53. Miller and Bluestone, "Prospects for Service Sector Growth," 146.

54. Quinn and Gagnon, "Will Services Follow Manufacturing into Decline?" (p. 103).

55. Ibid., 96.

56. Ibid., 101.

57. Reich, *The Work of Nations,* 85.

58. Joseph Cortright, "Old World, New Ideas: Business Assistance Lessons from Europe," *Report to the Legislative Committee on Trade and Economic Development,* Oregon Legislature, April 1990.

59. Ibid., 10.

60. Kirn, "Growth and Change," 355.

61. Miller and Bluestone, "Prospects for Service Sector Growth," 148; Glenn V. Fuguitt et al., *Rural and Small Town America* (New York: Russell Sage

Foundation, 1989).

62. Glasmeier, *Bypassing America's Outlands*, 21; Glasmeier and Howland, *From Combines to Computers: Rural Services and Development in the Information Age* (Albany: State University of New York Press, 1995).

63. Miller and Bluestone, "Prospects for Service Sector Growth," 142.

64. Glasmeier, *Bypassing America's Outlands*, 24.

65. Ibid., 25–26.

66. Kirn, "Growth and Change," 370; Glasmeier and Howland.

67. Ibid., 369.

68. Miller and Bluestone, "Prospects for Service Sector Growth," 146.

69. Glasmeier, *Bypassing America's Outlands*, 34.

70. Margaret G. Thomas, *Profiles in Rural Economic Development: A Guidebook of Selected Successful Rural Area Initiatives* (Midwest Research Institute: Kansas City, MO, April 1988), 31.

71. Glasmeier, *Bypassing America's Outlands*, 18.

72. Glasmeier and Howland, *Services and Rural Development*.

73 Ibid.

74. Glasmeier, *Bypassing America's Outlands*, 20.

75. Miller and Bluestone, "Prospects for Service Sector Growth," 154.

76. See the description of Kearney, Nebraska in Sharon Strover and Frederick Williams, *Rural Revitalization and Information Technologies in the United States*, The University of Texas at Austin, November 1991.

77. Glasmeier, *Bypassing America's Outlands*, 33.

78. Kirn, "Growth and Change," 355 and footnote 1, 370.

79. Glasmeier and Howland, *Services and Rural Development*.

80. W.B. Beyers, M.J. Alvine, and E.G. Johnsen, "The Service Economy: Export of Services in the Central Puget Sound Region," Central Puget Sound Economic Development District, Seattle, WA, April 1985; Stephen M. Smith, "Diversifying Smalltown Economies with Nonmanufacturing Industries, *Rural Development Perspectives*, 2:1, Oct. 1985; 18–21; Stephen Smith, "Comparison of Nonlocal Market Orientation of Rural Service and Manufacturing Businesses," Staff Paper 186, Agricultural Economics and Rural Sociology Department, College of Agriculture, The Pennsylvania State University, University Park, PA, June 1990. The results of these studies, however, are not conclusive. The majority of service firms in both cases were not significantly export-oriented.

81. Thierry Noyelle, "The Rise of Advanced Services," *Journal of the American Planning Association*, 49:3, 1983, 280–290; Roger F. Riefler, "Implications of Service Industry Growth for Regional Development Strategies," *Annals of Regional Science*, 10:2, 1976, 88–104.

82. Glasmeier, *Bypassing America's Outlands*, 18.

83. Robert W. Gilmer et al., "The Service Sector in a Hierarchy of Rural Places: Potential for Export Activity," *Land Economics*, 65:3, Aug. 1989, 217–227.

84. Smith, "Comparison of Nonlocal Market Orientation," 15.

85. Glasmeier and Howland, *Services and Rural Development*. The medical center

example, however, is unusual because most health dollars do not come out of the pockets of local residents the way that restaurant or auto repair dollars do. Medical centers are an important channel for export dollars from third-party payers in the form of insurance companies and the government (through Medicare and Medicaid).

86. Ibid.
87. Robert Kuttner, "The Declining Middle," *The Atlantic*, July 1983, 60–72; Barry Bluestone and Bennett Harrison, "The Great American Job Machine: The Proliferation of Low Wage Employment in the U.S. Economy," paper prepared for the Joint Economic Committee, U.S. Congress, Dec. 1986.
88. Robert Z. Lawrence, "Sectoral Shifts and the Size of the Middle Class," *The Brookings Review*, Fall 1984, 3–11.
89. William O'Hare and Anne Pauti, "Declining Wages of Young Workers in Rural America," staff working paper (Washington, D.C.: Population Reference Bureau, May 1990), 14–15. Between 1979 and 1987, O'Hare and Pauti found that the proportion of young rural workers (aged 16 to 34) employed in middle-wage jobs declined 11 percent over the period, while the proportion employed in low-wage jobs increased by the same amount (pp. 8–9). In contrast, urban workers in the same age group experienced only a 4 percent shift toward low-wage work. Mean earnings for young rural workers fell 13 percent over the period, compared to a 1 percent rise in mean earnings for urban workers (p. 9).
90. Ibid., 14.
91. Ibid. In 1979, 25 percent of young rural workers held jobs in manufacturing and 28 percent held jobs in services. By 1987, the share in manufacturing had fallen to 22 percent and the share in services had risen one point, to 29 percent.
92. Frank S. Levy, *Dollars and Dreams: The Changing American Income Distribution* (New York: W.W. Norton & Co., 1988), p. 93.
93. Ibid., 80.
94. According to Levy, this break in the income trend, "26 years of income growth followed by 12 years of income stagnation … is the major economic story of the postwar period" (p. 17).
95. Ibid., 100.
96. Shirley Porterfield, "Service Sector Offers More Jobs, Lower Pay," *Rural Development Perspectives*, 6:3, June/Sept. 1990, table 3.
97. O'Hare and Pauti, "Declining Wages of Young Workers," 13–14.
98. Riddle, *Service-led Growth*.
99. Edward R. Bergman, "Urban and Rural Considerations in Southern Development," *Rural Flight/Urban Might: Economic Development Challenges for the 1990s*, Cross-Cutting Issue Report No. 3, 1986 Commission on the Future of the South (Research Triangle Park, NC: Southern Growth Policies Board, 1986), 21.
100. ERS 1991, 8–9.
101 David Harrison and Jonathan Seib, "Toward 'One Washington': Strengthening

Rural–Urban Economic Linkages," *A Northwest Reader: Options for Rural Communities* (Seattle: Northwest Policy Center, University of Washington, Graduate School of Public Affairs, 1988).

102 Kenny Johnson, "The Southern Stake in Rural Development: An Introductory Overview," *Rural Flight/Urban Might: Economic Development Challenges for the 1990s,* Cross-Cutting Issue Report No. 3, 1986, 16. He offers the example of Greene County, Alabama, a rural county within a 30-mile radius of three metro areas with more viable job markets: Tuscaloosa and Demopolis, Alabama and Columbus, Mississippi.

103. Public and private entrepreneurs, the individuals who initiate growth and change, represent precisely those traits that threaten continuity. As Ron Shaffer and Gene F. Summers describe them: "Individuals likely to engage in entrepreneurial innovation have a minimal commitment to existing norms and institutional arrangements. Because they have this minimal commitment, they can perceive alternative behavioral patterns and ways of doing things" (p. 9).

104. Harrison and Seib, "Toward 'One Washington.'"

Chapter 8

1. The Congressional Office of Technology Assessment (OTA) 1988, 265. Other studies include food, health, housing, transportation, clothing and personal care, education, personal business, and communication.

2. Uel Blank, *The Community Tourism Imperative* (State College, Pennsylvania: Venture Publishing, Inc., 1989), table 2.2.

3. Janet Ware, "Unlocking Tourism's Potential," *American City and County,* May 1987, 96.

4. Jeff Blyskal, "Tour Wars," *Forbes,* July 2, 1984, 46.

5. U.S. Congress, "Economic Impact of Tourism," hearings before the Subcommittee on Business, Trade, and Tourism of the Senate Committee on Commerce, Science, and Transportation, 97th Congress, second session (Washington, D.C.: U.S. Government Printing Office, 1982); see Frechtling in.

6. Ibid., see Neville in.

7. Donna Tuttle, Undersecretary for Travel and Tourism, U.S. Department of Commerce. Testimony before the Committee on Commerce, Science, and Transportation (Washington, D.C.: U.S. Government Printing Office, 99th Congress, 1986).

8. Blank, *Community Tourism Imperative,* 1.

9. Henry Kelly, Office of Technology Assessment. Testimony before the Senate Committee on Commerce, Science, and Transportation (Washington, D.C.: U.S. Government Printing Office, 99th Congress, 1986); Herman Kahn, Hudson Institute. Testimony before the Senate Committee on Commerce, Science, and Transportation (Washington, D.C.: U.S. Government Printing Office, 97th Congress, 1982).

10. U.S. Travel and Tourism Administration (USTTA), U.S. Department of

Commerce, *A Strategic Look at the Travel and Tourism Industry* (Washington, D.C.: U.S. Government Printing Office, Feb. 1989).

11. Frank Fish, "Tourism: Planning for Its Development," *Commentary,* National Council for Urban Economic Development, Spring 1985, 17.

12. Ibid.

13. Stuart A. Rosenfeld et al., *Making Connections: "After the Factories" Revisited* (Research Triangle Park, NC: Southern Growth Policies Board, Feb. 1989).

14. DeWitt John et al., *A Brighter Future for Rural America?* (Washington, D.C.: National Governors' Association, Center for Policy Research, 1988).

15. *Barron's,* 60:2, Jan. 14, 1980, 39.

16. Randall S. Anderson et al., "Contribution of State Parks to State Economies," *Parks and Recreation,* 21:10, Oct. 1986, 6263.

17. John C. Bergstrom et al., "Economic Impacts of Recreational Spending on Rural Areas: A Case Study," *Economic Development Quarterly,* 4:1, Feb. 1990, 29–39.

18. Ibid., table 4, p. 37.

19. Phyllis Myers, *State Parks in a New Era: Volume 3, Strategies for Tourism and Economic Development* (Washington, D.C.: The Conservation Foundation, 1989), 22.

20. Gael Stahl, "Audit Lists Downside of Tourism: seasonal, low-paying jobs," *Tennessee Town & City,* 40:10, May 1989, 6.

21. Mark Drabenstott and Lynn Gibson, *Rural America in Transition* (Kansas City: The Federal Reserve Bank of Kansas City, Research Division, April 1988).

22. For a few examples, see Deen Boe, "Outdoor Recreation in Economic Development," background paper submitted to Task Force on Rural Development, Washington, D.C.: National Governors' Association, 1988; Fish, "Tourism: Planning"; Thomas J. Martin, "The Impact of Tourism," *American City and County* 102:12, Dec. 1987; Myers, *State Parks in a New Era:* Volume 3, Strategies for Tourism and Economic Development, 1989; John Sem, ed., *Using Tourism and Travel as a Community and Rural Revitalization Strategy,* Proceedings of National Extension Workshop, University of Minnesota, Aug. 1989; Lawrence R. Simonson et al., "So Your Community Wants Travel/Tourism? Guidelines for Attracting and Serving Visitors," publication CD-BU-3443, University of Minnesota, 1988; Margaret G. Thomas, "A Guide to Rural Economic Development through Tourism and Wildlife-based Recreation," chapter VI in *Recouples,* Midwest Research Institute, 1990; University of Missouri, *Guidelines for Tourism Development,* revised and expanded, 1986; and Glenn Weaver, *Inventorying the Tourism Package,* Tourism Development Series, Recreation Extension, University of Missouri, c. 1986.

23. Peter H. Gray, "The Contributions of Economics to Tourism," *Annals of Tourism Research* 9:2, 1982.

24. Blank, *Community Tourism Imperative,* 37.

25. Ware, "Unlocking Tourism's Potential."

26. Spiro G. Patton, "Tourism and Local Economic Development: Factory

Outlets and the Reading SMSA," *Growth and Change* 16:3, July 1985, 64–73.

27. For a discussion of rural industrial tourism, see Simonson, in Sem (*Using Tourism,* 120–124).

28. In tourism projects based on both cultural and historical assets, local leaders should be aware of the potential conflicts that may arise between and among preservationists, developers, and tourism professionals. Difficult questions emerge in the planning of "heritage tourism" efforts regarding the right balance of protection and promotion of these assets. The National Trust for Historic Preservation provides extensive technical assistance to communities interested in pursuing history and culture-based tourism development. See "The National Trust and Heritage Tourism," a background paper available from the National Trust offices in Washington, D.C.

29. For guidelines on developing festivals and special events, see Simonson, in Sem (*Using Tourism,* 174–176), and Weaver ("Creating and Managing Hometown Special Events," *Small Town,* Nov.-Dec. 1988, 5–10).

30. Blank, *Community Tourism Imperative,* 28–31.

31. See Moyer in Sem, *Using Tourism and Travel,* 116–119.

32. See Weaver, *Inventorying the Tourism Package,* in particular.

33. Fish, "Tourism," 17.

34. Ibid. Blank (*Community Tourism Imperative,* 101–102) makes the point that all tourist attractions are manufactured in the sense that human activity is what turns a natural resource into a recreational resource by providing access, enhancements, and related services.

35. University of Missouri, *Guidelines,* 1986.

36. Guidelines for conducting cost-benefit analyses and developing income multipliers can be found in University of Missouri *Guidelines,* 56–64. Fish ("Tourism: Planning") offers a model of a visitation and expenditure projection study for an urban park that might be replicated for rural communities (p. 19.).

37. According to the University of Missouri manual (ibid.), "User studies of numerous recreation facilities show that use begins locally and expands outward in proportion to the uniqueness of the attraction and the visibility or promotion the attraction gets" (p. 12).

38. Barbara A. Koth and Glenn M. Kreag, "Community Travel and Tourism Marketing," publication CD-FO-3272 (St. Paul, MN: Tourism Center, Minnesota Extension Service, University of Minnesota, 1987).

39. Blank, *Community Tourism Imperative,* 88.

40. Ibid. New businesses may enjoy longer life spans in rural areas, however. James Miller ("New Rural Businesses") has shown that, during the period 1980–86, new establishments in nonmetro areas had higher survival rates than those in metro areas.

41. Alan S. Gregerman, "Rekindling the Future: Creating a More Entrepreneurial Environment," *Commentary,* National Council for Urban Economic Development, 14:4, Winter 1991, 3.

42. Ibid., 5.

43. Thomas, *Profiles in Rural Economic Development: A Guidebook of Selected Successful Rural Area Initiatives* (Kansas City, MO: Midwest Research Institute, April 1988).

44. Boe, "Outdoor Recreation in Economic Development."

45. For more information on B&B development, see Espeseth et al. in Sem, *Using Tourism*, 134–152.

46. See, in particular, Phyllis Myers (*State Parks in a New Era:* Volume 3, 1989) on the northern Berkshires in Massachusetts and Boe ("Outdoor Recreation") on central Oregon.

47. Myers, *State Parks in a New Era*, 18–19.

48. Ibid., 19.

49. Thomas, *Profiles*.

50. For a list of agencies that may provide assistance for tourism-related projects, see University of Missouri *Guidelines*, 1986, 171–204.

51. See Gitelson in Sem, *Using Tourism and Travel*, 9–17.

52. See University of Missouri *Guidelines*, chapter 6, for a list of relevant federal programs.

53. Simonson et al., "So Your Community Wants Travel/Tourism?

54. Blank, *Community Tourism Imperative*, 137–138.

55. Blank (ibid.) notes a few exceptional states and provinces that have made progress in developing tourism plans: Hawaii, Ontario, New Mexico, Florida, and Michigan (pp. 177–178).

56. Barbara A. Koth, "Evaluating Tourism Advertising with Cost-Comparison Methods," publication CD-FO-3372, University of Minnesota, 1987; Koth, "Tourism Advertising: Some Basics," publication CD-FO-3311, University of Minnesota, 1987;Koth and Glenn M. Kreag, "Community Travel and Tourism Marketing," publication CD-FO-3272, University of Minnesota, 1987; Don Breneman et al., "Tourism Brochures to Boost Business," publication CD-FO-3273, University of Minnesota, 1987; University of Missouri *Guidelines*, 1986.

57. See Gunn in Sem, *Using Tourism and Travel*, 22.

58. At the bottom of the 1980 recession when total national employment fell by 200,000, travel industry employment increased.

59. Michal Smith: *The Impact of Tourism on Rural Women in the Southeast* (Lexington, KY: Southeast Women's Employment Coalition, Aug. 1989).

60. The extent of potential productivity increases in this sector of the economy may be smaller than it first appears. In testimony before Congress, Henry Kelly of the Congressional Office of Technology Assessment noted that hotels hired one employee for every five guest rooms in 1933; in 1982 the ratio was one employee for every two rooms (Kelly, in U.S. Congress hearings 1986). The reasons for the apparently dramatic drop in productivity are complex and include the fact that hotel customers expect and receive many more different types of services today than they did in the 1930s.
    Kelly also predicted only slow progress in productivity gains for the tourism industry. Where the quality of the tourist's experience is important, it is diffi-

cult to find ways of replacing service and retail workers. Technology will play a smaller role here than in other sectors, and the tourism industry is likely to remain highly labor intensive.

61. Hunt, in U.S. Congress, "Economic Impact of Tourism," hearings before Subcommittee on Business, Trade, and Tourism, 97th Congress, second session, 1982.

62. Alan S. Gregerman, "Rekindling the Future: Creating a More Entrepreneurial Environment," *Commentary*, National Council for Urban Economic Development, 14:4, Winter 1991, 6.

63. Steve Quick and Robert Friedman, "The Safety Net as Ladder: Transfer Payments and Economic Development, Executive Summary" (Washington, D.C.: The Corporation for Enterprise Development, Oct. 1984), 15–17.

64. Smith, *Behind the Glitter*, 1989.

65. Quoted by Peter McCoy, Undersecretary for Travel and Tourism, U.S. Department of Commerce. Testimony before the Senate Committee on Commerce, Science, and Transportation (Washington, D.C.: U.S. Government Printing Office, 97th Congress, 1982)

66. Bergstrom et al., "Economic Impacts," 29–39.

67. Myers, *State Parks*, 3-8.

68. Ibid., pp. xii, 3–8.

69. Barbara Ellen Smith, "Questions about Tourism," *Southern Exposure*, Southwest Women's Employment Coalition, c. 1989.

70. Ibid.; Smith, *Behind the Glitter*, 1989.

71. Thomas, "A Guide to Rural Economic Development."

72. Smith, *Behind the Glitter*, 1989.

Chapter 9

1. Bill Richards, "An Influx of Retirees Pumps New Vitality into Distressed Towns," *Wall Street Journal*, 212:25, Aug. 5, 1988.

2. Population Reference Bureau, "U.S. Population, Where We Are; Where We're Going," Bulletin 1982, 29–32.

3. Leon F. Bouvier, "America's Baby Boom Generation: the Fateful Bulge," Bulletin of the Population Reference Bureau, Washington, D.C., 1984, 30.

4. Jeanne C. Biggar, "The Graying of the Sunbelt: A Look at the Impact of U.S. Elderly Migration," Population Trends and Public Policy, no. 6 (Washington, D.C.: Population Reference Bureau, Inc., Oct. 1984), 3.

5. Robert A. Hoppe, "The Elderly's Income and Rural Development: Some Cautions," *Rural Development Perspectives* 7:2, Feb.–May 1991, 30.

6. Biggar, "Graying of the Sunbelt," 1.

7. Everett S. Lee, "Migration of the Aged," *Research on Aging* 2:2, June 1980.

8. William Serow, "Why the Elderly Move: Cross National Comparisons," *Research on Aging*, Dec. 1987.

9. Ellen S. Bryant and Mohammed El-Attar, "Migration and Redistribution of the Elderly: A Challenge to Community Services," *Gerontologist* 24:6, Dec.

1984.

10. T.D. Hogan, "Determinants of the Seasonal Migration of the Elderly to Sunbelt States," *Research on Aging*, March 1987.

11. Serow and Charity, "Return Migration of the Elderly in the United States," *Research on Aging*, June 1988.

12. Biggar, "Graying of the Sunbelt," 8.

13. Hogan, "Determinants of Seasonal Migration."

14. John A. Krout, *The Aged in Rural America* (New York: Greenwood Press, 1986).

15. Hoppe, "The Elderly's Income," 29–30.

16. Ibid.

17. Included in retirement-related transfers are the Social Security Old Age, Survivor's, and Disability Insurance Program; Medicare; and Federal Employees' Retirement and Disability.

18. Gary W. Smith and Robert A. Chase, "Shifts in Personal Income Composition: The Graying of the Northwest," *Pacific Northwest Executive*, January 1991, 9.

19. Melinda Beck, "The Geezer Boom," *Newsweek*, Special Issue, vol. 114, Winter 1989/Spring 1990, 62+.

20. See Krout, *The Aged;* Krout, ed., *Journal of Rural Studies*, 4:2, 1988 (entire issue devoted to elderly concerns); Raymond T. Coward and Gary R. Lee, eds., *The Elderly in Rural Society* (New York: Springer Publishing Co., 1985); Nina Glasgow and Calvin Beale, "Rural Elderly in Demographic Perspective," *Rural Development Perspectives* 3:1, 22–26, 1985.

21. Susan S. Meyers, "Economic Status of Elderly Is a More Severe Problem in Rural Areas," *Sociology of Rural Life* 9:3, Minnesota Extension Service, Fall 1987.

22. Krout, *The Aged.*

23. U.S. Congress, "Future of the Rural Elderly," hearing before the Select Committee on Aging, House of Representatives, 100th Congress, second session, Comm. Pub. no. 100-690, June 13, 1988 (Washington, D.C.: U.S. Government Printing Office).

24. Krout, *The Aged.*

25 Glasgow and Beale, "Rural Elderly," 25.

26. Ibid.

27. Ibid.

28. U.S. Congress, "Future of Rural Elderly."

29. Glasgow and Beale, "Rural Elderly," 23.

30. Calvin L. Beale and Glenn V. Fuguitt, "Decade of Pessimistic Nonmetro Population Trend Ends on Optimistic Note," *Rural Development Perspectives* 6:3, June–September 1990, 16.

31. Barbara Vobejda , "For the New Retirees, Out-of-the-Way Places: Rural, Small-Town Communities Benefiting," *The Washington Post*, December 1990.

32. Ibid.

33. Glasgow and Beale, "Rural Elderly," 23–24.

34. Stuart A. Rosenfeld et al., *Making Connections: "After the Factories" Revisited* (Research Triangle Park, NC: Southern Growth Policies Board, Feb. 1988).

35. DeWitt John et al., *A Brighter Future for Rural America?* (Washington, D.C.: National Governors' Association, Center for Policy Research, 1988).

36. Mark Drabenstott and Lynn Gibson, *Rural America in Transition* (Kansas City: The Federal Reserve Bank of Kansas City, Research Division, April 1988).

37. Beale and Fuguitt, "Decade of Pessimistic Nonmetro Population Trends," figure 5.

38. Richard J. Reeder and Nina L. Glasgow, "Nonmetro Retirement Counties' Strengths and Weaknesses," *Rural Development Perspectives* 6:2, February–May 1990, 13.

39. Ibid., 12. Roughly one-third of all nonmetro retirement counties fit the "mature" classification.

40. Ibid., figures 2–5.

41. Glasgow, "Attracting Retirees as a Community Development Option," *Journal of the Community Development Society* 21:1, 1990.

42. Hoppe, "The Elderly's Income"; this is the number of Americans aged 65 or over with incomes four or more times the poverty level.

43. Reeder and Glasgow, "Nonmetro Retirement Counties."

44. Hoppe, "The Elderly's Income," 31.

45. Julie Rovner, "No Help from Congress on a Near-Term Solution for Long-Term Care. But states are going ahead with other new ideas that don't require a federal permission slip." *Governing,* June 1990, 21–27.

46. Ibid.

47. Bryant and El-Attar, "Migration and Redistribution."

48. Gene F. Summers and Thomas A. Hirschl, "Retirees as a Growth Industry," *Rural Development Perspectives,* 1:2, Feb. 1985. 13–16.

49. Elliott Dubin and Norman J. Reid, "Federal Funds to Rural Areas: Fair Share? Right Mix?" background paper submitted to the Task Force on Rural Development (Washington, D.C.: National Governors' Association, 1988).

50. Robert D. Plotnick, "Small Community Economic Development: Can Income Transfers Help?" *A Northwest Reader: Options for Rural Communities* (Seattle: Northwest Policy Center, University of Washington, Graduate School of Public Affairs, 1988); Hoppe, "The Elderly's Income." By contrast, other types of transfers—unemployment insurance (UI) and welfare (including Aid to Families with Dependent Children (AFDC), Medicaid, and food stamps)—in their current forms offer little more than the short-term income boost described by Dubin and Reid.

51. Eldon Smith cited in Thomas A. Hirschl and Gene F. Summers, "Retirees as Growth Industry," *Rural Development Perspectives,* Feb. 1985, 14–15.

52. Hirschl and Summers (ibid.) note that these estimates may overstate the effect of transfer income on job creation (p. 15). Smith, in his study, looked at the effect of total spending by the elderly on local economic growth and assumed (a big assumption) that all of their income was represented by pension or transfer income. Even if he overestimates effects by 50 percent, however

(which Hirschl and Summers argue is possible), the difference in job creation potential is very large.

53. Ibid.

54. Krout, *The Aged.*

55. Reeder and Glasgow, "Nonmetro Retirement Counties."

56. Hirschl, "Retirement Transfers and Local Wage Rates," *Community Economic Vitality: Major Trends and Selected Issues* (Ames, IA: The North Central Regional Center for Rural Development, Iowa State University, 1988), 55–60.

57. Richards, "An Influx of Retirees."

58. Reeder and Glasgow, "Nonmetro Retirement Counties," 15.

59. Using a per pupil figure might produce a smaller gap. The per pupil figure adjusts for the fact that retirement communities have relatively smaller student populations than other nonmetro communities.

60. Reeder and Glasgow, "Nonmetro Retirement Counties," 15.

61. Ibid., 16–17.

62. Ibid., 17.

Chapter 10

1. David N. Allen and Victor Levine, Nurturing Advanced Technology Enterprises: Emerging Issues in State and Local Economic Development Policy (New York: Praeger Publishers, 1986), 29.

2. Edward J. Malecki, "Research and Development and the Geography of High-Technology Complexes," in John Rees, ed., *Technology, Regions, and Policy* (Totowa, NJ: Rowman & Littlefield, 1986), 64–67.

3. Amy Glasmeier, *Bypassing America's Outlands: Rural America and High Technology* (Austin: The University of Texas at Austin, Graduate Program in Community and Regional Planning, October 1988a); OTA 1984; and Catherine Armington, "The Changing Geography of High-Technology Businesses," in John Rees, ed., *Technology, Regions, and Policy* (Totowa, NJ: Rowman & Littlefield, 1986) 75–93.

4. Malecki, "High Technology and Local Economic Development," *Journal of the American Planning Association,* Summer 1984, 262-269; and Armington, "The Changing Geography."

5. Glasmeier, *Bypassing America's Outlands.*

6. Armington, "Changing Geography."

7. Stuart Rosenfeld et al., *Reviving the Rural Factory: Automation and Work in the South* (Research Triangle Park, NC: Southern Growth Policies Board, May 1988), 22.

8. Ibid., vi.

9. Glasmeier, *Bypassing America's Outlands,* 19.

10. Armington, "Changing Geography."

11. Glasmeier, *The High-Tech Potential: Economic Development in Rural America* (New Brunswick, NJ: Center for Urban Policy Research, Rutgers, the State University of New Jersey, 1991), 25–26.

12. Armington, "Changing Geography," 87.

13. Glasmeier, *Bypassing America's Outlands,* 20.

14. Malecki, "High Tech Economics: Hope or Hyperbole?" Current, March/April 1988, 36–40.

15. Roger Vaughan and Robert Pollard, "State and Federal Policies for High-Tech Development," in John Rees, ed., *Technology, Regions, and Policy* (Totowa, NJ: Rowman & Littlefield, 1986), 269.

16. Allen and Levine, *Nurturing Advanced Technology,* 44. The idea of rapid growth from a very small base applies here at the firm level. Again, the phenomenon exaggerates the scale of real gains.

17. Glasmeier, *Bypassing America's Outlands,* 19–20.

18. Ibid., 19, 22.

19. Ibid., 19.

20. McCrossen, "As growth tapers off," C76.

21. John Browning, "Information Technology Survey: The ubiquitous machine," *The Economist,* June 16, 1990, 5.

22. Philip Shapira, "Modern Times: Learning from State Initiatives in Industrial Extension and Technology Transfer," *Economic Development Quarterly* 4:3, Aug. 1990, 186; John Rees, Ronald Briggs, and Raymond Oakey, "The Adoption of New Technology in the American Machinery Industry," in John Rees, ed., *Technology, Regions, and Policy* (Totowa, NJ: Rowman & Littlefield, 1986), 193.

23. Survey done in 1982, Rees, Briggs, and Oakey, "Adoption of New Technology," 193.

24. Rosenfeld et al., *Reviving the Rural Factory,* 25.

25. Ibid. Part of this discrepancy, however, may be because the Japanese definition of what qualifies as a robot is broader than that used in the United States and elsewhere.

26. Koretz, "Will Direct Foreign Investment Help on the Trade Front?" *Business Week,* Dec. 16, 1991, 20.

27. Stephen M. Smith and David L. Barkley, "Contributions of High-Tech Manufacturing to Rural Economies," *Rural Development Perspectives* 5:3, June 1989, 7.

28. Glasmeier, *Bypassing America's Outlands.*

29. Ibid., 28–31.

30. Ibid.

31. Ibid., 38.

32. Other parts of the defense sector, however, do have a strong rural component. Military bases, for example, employ a large number of rural residents across the country. The closing of a base can be a devastating experience for a small community.

33. Glasmeier, "Factors Governing the Development of High Tech Industry Agglomerations: A Tale of Three Cities," *Regional Studies* 22:4, August 1988, 288–289.

34. Ibid.

35. Smith and Barkley, "Contributions of High-Tech Manufacturing," 9.
36. Rosenfeld et al., *Reviving the Rural Factory.*
37. Southern Growth Policy Board (SGPB) survey, vii.
38. Care must be taken in generalizing from these results about other parts of the country. Rees, Briggs, and Oakey ("Adoption of New Technology") found that, despite its high rate of job growth over the past 15 years, the South showed the lowest rate of process innovation deployment of any of the four census regions as of 1982 (pp. 200–201). The North Central region ranked first, followed by the Northeast, the West, and the South.
39. Rees, Briggs, and Oakey, "Adoption of New Technology," 202–203.
40. Ibid.
41. Vaughan and Pollard, "State and Federal Policies for High-Tech Development," 268–269.
42. Ibid.
43. Malecki, "High-Tech Economics," 37.
44. Malecki, "Geography of High-Tech Complexes," 68–69.
45. Ibid.
46. Smith and Barkley, "Contributions of High-Tech Manufacturing," 10.
47. Barkley, "The Decentralization of High-Technology Manufacturing to Nonmetropolitan Areas," Growth and Change, 19:1, Winter 1988, 24.
48. Ibid., 18.
49. Ibid., 19; Glasmeier, *The High-Tech Potential: Economic Development in Rural America,* and *Bypassing America's Outlands.*
50. Malecki, "Geography of High-Tech Complexes," 64–66.
51. R.P. Oakey and S.Y. Cooper, "High Technology" Industry Agglomeration and the Potential for Peripherally Sited Small Firms," *Regional Studies* 23:4, 1989, 348–349.
52. Mark Satterthwaite, "Location Patterns of High-Growth Firms," *Economic Development Commentary,* Council for Urban Economic Development, 12:1, Spring 1988, 9; Malecki, "High-Tech Economics," 37; John Rees and Howard A. Stafford, "Theories of Regional Growth and Industrial Location: Their Relevance for Understanding High-Technology Complexes," in John Rees, ed., *Technology, Regions, and Policy* (Totowa, NJ: Rowman & Littlefield, 1986), 43.
53. Ann R. Markusen, "Defense Spending and the Geography of High-Tech Industries," in John Rees, ed., *Technology, Regions, and Policy* (Totowa, NJ: Rowman & Littlefield, 1986), 114. While this result is striking, Markusen believes that more research is needed to definitively prove a causal link between military spending and regional restructuring of industry (pp. 114–115).
54. Vaughan and Pollard, "State and Federal Policies," 270.
55. Oakey and Cooper, "High Technology Industry," 349.
56. Satterthwaite, "Location Patterns," 8–9.
57. Clarke, *Revitalizing State Economics,* 57.
58. Robert D. Atkinson, "Ten Lessons for Successful State Technology Planning," *Economic Development Commentary* 14:2, Summer 1990, 20.

59. Ibid., 27.
60. Barkley, "Decentralization of High-Technology," 16.
61. Vaughan and Pollard, "State and Federal Policies," 269.
62. David Osborne, "Refining State Technology Programs: The past decade of creative experimentation has produced some useful lessons." *Issues in Science and Technology* 6:4, Summer 1990, 56.
63. Clarke, *Revitalizing State Economics,* 74.
64. Osborne, "Refining State Technology Programs," 56.
65. Malecki, "High-Tech Economics," 36.
66. Ibid., 37.
67. Atkinson, "Ten Lessons," 22–23.
68. Osborne, "Refining State Technology Programs," 57.
69. Atkinson, "Ten Lessons," 22.
70. Center for Rural Affairs, *Half a Glass of Water: State Economic Development Policies and the Small Agricultural Communities of the Middle Border* (Walthill, NE: Center for Rural Affairs), March 1990, 75.
71. Ibid., 96.
72. Ibid., 75–76. Exceptions include research and development centers in Minnesota, Iowa, and Nebraska dedicated to agriculture, food processing, and gasohol (p. 97). These programs are likely to yield some benefits for rural areas of their states. In addition, the Greater Minnesota Corporation, a quasi-public product development corporation, "has a legislative mission to build on the state's rural economy, and it may bring high-tech development to small towns" (pp. 32–34, 76).
73. Ibid., 97.
74. Ibid., 99. Going a step further, the Center for Rural Affairs (*Half a Glass of Water*) also suggests that many states' current infatuation with "more glamorous applications of these strategies" to high-risk, high-tech industries diverts resources that might better be used in support of "plainer, more homespun approaches involving small business, innovation, and research" (p. 73). Exceptions to this rule include state-backed investment in developing milkweed fiber as a substitute for goose and duck down filling in a small Nebraska community and a locally sponsored investment in a pork rind processing plant in a small Iowa town (p. 76).
    Rosenfeld, et al. (1988) make a similar point when they recommend that state R&D investments be channeled to industries with heavy concentrations in the rural South, most of which do not qualify as high tech or high growth but do play a vital role in local economies (p. 137).
75. Satterthwaite, "Location Patterns," 11.
76. Smith and Barkley, "Contributions of High-Tech Manufacturing," 8.
77. Rees and Stafford, "Theories of Regional Growth and Industrial Location," 30.
78. Gregory A. Daneke, "Technological Entrepreneurship as a Focal Point of Economic Development Policy: A Conceptual Reassessment," *Policy Studies Journal,* 17:3, Spring 1989, 648–651.

79. Satterthwaite, "Location Patterns," 10.
80. Clarke, *Revitalizing State Economics*, 65. In an evaluation of economic oppor-tunity strategies focused on poor, inner-city neighborhoods, Alan Okagaki (1988) also has identified learning as one of the key elements in "the process of individual economic advancement and the ways neighborhoods foster or retard it" (p. 4). Learning in this context goes far beyond basic academic knowledge and job skills to include "learning about the world-at-large and en-visioning where one wants to fit into it"—a process of breaking through the geographic, social, and economic isolation that characterizes life in poor, inner-city neighborhoods (pp. 3–4).
81. Rosenfeld et al., *Reviving the Rural Factory*; Rees et al., "Adoption of New Technology."
82. Ibid., 32; Rees, Briggs, and Oakey, "Adoption of New Technology," 194-196.
83. Rosenfeld et al., *Reviving the Rural Factory*, 41.
84. Rees, Briggs, and Oakey, "Adoption of New Technology," 197.
85. Rosenfeld et al., *Reviving the Rural Factory*, 48-49.
86. Based on telephone conversations with officials in Illinois and New York, 1988.
87. Rees, Briggs, and Oakey, "Adoption of New Technology," 215.
88. Rees and Stafford, "Theories of Regional Growth," 30–31.
89. Rosenfeld et al., *Reviving the Rural Factory*, vii.
90. Ibid., 39.
91. Ibid., 25.
92. Shapira, "Modern Times," 197.
93. Koretz, "Will Direct Foreign Investment Help?"
94. Edward M. Graham, "Foreign Direct Investment in the United States and U.S. Interests," *Science*, 254:5039, Dec. 20, 1991, 1743.
95. Shapira, "Modern Times," 188.
96. Clarke, *Revitalizing State Economies*, 65, 68.
97. Shapira, "Modern Times," 188–189.
98. Ibid.
99. Rosenfeld et al. *Reviving the Rural Factory*, 135.
100. Shapira, "Modern Times," 200.
101. Ibid.
102. Ibid., 199.
103. Ibid.
104. Rosenfeld et al., *Reviving the Rural Factory*, 136–137.
105. Shapira, "Modern Times"; ibid., 200.
106. Rosenfeld et al., *Reviving the Rural Factory*, 138–139.
107. Ibid., 140-141.
108. Smith and Barkley, "Contributions of High-Tech Manufacturing," 8–9.
109. Ibid.
110. Rosenfeld et al., *Reviving the Rural Factory*, 67–74.
111. Ibid., 74–96.

Chapter 11

1. Case studies show that public institutions already have adopted a leadership role in telecommunications applications in many rural areas.
2. Edward Carr, "Telecommunications Survey: The message-makers," *The Economist* 314:7653, March 10, 1990, 5.
3. Ibid., 34.
4. Ibid., 6.
5. "A Scramble for Global Networks," special report on telecommunication, *Business Week* March 21, 1988.
6. Ibid., 3
7. Ibid., 2–3. There is another side to the bypass debate. While the disadvantages for the traditional carriers are obvious, some communities may actually benefit from the opportunities for piggybacking onto the new, private systems and gaining access to enhanced services never before available to them. One large company's decision to build a telecommunications bypass can open up vast opportunities for neighboring businesses and change the direction of a local economy.
8. Cuomo Commission on Trade and Competitiveness, *The Cuomo Commission Report* (New York: Simon and Schuster, 1988), 154.
9. Carr, "Telecommunications Survey," 14
10. Cuomo Commission Report, 154.
11. Carr, "Telecommunications Survey," 14.
12. A high percentage of long distance telephone traffic now travels over fiber-optic networks stretching between central exchanges in different locales. However, transmission from the central switching office to the home or business still runs along traditional copper wires. The next step in completing the fiber-optic network—installing that "last mile" of fiber—is highly controversial. Given the uncertain costs and benefits, experts do not agree about the wisdom of pursuing that goal in the near future. (See special issue of *Public Utilities Fortnightly* on fiber optics, August 16, 1990.)
13. This additional step in communications deregulation would create yet another arena of competition for telecommunications firms—this time in cable TV and video services. Allowing telecommunications firms entrance to this market would increase the profitability of running fiber-optic networks directly to homes and businesses and surely would hasten completion of "the last mile" (Marshal Yates, "The Promise of Fiber Optics," 1990, 14–15).
14. See especially Malecki, "High-Tech Economics."
15. Frederick Williams, "Telecommunications and U.S. Rural Development: An Update," paper prepared for the Aspen Institute Seminar on Telecommunications and Rural Development, Queenstown, Maryland, March 25–27, 1991.
16. Sharon Strover and Williams, *Rural Revitalization and Information Technologies in the United States* (Austin, TX: Center for Research on Communication Technology and Society, The University of Texas at Austin, Nov. 1991),

chapter 4.

17. Center for Rural Affairs 1990, 80–81.

18. Don A. Dillman et al., "Is Being Rural a Barrier to Job Creation in the Information Age?" *A Northwest Reader: Options for Rural Communities* (Seattle: Northwest Policy Center, University of Washington, Graduate School of Public Affairs, 1988.)

19. Williams, "Telecommunications and U.S. Rural Development."

20 Dillman et al., "Is Being Rural a Barrier?" 74.

21. For details, see "Many Rural Regions Are Growing Again; the Reason: Technology," *Wall Street Journal,* November 21, 1994, Al.

22. James Bennet, "Power Failure: Rural electric and telephone programs show that good government programs never die—they just get more expensive," *The Washington Monthly* 22:6–7, July/Aug. 1990, 12, 14–15.

23. Edwin B. Parker et al., *Rural America in the Information Age: Telecommunications Policy for Rural Development* (Lanham, MD: University Press of America and The Aspen Institute, 1989), 68.

24. Ibid., 67.

25. Ibid.

26. Although national conversion to the new digital switches is a high priority for telephone companies, the process is just starting. At the beginning of 1989, less than one-third of the lines owned by the Bell system's seven Regional Holding Companies had gone digital. However, the Bell companies were planning to spend more than $4 billion in 1989 alone to purchase and install the new switches. Pressure from businesses that want to transmit data over the telephone lines is spurring the conversion to digital switches. Urban and some suburban areas with heavy concentrations of business customers are likely to be the biggest beneficiaries for the foreseeable future (H. Terrence Riley, "Monarchy gives way to oligopoly—is democracy next?" *Industry Surveys,* Standard & Poor's, Oct. 5, 1989, T39).

    Those rural areas served by independent companies, however, may actually enjoy greater access to digital technology. Parker et al. (*Rural America in the Information Age*) report 1989 figures from *Telephone* magazine that show the large independent telephone companies with higher overall rates of digital switching (50.6 percent) than the regional Bell companies (34 percent) (pp. 80–81). Unfortunately, data is not available to determine what percentage of these switches serve rural communities.

27. This is most important for the speed and reliability of data transmission (Parker et al., *Rural America,* 82).

28. Ibid., 86.

29. Ibid., 83–85.

30. Robert H. Wilson and Paul E. Teske, "Telecommunications and Economic Development: The State and Local Role," *Economic Development Quarterly* 4:2, May 1990, 160.

31. Some observers expect deregulation of local networks to begin soon.

32. Gail Garfield Schwartz, "Telecommunications and Economic Development Policy," *Economic Development Quarterly* 4:2, May 1990, 86.

33. Wilson and Teske, "Telecommunications," 170; Jill Hills, "The telecommunications rich and poor," *Third World Quarterly* 12:2, April 1990, 73.

34. "A Scramble for Global Networks," *Business Week*, March 21, 1988, 143.

35. Carr ("Telecommunications Survey"), however, warns that telecommunications companies should not focus on large users at the expense of serving smaller firms (p. 35). In the context of the three-way competition among phone companies, computer companies, and private networks, he argues, phone companies may be best suited and have the most success providing service to the small business market.

36. Strover and Williams, *Rural Revitalization*, chapters 3 and 4.

37. Wilson and Teske, "Telecommunications," 171.

38. Schwartz, "Telecommunications," 86.

39. Parker et al., *Rural America*, 54.

40. Ibid., 55, 60–61. The FCC has already begun to revise its attitudes about rate setting. In 1989, they shifted from a rate-of-return regulatory scheme for AT&T's long-distance service to a price cap scheme. In this way , the company is allowed to pursue higher profit margins by improving efficiency, but customers are protected from dramatic price increases by the cap. The next step in price deregulation—abandoning the cap—would have the most dramatic effect on rural telephone bills.

41. Williams, "Telecommunications."

42. Parker et al., *Rural America*.

43. Dillman et al., "Is Being Rural a Barrier?" Table 3.

44. Ibid., 76.

45. Strover and Williams, *Rural Revitalization*.

46. Ibid., chapter 4. Since then, however, Nebraska has become a telecommunications success story (see "Many Rural Regions Are Growing Again").

47. Ibid., chapter 6.

48. Ibid., chapter 4.

49. Ibid., chapter 3.

50. Ibid., chapter 3.

51. Ibid., chapter 5.

52. Heather E. Hudson, "Telecommunications Policy: The State Role, a National Overview," paper for the Aspen Institute, September 1990, 14–16.

53. Parker et al., *Rural America*, 34.

54. Jill Hills makes a similar point about the tendency of developing countries to underinvest in telecommunications technology ("Telecommunications rich and poor," 78–79). Here, the problem seems to be a combination of inadequate financing options, lack of foreign exchange, dependence on industrialized countries for technical personnel and information, mismatch between available equipment and developing countries' needs, and excessive government control.

55. Parker et al., *Rural America*, 9.

56. Ibid., 34–35.

57. Ibid., 31.

58. Ibid., 32.

59. Hills, "Telecommunications rich and poor," 77.
60. Ibid., 76.
61. Parker et al., *Rural America*, 33.
62. Ibid., 43–50.
63. Schwartz, "Telecommunications," 87.
64. Ibid., 85.
65. Wilson and Teske, "Telecommunications," 170.
66. Bennet, "Power Failure," 18–19.
67. Ibid.
68. Ibid.
69. Parker et al., *Rural America*, 91.
70. Ibid., 94–97.
71. Ibid., 97.
72. Ibid., 97–99.
73. Ibid., 100–101.
74. Ibid., 92–102.
75. Schwartz, "Telecommunications," 88.
76. Heather E. Hudson, "The Role of the Public Sector in Rural
    Telecommunications," paper prepared for The Aspen Institute, c. 1991.
    Hudson has identified examples in which the federal government already serves
    this function. She reports that the Internal Revenue Service requires that its tele-
    phone-based information centers locate only in areas with access to optical-fiber
    networks (p. 16).
       Strover and Williams describe how the process has worked in urban areas.
    Omaha, today considered the "800 Capital of the World" because of its domi-
    nance in telemarketing, owes its superior telecommunications infrastructure to
    the Air Force's Strategic Air Command (SAC) headquarters located in Omaha.
77. Schwartz, "Telecommunications," 88–89.
78. Ibid., 87–88.
79. Ibid., 89.
80. Strover and Williams, *Rural Revitalization,* chapter 3.
81. Ibid., chapter 6.
82. As Robert Reich (*The Work of Nations*) puts it, "The 'information revolution'
    may have rendered some of us more productive, but it has also produced huge
    piles of raw data which must be processed in much the same monotonous way
    that assembly-line workers and, before them, textile workers processed piles of
    other raw materials" (p. 175).
83. Strover and Williams, *Rural Revitalization,* chapter 6.

Conclusion

 1. Spencer Rich, "Low-Paying Jobs Up Sharply in Decade, U.S. Says," *The
    Washington Post,* May 12, 1992, A7; Jason DeParle, "Report, Delayed Months,
    Says Lowest Income Group Grew Sharply," *The New York Times,* May 12,
    1992, p. A15.

2. This is what is missing in the accounts of rural preservationists like Wendell Berry who seems to believe that generational continuities can be achieved without significant changes in economic activities and social relationships (Berry 1990). Because such arguments fail to acknowledge the embeddedness of rural America, they represent the triumph of nostalgia over analysis.

3. For an illustration of this thesis, see Hugh M. Raup, "The View from John Sanderson's Farm: A Perspective for the Use of the Land," *Forest History* 10:1, April 1966, 2–11.

4. Daniel Kemmis, *Community and the Politics of Place* (Norman, OK: University of Oklahoma Press, 1990).

5. Raup, "The View," 6.

6. See Robert Greenstein and Isaac Shapiro in Cynthia M. Duncan, ed. *Rural Poverty in America* (New York: Auburn House, 1992).

7. Jeremy D. Rosner, *A Progressive Perspective on Health Care Reform* (Washington, D.C.: Progressive Foundation, 1992).

Bibliography

Allen, David N., and Victor Levine. *Nurturing Advanced Technology Enterprises: Emerging Issues in State and Local Economic Development Policy.* New York: Praeger Publishers, 1986.

Anderson, Leslie. *Tourism and Local Economic Development: A Bibliography.* Monticello, Illinois: Vance Bibliographies, 1988.

Anderson, Randall S., Jay A. Leitch, and John F. Mittleider. "Contribution of State Parks to State Economies." *Parks and Recreation,* vol. 21, no. 10, Oct. 1986, pp. 62–63.

Appleby, Joyce. "Commercial Farming and the Agrarian Myth in the Early Republic," *The Journal of American History* 68, March 1982, pp. 833–849.

Archibugi, F., and P. Nijkamp. *Economy and Ecology: Towards Sustainable Development.* Dordrecht: Kluwer, 1989.

Armington, Catherine. "The Changing Geography of High-Technology Business," in John Rees, ed., *Technology, Regions, and Policy.* Totowa, NJ: Rowan & Littlefield, 1986, pp. 75–93.

Arndt, H.W. *Economic Development: The History of an Idea.* Chicago: University of Chicago Press, 1987.

Atkinson, Robert D. "Ten Lessons for Successful State Technology Planning." *Economic Development Commentary,* vol. 14, no. 2, Summer 1990, pp. 20–28.

Baily, Martin Neil, and Margaret M. Blair. "Productivity and American Management," in Robert E. Litan, Robert Z. Lawrence, and Charles l. Schultze, eds. *American Living Standards: Threats and Challenges.* Washington, D.C.: The Brookings Institution, 1988, pp. 178–214.

———— and Alok K. Chakrabati. *Innovation and the Productivity Crisis.* Washington, D.C.: The Brookings Institution, 1988.

———— and Robert J. Gordon. "The Productivity Slowdown, Measurement Issues, and the Explosion of Computer Power." *Brookings Paper on Economic Activity,* 2:1988.

Barancik, Scott. "The Rural Disadvantage: Growing Income Disparities Between Rural and Urban Areas." Washington, D.C.: Center on Budget and Policy Priorities, 1990.

Bardhan, Pranab. "Comments on 'Development Economics: What Next?'" in Gustav Ranis and T. Paul Schultz, *The State of Development Economics: Progress and Perspectives.* New York: Basil Blackwell, 1988, pp. 137–138.

Bar-El, Ralph, and Daniel Felsenstein. "Technological Profile and Industrial Structure: Implications for the Development of Sophisticated Industry in Peripheral Areas," *Regional Studies,* vol. 23, no. 3, pp. 253–266.

Barkema, Alan D., Mark Drabenstott, and Julie Stanley. "Processing Food in Farm States: An Economic Development Strategy for the 1990s." *Economic Review*, Federal Reserve Bank of Kansas, July/Aug. 1990, pp. 5–23.

Barkley, David L. "The Decentralization of High-Technology Manufacturing to Nonmetropolitan Areas." *Growth and Change*, vol. 19, no. 1, Winter 1988, pp. 13–30.

Barrett, Todd. "The Country Connection: Tiny phone firms boom." *Newsweek*, vol. 114, no. 12, Sept. 18, 1989, p. 47.

Bauer, P.T. *Dissent on Development.* London: Weidenfeld and Nicolson, 1972.

———. "N.H. Stern on Substance and Method in Development Economics." *Journal of Development Economics* 2,4 1975 pp. 387–405.

Beale, Calvin L., and Glenn V. Fuguitt. "Decade of Pessimistic Nonmetro Population Trends Ends on Optimistic Note." *Rural Development Perspectives*, vol. 6, no. 3, June–September 1990, pp. 14–18.

Beck, Melinda. "The Geezer Boom." *Newsweek* Special Issue, vol. 114, Winter 1989/Spring 1990, pp. 62+.

Begley, Sharon, et al. "E pluribus, plures. Without Leadership from Washington, the States Set the Environmental Agenda for the Nation." *Newsweek*, November 13, 1989, pp. 70–72.

Beitz, Charles R. "Democracy in Developing Societies," in Peter G. Brown and Henry Shue, eds. *Boundaries: National Autonomy and Its Limits.* Totowa, NJ: Rowman and Littlefield, 1981.

Bellah, Robert N., Richard Madsen, William M. Sullivan, Ann Swidler, and Steven M. Tipton. *Habits of the Heart: Individualism and Commitment in American Life.* New York: Harper & Row, 1985.

Bender, Lloyd D. "The Role of Services in Rural Development Policies." *Land Economics*, vol. 63, no. 1, Feb. 1987, pp. 62–71.

Bennet, James. "Power Failure; Rural electric and telephone program shows that good government programs never die—they just get more expensive." *The Washington Monthly*, vol. 22, no. 6-7, July/Aug. 1990, pp. 12–21.

Berger, Suzanne, Michael L. Dertouzos, Richard K. Lester, Robert M. Solow, and Lester C. Thurow. "Toward a New Industrial America." *Scientific American* vol. 260, no. 6, June 1989, pp. 39–47.

Bergman, Edward R. "Urban and Rural Considerations in Southern Development," in *Rural Flight/Urban Might: Economic Development Challenges for the 1990s.* Cross-Cutting Issue report No. 3, 1986 Commission on the Future of the South. Research Triangle Park, NC: Southern Growth Policies Board, 1986, pp. 7–12.

Bergstrom, John C., H. Ken Cordell, Gregory A. Ashley, and Alan E. Watson. "Economic Impacts of Recreational Spending on Rural Areas: A Case Study." *Economic Development Quarterly*, vol. 4, no. 1, Feb. 1990, pp. 29–39.

Berry, Brian J.L. "Strategies, Models, and Economic Theories of Development in Rural Regions." *Agricultural Economic Report No. 127*, ERS-USDA, December 1967.

Berry, Wendell. "An Argument for Diversity." *What Are People For? Essays by Wendell Berry.* San Francisco: North Point Press, 1990, pp. 109–122.

Beyers, W.B., M.J. Alvine, and E.G. Johnsen. "The Service Economy: Export of Services in the Central Puget Sound Region." Central Puget Sound Economic Development District, Seattle, WA. April, 1985.

Bhagwati, Jagdish N. "Development Economics: What Have We Learnt?" in Krishna Ahooja-Patel et al., eds., *World Economy in Transition*. Oxford: Pergamon Press, 1986.

———. "Directly Unproductive, Profit-Seeking (DUP) Activities." *Journal of Political Economy* 90. October 1982, pp. 988–1002.

Biggar, Jeanne C. "The Graying of the Sunbelt: A Look at the Impact of U.S. Elderly Migration." *Population Trends and Public Policy, No. 6.* Washington, D.C.: Population Reference Bureau, Inc., Oct. 1984.

Blackley, Paul R. "Urban-Rural Variations in the Structure of Manufacturing Production." *Urban Studies* vol. 23, no. 6, Dec. 1986, pp. 471–483.

Blank, Uel. *The Community Tourism Imperative.* State College, Pennsylvania: Venture Publishing, Inc., 1989.

Bloomquist, Leonard E. "Performance of the Rural Manufacturing Sector," in David L. Brown et al., eds., *Rural Economic Development in the 1980s: Prospects for the Future,* RDRR-69. Economic Research Service, U.S. Department of Agriculture. Washington, D.C.: Government Printing Office, Sept. 1988, pp. 49–75.

Bluestone, Barry, and Bennett Harrison. *The Deindustrialization of America.* Boston, MA: Basic Books, 1982.

——— and Bennett Harrison. "The Great American Job Machine: The Proliferation of Low Wage Employment in the U.S. Economy," paper prepared for the Joint Economic Committee, U.S. Congress, Dec. 1986.

Bluestone, Herman, and Stan G. Daberkow. "Employment Growth in Nonmetro America: Past Trends and Prospects to 1990." *Rural Development Perspectives,* vol 1, issue 3, June 1985, pp. 20+.

——— and Celeste A. Long. "Growth Falters in Most Rural Counties: Manufacturing Both Hero and Goat." *Rural Development Perspective,* vol. 5, issue 2, Feb. 1989, pp. 8–10.

——— and Paul R. Myers. "Rural Manufacturing Counties on Upswing Again." *Rural Development Perspectives,* vol. 4, issue 1, Oct. 1987.

Blyskal, Jeff. "Tour Wars." *Forbes,* July 2, 1984.

Boe, Deen. "Outdoor Recreation in Economic Development," background paper submitted to the Task Force on Rural Development. Washington, D.C.: National Governors' Association, 1988.

Bonnen, James T. "U.S. Perspective on the Interest Group Base of Rural Policy: People , Agriculture, the Environment," paper prepared for the International Symposium on Economic Change, Policies, Strategies and Research Issues, Aspen Colorado, July 4–7 1990.

Bouvier, Leon F. "America's Baby Boom Generation: The Fateful Bulge." *Population Bulletin,* Population Reference Bureau, Washington, D.C. April 1980.

Breneman, Don, Barbara Koth, and Glenn Kreag. "Tourism Brochures to Boost Business," publication CD-FO-3273. St. Paul, Minnesota: Tourism Center, Minnesota Extension Service, University of Minnesota, 1987.

Brown, David L., and Kenneth L. Deavers. "Rural Change and the Rural
    Economic Policy Agenda for the 1980s," in David L. Brown et al., eds., *Rural
    Economic Development in the 1980s: Prospects for the Future,* RDRR-69.
    Economic Research Service, U.S. Department of Agriculture. Washington,
    D.C.: U.S. Government Printing Office, Sept. 1988, pp. 1–28.

Browning, John. "Information Technology Survey: The ubiquitous machine." *The
    Economist,* June 16, 1990, pp. 5–20.

Bryan, Governor Richard H. "Nation's Governors Raise Tourism on Public
    Agenda." *State Government News,* vol. 30, no. 5, May 1987, pp. 4–5.

Bryant, Ellen S., and Mohammed El-Attair. "Migration and Redistribution of the
    Elderly: A Challenge to Community Services." *Gerontologist,* vol. 24, no. 6,
    Dec. 1984, pp. 634+.

Burgess, John. "Flood of Money Into U.S. Slows to a Trickle." *The Washington
    Post,* Oct. 7, 1990, pp. H1+.

Bury, J.B. *The Idea of Progress.* New York: Dover, 1955.

Campbell, Gary A. "The Response of U.S. Copper Companies to Changing
    Market Conditions." *Resources Policy,* vol. 15, no. 4, Dec. 1989, pp. 321–337.

Carlin, Thomas A. "Rural Areas Weaning Themselves from Farming." *Rural
    Development Perspectives,* vol. 4, issue 1, Oct. 1987, pp. 24–28.

Caro, Robert. *The Power Broker.* New York: Vintage, 1975.

Carr, Edward. "Telecommunications Survey: The message-makers," *The Economist*
    vol. 314, no. 7645, March 10, 1990, pp. 5–36.

Carriker, Roy. "Linking Natural Resource Policies with Rural Development Goals."
    Rural Development Perspectives, vol. 6, no. 1, October 1989, pp. 13–16.

Castle, Emery. "Policy Options for Rural Development in a Restructured Rural
    Economy," in Gene Summers, John Bryden, Kenneth Deavers, Howard
    Newby, and Susan Sechler, eds., *Agriculture and Beyond: Rural Economic
    Development.* Madison: University of Wisconsin College of Agricultural and
    Life Sciences, 1987.

Center for Community Change. *Searching for "The Way That Works": An Analysis of
    FmHA Rural Development Policy and Implementation.* Washington, D.C.:
    Aspen Institute, 1990.

Center for Resource Economics. *Farm Bill 1990: Agenda for the Environment and
    Consumers.* Washington, D.C.: Island Press, 1990.

Center for Rural Affairs. *Half a Glass of Water: State Economic Development Policies
    and the Small Agricultural Communities of the Middle Border.* Walthill, NE:
    Center for Rural Affairs, March 1990.

Chambers, Robert. *Rural Development: Putting the Last First.* New York: Longman,
    1983.

"Clean Air Act." *Congressional Digest* vol. 69, no. 3, March 1990, pp. 65–72+.

Clarke, Marianne K. *Revitalizing State Economies.* Washington, D.C.: National
    Governors' Association, 1986.

Clarke, Susan E., and Gary L. Gaile. "Moving Toward Entrepreneurial Economic
    Development Policies: Opportunities and Barriers." *Policy Studies Journal* 17,
    3. Spring 1989, pp. 574–958.

Clifford, Patrick. "Health and Migration of the Elderly." *Research on Aging* vol. 2, no.2, June 1980, pp. 233–242.

Cloud, David S. "Conferees Forced to Seek New Ideas in Farm Bill." *Congressional Quarterly,* Oct. 20, 1990, pp. 3491–3495.

"Coal production closing in on one billion mark." *Industry Surveys, Standard & Poor's,* Oct. 19, 1989, pp. R27–R32.

Cocheba, Donald J., Robert W. Gilmer, and Richard S. Mack. "Causes and Consequences of Slow Growth in the Tennessee Valley's Service Sector." *Growth and Change,* vol. 17, no 1, Jan. 1986, pp. 51–65.

Coffey, William J., and Mario Polese. "Local Development: Conceptual Bases and Policy Implications." *Regional Studies,* 2. (April 1985), pp. 85–93.

Cohen, Stephen S., and John Zysman. *Manufacturing Matters: The Myth of the Post-Industrial Economy.* New York: Basic Books, 1987.

———."Why Manufacturing Matters: The Myth of the Post-Industrial Economy." *California Management Review,* vol. 29, no. 3, Spring 1987, pp 9–26.

Connell, John, Biplab Dasgupta, Roy Laishley, and Michael Lipton. *Migration from Rural Areas: The Evidence from Village Studies.* Delhi: Oxford University Press, 1976.

Cook, Paul, and David Hulme. "The Compatibility of Market Liberalization and Local Economic Development Strategies." *Regional Studies* 22, 3. June 1988, pp. 221–231.

Cortright, Joseph. "Old World, New Ideas: Business Assistance Lessons from Europe." *Report to the Legislative Committee on Trade and Economic Development,* Oregon Legislature, April 1990.

Crompton, John L., and Sarah L. Richardson. "The Tourism Connection: Where Public and Private Leisure Services Meet." *Parks and Recreation,* vol. 21, no. 10, Oct. 1986, pp. 62–63.

The Cuomo Commission on Trade and Competitiveness. *The Cuomo Commission Report.* New York: Simon and Schuster, 1988.

Dahl, Robert. *Who Governs?* New Haven: Yale University Press, 1961.

Daly, Herman E. "The Economic Growth Debate: What Some Economists Have Learned But Many Have Not." *Journal of Environmental Economics and Management* 14, 4. December 1987, pp. 323–336.

Daneke, Gregory A. "Technological Entrepreneurship as a Focal Point of Economic Development Policy: A Conceptual Reassessment." *Policy Studies Journal,* vol. 17, no. 3, Spring 1989, pp. 643–655.

Daniels, Thomas L. "The Goals and Values of Local Economic Development Strategies in Rural America." *Agriculture and Human Values* 8, 3. Summer 1991, pp. 3–9.

Datta-Chauduri, Mrinal. "Market Failure and Government Failure." *Journal of Economic Perspectives* 4, 3. Summer 1990, pp. 25–39.

de Janvry, Alain, Robin Marsh, David Runsten, Elisabeth Sadoulet, and Carol Zabin. *Rural Development in Latin America: An Evaluation and a Proposal.* San Jose, C.R.: Instituto Interamericano de Cooperacion para la Agricultural, 1989.

————, David Runsten, and Elisabeth Sadoulet. "Toward a Rural Development Program for the United States: A Proposal," in Summers, Bryden, Deavers, Newby, and Sechler, eds., *Agriculture and Beyond: Rural Economic Development.* Department of Agricultural Journalism, University of Wisconsin-Madison, 1989.

de Tocqueville, Alexis. *Democracy in America.* Garden City, NY: Doubleday, 1969.

Deavers, Kenneth L. "Rural Development in the 1990s: Data and Research Needs," paper prepared for the Rural Social Science Symposium, AAEA, Baton Rouge, Louisiana, July 28–29, 1989.

"Delaware Tourism Study Proves Visitor Tax Receipts Exceed State Service Costs: Seen as Nationally Projectable." *Barron's*, vol. 60, no. 2, Jan. 14, 1980, p. 39.

DeParle, Jason. "Report, Delayed Months, Says Lowest Income Group Grew Sharply." *New York Times*, May 12, 1992, A15.

Dertouzos, Michael L., Richard K. Lester, Robert M. Solow, et al. *Made in America; Regaining the Productive Edge.* Cambridge, MA: MIT Press, 1988.

Dillman, Don A., Donald M. Beck, and John C. Allen. "Is Being Rural a Barrier to Job Creation in the Information Age?" in *A Northwest Reader: Options for Rural Communities.* Seattle: Northwest Policy Center, University of Washington, Graduate School of Public Affairs, 1988.

Doeringer, Peter B., and David G. Terkla. "Turning Around Local Economies: Managerial Strategies and Community Assets." *Journal of Policy Analysis and Management* 9, 4. 1990, pp. 487–506.

Drabenstott, Mark, and Alan D. Barkema. "A Turning Point in the Farm Recovery?" *Economic Review*, vol. 76, no. 1, Jan./Feb. 1991, pp. 17–31.

———— and Lynn Gibson. *Rural America in Transition.* Kansas City: The Federal Reserve Bank of Kansas City, Research Division, April 1988.

Drucker, Peter F. "The Changed World Economy." *Foreign Affairs*, vol. 64, no. 4, Spring 1986, pp. 768–791.

————. *The New Realities.* New York: Harper and Row, 1989.

Dubin, Elliott, and Norman J. Reid. "Federal Funds to Rural Areas: Fair Share? Right Mix?," background paper submitted to the task Force on Rural Development. Washington, D.C.: National Governors' Association, 1988.

Duncan, Cynthia M. *Rural Poverty in America.* New York: Auburn House, 1992.

Durbin, Kathie, and Paul Koberstein. "Northwest Forests: Day of Reckoning." Special section of *The Oregonian*, Oct. 15, 1990.

Dutt, Amitava Krishna. "Sectoral Balance in Development: A Survey." *World Development* 18, 6. June 1990, pp. 915–930.

Eckstein, Albert J., and Dale M. Heien. "Causes and Consequences of Service Sector Growth." *Growth and Change* vol. 16, no. 2, April 1985, pp. 12–17.

Economic Research Service (ERS), U.S. Department of Agriculture. *Education and Rural Economic Development: Strategies for the 1990s.* Agriculture and Rural Economy Division, ERS Staff Report No. AGES, 9153, September 1991.

————. "The Status of the Rural Economy," July 1994.

Ehrensaft, Philip, and David Freshwater. "Direct and Indirect Development Policy in a Neo-Conservative North America" (unpublished: on file with the authors).

Ellefson, Paul V. *Forest Resource Economics and Policy Research.* Boulder, CO: Westview Press, 1989.

Elo, Irma T., and Calvin L. Beale. *Natural Resources and Rural Poverty. An Overview.* Resources for the Future, Inc.: Washington, D.C., c. 1983.

"Environmental issues shake up the industry." *Industry Surveys, Standard & Poor's* Dec. 14, 1989, pp. B81–B84.

"The factory of the future." *The Economist,* April 5, 1986, pp. 97–99.

Fallows, James. *More Like Us.* Boston: Houghton Mifflin, 1989

Findlay, Ronald. "Trade, Development, and the State," in Ranis and Schultz, eds., *The State of Development Economics: Progress and Perspectives.* New York: Basil Blackwell, 1988.

Fish, Frank. "Tourism: Planning for Its Development," *Commentary,* National Council for Urban Economic Development, Spring 1985, pp. 17–22.

Fisher, Peter S. "Risk Capital and Rural Development," in *Toward Rural Development Policy for the 1990s: Enhancing Income and Employment Opportunities,* a symposium sponsored by the Congressional Research Service for the Joint Economic Committee, U.S. Congress. 101st Congress, first session, Senate Print 101–50, 1989.

Fishlow, Albert. "The Latin American State," *Journal of Economic Perspectives* 4,3. Summer 1990, pp. 61–74.

———. "Review of Handbook of Development Economics." *Journal of Economic Literature* 29. December 1991, pp. 1728–1737.

Flora, Cornelia B., and Jan L. Flora. "Developing entrepreneurial rural communities," *Sociological Practice* 8 (1990), pp. 197–207.

"The Forest Service: Time for a Little Perestroika." *The Economist,* March 10, 1990, p. 28.

Franklin, Karen. "Timber! The Forest Disservice." *The New Republic,* Jan. 2, 1989, pp. 12–14.

Frohlich, Norman, and Joe A. Oppenheimer. *Political Leadership and Collective Goods.* Princeton: Princeton University Press, 1971.

Fuguitt, Glenn V., David L. Brown, and Calvin L. Beale. *Rural and Small Town America.* New York: Russell Sage Foundation, 1989.

Fuller, Tony. "Local Development Strategies: A Canadian Perspective," paper prepared for the International Symposium on Economic Change: Policies, Strategies, and Research Issues," Aspen Colorado, July 4–7, 1990.

Ganiatsos, Tom. "Transfer of Technology: Theory and Policy," in Ahooja-Patel et al., *World Economy in Transition,* pp. 229–251.

Gilmer, Robert W., Stanley R. Keil, and Richard S. Mack. "The Service Sector in a Hierarchy of Rural Places: Potential for Export Activity." *Land Economics,* vol. 65, no. 3, Aug. 1989, pp. 217–227.

——— and Allan G. Pulsipher. "Structural Change in Southern Manufacturing: Expansion in the Tennessee Valley." *Growth and Change,* vol. 20, no. 2, Spring 1989, pp. 62–70.

Gittell, Ross. "Managing the Development Process: Community Strategies in Economic Revitalization." *Journal of Policy Analysis and Management* 9, 4. 1990, pp. 507–531

Glasgow, Nina L. "Attracting Retirees as a Community Development Option." *Journal of the Community Development Society*, vol. 21, no. 1, 1990.

————— and Calvin L. Beale. "Rural Elderly in Demographic Perspective." *Rural Development Perspectives*, vol. 3, no. 1, Oct. 1985, pp. 22–26.

Glasmeier, Amy. *Bypassing America's Outlands: Rural America and High Technology.* Austin: The University of Texas at Austin, Graduate Program in Community and Regional Planning, October 1988.

—————. "Factors Governing the Development of High Tech Industry Agglomerations: A Tale of Three Cities." *Regional Studies*, vol. 22, no. 4, August 1988, pp. 287–301.

—————. *The High-Tech Potential: Economic Development in Rural America.* New Brunswick, NJ: Center for Urban Policy Research, Rutgers, the State University of New Jersey, 1991.

————— and Gayle Borchard. *The Service Economy and Rural America: A Literature Review.* Washington, D.C.: Aspen Institute, Rural Economic Development Policy Project, July 1988.

————— and Norman Glickman. "Foreign Investment Boosts Rural Economies." *Rural Development Perspectives*, vol. 6, no. 3, June/Sept. 1990, pp. 19–25.

————— and Michael Conroy. "Global Squeeze on Rural America: Opportunities, Threats, and Challenges from NAFTA, GATT, and the Processes of Globalization." Institute for Policy Research and Evaluation. The Pennsylvania State University, 1994.

————— and Marie Howland. *From Combines to Computers: Rural Services and Development in the Information Age.* Albany: State University of New York Press, 1995.

"Good times are back on the farm, for a bit." *The Economist*, March 10, 1990, pp. 25–26.

Goode, F.M. "Rural Industrial Location vs. Rural Industrial Growth." *The Annals of Regional Science*, vol. 23, no. 1, 1989, pp. 59–68.

Gomory, Ralph E., and Roland W. Schmitt. "Science and Product." *Science*, vol. 240, May 27, 1988, pp. 11331+.

Gorham, Lucy, and Bennet Harrison. "Working Below the Poverty Line: The Growing Problem of Low Earnings in Rural and Urban Regions across the United States." Washington, D.C.: The Aspen Institute, 1990.

Graham, Edward M. "Foreign Direct Investment in the United States and U.S. Interests." *Science*, vol. 254, no. 5039, December 20, 1991, pp. 1740–1745.

Gray, Peter H. "The Contributions of Economics to Tourism." *Annals of Tourism Research*, vol. 9, no. 2, 1982.

Greenstein, Robert, and Isaac Shapiro. "Policies to Alleviate Rural Poverty." *Rural Poverty in America.* New York: Auburn House 1992.

Gregerman, Alan S. "Rekindling the Future: Creating a More Entrepreneurial Environment." *Commentary*, National Council for Urban Economic Development, vol. 14, no. 4, Winter 1991.

Hahn, Robert W., and Wilbur A. Steger. *An Analysis of Jobs-at-Risk and Job Losses Resulting from the Proposed Clean Air Act Amendments.* Pittsburgh: CONSAD Research Corporation for the Business Roundtable, Feb. 20, 1990.

Happel, S.K., T.D. Hogan, et al. "Economic Impact of Elderly Winter Residents in the Phoenix Area." *Research on Aging,* March 1988, pp. 119–133.

Harrison, Bennett, and Maryellen R. Kelley. "The New Industrial Culture: Journeys Toward Collaboration." *The American Prospect,* Winter 1991, pp. 54–61.

Harrison, David, and Jonathan Seib. "Toward 'One Washington': Strengthening Rural–Urban Economic Linkages," in Northwest Policy Center, *A Northwest Reader: Options for Rural Communities.* Seattle: University of Washington, 1988, chapter 6.

Hatch, C. Richard. "Flexible Manufacturing Networks: Cooperation for Competitiveness in a Global Economy." Washington, D.C.: The Corporation for Enterprise Development, 1988.

Helm, Dieter, ed. *The Economic Borders of the State.* Oxford: Oxford University Press, 1989.

Hibbard, Michael. "Community Beliefs and the Failure of Community Economic Development." *Social Service Review* 60, 2, pp. 183–200.

Hills, Jill. "The telecommunications rich and poor." *Third World Quarterly,* vol. 12, no. 2, April 1990, pp. 71–90.

Hirschl, Thomas A. "Retirement Transfers and Local Wage Rates," in *Community Economic Vitality: Major Trends and Selected Issues.* Ames, IA: The North Central Regional Center for Rural Development, Iowa State University, 1988, pp. 55–60.

———— and Gene F. Summers. "Retirees as a Growth Industry." *Rural Development Perspectives,* Feb. 1985, pp. 13–16.

Hirschman, Albert. *Essays in Trespassing: Economic to Politics and Beyond.* Cambridge: Cambridge University Press, 1981.

————. *Exit, Voice, and Loyalty.* Cambridge, MA: Harvard University Press, 1970.

————. *Rival Views of Market Society.* New York: Viking, 1986.

————. *The Strategy of Economic Development.* New York: Yale University Press, 1958.

Hogan, T.D. "Determinants of the Seasonal Migration of the Elderly to Sunbelt States." *Research on Aging,* March 1987, pp. 115+.

Hogendorn, Jan. *Economic Development.* New York: Harper and Row, 1987.

Hoover, Edgar M. "Some Old and New Issues in Regional Development," in E.A.G. Robinson, ed., *Backward Areas in Advanced Countries.* London: Macmillan, 1969.

Hoppe, Robert A. "The Elderly's Income and Rural Development: Some Cautions." *Rural Development Perspectives,* vol. 7, no. 2, February-May 1991, pp. 27–32.

Howe, Charles. "On the Theory of Optima; Regional Development Based on an Exhaustible Resource." *Growth and Change* 18,2. Spring 1987, pp. 53–68.

Hudson, Heather E. "Telecommunications Policy: The State Role, A National Overview." Paper for the Aspen Institute, September 1990.

————. "The Role of the Public Sector in Telecommunication." Paper for the Aspen Institute, 1991.

Humphrey, Craig R., Rodney A. Erickson, and Richard E. McCluskey. "Industrial Development Groups, External Connections, and Job Generation in Local Communities." *Economic Development Quarterly* vol. 3, no. 1, Feb. 1989, pp. 32–45.

Hunt, John D. "Tourism Comes of Age in the 1980s." *Parks and Recreation*, vol. 21, no. 10, October 1986, pp. 30–36+.

Israilevich, Philip R., and William A. Testa. "The Geography of Value Added." *Economic Perspectives*, Federal Reserve Bank of Chicago, vol. 13, issue 5, Sept./Oct. 1989, pp. 2+.

Jacobs, Jane. *Cities and the Wealth of Nations.* New York: Vintage, 1985.

Jaffee, David. "Export Dependence and Economic Growth: A Reformulation and Respecification." *Social Forces* 64, 1. September 1985, pp. 102–118.

John, DeWitt. *Shifting Responsibilities: Federalism in Economic Development.* Washington, DC.: National Governors' Association, 1987.

————, Sandra S. Batie, and Kim Norris. *A Brighter Future for Rural America?* Washington D.C.: National Governors' Association, Center for Policy Research, 1988.

———— and Kim Norris. "Rural Communities; State Governments Can Help." *Choices* 4, 2. Second Quarter 1989, pp. 12–15.

Johnson, Kenny. "The Southern Stake in Rural Development: An Introductory Overview," in *Rural Flight/Urban Might: Economic Development Challenges for the 1990s,* Cross-Cutting Issue Report No. 3, 1986, Commission on the Future of the South. Research Triangle Park, NC: Southern Growth Policies Board, 1986, pp. 13–20.

Johnson, Thomas G., David S. Kraybill, and Brady J. Deaton. "Improvements in Well-Being in Virginia Coalfields Hampered by Low and Unstable Income." *Rural Development Perspectives*, vol. 6, no. 1, Oct. 1989, pp. 37–41.

Johnston, Bruce F., and William C. Clark, *Redesigning Rural Development: A Strategic Perspective.* Baltimore: Johns Hopkins, 1982.

Johnston, William B., and Arnold E. Packer. *Workforce 2000: Work and Workers for the Twenty-first Century.* Indianapolis, IN: Hudson Institute, June 1987.

Kahley, William J. "U.S. and Foreign Direct Investment Patterns." *Economic Review.* Federal Reserve Bank of Atlanta, vol. 74, no. 6, Nov./Dec. 1989, pp. 42–57.

Kale, Steven R. "Theoretical Contributions to the Understanding of U.S. Nonmetropolitan Economic Change." *Economic Development Quarterly* 3, 1. February 1989, pp. 58–69.

———— and Richard E. Lonsdale. "Recent Trends in U.S. and Canadian Nonmetro Manufacturing." *Journal of Rural Studies*, vol. 3, no. 1, 1987, pp. 1–13.

Kane, Matt, and Peggy Sand. *Economic Development: What Works at the Local Level.* Washington, D.C.: National League of Cities, 1988.

Keegan, Charles E., III, and Paul E. Polzin. "Trends in the Wood and Paper Products Industry: Their Impact on the Pacific Northwest Economy." *Journal of Forestry,* vol. 85, no. 11, Nov. 1987, pp. 31–36.

Kelley, Maryellen R., and Harvey Brooks. "From Breakthrough to Followthrough," *Issues in Science and Technology* vol. 5, no. 3, Spring 1989, pp. 42–47.

Kemmis, Daniel. *Community and the Politics of Place.* Norman, OK: University of Oklahoma Press, 1990.

Kendrick, John W. "Service Sector Productivity." *Business Economics* vol. 22, no. 2, April 1987, pp. 18–24.

Killian, Molly S., and Thomas F. Hady. "What Is the Payoff for Diversifying Rural Economies?" *Rural Development Perspectives,* vol. 4, issue 2, Feb. 1988, pp. 2–7.

———— and Timothy S. Parker. *Education and Local Employment Growth in a Changing Economy,"* in *Education and Rural Economic Development: Strategies for the 1990s.* Agriculture and Rural Economy Division, Economic Research Service, U.S. Department of Agriculture, ERS Staff Report No. AGES 9153, September 1991, pp. 93–121.

Kirk, Robert. "Are Business Services Immune to the Business Cycle?" *Growth and Change,* vol. 18, no. 2, Spring 1987, pp. 15–23.

Kirkland, Richard I., Jr. "Are Service Jobs Good Jobs?" *Fortune,* vol. 111, no. 12, June 10, 1985, pp. 38–43.

Kirn, Thomas J. "Growth and Change in the Service Sector of the U.S.: A Spatial Perspective." *Annals of the Association of American Geographers,* vol. 77, no. 3, 1987, pp. 353–372.

Knapp, Elaine S. "States Lure Billions in Tourist Dollars." *State Government News,* vol. 30, no. 5, May 1987, pp. 8–10.

Koretz, Gene. "U.S. high-tech trade may be headed for the doldrums." *Business Week,* April 16, 1990, p. 18.

————. "Has high-tech America passed its high-water mark?" *Business Week,* Feb. 5, 1990, p. 18.

————. "Will Direct Foreign Investment Help on the Trade Front?" *Business Week,* December 16, 1991, p. 20.

Kosters, Marvin H., and Murray N. Ross. "Job Quality and Service Sector Employment: The New Conventional Wisdom Is Wrong." *The Service Economy,* Coalition of Service Industries, Washington, D.C., vol. 2, no. 1, Dec. 1987, pp. 1–4.

Koth, Barbara A. "Evaluating Tourism Advertising with Cost-Comparison Methods," publication CD-FO-3372. St. Paul, Minnesota: Tourism Center, Minnesota Extension Service, University of Minnesota, 1987.

————. "Tourism Advertising: Some Basics," publication CD-FO-3311. St. Paul, Minnesota: Tourism Center, Minnesota Extension Service, University of Minnesota, 1987.

———— and Glenn M. Kreag. "Community Travel and Tourism Marketing," publication CD-FO-3272. St. Paul, Minnesota: Tourism Center, Minnesota Extension Service, University of Minnesota, 1987.

Kriz, Margaret E. "Turbulence Ahead for Clean Air Act?" *National Journal,* Jan. 17, 1990, pp. 223–224.

————. "Last Stand on Timber. A Bush Administration plan to restrict money-losing sales in national forests fans a conflict between timber interests and environmental groups over the future of the forest system." *National Journal*, March 3, 1990, pp. 508–512.

———. "Dunning the Midwest. After snubbing past offers to share the cost of controlling acid rain, the Midwest is getting stuck with the tab in this year's showdown over clean air legislation." *National Journal*, April 14, 1990, pp. 893–895.

Krout, John A. *The Aged in Rural America.* New York: Greenwood Press, 1986.

———, ed. *Journal of Rural Studies*, vol. 4, no. 2, 1988, pp. 99–168; entire issue devoted to elderly concerns.

Krueger, Anne O. "Government Failures in Development." *Journal of Economic Perspectives* 4, 3. Summer 1990, pp. 9–23.

Kuehn, John A. "Retirement: A Growing Part of Rural Economies." *Rural Development Perspectives,* vol. 2, no. 2, Feb. 1986, pp. 36–37.

Kutscher, Roland E., and Valerie A. Personick. "Deindustrialization and the Shift to Services." *Monthly Labor Review*, vol. 109, no. 6, June 1986, pp. 3–13.

Kuttner, Robert. "The Declining Middle," *The Atlantic,* July 1983, pp. 60–72.

Labaton, Stephen. "$5 Billion '91 Loss Seen for U.S. Fund Insuring Deposits." *The New York Times,* December 17, 1990, A1.

Ladd, Helen F. "Introduction to Symposium on Managing Local Development." *Journal of Policy Analysis and Management* 9,4. 1990, pp. 484–486.

Lawrence, Robert Z. "Sectoral Shifts and the Size of the Middle Class." *The Brooking Review* 3:1, Fall 1984, pp. 3–11.

Lee, Everett S. "Migration of the Aged." *Research on Aging* 2:2. June 1980.

Lee, Gary R., and Marie L. Lassey. "The Elderly," in Don A. Dillman and Daryl J. Hobbs, eds., *Rural Society in the U.S.: Issues for the 1980s.* Boulder, CO: Westview Press, 1982.

Leeson, P.F., and M.M. Minogue, eds. *Perspectives on Development: Cross-disciplinary themes in development studies.* Manchester: Manchester University Press, 1988.

Leipert, Christian. "Social Costs of Economic Growth." *Journal of Economic Issues* 20, 1. March 1986, pp. 109–131.

Leipziger, Danny M. *Basic Needs and Development.* Oelgeschlager, Gunn, and Hain, 1981.

Leman, Chris. "A Natural Resources Strategy for the 1990s," in *Northwest Region Watch,* Northwest Policy Center, Seattle, WA.

Levy, Frank S. *Dollars and Dreams: The Changing American Income Distribution.* New York: W.W. Norton & Co., 1988.

———, and Richard C. Michel. *The Economic Future of American Families: Income and Wealth Trends.* Washington, D.C.: Urban Institute Press, 1991.

Lindblom, Charles E. *Politics and Markets.* New York: Basic Books, 1977.

Lloyd, Robert C., and Kenneth D. Wilkinson. "Community Factors in Rural Manufacturing Development." *Rural Sociology*, vol. 50, no. 1, Spring 1985, pp. 27–37.

McConnell, Grant. *Private Power and American Democracy in America.* New York: Vintage, 1966.

McCrossen, Melanie. "As growth tapers off, the industry looks to networking." *Industry Surveys,* June 15, 1989, pp. C75–C78.

McDowell, George R. "Local Development Strategies: Do We Do What We Know, Do We Know What We Are Doing?" paper prepared for International Symposium on Economic Change, Aspen Colorado, July 4–7, 1990.

McGranahan, David A. Introduction to *Education and Rural Economic Development: Strategies for the 1990s.* Agriculture and Rural Economy Division, Economic Research Service, U.S. Department of Agriculture, ERS Staff Report No. AGES 9153, September 1991, pp. 1–12.

———. "Changes in Age Structure and Rural Community Growth." *Rural Development Perspectives,* vol. 1, no. 3, June 1985, pp. 21–25.

———. "Recent Rural Employment Gains." *Rural Development Perspectives,* vol. 5, issue 1, Oct. 1988, pp. 44–45.

———. "Rural Workers in the National Economy," in David L. Brown et al., eds., *Rural Economic Development in the 1980s: Prospects for the Future,* RDRR-69. Economic Research Service, U.S. Department of Agriculture. Washington, D.C.; Government Printing Office, Sept. 1988, pp. 29–47.

——— and Linda M. Ghelfi. "The Education Crisis and Rural Stagnation in the 1980s," in *Education and Rural Economic Development: Strategies for the 1990s.* Agriculture and Rural Economy Division, Economic Research Service, U.S. Department of Agriculture, ERS Staff Report No. AGES 9153, September 1991, pp. 40–92.

Majchrowicz, T. Alexander. "Rural Areas Fall Further Behind in Jobs." *Rural Development Perspectives,* vol. 5, issues 2, pp. 34–36.

Malecki, Edward J. "High Technology and Local Economic Development." *Journal of the American Planning Association.* Summer 1984.

———. "High-Tech Economics: Hope or Hyperbole?" *Current,* no. 301, March/April 1988.

Malizia, Emile. "Economic Development in Smaller Cities and Rural Areas." *Journal of the American Planning Association* 51, 4. Autumn 1986, pp. 489–499.

Markley, Deborah. "Availability of Capital in Rural America: Problems and Options," background paper submitted to the Task Force on Rural Development, National Governors' Association, Washington, D.C., 1988.

Marshall, J.N. "Business Services, the Region, and Regional Policy." *Regional Studies,* vol. 19, no. 4, Aug. 1985, pp. 353–363.

Martin, Thomas J. "The Impact of Tourism." *American City and County,* vol. 102, no. 12, December 1987, pp. 48+.

Mathews, Jessica. "The New Dogma of Environmentalism." *Washington Post,* January 3, 1991, A21.

Meier, Gerald, M. *Emerging from Poverty: The Economics That Really Matters.* New York: Oxford University Press, 1984.

——— and Dudley Seers, eds. *Pioneers in Development.* New York: Oxford University Press, 1984.

Meyer, Peter B., and Michael Burayidi. "Is Value Conflict Inherent in Rural

Economic Development? An Exploratory Examination of Unrecognized Choices." *Agriculture and Human Values* 8, 3. Summer 1991, pp. 10–18.

Meyers, Susan S. "Economic Status of Elderly Is a More Severe Problem in Rural Areas." *Sociology of Rural Life*. Minnesota Extension Service, Agricultural Experiment Station, Fall 1987, vol. 9, no. 3.

Miller, James P. "New Rural Businesses Show Good Survival and Growth Rates." *Rural Development Perspectives* vol. 7, no. 3, June-September 1991, pp. 25–29.

———. "Rethinking Small Business as the Best Way to Create Rural Jobs." *Rural Development Perspectives*, vol. 1, no. 2, Feb. 1985, pp. 9–12.

——— and Herman Bluestone. "Prospects for Service Sector Employment Growth in Nonmetro America," in David L. Brown et al., eds., *Rural Economic Development in the 1980s: Prospects for the Future*, RDRR-69. Economic Research Service, U.S. Department of Agriculture. Washington, D.C.: U.S. Government Printing Office, Sept. 1988, pp. 135–158.

Millman, Joel. "There's Your Solution." *Forbes*, January 7, 1991, pp. 72, 76.

Milward, H. Brinton, and Heidi Hosbach Newman. "State Incentive Packages and the Industrial Location Decision." *Economic Development Quarterly*, vol. 3, no. 3, Aug. 1989, pp. 203–222.

Misra, R.P., and M. Honjo, *Changing Perceptions of Development Problems*. Hong Kong: Maruzen Asia, 1981.

Moore, Geoffrey H. "The Service Industries and the Business Cycle." *Business Economics*, vol. 22, no. 2, April 1987, pp. 12–17.

———. "Unemployment in the Service Industries Is Lower in Good Times and Bad." *The Service Economy*, Coalition of Service Industries, Washington, D.C., vol. 1, no. 4., Sept. 1987, pp. 1–3.

Morris, Charles, and Mark Drabenstott. "Rethinking the Rural Credit Gap." *Rural Development Perspectives*, vol. 7, no. 1, Oct.-Jan. 1991, pp. 20–25.

Morrison, Peter A. *A Taste of the Country: A Collection of Calvin Beale's Writings*. University Park: The Pennsylvania State University Press, 1990, p. 18.

Myers, Phyllis. *State Parks in a New Era: Volume 3, Strategies for Tourism and Economic Development*. Washington, D.C.: The Conservation Foundation, 1989.

Nelson, Richard. "Incentives for Entrepreneurship and Supporting Institutions," in Bela Balassa and Herbert Giersch, eds., *Economic Incentives*. New York: St. Martin's, 1986, pp. 173–187.

North, Douglass. "Location Theory and Regional Economic Growth." *Journal of Political Economy* 63. 1955, pp. 243–258.

Norton, R.D. "Reindustrializaiton and Economic Development Strategy," *Economic Development Quarterly*, vol. 3, no. 3, Aug. 1989, pp. 188–202.

Nothdurft, William E. *Renewing America*. Washington, D.C.: Council of State Planning Agencies, 1984.

——— and Mark Popovich. "Bucking the System: Lessons from One Foundation's Investments in Agricultural Diversification." Report to the Northwest Area Foundation, St. Paul, MN, 1991.

Noyelle, Thierry. "Economic Transformation." *Annals of the American Academy of Political and Social Science*, 488, Nov. 1986.

————. "The Rise of Advanced Services." *Journal of the American Planning Association*, vol. 49, no. 3, 1983 pp. 280–290.

Oakey, R.P., and S.Y. Cooper. "High Technology Industry, Agglomeration and the Potential for Peripherally Sited Small Firms." *Regional Studies,* vol. 23, no. 4, 1989, pp. 347–360.

Ocampo, Jose Antonio. "New Developments in Trade Theory and LDCs." *Journal of Development Economics* 22, 1. June 1986, pp. 129–170.

O'Farrell, P.N., and D.M. Hitchens. "Producer Services and Regional Development: Key Conceptual Issues of Taxonomy and Quality Measurements." *Regional Studies*, vol. 24, no. 2, April 1990, pp. 163–171.

O'Hare, William, and Anne Pauti. "Declining Wages of Young Workers in Rural America," staff working papers. Washington, D.C.: Population Reference Bureau, May 1990.

Okagaki, Alan. "Windows on the World: Best Practice in Economic Opportunity Strategy." *Entrepreneurial Economy Review,* Corporation for Enterprise Development, Nov. 1988, pp. 3–19.

Okun, Arthur. *Equity and Efficiency: The Big Tradeoff.* Washington, D.C.: The Brookings Institution, 1975.

Olson, Jr., Mancur. *The Logic of Collective Action: Public Goods and the Theory of Groups.* Cambridge, Mass.: Harvard University Press, 1965.

O'Neill, Dave M. "We're Not Losing Our Industrial Base." *Challenge,* vol. 30, no. 4, Sept./Oct. 1987, pp. 19–25.

Osborne, David. "Refining State Technology Programs: The past decade of creative experimentation has produced some useful lessons." *Issues in Science and Technology,* vol. 6, no. 4, Summer 1990, pp. 55–61.

————. "Reinventing D.C.: How Sharon Pratt Dixon Can Turn the City Around." *The Washington Post Magazine,* December 9, 1990, p. 19.

———— and Ted Gaebler. *Reinventing Government.* Reading, MA: Addison-Wesley, 1992.

Parker, Edwin B., Heather E. Hudson, Don A. Dillman, and Andrew D. Roscoe. *Rural America in the Information Age: Telecommunications Policy for Rural Development.* Lanham, MD: University Press of America and The Aspen Institute, 1989.

Patton, Spiro G. "Tourism and Local Economic Development: Factory Outlets and the Reading SMSA." *Growth and Change,* vol. 16, no. 3, July 1985, pp. 64–73.

Peck, John E., and Brian R. Shappell. "The Income Impact of the Shift to Service Industry: A Case Study." *Economic Development Review,* vol. 4, no. 2, Summer 1986, pp. 11–15.

Piore, Michael J., and Charles F. Sabel. *The Second Industrial Divide: Possibilities for Prosperity.* New York: Basic Books, 1984.

Plotnick, Robert D. "Small Community Economic Development: Can Income Transfers Help?" in *A Northwest Reader: Options for Rural Communities.* Seattle: Northwest Policy Center, University of Washington, Graduate School of Public Affairs, 1988.

Policy for Rural Development. Lanham, MD: Aspen Institute/University Press of America, 1989.

Pollack, Susan, and Shelley Pendleton. "Nonmetro Unemployment Tied to Major Industries in Region." *Rural Development Perspectives,* vol. 3, issue 1, Oct. 1986.

Population Reference Bureau. "U.S. Population: Where We Are; Where We're Going." Bulletin 1982.

Porterfield, Shirley. "Service Sector Offers More Jobs, Lower Pay." *Rural Development Perspectives,* vol. 6, no. 3, June/Sept. 1990, pp. 2–7.

Putnam, Robert D. "Bowling Alone: America's Declining Social Capital." *Journal of Democracy,* vol. 6, no. 1, January 1995, pp. 65–78.

———. "The Prosperous Community: Social Capital and Public Life." *The American Prospect* 13, Spring 1993, pp. 35–42.

Pytte, Alyson. "A Decade's Acrimony Lifted in the Glow of Clean Air." *Congressional Quarterly,* Oct. 27, 1990, pp. 3587–3592.

Quick, Steve, and Robert Friedman. "The Safety Net as Ladder: Transfer Payments and Economic Development, Executive Summary." Washington, D.C.: The Corporation for Enterprise Development, Oct. 1984.

Quinn, James Brian, and Christopher E. Gagnon. "Will Services Follow Manufacturing Into Decline?" *Harvard Business Review,* Nov./Dec. 1986, pp. 95–103.

Raup, Hugh M. "The View from John Sanderson's Farm: A Perspective for the Use of the Land." *Forest History* 10, 1 April, 1966, pp. 2–11.

Ray, Cadwell L., and R. Lynn Rittenoure. "Recent Regional Growth Patterns: More Inequality." *Economic Development Quarterly,* vol. 1, no. 3, 1987, pp. 240–248.

Redclift, Michael. *Sustainable Development: Exploring the Contradictions.* London: Methuen, 1987.

Reeder, Richard J., and Nina L. Glasgow. "Nonmetro Retirement Counties' Strengths and Weaknesses." *Rural Development Perspectives,* vol. 6, no. 2, February-May 1990, pp. 12–17.

Rees, John, ed. *Technology, Regions, and Policy.* Totowa, NJ: Rowman & Littlefield, 1986.

Reich, Robert B. "Who Is Us?" *Harvard Business Review* January-February 1990: 53–64.

———. "The Real Economy." *The Atlantic* February 1991, pp. 35–52.

———. *The Work of Nations: Preparing Ourselves for 21st-Century Capitalism.* New York: Knopf, 1991.

Reid, Norman J., and Elliott Dubin. "Federal Funds to Rural Areas: Fair Share? Right Mix?" background paper submitted to the Task Force on Rural Development. Washington, D.C.: National Governors' Association, 1988.

Reimund, Donn A., and Fred Gale. *Structural Change in the U.S. Farm Sector, 1974-87: 13th Annual Family Farm Report to Congress.* Agriculture and Rural Economy Division, Economic Research Service, U.S. Department of Agriculture. Agriculture Information Bulletin No. 647, May 1992.

——— and Mindy Petrulis. "Performance of the Agricultural Sector," in David L.

Brown et al., eds., *Rural Economic Development in the 1980s: Prospects for the Future,* RDRR-69. Economic Research Service, U.S. Department of Agriculture. Washington, D.C.: U.S. Government Printing Office, Sept. 1988, pp. 77–101.

Rich, Spencer. "Low-Paying Jobs Up Sharply in Decade, U.S. Says." *Washington Post,* May 12, 1992, A7.

Richards, Bill. "An Influx of Retirees Pumps New Vitality Into Distressed Towns." *The Wall Street Journal,* vol. 212, no. 25, Aug. 5, 1988, pp. 1+.

————. "Many Rural Regions Are Growing Again; A Reason: Technology. *The Wall Street Journal,* Nov. 21, 1994, Al.

Riddle, Dorothy I. *Service-led Growth: The Role of the Service Sector in World Development.* New York: Praeger Publishers, 1986.

Riefler, Roger F. "Implications of Service Industry Growth for Regional Development Strategies." *Annals of Regional Science,* vol. 10, no. 2, 1976, pp. 88–104.

Riley, H. Terrence, III. "Monarchy gives way to oligopoly—is democracy next?" *Industry Surveys, Standard & Poor's,* Oct. 5, 1989, pp. T15–T16 and T38–T40.

Robinson, E.A.G., ed. *Backward Areas in Advanced Countries.* London: Macmillan, 1969.

Rose, Adam, Brandt Stevens, and Gregg Davis. *Natural Resource Policy and Income Distribution.* Baltimore: Johns Hopkins University Press, 1988.

Rosenfeld, Stuart A., Edward M. Berman, and Sarah Rubin. *Making Connections: "After the Factories" Revisited.* Research Triangle Park, NC: Southern Growth Policies Board, Feb. 1989.

————, Emil E. Malizia, and Marybeth Dugan. *Reviving the Rural Factory: Automation and Work in the South.* Research Triangle Park, NC: Southern Growth Policies Board, May 1988.

Rosewicz, Barbara, and Rose Gutfeld. "Clean Air Legislation Will Cost Americans $21.5 Billion a Year." *The Wall Street Journal,* March 28, 1990, pp. 1+.

Rosner, Jeremy D. *A Progressive Perspective on Health Care Reform.* Washington, D.C.: Progressive Foundation, 1992.

Ross, Doug. "Thinking About Rural Economic Development in the 1990s," paper prepared for the CSPA Rural Development Academy, Spring 1990.

Rostow, Walt W. "Economic Growth and the Diffusion of Power." *Challenge* 29, 4 September-October 1986, pp. 29–37.

Rothwell, Roy. "The Role of Technology in Industrial Change: Implications for Regional Policy." *Regional Studies,* vol. 16, no. 5, Oct. 1982, pp. 361–369.

Rovner, Julie. "No Help from Congress on a Near-Term Solution for Long-Term Care. But states are going ahead with other new ideas that don't require a federal permission slip." *Governing,* June 1990, pp. 21–27.

Sachs, Wolfgang. "On the Archaeology of the Development Idea." Essay Two (English translation by the Science, Technology, and Society Program, Pennsylvania State University, unpublished).

Sagoff, Mark. "The Concept of Overlapping Consensus as an Organizing Principle for International Regime Formation and Environmental Management" (Institute for Philosophy and Public Policy, University of Maryland at College Park, unpublished).

――. "Has Nature a Good of Its Own?" (Institute for Philosophy and Public Policy, University of Maryland at College Park, unpublished).

――. "The Humanities and Sustainable Development" (Institute for Philosophy and Public Policy, University of Maryland at College Park, unpublished).

Satterthwaite, Mark. "Location Patterns of High-Growth Firms." *Economic Development Commentary*, Council for Urban Economic Development, vol. 12, no. 1, Spring 1988, pp. 7–11.

Savage, J.A. "Timber Companies Can't See the Forest for the Trees." *Business and Society Review*, no. 74 Summer 1990, pp. 44–47.

Schmandt, Jurgen, Frederick Williams, Robert Wilson, and Sharon Strover, eds. *Telecommunications and Rural Development: A Study of Private and Public Sector Innovation.* New York: Praeger Publishers, 1991.

Schoenberger, Erica. "Foreign Manufacturing Investment in the United States." *Commentary*, National Council for Urban Economic Development, vol. 13, no. 3, Fall 1989, pp. 26–29.

Schultze, Charles L. "Industrial Policy: A Solution in Search of a Problem." *California Management Review*, vol. 25, no. 4, Summer 1983, pp. 5–15.

Schwartz, Gail Garfield. "Telecommunications and Economic Development Policy." *Economic Development Quarterly*, vol. 4, no. 2, May 1990, pp. 83–91.

Scott, Frank A., Jr., Mark C. Berger, and Glenn C. Blomquist. "Impacts of Air Pollution Control Strategies in Kentucky." *Growth and Change*, vol. 19, no. 2, Spring 1988, pp. 40–54.

"A Scramble for Global Networks: Companies are spending big on worldwide communications systems." *Business Week*. Special report on telecommunications, March 21, 1988 pp. 140+.

Sem, John, ed. *Using Tourism and Travel as a Community and Rural Revitalization Strategy.* Proceedings of the National Extension Workshop. Minneapolis, Minnesota; Tourism Center, Minnesota Extension Service, University of Minnesota, August 1989.

Sen, Amartya. *Commodities and Capabilities.* Amsterdam: Elsevier, 1985.

――. "Development: Which Way Now?" in *Resources, Values, and Development.* Cambridge, MA: Harvard University Press, 1984.

――. *Resources, Values, and Development.* Cambridge, MA: Harvard University Press, 1984.

――. *The Standard of Living.* Cambridge: Cambridge University Press, 1987.

Serow, William. "Why the Elderly Move: Cross National Comparisons." *Research on Aging*, Dec. 1987, p. 582+.

―― and Douglas A. Charity. "Return Migration of the Elderly in the United States." *Research on Aging*, June 1988, p. 155+.

Shaffer, Ron, and Gene F. Summers. "Community Economic Vitality," in *Community Economic Vitality: Major Trends and Selected Issues.* Ames, IA: The

North Central Regional Center for Rural Development, Iowa State University, 1988.

Shapira, Philip. "Modern Times: Learning from State Initiatives in Industrial Extension and Technology Transfer." *Economic Development Quarterly,* vol. 4, no. 3, Aug. 1990, pp. 186–202.

Shapiro, Helen, and Lance Taylor. "The State and Industrial Strategy." *World Development* 18, 6. June 1990, pp. 861–878.

Shapiro, Isaac, and Robert Greenstein, "Fulfilling Work's Promise: Policies to Increase Incomes of the Rural Working Poor." Washington, D.C.: Center on Budget and Policy Priorities, 1990.

Shimada, Haruo, and John Paul MacDuffie. "Industrial Relations and 'Humanware': Japanese Investments in Automobile Manufacturing in the United States." Sloan School of Management, M.I.T., Dec. 1986.

Shribman, David. "Iowa Towns Shrivel as the Young People Head for the Cities." *The Wall Street Journal,* April 24, 1991, A1.

Siegel, Barry. "Hawaii: To Grow or Not to Grow." *Los Angeles Times,* Feb. 3, 1984, section 1, p.1.

Simons, Marlise. "Europeans Begin to Calculate the Price of Pollution." *New York Times,* December 9, 1990, E3.

Simonson, Lawrence R., Barbara A. Koth, and Glenn M. Kreag. "So Your Community Wants Travel/Tourism? Guidelines for Attracting and Serving Visitors," publication CD-BU-3443. St. Paul, Minnesota: Tourism Center, Minnesota Extension Service, University of Minnesota, 1988.

Smith, Andrew. "Whither Copper Prices? Golden Years or a Return to Bust?" *Resources Policy,* vol. 15, no. 4, Dec. 1989, pp. 314–320.

Smith, Barbara Ellen. "Questions About Tourism." *Southern Exposure.* Southwest Women's Employment Coalition, c 1989.

Smith, Gary W., and Robert A. Chase. "Shifts in Personal Income Composition: The Graying of the Northwest." *Pacific Northwest Executive,* January 1991.

Smith, Michal. *Behind the Glitter: The Impact of Tourism on Rural Women in the Southeast.* Lexington, KY: Southeast Women's Employment Coalition, August 1989.

Smith, Stephen. "Comparison of Nonlocal Market Orientation of Rural Service and Manufacturing Business." Staff Paper 186, Agricultural Economics and Rural Sociology Department, College of Agriculture, The Pennsylvania State University, University Park, PA, June 1990.

———. "Diversifying Smalltown Economies with Nonmanufacturing Industries." *Rural Development Perspectives,* vol. 2, no. 1, Oct. 1985, pp. 18–21.

——— and David L. Barkley. "Contributions of High-Tech Manufacturing to Rural Economies." *Rural Development Perspectives,* vol. 5, issue 3, June 1989, pp. 6–11.

Stabler, Jack C. "Non-Metropolitan Population Growth and the Evolution of Rural Service Centers in the Canadian Prairie Region." *Regional Studies,* vol. 21, no. 1, Feb. 1987, pp. 43–53.

Stahl, Gael. "Audit lists downside of tourism: seasonal, low-paying jobs." *Tennessee*

Town & City, vol. 40, no. 10, May 22, 1989, p. 6.

Staniland, Martin. *What Is Political Economy?* New Haven: Yale University Press, 1985.

Starobin, Paul. "Foggy Forecasts. So, how much is the new clean air legislation going to cost? Even the experts don't have much of a clue, and their computer models have missed the mark before." *National Journal,* May 19, 1990, pp. 1212–1215.

Stegner, Wallace. *Where the Bluebird Sings to the Lemonade Springs: Living and Writing in the West.* New York: Random House, 1992.

Stern, Nicholas H. "Professor Bauer on Development." *Journal of Development Economics* 1, 3. 1974, pp. 191–211.

———. "The Economics of Development: A Survey." *The Economic Journal* 99. September 1989, pp. 597–685.

Stokes, Bruce. "End of the Boom." *National Journal,* Oct. 13, 1990, pp. 2457–2460.

Street, James H. "The Institutionalist Theory of Economic Development." *Journal of Economic Issues* 21, 4. December 1987, pp. 1861–1887.

Strover, Sharon, and Frederick William. *Rural Revitalization and Information Technologies in the United States.* Austin, TX: Center for Research on Communication Technology and Society, The University of Texas at Austin. November 1991.

Sullivan, Gene D. "FYI: The 1990 Farm Bill." *Economic Review,* vol. 76, no. 1, Jan./Feb. 1991, pp. 22–29.

——— and David Avery. "Southern Manufacturing: Recent Changes and Prospects." *Economic Review,* Federal Reserve Bank of Atlanta, vol. 74, no. 1, January/February 1989, pp. 2–15.

Summers, Gene F., and Thomas A Hirschl. "Retirees as a Growth Industry." *Rural Development Perspectives,* vol. 1, no. 2, Feb. 1985, pp. 13–16.

Swaim, Paul L., and Ruy A. Teixeira. "Education and Training Policy: Skill Upgrading Options for the Rural Workforce," in *Education and Rural Economic Development: Strategies for the 1990s.* Agriculture and Rural Economy Division, Economic Research Service, U.S. Department of Agriculture, ERS Staff Report No. AGES 9153, September 1991, pp. 122–162.

Tanner, Marsha. "State Parks Offer Diversity, Challenge." *State Government News,* vol. 30, no. 5, May 1987, pp. 14–15+.

Taylor, Ronald B. "Kauai Islanders Stop Developers' $50-Million Gamble in Mid-Sprawl." *Los Angeles Times,* April 30, 1983, section 1, p. 15.

Teixeira, Ruy A., and Lawrence Mishel. "Upgrading Workers' Skills Not Sufficient to Jump-Start Rural Economy." *Rural Development Perspectives,* vol. 7, no. 3, June-September 1991.

Thomas, Margaret G. "A Guide to Rural Economic Development through Tourism and Wildlife-based Recreation." Chapter VI in *Recouples: Natural Resource Strategies for Rural Economic Development.* Kansas City, Missouri: Midwest Research Institute, 1990.

————. *Profiles in Rural Economic Development:* A *Guidebook of Selected Successful Rural Area Initiatives.* Midwest Research Institute: Kansas City, MO, April 1988.

Thompson, Joel A., and Mark W. Lanier. "Measuring Economic Development: Economic Diversification as an Alternative to Standard Indicators." *Policy Studies Review*, 1. Autumn 1987, pp. 77–90.

Thurow, Lester. "The Big Lie That Caused the Budget Catastrophe." *Washington Post*, October 7, 1990, D5.

————. *The Zero-Sum Solution.* New York: Simon and Schuster. 1985.

Tickamyer, Ann R., and Cynthia M. Duncan. "Poverty and Opportunity Structure in Rural America." *Annual Review of Sociology* 16 (1990), pp. 67–86.

Tierney, John. "Betting the Plant." *New York Times Magazine*, December 2, 1990, p. 52.

Toft, Graham S. "Urban Development: Radical Perspectives on a Perennial Problem." *The Entrepreneurial Economy Review* 8, 4 January/February 1990, pp. 13–19.

Tomaskovic-Devey, Donald, with Rosemary Ritzman. *Back to the Future? Human Resources and Economic Development Policy for North Carolina.* Raleigh, NC: North Carolina State University, Department of Sociology, Spring 1990.

————. *Sundown on the Sunbelt? Growth Without Development in the Rural South.* Raleigh, NC: North Carolina State University, Department of Sociology, October 1991.

Toohey, William D. "Tourism Works for States." *State Government News*, vol. 30, no. 5, May 1987, pp. 6–7+.

Toye, John. *Dilemmas of Development: Reflections on the Counter-Revolution in Development Theory and Policy.* Oxford: Basil Blackwell, 1987.

Trumka, Richard L. Statement on Acid Rain Control Legislation before the Subcommittee on Energy and Power, Committee on Energy and Commerce, U.S. House of Representatives, Sept. 7, 1989. Washington, D.C.: United Mine Workers of America.

Tucker, Stanley. "Bright Future for Coal." *Petroleum Economist*, vol. 16, no. 10, Oct. 1989, pp. 315–317.

Tyson, Laura D'Andrea. "They Are Not Us: Why American Ownership Still Matters." *The American Prospect*, Winter 1991, pp. 37–49.

U.S. Congress. "Economic Impact of Tourism." Hearings before the Subcommittee on Business, Trade, and Tourism of the Senate Committee on Commerce, Science, and Transportation, 97th Congress, second session. Washington, D.C.: U.S. Government Printing Office, 1982.

————. "Future of the Rural Elderly." Hearing before the Select Committee on Aging, House of Representatives, 100th Congress, second session, June 13, 1988. Washington, D.C.: Government Printing Office, Comm. Pub. No. 100-690.

————. "Promotion of Domestic Tourism," Hearings before the Subcommittee on Business, Trade, and Tourism of the Senate Committee on Commerce, Science, and Transportation, 99th Congress, second session. Washington,

D.C.: U.S. Government Printing Office, 1986.

———. Congressional Research Service (CRS). "Toward Rural Development Policy for the 1990s: Enhancing Income and Employment Opportunities," a symposium sponsored by CRS at the request of the Joint Economic Committee, 101st Congress, first session. Washington, D.C.: U.S. Government Printing Office, Senate Print 101-50, 1989.

———. Office of Technology Assessment. *Technology and the American Economic Transition: Choices for the Future.* OTA-TET-283. Washington, D.C.: U.S. Government Printing Office, May 1988.

———. Office of Technology Assessment. *Copper: Technology and Competitiveness.* OTA-E-367. Washington, D.C.: U.S. Government Printing Office, Sept. 1988.

———. Office of Technology Assessment. *Energy Use and the U.S. Economy,* OTA-BP-E-57. Washington, D.C.: U.S. Government Printing Office, June 1990.

U.S. Travel and Tourism Administration (USTTA), U.S. Department of Commerce. *A Strategic Look at the Travel and Tourism Industry.* Washington, D.C.: U.S. Government Printing Office, Feb. 1989.

University of Missouri, Department of Recreation and Park Administration, University Extension. *Guidelines for Tourism Development:* Appraising Tourism Potential, Planning for Tourism, Assessing Product and Marketing, Marketing Tourism, Visitor Services, Sources of Assistance. Revised and expanded, 1986.

Verity, John W. "Another Crunch for Computer Makers." *Business Week,* January 8, 1990, p. 97.

Vobejda, Barbara. "For the New Retirees, Out-of-the-Way Places: Rural, Small-Town Communities Benefiting." *The Washington Post,* December, 1990.

———. "In West Virginia, The Great Divide." *The Washington Post,* January 7, 1991, A1.

von Furstenberg, George M. "High-Tech Industries and Economic Growth." *Business Economics,* vol. 21, no. 3, July 1986.

Ware, Janet. "Unlocking Tourism's Potential." *American City and County,* May 1987, p. 96.

Weaver, Glenn. *Inventorying the Tourism Package.* Tourism Development Series, Recreation Extension, University of Missouri, c 1986.

———. "Creating and Managing Hometown Special Events." *Small Town,* November-December 1988, pp. 5–10.

Weber, Bruce A., Emery N. Castle, and Ann L. Shriver. "Performance of Natural Resource Industries," in David L. Brown et al., eds., *Rural Economic Development in the 1980s: Prospects for the Future,* RDRR-69. Economic Research Service, U.S. Department of Agriculture. Washington, D.C.: U.S. Government Printing Office, Sept. 1988, pp. 103–33.

Webster, Elaine, Edward J. Mathis, and Charles E. Zeck. "The Case for State-Level Export Promotion Assistance: A Comparison of Foreign and Domestic Export Employment Multipliers." *Economic Development Quarterly,* vol. 4, no. 3, August 1990, pp. 203–210.

Westphal, Larry E. "Industrial Policy in an Export-Propelled Economy: Lessons from South Korea's Experience." *Journal of Economic Perspectives* 4, 3. Summer 1990, pp. 41–59.

Williams, Frederick. "Telecommunications and U.S. Rural Development: An Update," paper prepared for the Aspen Institute Seminar on Telecommunications and Rural Development, Queenstown, Maryland, March 25–27, 1991.

Wilson, David L. "Boom Years for U.S. Tourist Industry." *National Journal*, June 2, 1990, p. 1367.

Wilson, Robert H., and Paul E. Teske. "Telecommunications and Economic Development: The State and Local Role." *Economic Development Quarterly*, vol. 4, no. 2, May 1990, pp. 158–174.

Wiseman, Robert F. "Why Older People Move: Theoretical Issues." *Research on Aging* vol. 2, no. 2, June 1980, pp. 141–154.

Woo, Wing Thye. "The art of economic development: markets, politics, and externalities." *International Organization* 44, 3. Summer 1990, pp. 403–429.

Wright, Gavin. "The Origins of American Industrial Success, 1979–1940." *American Economic Review* 80, 4. September 1990, pp. 651–668.

Yates, Marshal. "The Promise of Fiber Optics." *Public Utilities Fortnightly*, vol. 126, no. 4, Aug. 16, 1990, pp. 14–15.

Young, Ruth C., and Joe D. Francis. "Who Helps Small Manufacturing Firms Get Started?" *Rural Development Perspectives,* 6:1, Oct. 1989, 21–25.

Index